The Tudor Prophecy

The Tudor Prophecy

a novel

Julie K. Strong

The Tudor Prophecy
Copyright © 2025 Julie K. Strong

All rights reserved under international copyright conventions. No part of this publication may be reproduced, stored in or introduced into a retrieval system, or transmitted in any form, or by any means, without the prior written permission of the author.

First published in 2024 by

Halifax, NS, Canada
www.ocpublishing.ca

Edited by Marianne Ward
Cover illustration by Rebecca Wilson
Cover and interior book design by David W. Edelstein

ISBN 978-1-989833-49-0 (Paperback edition)
ISBN 978-1-989833-50-6 (eBook edition)

In honour of the Old Ones.

The Kingdom of England

he cousins reached the chestnut tree and dropped to the grass, panting, and leaned back against its trunk. A crow, disturbed among the topmost branches, cawed in protest. Had it been interested in living flesh it would have noticed Hester, a young woman with hazel eyes wearing a red woolen dress and a white coif over her hair. It would also have observed Alice, slightly younger, garbed in blue silk and a black satin hood. But the crow, interested only in the dead, flew away.

"I have waited all day to show you," gasped Hester, withdrawing a parchment from her sleeve. "I have an audience with His Majesty tomorrow!"

Alice's eyes widened and her hand flew to her mouth. "Surely you jest!"

Hester frowned at this response and stared up at the chestnut tree's canopy of pink-and-white flowers. The tree had been late to bloom this year of Our Lord, 1541. It had been a harsh winter, and folks whispered this was God's punishment of England. King Henry VIII should never have defied the Holy Father in Rome and installed himself as Head of the Church. But folks whispered softly, for fear of losing their tongues to a steel blade.

A petal drifted onto Hester's skirt. "In the legends of King Arthur, the knight always weds the damsel who heals him. And I shall heal His Majesty's leg ulcers." She spoke vehemently, then under her breath murmured, "I must, for I have no other recourse." She twirled the petal between fingers and thumb a moment before crushing it. "Father will send for me soon, and I do not want to return to Wales to marry a gentleman farmer of his choosing." *Wales. The very name sounds dismal.*

The young women sat halfway up a hill overlooking Hartbourne, the ancestral home of Sir Hugh, Alice's father, situated near Richmond, ten miles south of London. The old stone mansion was surrounded by fields in which workers scythed the first of the new hay, sending the fragrance upwards.

"Do you forget the King has a wife already?" asked Alice, taking out her embroidery.

"Cat Howard?" Hester sniffed, grimacing. "They are wed near a year and she is not yet with child. She is barren." Hester dropped her voice. "And 'tis said she has a paramour at court." She looked around to ensure they were alone, then louder asserted, "Besides, she was penniless when the King wed her, so he will not mind my being so. And I am the same age now that she was when he married her—seventeen." Hester stared above at a solitary cloud that drifted, white and fluffy, in a perfect blue sky. Blue was the colour of the Virgin Mary's mantle, and it seemed fitting that the month of May was dedicated to Our Lady.

"I know you are doing this for Dickie," said Alice, her eyes softening as she touched her cousin's arm. "If Father comes to grief and Mother and I are forced to leave Hartbourne, we women may find refuge in the remains of a convent, but…"

"Dickie would not be permitted," concluded Hester, her eyebrows knitted together. "But," she added with a gnawing of envy in her gut, "you are an heiress, you would not remain there for long."

"If Henry takes our land, I shall. But I would love to have a family. Mother worries I shall marry a Protestant and damn my soul for eternity." Alice sighed, then laughed. "I shall not meet any men, Protestant or otherwise, in a nunnery." She pouted. "But have you thought how any woman could have marital…. The King is so huge larded, every prize hog in the land is called Harry after him." Alice selected a strand of crimson thread for the poppies bordering the figure of St. Anne teaching her daughter, the Virgin Mary, to read.

Hester pretended not to hear and stretched her arms above her head. This last winter had seen her develop from a wild colt of a girl into a comely young woman. Fresh stitching ran down the sides of her bodice, where the seams had been let out again just the previous week. Hester knew Alice spoke truth about the King's huge bulk, but she squeezed her eyes shut and focused on enjoying the warmth of the spring sun on her face.

"I am tired, for I was singing lullabies to Dickie until past midnight. John is a great help, but he does not understand Dickie's fear of the dark, or that he doesn't like getting soap in his eyes when his hair is washed." Hester brushed away a fly that landed on her forehead.

"You have been like a mother to him, bathing him, helping him dress," said Alice, "but now John can—ouch!"

Hester sat up. "Are you hurt?"

"I jabbed my finger, but it is fine. What I was saying is that John has only been with us a week, and—but look, here comes Dickie."

A pale-faced boy, small for his thirteen years, limped up the hill. He wore a brown woolen jacket belted at the waist over grey hose.

"His knees are covered in mud. He must have taken a fit and fallen," said Alice.

"He barely goes two days together now without one," said Hester, rising to greet him.

Dickie embraced her and a clod of mud smeared onto her dress. "Hessie, I am sorry, I have dirtied your pretty dress."

"Never mind," said Hester, smiling. "It will dry and brush off. But where is John?"

Dickie pointed down the hill to where a red-faced young man puffed his way up to them.

"I'm not a baby," said Dickie, scowling. "I don't need a minder."

"You have fits, remember," said Hester.

"Don't fuss. Look what I brought you." He unwrapped a small bundle of red flannel to reveal a brown speckled egg. Hester became aware of a sweet, sharp smell and saw the wet stain creeping down Dickie's hose. *Oh, dear Lady, he has pissed himself and doesn't even know it.*

"It's lovely, dear heart," enthused Hester, willing her smile wider. The egg was still warm with one fluffy white feather stuck to it.

Dickie gave a lopsided grin and flung himself on the grass. He tossed a handful of petals in the air. "You like today's present even better than yesterday's? I forget what it was."

Yesterday's present had been a dried-up frog with one leg, and the day before's a dead fledgling dropped from its nest. Dickie rubbed at his muddy knees. "I slipped in a puddle, but I did not take a fit and crack my head open, like last time. See, it is all mended." He brushed a shock of fair hair away from his forehead. A livid scar ran down the centre.

Hester reached over and touched it. "Yes. It is healing, thanks to Aunt Maud's salves."

John arrived, mopping his face with a handkerchief. It would have been a handsome face, save for the deep pockmarks on his cheeks.

"Ladies," he greeted them, removing his cap and bowing. He turned to Dickie. "Master Dickon, why did you run off? I have searched everywhere for you."

"I wanted to go to the henhouse, and I knew you wouldn't let me because last time I forgot to shut the door and the hens escaped." Dickie examined a blade of grass and then chewed on it. "So I waited till you were kissing the dairy maid, behind the barn, then went to fetch my sister's present." He pointed at the egg lying on the grass. "And I remembered to shut the door."

Hester frowned at John. "Master Dickon could have wandered to the pond and fallen in."

"I beg pardon, Mistress." Turning to Dickie, he groaned. "Come along and we will get you clean hose."

"I don't want to." Dickie sat upright and folded his arms over his chest. Although small, he was strong—it would take two men to move him by force.

"I have honeycomb in my pocket," wheedled John.

"I want some." Dickie sprang up and accompanied John back down the hill.

"You really like your present, don't you Hessie?" shouted Dickie from below.

"Of course I do, silly goose!" she called back.

As Dickie limped past a field, a few workers leaned against their hoes and signed themselves with the cross.

"I hate when they do that!" cried Hester. "As if Dickie were possessed by a demon or carried the pestilence. He needs more than one caretaker now. I must succeed with the King. Otherwise it's the Bedlam for him." She clenched her jaw.

"I know," whispered Alice, in sympathy.

"Where the keeper will charge visitors a penny to see him normal and a shilling when he takes a fit." Hester's voice was tight with anger.

"In any case, there can be no harm in your going tomorrow to the King," assured Alice. "For you are the same age as Queen Catherine and just as pretty. Why should you not catch his fancy?"

But can I keep it, and keep it strongly enough that he will want to marry me? thought Hester. And there was the other reason she must marry the King. She must not die in childbirth. She must not leave a motherless child behind, as she was left behind when her own mother died. Also, she must not abandon Dickie, who would always be a child. Hester brought her hand to her mouth and bit down on her fingernails. *I will beg the King for the use of Our Lady of Westminster's girdle.* That belt contained splinters of Christ's cross woven into the fabric. Queen Katherine, Henry's first queen, had worn it during each delivery and had survived six pregnancies, though only Mary had lived. Hester wondered if Anne Boleyn, his second queen, had worn it, for she too had survived childbirth. But definitely Jane Seymour, as a good Protestant, had not and died the week after birthing sickly Prince Edward.

If only Mother had used the girdle, mayhap she would have lived. But it was a boon conferred only on the nobility. Moreover, the

King had declared such relics to be Romish idolatry. Yet even so, surely Henry would relent. He needed but one healthy son, and if the mother also survived, surely he could bend his conscience a little? That the King's conscience was known to be pliable gave her hope.

Hester relaxed against the tree's trunk. The warmth of the sun lulled her into a doze. She half-woke and glimpsed a horse-shaped cloud, its mane streaming behind it, then fell back asleep.

A white mare lay in a huge bed, its skin pale as the snowy linen bolsters propping up her head. A green silk shawl draped around the horse's shoulders. It was too still to be sleeping. Hester approached, crying. "No, no, she is only asleep! She can't be..." She would not let herself think the word "dead," but it crashed over her. "She's dead, dead, dead."

A red bull leaped onto the bed and ripped the mare through the belly, drenching the sheets in blood. An enormous black slug crawled out of the wound. The bull tore down the bed frame, snapping the four posts, and the canopy collapsed. The slug crept toward Hester, trailing blood and slime. Its open mouth revealed huge fangs. There was nowhere for her to hide.

Hester awoke shivering and the dream vanished. She looked up and saw clouds covering the sun and Alice folding her embroidery.

"'Tis about to rain!" said Alice.

They shook themselves, dislodging chestnut petals, which floated to the ground.

"Oh, no!" cried Hester, as she heard a crack beneath her foot. A raven from the rookery uttered a raucous, half-mocking cry. It clanged in Hester's ears. "What a fool! I have ruined Dickie's present!" Tears sprang to her eyes as she wiped shards of eggshell from the sole of her shoe onto the grass.

"He will have forgotten by now," said Alice, touching her cousin's arm.

Hester nodded. They ran down to the manor house as drops began to fall.

"You will not tell about tomorrow?" implored Hester as they approached the doorway.

Alice shook her head. "No, Mother and Father have worries enough already."

Goody stood at the entrance, clucking. "You could have been drenched, the pair of you." Their nurse tucked a strand of Alice's nasturtium-red hair behind her hood. "Lady Alice, your nose is covered in freckles. They are calling out for lemon juice, but later, for your Lady mother awaits you in the solar."

Hester scowled. *Of course Lady Alice is tended to first.* She then berated herself for the sin of envy. She began to chew on her fingernails.

"Now, Mistress Hester, stop that. And hasn't Sir Hugh been calling for you this past hour? Just look at your dress, covered in mud!"

Goody brushed Hester down and shooed her toward Sir Hugh Grantmire's library door. No one entered this sanctum sanctorum unbidden, and Hester knew she could have been summoned for only one reason. Uncle had learned of her plan.

 footman opened the door, and Hester stepped inside. The smell of leather, burning applewood, and old dog permeated the air. Sir Hugh, a portly man in his early fifties, paced at the far end of the room, stroking his grizzled beard. His cap was askew and his white collar rumpled. Hester could hear her uncle talking to himself.

"Poor Margaret, may she rest in peace with the angels," muttered Sir Hugh. "I should never have allowed her to elope with Dafydd Vaughan, though 'twas said the man could charm birds down from the trees. And now her daughter, set on an even wilder course."

Hester bit down on her nails, thought better of it, and tugged a tendril free from her coif and twisted it around her finger. Rain splattered on the mullioned windows, and the footman closed the heavy damask curtains. He lit beeswax candles set in silver sconces on the walls and bowed himself out. A fire blazed in the hearth, its light glinting off shelves of legal volumes. Beside the fire stood two cushioned chairs on either side of a mahogany table.

Sir Hugh, noticing her presence, gestured her to a chair. Hester curtseyed and sat. She saw a parchment on the table, identical to her own. Her heart raced and her hands shook. To cover her confusion, she leaned down to stroke Shep, the old dog, dozing by the fire.

"Thank you for coming, niece. I have but an hour before I must away to London town." Sir Hugh sat and Shep moved toward him. They looked rather alike, Sir Hugh with his bushy eyebrows and Shep with his grey, springy fur.

Hester felt a pang of abandonment and clasped her trembling hands in her lap.

"I confess I have not been paying mind to you and Alice recently," said Sir Hugh, "but this proposed venture of yours is both foolhardy and dangerous, and I must forbid it."

"But, Uncle," Hester began to protest, her brow furrowing.

"It is well," continued Sir Hugh, "that Lady Maud has taught you how to heal the villagers of their ailments. It is her duty as lady of the manor to provide liniments, cordials, and such like to tenants in need, but you are not lady of the manor, and offering to minister to the King is beyond comprehension!" He blew out his cheeks in exasperation.

No, thought Hester, *I am not a lady.* She stared into the fire. *Uncle can't understand how it feels to be called "Mistress" while my younger cousin is always "Lady Alice." This is my one chance for greatness. And for life itself, for if ever I were to be with child...*

Sir Hugh, irritated by Hester's inattention, brandished the document toward her. Hester ducked as if it were a loaded musket. "As your guardian I received a copy of the letter sent you from His Majesty."

Hester stammered, "I can explain, Uncle..."

"Yea, but by the Mass, however did you gain this summons?"

Hester felt the guilty flush arise from her breast. Despite her efforts at suppression, the scarlet betrayer crept inexorably upwards until it had tinged her face and neck crimson. She gulped. "I sent his niece, Lady Frances, a necklace to ensure he received my letter." The words tumbled from her lips. "I wrote saying how Aunt Maud had trained me in the healing arts, and as His Majesty was descended from King Arthur—"

"So you fed his vanity!" Sir Hugh snorted. He ran his hand through his hair, making it even more dishevelled.

Hester rushed on. "And how Arthur's half-sister Morgana had healed him, so why not permit a woman to dress his leg ulcers?"

"By all the virgin martyrs of Heaven!" exclaimed Sir Hugh.

"Morgana le Fay was a powerful witch! Did you not think about my work in the courts trying to keep women healers safe from the charge of witchcraft?"

Hester's eyelids drooped and she hung her head. "No, Uncle, I am sorry. I did not think."

Sir Hugh frowned. "It goes slow. It will be at least next summer before the bill becomes law." He kicked at a log, and Shep startled as sparks scattered in the grate. "Let me speak plain, niece. You are a handsome young woman, and when you are kneeling down putting a dock-leaf poultice or whatever it is that you, by Saint George, propose to use on Henry's festering wound, he will see your breasts peeping up over the lace of your bodice. And whatever Harry sees, he wants."

"Uncle, I can conduct myself with decorum, even—"

"His word is law!" Sir Hugh leaned forward and spat into the fire. The gobbet of saliva struck a glowing log, hissed a moment, and was no more. He took a slow in-breath. "I have been summoned to council in Westminster. I am elevated to senior cleric in this bill to defend wise women and can no longer avoid swearing the King's Oath."

"Oh, no!" gasped Hester. "We knew that this might happen someday, but already?"

Every schoolchild knew that all in positions of responsibility must formally acknowledge Henry as Supreme Head of the Church. Refusal was treason and meant death and confiscation of lands.

"Henry has coveted Hartbourne for years," growled Sir Hugh. "But your aunt and I agree. We cannot betray our faith." Shep whimpered and kicked his legs, and Sir Hugh stroked him behind the ears. "I do not want to follow my old friend and mentor Sir Thomas More to the block, but if needs must be…"

Hester frowned and clenched her fists. Sir Hugh had a beautiful home and family—and an adoring dog. What was the old religion that he was prepared to die for it?

"I would not be telling you this were it not that I also received a letter today, from your father." He pulled a parchment from his sleeve. "He requests your return to him in North Wales, and your escort should arrive any day now."

"Any day?" Hester echoed, her heart sinking. "And does Father mention Dickie?"

"No, my dear." Sir Hugh sighed. "You know if Dickie were to travel, the journey would take weeks as he cannot ride." The pair sat in silence except for Shep's steady breathing and the crackle of the fire. It hung unsaid between them that Dafydd had no interest in seeing his son. Hester felt a blaze of anger toward him and curled the tendril of hair tighter around her finger.

"I, your aunt, and your cousin here at Hartbourne will miss you greatly." He reached over and took Hester's hand. "But you will be able to pay your respects at your mother's grave in Holywell, once you cross into Wales."

But why should I want to go there? I have no memory of her and I have only this one chance with the King. "Oh, please, Uncle, reconsider. You have been a true father to me. My father in Wales is a…" She was too ashamed to say the word "lunatic." Her only memories of him were of his rampage following his wife's death. Hester breathed in, and for a moment the smoke from the hearth was from the bonfire on which her father had burned all her mother's clothes and possessions. Hester choked and tears started in her eyes.

Sir Hugh took both her hands in his. "I am sure he has a good home to offer you, although the King seized most of his family's lands." Bitterness gravelled his voice as he added, "Like he may soon seize ours." Hester uttered a moan and Sir Hugh spoke more gently. "And I expect he has a fine suitor awaiting you."

Hester's thoughts raced. *Without Our Lady of Westminster's girdle, I will be married and dead within twelve months.*

"Now, my dear," concluded Sir Hugh, "promise you will not venture to Hampton Court the morrow but will stay home, like a good girl."

Hester stared into the fire at the ruby-red coals. She imagined devils in Hell flinging pitchforks at sinners, searing their flesh and mocking as they writhed in agony, screaming for mercy that would never come. Sinners such as herself, who lied to their loved ones. She cursed herself for what she was about to do, but something hardened inside her. Sir Hugh knew nothing of how it felt to be envy-blistered of those with true parents and prospects. Besides, Sir Hugh would owe her a huge debt of gratitude once she had succeeded with the King. Surely Henry would not execute his new bride's beloved uncle over such trivial reason as an oath.

Hester squeezed her fists so tightly that her nails, bitten as they were, dug into her palms. The pain steadied her. "Very well," she said, "I shall not go the King." Her eyes narrowed, and inside she prayed, *Dear Blessed Virgin, I will confess and be shriven, I swear it. But later, not now.*

"That's my sweet niece," replied Sir Hugh. "Now promise me to say no word to your aunt of what takes me to London tonight. She believes I go about my usual work, and why alarm her before I have even met with the council? And she does tend to worry, so."

Hester nodded—at least she could keep that promise. Sir Hugh rose and so did Hester. She curtseyed. She felt sick to her stomach with sin as she walked toward the door.

Sir Hugh opened it for her and she curtseyed again. He bent to kiss her forehead and signed her with the cross. "God bless you," he said.

Hester stood in the hallway glaring at the portraits of Sir Hugh's ancestors that lined the walls. *Why can Uncle not outwardly conform to the King's religion and privately keep his own faith? Does he wish to become another martyr like Sir Thomas More?* She recalled the King's ordering More's head preserved in cumin so the crows would not peck at it where it sat, impaled upon Tower Bridge. The traitor's head was to remain intact as warning to other obdurate subjects. Hester chuckled at the idea of a pickled head. But then she could not dismiss the image of a shrivelled skull plastered with black hair. A wave of nausea struck her and she sank onto a bench.

Hester is little—it took all her strength to push open the door to Mother's room. She knew only grown women were allowed in there and she should not go in, but she was worried about Mother. Hester knew that women took to their chamber a few weeks before they were due to have a baby. But why was Mother in there now, on the first of May? She had said the baby would come out in mid-June. Once she was inside the room she heard a frightful scream. Was Mother making that terrible sound? What were those two women doing, taking a black, blood-covered thing from between Mother's bent legs? Blood drenched the white linen sheets and splattered over the floor. Hester screamed at the women to make that devil stop hurting Mother. Another woman shoved Hester out the room; the door slammed shut in her face. Her mother gave a harrowing cry, "Our Lady, help me!" then silence.

Hester sat down outside the door, listening.

A voice called out, "It's a boy! Heaven be praised!" A pause. Then, "But it's blue and not breathing!"

Another voice: "Quick, Martha, clear its throat. Dear Lord, she's bleeding far too much."

Hester heard a feeble cry, like a kitten mewling. "Warm him up, but best baptize him, in case. Please, God, let it stop! Mistress! Lady Margaret! Wait until we can call the priest!"

A wail of anguish, then, "She's gone! Lord have mercy on her soul."

Hester could make out a murmuring, "I baptize thee Dickon, *in nomine Patris et Filii et Spiritus Sancti*, Amen." Then the only sound was of women sobbing.

Hester knew something really bad had happened. She chewed on her fingernails to try to stop the sick emptiness in her stomach.

She felt so bad inside and there could be only one reason for it. She must have done something bad. Of course! She had opened the door. If only she hadn't opened the door just at that moment, everything would have been alright. She had not meant for the bad thing to happen, and she wished with all her heart she had not opened the door. But it was too late for wishing now, and she would have to live with what she had done.

he great clock chimed the hour. Hester was late for prayers. She ran upstairs to Lady Maud's chamber, wondering, *How will I persuade Aunt Maud to allow me appear at court tomorrow?* She promised the coat of arms hanging above the balustrade, *I swear when I am queen, I will make amends to Sir Hugh and commission a statue of Our Lady for Mother's tomb.*

As Hester entered the solar, she glanced up at a gold-embroidered tapestry of a unicorn resting its head in a maiden's lap. Hester's breath caught in her throat. Now forsworn, she was no less criminal than that treacherous young woman. In the background, hunters peeped out from behind a bush, about to seize the slumbering beast and cut off its horn. *Oh, if Father hadn't laid his horn in Mother's lap a second time, she would not have died. No, I must not think of that now. Henry's horn is old and mayhap will work but the once. Just one healthy son, please God.*

Three women were gathered around an oval table. Lady Maud sat at the head on a hard-backed willow chair. On her right sat Lady Joyce, her widowed older sister; on her left sat Alice. Hester curtseyed and took a seat beside her cousin. Alice squeezed her hand and whispered, "Mother said your father has sent for you." Hester nodded and returned the pressure.

Lady Maud paused in reading aloud from her missal. Her face was still comely, although etched with lines of care. A slender woman, she wore a plain grey robe, which, along with her crucifix, gave her more the appearance of a lady abbess than mistress of a noble household.

"Dear Hester, you will be greatly missed," said she.

Guilt painted Hester's face red as a robin's breast and she stared down at the table, hoping others would not notice her flush.

"Today's study is the Flight of the Holy Family," continued Lady Maud.

The picture of Mary in robes of cerulean blue gave Hester an idea. "Excuse me, Aunt Maud, may I go to Hampton Court to hear Mass tomorrow? It is the feast of the Queenship of the Blessed Virgin, and I wish to offer up prayers for the repose of my mother's soul." *I am already damned for lying, so what is one more?*

Alice's green eyes widened in surprise.

Lady Maud turned to her sister. "Who preaches tomorrow?"

Lady Joyce was assistant keeper of the queen's wardrobe. She wore a voluminous pink damask gown; an opal necklace lay half-buried between her ample breasts. "Bishop Gardiner," she said, frowning, "one of the last to accept the King's religion."

"I believe he is still a true Catholic at heart," said Lady Maud. "Will you accompany Alice and Hester?"

"The King doesn't trust Gardiner, so I shall hold back, but the girls can hear him, since you so wish it."

Lady Maud nodded and stood; the women followed her to a niche beside the window covered by a white silk curtain. Alice withdrew it and they knelt before an altar on which stood a small crucifix. Christ's fingers curled in paroxysms around the nails piercing His hands, and His face was contorted in agony. Beside the crucifix was an exquisite, twelve-inch-high alabaster Madonna cloaked in blue satin, a diadem of rubies upon her head. Her expression was of utmost serenity.

Lady Maud recited the antiphon.

Salve, Regina, Mater misericordiae,
Vita, dulcedo, et spes nostra, salve.
Ad te clamamus exsules filii Hevae
Ad te suspiramus, gementes et flentes
In hac lacrimarum valle...

Hester pondered the words in English. *O Queen, Mother of Mercy, our life, our sweetness, and our hope. We, Eve's children, mourning and weeping in this vale of tears, call out to thee.* She stared at her fingernails, bitten to the quick. Why should this world be a vale of tears? But, regardless, she must stop biting her nails before they bled. The King would not wish to be attended by someone with horrid, bleeding fingernails.

The women intoned the final "*amicus Virgo Maria, ora pro nobis*" and crossed themselves. *And especially pray for me, Blessed Virgin, come the morrow,* thought Hester.

Lady Maud led the way to a side chamber where supper awaited. On the table sat a poached salmon, a game pie, and wassail bread with marmalade. Hester took her seat facing the salmon, which stared at her with baleful eye.

Lady Maud handed a piece of fish to her sister. "Hester and I are reading Plato's *Republic* in Greek. Her Latin is excellent, too, and she knows Ovid's *Metamorphoses* by heart." She frowned and twisted her wedding ring. "I wish Alice showed more interest in the Classics. Her Latin is quite good, but she knows very little Greek."

Alice blushed and Lady Maud turned to Hester. "You must take the *Republic* with you to Wales."

"I see no reason for this learning in women," said Lady Joyce. "You studied with Sir Thomas More's daughters, but did his ancient books avail him in the end?" She speared another piece of salmon. "Delicious, and Alice, that silk gown is most becoming on you."

"I wish you would not bestow such handsome gifts upon her, sister." Lady Maud pursed her lips and changed the subject. "I have been studying some of Hippocrates's texts. He claims the falling sickness is due to a disorder in the brain and no whit is the Devil to blame. If the common folk knew this, they would, I am sure, show some compassion toward my poor nephew. Instead they treat Dickon as worse than a leper."

Hester cast her aunt a grateful smile.

"That is all very well," said Lady Joyce, "but I wish you would stop brewing physic for your tenants. Are you not afraid of being charged with witchcraft?" All four women crossed themselves.

"No," replied Lady Maud, "for our dear departed mother succoured likewise her tenants. It is the solitary wise women who face persecution, but Sir Hugh is even now riding for London to prepare a parliament bill to preserve their safety."

Hester gulped and pushed away the remains of her meal.

Lady Joyce coughed. "Sister, speaking of your husband, has he rethought conforming to the King's religion?"

"No." Lady Maud frowned. "He has not. Should he be arrested and we women forced to leave Hartbourne, we would find refuge with the nuns evicted from Wilton Abbey two years ago." She turned to Hester. "I am most sorry this would exclude Dickie, but remember, dear heart, we must suffer for our faith only a short time here on Earth before enjoying Paradise for eternity."

Hester nodded and clenched her hands under the tablecloth. *Blessed Lady, help me win the King's affection and save Dickie.*

Lady Joyce groaned. "To leave all this!" She gestured toward the tapestries and fine oak furnishings. "And Heaven defend us when Henry discovers his dear Catherine Howard is wanton and recalls that Anne Boleyn was a Howard too. Our family is doomed!"

"We are just second cousins to the queen through our mother and shall not suffer for that poor, wicked girl's disgrace." Lady Maud crumbled bread on her plate.

"But Anne Boleyn destroyed our religion!" exclaimed Lady Joyce, spearing another piece of salmon.

"Do you ever wonder what will befall Anne's daughter, little Elizabeth?" asked Lady Maud.

"A bastard cut out of the succession?" sneered Lady Joyce. "Some lordling will be found to wed her. She will be ridden hard till she whelps her tenth and dies from exhaustion."

Lady Maud sighed and turned to Alice and Hester. "You may be excused."

Hester knelt to receive her aunt's blessing and inhaled her fragrance of lily of the valley.

"Your hair has come loose," said Lady Maud, tucking the strand back under Hester's coif. "It is bright and shiny like the raven's wing."

The raven is a bird of ill omen, thought Hester. She felt a sudden urge to confess her plan to her aunt, but resisted. *This is my only chance at fortune*, she told herself again. *My only chance.*

The cousins set their candles on a side table in their chamber. A trio of moths tapped on the outside of the windowpane.

Alice sat on the bed they shared. "I shall miss you very much," said she.

Hester wondered whether to tell Alice of Sir Hugh's troubles. But how could she tell Alice when she had promised not to tell Lady Maud? Overwhelmed by doubt and guilt, she sought refuge in flippancy. "How can I go to Wales when I am soon to be Queen of England?"

Alice realized she would get no sense from her cousin this night. "Will you unfasten my kirtle, then, Your Majesty?"

Hester laughed and did so. The cousins unlaced each other's sleeves and bodices, and clad only in their smocks, dived under the blankets and rubbed their feet over the sheets for warmth.

"Oh, I nearly forgot!" exclaimed Hester. She retrieved the King's letter from her gown pocket. She kissed it and placed it under the bolster. Hester unfastened her braids and handed Alice a hairbrush. Alice knelt behind and, placing one hand on Hester's scalp, brushed out her cousin's hair with long, even strokes. "Your hair is soft, while mine is like straw."

"Your hair is not like straw," replied Hester, "it's more like hay."

Alice rapped Hester's head with the back of the brush, then resumed her task. Hester relaxed into the trance of being stroked.

"Perhaps Mother could find a way for you to stay with us?" asked Alice, softly. She put her hand on her cousin's shoulder and the warmth made Hester want to weep; she was glad that the dimming light hid her tears. Hester waved a hand in front of her face as if to dispel the ghost of a long forgotten memory.

"It is too late; I am committed to the King tomorrow," said Hester, her heart racing. "By the afternoon, I trust I shall be his promised bride." Her hand shook as she reached for a little painting on the windowsill. "Here is Saint Margaret emerging from the dragon. Swear on it that you will keep my secret, and if you fail me, may a dragon devour you forever."

Alice hesitated. "I swear. But, sweet coz, you are frenzied like a bear staked for baiting."

Hester realized she was panting. She seized Alice's arm. "I know as much as his physicians. They treat his leg ulcers with ground pearls, which is useless."

Alice laughed. "Casting pearls before swine!"

"Shush! I know, thanks to Aunt Maud, that borage, calendula, and blessed thistle will heal his morbels. We have seen huge sores…"

"Yes, but on farmers and millers, not on…"

Hester ignored her and lay down. "And if I succeed, Dickie shall have his own apartments and hens and a henhouse, and your family will keep Hartbourne. Also I shall give a purse of gold to the poor of Westminster because Our Lady's girdle will afford me safe deliverance of the King's son."

Alice, realizing that counsel to her cousin was water running from a duck's back, shut her eyes and soon fell asleep.

Hester's mind would not cease its whirring. *My plan must not fail, for if it does I will likely be dead in childbed by next Michaelmas, and Dickie, every remaining minute of his life, will wish he were dead.*

She climbed out of bed to check the contents of her linen script.

Its pouches contained herbs and a phial each of poppyseed juice and rosewater. The phial of rosewater was only half full so she replenished it from her medicine chest. She inhaled the fragrance of roses then slipped back under the bedclothes and fell into a doze.

Hester dreamed she was in her old home in Wales and was lying in a huge bed with light shining on her through the window. She could smell Mother's scent of roses. Suddenly a wolf appeared. Frightened, she looked for Mother. Then Hester was standing in the garden, but the plants had grown huge and a mouse in a branch sang "To Heaven," over and over. *Mother always said our garden was Heaven, so she has to be somewhere nearby.* She must be playing their favourite game of hide-and-go-seek. Hester looked behind an old bench, but all she saw was a tiny green cat. Then she saw a large rose bush in the middle of the lawn. *Of course, Mother is hiding behind that bush.* She could even see the red of her dress peeping through the leaves. She crept up to the bush and raced around to the other side. "Ha! I have found you now!" she cried, but instead of Mother, it was a red snake. Hester ran from it, frantic, calling out, "Mother! Come out, Mother, wherever you are! Please come out." Once she found Mother, she would tell her how angry she was with her for frightening her. Mother shouldn't have tricked her like that; she had ruined their special game. In her dream the snake turned into a bundle of black rags. The bundle hissed, "It is your fault Mother has gone away. It is because you were angry with her. What a bad girl you are."

"Stop! Stop!" cried Hester. "I am sorry, I did not mean to be angry. Please let her come back so I can tell her myself."

The voice mocked her. "Too late for that now. You have learned what happens to wicked little girls. No one wants to be with them. Nobody will ever want to be with you. You will never, ever be loved again."

Hester woke, her heart thumping and tears pouring down her face. She scolded herself for her stupidity. Mother had been dead for thirteen years, why cry about her now?

he stifling hot privy chamber reeked of perfumes: rosewater, ambergris, and civet musk with an underlay of fetid flesh. Dozens of beeswax candles set in gold candelabra lit the room. The King, wearing a yellow silk nightshirt, reclined in his purple canopied bed. Using a gold spoon he stirred honey into a goblet of hippocras. He drained it and thrust it toward Will Somers, his jester. Will was clad in a green jerkin, which ill-concealed his hunchback. That, plus his bulging forehead and protruding jaw, made him appear more brute than human. He took the goblet and handed the King a silver platter of sugarplums.

"To which grasping lord have I granted an audience tomorrow?" mumbled Henry, his mouth full.

"None, Sire. Only to one Hester Vaughan, niece to Sir Hugh Grantmire."

"Ah, the lawyer who refuses to acknowledge me as Head of the Church. He who may soon be without his own head."

Will guffawed obediently.

"Your Majesty is no doubt aware that she is kinswoman to Queen Catherine."

Henry scowled and his eyes narrowed. "But of course, and where was Madam last month when my leg pained so badly I had to travel my court in a litter?" He snorted. "Amusing herself with her fine gentlemen." He cried out as a spasm of pain shot through his calf. "Oh my wretched leg!" Will refilled Henry's goblet. "No, the queen is just high-spirited," Henry said and gave a little chuckle, then his lips puckered and he growled, "God's teeth, have I been tricked, bewitched again, like by Anne? How everyone would mock me if…No, Catherine is my sweet little wife, who worships me," he murmured. Aloud he commanded, "Remind me to commission another diamond necklace for Her Majesty."

Will bowed. "As you command, Sire."

"My wine is cold," said Henry. He frowned and his jaw tightened. The jester withdrew a poker from the blazing fire and plunged it in the goblet for a few seconds. Henry quaffed the remainder in two gulps.

He tugged a ruby ring from his index finger. "Mother's ring. It is like unto yesterday when I first wore it," he mused. "I was nearly twelve and my elder brother, Arthur, newly buried. Mother was draped in black velvet, and I was sitting at her feet with my head in her lap against her big belly. I stroked her skirt and she ran her hands through my hair. I told her I had killed three deer in her honour that morning. Her ring caught in my hair. She laughed and asked if I would like to try it on. It fell off my finger, but Mother said one day it would fit me and be mine, and I said, 'But not, please God, for many years yet to come.' Then I sang a psalm and she joined in with the verse, 'Deliver my soul from the sword and my life from the power of the dog.'"

Henry wiped a hand over his forehead. "Then she said I was now her only son and how much she loved me. But then she sighed. Oh I remember that weary sigh. To cheer her, I told her she was the Lady of my heart and I was her own true Sir Knight. I promised to protect all damsels for her honour, and she smiled at me. Just then Father came in; he scowled as I bowed to him. He snarled at me to be gone, for I was tiring Mother. He only ever loved Arthur. I wanted to kiss Mother good night, but I was afraid of angering Father. I wish I had defied him. It was the very next morning she died." Henry sobbed. "It was your birthday, Mother. You dead and the baby too." Tears ran down the furrows of his jowls, and he reached for the linen napkin Will had ready.

Henry shook his fist at the ceiling. The veins stood out on his forehead. "I prayed to the Virgin to save Mother, but she ignored me. God, you should not have taken the best of mothers. But where is the mother of God now? She is gone. All her images smashed. We are even. No, nothing will ever replace mine."

The wine took its effect. The King fell asleep. Will took the ring and empty cup from Henry's hand and snuffed the candles.

※

Hester fell back asleep. The bundle of rags became a witch who tied a red silk handkerchief close around Hester's neck. Hester tried to rip the handkerchief off, but it turned into a ruby pendant pressing into her throat. The more she clawed at it, the harder it pressed. She tried to scream but could make no sound.

Hester woke to a cock crowing and leaped out of bed and drew back the curtains. In the mist-covered fields a family of rabbits cavorted, their white tails bobbing up and down.

Alice woke and bid her cousin good morrow just as the sun's first rays shone through the window, emblazoning the room.

"We must dress!" exclaimed Hester. "We cannot be late. Should I wear my blue dress or the green?"

"We should pray first." Alice knelt, as did Hester. The only prayer that came to Alice was "Salve Stella Maris," the orison drowning sailors made to Our Lady, imploring her to receive their souls.

Hester cried, "Amen," sprang up, and donned her best chemise of fine lawn. Alice fastened the bodices to reveal an edge of Brussels lace and a hint of cleavage. "Today would have been Mother's birthday," said Hester, her brows contracting. "We are both Geminis."

"Then Aphrodite is the ruling deity of you both," said Alice, helping Hester into the reed-stiffened petticoat.

"Indeed," replied Hester. "Father met Mother at Sir Thomas More's house and they eloped the following week."

Alice fastened the silver-embroidered damask underskirt. "Now all that is required is for you to Aphrodite the King," said she, smiling.

Hester lifted her blue velvet dress from the chest. As she nuzzled against its softness a few dried rose petals fell to the floor. The dress fit snugly, flaring out over her hips. Alice attached the sleeves and folded them back to reveal the same silver pattern as on the underskirt. Then she braided her cousin's hair and set a black satin hood with a pearl biliment on her head.

"I shall wear Mother's sapphire pendant," said Hester, but her hands trembled, so Alice fastened it behind her neck. "Look at my fingernails. They are bitten down to the quick."

"Do not be discomfited, dear heart. Soon your fingers will be so laden with jewels you will lack strength enough to raise them to your mouth." Alice stroked Hester's hand. "And your pendant is beautiful. I know how much you treasure it."

Hester gave a tiny smile. "Yes, Father sent it with me to Hartbourne. It has been in the Vaughan family for centuries, dating back to Ednyfed Fychan, who was also the King's ancestor. It is strange to think we are related."

"Have courage," said Alice, straightening the gem at Hester's throat. "So long as you are not first cousins you can still marry."

A wave of gratitude passed through Hester and tears welled in her eyes.

"Oh, dear, do not cry," warned Alice. "The King must not see red eyes as well as bitten fingernails."

Hester laughed and placed her script and the King's summons in her dress pocket. She recited in her head, *Mallow for soothing the pain, and sphagnum moss for drying the ulcer.* "Alice, this is my only chance. Wish me good fortune."

Alice kissed her softly on the forehead. "The blessing of Our Lady and Saint Luke the physician be upon you, now and at the hour of your..." She faltered for she did not like to say the word *death*. "At the hour of your need."

Strangely moved, Hester bobbed her head as if blessed by a priest. Hester helped Alice into a forest green dress with pale yellow underskirt. She braided her cousin's hair and pinned her hood in place. The cousins linked arms and proceeded downstairs. Sunlight blazed through a stained glass window, and for a second, Alice was tinted blue and Hester scarlet.

Goody stood at the foot of the stairs. "Why needs you be gadding off to Hampton Court? By Saint Michael and all the angels, cannot you say your prayers here at home?" She glowered at them both. "Lady Maud is at the mill, for Mistress Janet's waters broke an hour ago and the babe is two months early, and the midwife is delivering the blacksmith's wife right as we speak."

Hester felt relief at not having to see her aunt right now. She offered up a prayer for both mothers and their newborns.

Goody continued, "And she would have been glad of your help later on, preparing a liniment for Farmer Bates. He has the rheumatism very bad, saints bless him."

Alice nodded. "We shall return early afternoon. Please find Stewart and tell him to prepare the carriage."

"There's nary a half-dozen men left for your escort, since most went with Sir Hugh last night." Goody sniffed and turned on her heel.

The mention of Sir Hugh caused Hester's stomach to clench in a knot and she swayed.

Alice looked at her. "Sit here while I order breakfast from the buttery."

Hester lowered herself on a bench. She felt perspiration trickling down her back. What was she thinking of, intruding upon the King? Her mouth felt parched and her heart raced. *I could send word that I am indisposed. He would understand that my courses were upon me and so would not want me near him. He would soon forget about me, for I am no one to him, after all.*

Hester forced herself to stand up. "No, I am not a no one,"

she told a suit of armour, "and it will take more than my heart fluttering to stop me now."

Alice returned followed by a servant carrying bread and ale. Hester swallowed the bitter liquid but could not eat a bite of food. A clatter of hooves outside signalled the arrival of their carriage. Hester walked down the steps and fainted.

enry awoke and groaned. Will leaped from his truckle bed, wiping drool from his mouth.

"My leg pains like the Devil!" shouted Henry. "Summon my physicians. No, those fools are worthless." He groaned. "Send for my barber. Have to look good for the ladies. But by Saint George, Mistress Vaughan is not even a lady." He smoothed strands of thinning grey hair over his pate.

After the barber had trimmed Henry's beard and shaved his cheeks, the King called for a silver mirror. A pair of hooded, mud-coloured eyes, near obliterated by rolls of fat, stared back at him. He scowled in disgust, then blinked. "Rather fine for an old man," he declared.

"Your Majesty is in his prime," protested Will.

"A great monarch in his prime," echoed the barber.

Henry snorted. Two grooms assisted him into a fine white silk chemise and guided his legs into his nether hose. The younger groom's hands shook and his fingers brushed against the ulcer. Henry cried out, his eyes watering from pain and rage. He reached down and cuffed the youth. "Away with you, varlet!"

The elder groom stepped forward. "Pray permit me, your Majesty." With firm yet gentle hands he assisted the king into his breeches and then into a gold and black embroidered doublet. The groom pulled the fabric of the King's undershirt through slashings in the doublet's front and sleeves and clipped on jewelled aglets to keep the ruffles in place. Will attached a gold embroidered codpiece to the King's hose and helped him into a black surcoat with gold piping. The groom set a pearl-encrusted cap on Henry's head and brought forward a long

Venetian mirror. Henry stood before it, staring at his reflection, and nodded.

Henry VIII, King of England and Lord of Ireland, towered over his groom by a head, and Will barely reached his elbow. Both servants bowed low before the image in the glass. It was instinct—the glory and royal prestige of the realm emanated from this colossus of a man. Notwithstanding that he was but the great-grandson of an illegitimate child of John of Gaunt, fourth son of King Edward III, Henry had established himself in his people's minds as near divine.

He held out his hand and Will placed the ruby ring on his index finger.

"Bring me my harp, I shall play awhile."

※

Alice had held a phial of hartshorn to Hester's nose and supported her cousin to the waiting carriage. When Stewart, the groom, hastened to her side, Hester assured him she was quite well. Stewart was of middle age but had never married, avowing he preferred the company of horses to women. His pendulous upper lip and yellow teeth made him appear as much horse as man. His woolen jerkin was shabby and patched at the elbows, but he had a good, horsy smell about him.

"God's wounds!" declared Stewart. "You do look fine this morning, Mistress Vaughan. A true princess I would hazard you were, did I not know better."

Hester glanced at Alice and blushed. Alice gave a smile.

Stewart handed the young women a few withered apples. Hester offered one to Lady, a russet brown pony with white dappling on her flanks. Lady took the apple, and Hester felt her teeth nibble against her palm. Mirabel, the pony yoked beside Lady, pawed the ground, and Alice fed her an apple. Hester stroked Lady's muzzle and bent to kiss her warm velvet nose; the pony's chestnut brown eyes, fringed by long black eyelashes, met Hester's and bored into her heart.

"I will always love you, Lady," she whispered, running her hand through the pony's mane.

The coachman took his seat, and four gangly youths, outfitted in livery too big for them, mounted their shire horses and arranged themselves two before and two behind the carriage.

Stewart assisted Alice into the seat facing forward. A miasma of envy swirled in Hester's gut. *Alice always has precedence, even though she is younger.* Even worse was knowing that Alice was totally unaware of this gall of jealousy. Hester knew Alice would dispense with her rank in a heartbeat, like a used handkerchief, had she but known the suffering it caused her. If rank could be so disposed of.

They travelled the old Roman road along the banks of the River Thames. It was practically as intact as when it was first built, some fifteen hundred years before. It was said that any hole, dug to ten feet in the area, would yield Roman remnants.

The carriage passed a group of old willow trees whose long hanging branches swept the river's surface.

"Oh no!" gasped Hester.

"Are you unwell?" asked Alice in alarm.

"I forgot the powdered willow bark—Latin, *salix*. Every apothecary carries it."

"Surely you have enough for the King's poultice without that?"

"It relieves pain and fever, when taken by mouth."

Alice frowned. "Then surely his physicians will have given him sufficient already."

"Probably." Hester leaned back on the seat.

An hour later, the carriage arrived at Hampton Court Palace. It passed under the archway leading into the first courtyard. Two liveried servants appeared and bowed low, aware that only the very wealthy travelled by coach. But when they saw that its occupants were two unfamiliar young women and their escort mere yokels, their obsequious smiles curdled into smirks.

"I am Mistress Vaughan," declared Hester, as one helped her descend. "I have come to administer physic to His Majesty's Grace."

The men stared at her then broke into laughter before pointing the driver toward the stables. Boys appeared who led away their attendants' horses.

Hester blushed from shame and rage.

Alice whispered, "Take no mind." She assembled their escort and the party passed into the second archway. Alice slowed to admire the magnificent gold clock on the wall. "This was not here when we visited Aunt Joyce last Christmas."

The clock told the hour, the day, and the month, with all the astrological signs displayed around its circumference. Hester saw how the sun revolved around the earth. Why should not Henry revolve around her, once she had given him the healthy son he so craved? The clock hands pointed to eleven—one hour to pass before her audience. The group reached the stone staircase that led to the great hall and thence to the nobles' apartments.

"After we find Aunt Joyce we will hear Mass," said Alice.

"I do not wish her to know about my attending the King."

"Very well." Alice nodded. "But Mass is important. I am sure knights always prayed on the eve of battle." She squeezed Hester's arm.

A press of servants swarmed up the stairs, nearly unbalancing the women; it was dinnertime in hall. Alice signalled to their escort to clear a way, but even so men's elbows poked their shoulders, followed by gruff apologies. Women trod on their hems and tittered. The party entered the hall where the air was palpable with steam and the fragrance of roasted pork. Servers brought venison pasties and mince pies and set them on tables already loaded with roasted pigs' trotters and apple dumplings. Hester felt nauseated and her knees shook; she was glad they were hidden under her skirts.

Alice pointed to a tapestry above the door leading to Lady Joyce's apartments. "Look! It is Solomon and the Queen of Sheba."

Ah, I can imagine you in that role, discoursing the ancient Greeks with the King."

"No, do not say that! Uncle says there is a stained glass portrait of the Queen of Sheba in King's College chapel." Hester lowered her voice. "She has the face of Queen Catherine. I wish no likeness to her Majesty."

What have I done, coming here to the King at his court? Not only her knees, but her hands now shook. *I feel like a mouse entering the lion's den. But I remember the story of the mouse who plucked the thorn from the lion's paw. Please, Our Lady, help me be that mouse.*

The cousins smoothed their gowns while an attendant rapped on Lady Joyce's door. A groom dressed in blue satin admitted them. Two handsome young men bowed as Alice and Hester passed into the room. Lady Joyce sat at the head of a mahogany table, reading aloud to four women who worked their embroidery.

Alice kissed her aunt and Hester dipped a curtsey.

"Good morrow, niece, Mistress Vaughan." Lady Joyce cast a disdainful glance at their escort and beckoned to her own men. Selecting the two prettiest of her women, she turned to Alice. "Now I can show you to advantage at court."

Thus attended, they proceeded down the hall. Lady Joyce inclined her head toward two finely dressed ladies and dipped a slight curtsey to another. The party paused before the chapel entrance, adorned by painted, sculpted Tudor roses.

Hester considered the Tudor rose, that cunning combination of red Lancastrian and white Yorkist roses. It declared, "Be thankful you have Tudor kings to rule over you, for now there is peace, where before was only strife."

Lady Joyce whispered to Alice, "I shall wait at the entrance. It does no good to be seen here. Only the foolhardy or overrighteous come to hear a bishop the King mistrusts."

Hester's mouth felt dry. What if Henry discovered she had attended Mass celebrated by a cleric he found objectionable? She hesitated, but Alice took her hand and the cousins walked down the aisle, passing beneath great gold candelabra. Images of saints shone from stained glass windows in colours of amethyst, emerald, and ruby.

Hester felt a wave of terror pass through her body. *I wish I were home helping Aunt Maud in the distillery. Blessed Virgin, help me.* She became aware of sweat pooling in the small of her back and her underarms.

"Look at that window beside the altar," said Alice. Hester saw it depicted Mary Magdalene washing Christ's feet. She recognized the similarity between the prostitute's act and her own proposed ministrations to the King. She knew, in the depth of her bowels, she had made a terrible mistake. She clutched the royal letter tightly in her pocket, as if its ink could steel her blood.

The young women joined a small group of worshippers near the chancel. A fair-haired youth wearing a plumed hat smiled and bowed to them. Alice smiled and blushed as she dipped a curtsey.

Hester stared at a painting of the Nativity and thought, *How strange. Our Lady, giving birth to Jesus, suffered no pain at all, like cows giving birth in the fields. A cow utters a low moan, then a minute later licks the afterbirth from its young.* Hester crossed herself—surely it was blasphemy to compare the birth of Our Lord to that of a calf. Yet with cows, both mother and calf survived. She must obtain the holy girdle. Hester had accompanied Lady Maud to deliveries in the village, when the midwife was unavailable. Her aunt never gave physic to ease labour pains, for that was contrary to Scripture and was witchcraft besides. Yet a travailing woman's use of a holy relic was an act of piety. But that was before Henry abolished worship of the Mother of God and the saints and declared veneration of relics idolatry. It was most confusing. Hester's head ached and her stomach cramped. She wanted to bite her fingernails, but instead, to relieve her anxiety, she stroked the velvet of her skirt. Up and down, up and down. The rhythm and the softness soothed her.

Bishop Gardiner intoned, "On His garment and on His thigh is written: King of kings and Lord of lords."

A vision of Henry's legs appeared to Hester. Very soon she would be handling them. Again, she began to raise her hand to her mouth but forced it into the pocket containing her linen script. She clutched it so hard her fingers ached.

Mass ended with the blessing, "*Dominus vobiscum.*"

Hester could not rid her mind of the image of the King's legs. Panic overwhelmed her and she picked up her skirts and ran back up the aisle.

"You look as if you have seen a ghost!" exclaimed Alice, when she reached her cousin. "Are you ill?"

"No, just nervous." Hester could not admit, even to her closest friend, that she now realized she was set on a course of absolute folly.

Lady Joyce strode forward. "Hester Vaughan, what means this behaviour? Everyone is staring. Come away." The cousins followed her to a recess in the corridor. Lady Joyce waved her attendants away.

Hester took a deep breath. "I am summoned to His Majesty."

"What? Are you a lunatic, the same as your brother?"

Hester showed Lady Joyce the letter, whereupon that lady cried out and sank down on a bench. Her gentlewomen hurried to her. "Call their carriage!" she ordered.

"Lady Joyce," beseeched Hester, "if I can heal the King, our family will greatly benefit, whereas should I fail, it will be no worse than his physicians."

Lady Joyce ignored her. "Alice, I forbid your accompanying her any further."

"Begging your pardon, Aunt, but I have promised." Alice beckoned her escort and the four lanky youths took their positions.

Lady Joyce moaned. "I am obliged to stay with you, niece. You cannot appear unchaperoned at court. Consider your honour!"

Two grooms dressed in green-and-white Tudor livery admitted

the party to the watching chamber. The room was furnished with fine ivory-inlaid tables and chairs, and paintings of the King's ships adorned the walls. Murmured conversations took place in corners, in part obliterated by the scratching of quills on parchment as scribes took dictation from their noble masters.

Lady Joyce, Alice, and Hester sat on a red satin couch; Lady Joyce's women found stools and took out their embroidery. Hester was glad to sit. She felt aware of the weight of her gown, the layers of velvet and satin and the stiffened reed hoops of her petticoat. It was as if her very dress were trying to keep her anchored here in safety, away from the King.

The fair young man who had bowed to Alice in chapel approached. He wore a surcoat of blue velvet trimmed with fur, and high black leather boots. He brushed a wisp of hair away from his eyes, doffed his plumed hat, and bowed.

"Lady Joyce, good morrow. I trust you are in good health. I do not recollect seeing you in such company before."

Lady Joyce inclined her head and introduced him to her charges as Sir William of Bayston. The cousins rose and dipped curtseys. A faint blush tinted Alice's face as she met his gaze.

Her aunt lowered her voice. "A good man but a penniless Roman Catholic. He and his father would have been executed for refusing the oath but that William's grandfather sent a cask of claret to the Countess of Richmond, the King's grandmother, when she gave birth to His Majesty's father." She muttered under her breath, "The vagaries of this monarch." Lady Joyce looked around to ensure she had not been overheard. She ordered her women to bring her wine and hazelnuts from a sideboard spread with refreshments. Two young noblemen approached Alice, and Sir William stepped back. Lady Joyce smiled and introduced Alice to them as the only child of Sir Hugh Grantmire. Hester assumed that these two, unlike Sir William, were of families favoured by the King. Nonetheless, Lady Joyce did not provide their names; perhaps she had momentarily forgotten them.

The elder wore a pearl earring and the younger sported a yellow cloak. They bowed low to Alice.

"Permit me to say that your hair is the colour of spun gold, my lady," declared Pearl Earring, commenting on strands that had loosened from Alice's headdress. Alice reached to tuck them back behind her hood.

"No, leave those lustrous locks free," begged the youth. "'Twould be unspeakable cruelty to once more imprison them where they…," he paused, then blustered on, "where they cannot gladden the eyes of those privileged to behold such radiance."

Alice's cheeks and neck crimsoned. She left her hair as it was.

"And your eyes are like new verdant leaves on the ash tree," enthused Yellow Cloak.

Hester, watching the tableau, grimaced, and Sir William remarked, "You are not here to be courted, not with so sour an expression on your face."

"I have come hither to attend to His Majesty's health," she confided.

"Does he not have physicians enough that he must recourse to young women's remedies?" asked Sir William. "But I fear your face speaks for itself. The King enjoys the company of handsome young women." A wave of nausea roiled in Hester's stomach and she blanched. Sir William did not notice for he was staring at Alice.

"How are you and Lady Alice related? You are not sisters, for you look nothing alike." Sir William blushed. "I did not mean to infer that you are not pretty as she is. For you are, simply in a different way."

Hester could not help but smile at the knight's discomfiture. "Sir Hugh, Lady Alice's father, is my uncle and guardian."

"Somehow I doubt he knows of your presence here. And does your father know what you are about this day?"

Hester bristled. Her eyes flashed and she nearly spat the words. "My father is a nobleman in Wales, I shall have you know." She flushed from shame. Splotches of red dappled the upper part of her bosom. Where was her father when his only daughter was about to step into—she could not help but complete the thought—the lion's den? Struggling to regain her composure, Hester inquired, "And for what purpose are you here, Sir William?"

"His Majesty has confiscated my family's lands outside Shrewsbury. We cleave to Rome and are fortunate to still be among the living. I am come to plead for the restoration of a farm or two, so we shall not perish from want." He sighed. "I hope to catch the King's ear when he makes his afternoon procession around court." Sir William's brow furrowed. "May I take the liberty of advising you keep your escort close by when you attend His Majesty?"

Hester stole a glance at the door at the far side of the room, the door that led to the presence chamber and thence to the King's private apartments. She wished she could stay here with Alice and the others. Hester felt as if she were being swept away by a river in flood. She reckoned she could still bid a retreat, if she exerted all her strength, but fatigue penetrated the marrow of her bones, and it was easier to continue on, no matter the consequence. Her body swayed for a moment.

"Are you quite well, dear heart?" asked Alice, her brow clouded. She was flanked by her two admirers.

Hester forced a smile. "Yes, thank you."

In a condescending tone, Pearl Earring said, "So, Mistress Vaughan, we understand you will cure the King's morbels. Have the royal physicians no remedies to hand?"

Hester snorted. "Indeed, but they look to the heavens for guidance as to when to administer physic, as if feverfew relieved the headache only when the moon be waning."

Alice laughed, and Hester, having blustered herself into a state of readiness, said, "I shall take two attendants with me. Wish me luck." And in a softer voice, that only Alice could hear, she added, "Pray for me."

Yellow Cloak and Pearl Earring inclined their heads toward

Hester, and Sir William bowed, saying, "God's holy angels be with you, Mistress Vaughan, as you treat His Majesty's ulcers."

Hester scrutinized his face, unsure if he were mocking her. But all she saw was concern. She was momentarily nonplussed. "Thank you, kind sir," she returned. Yet his good wishes caused her heart to falter. It was as if she needed opposition in order to act, and when it was not forthcoming, she was helpless. It was like pushing with all your might against a closed door, and when it suddenly opened from the other side, you fell down in a heap.

Hester glanced over at Lady Joyce, cracking and eating hazelnuts one after the other. She was drinking her second glass of wine and, catching Hester's eye, glared at her. Hester strode toward the door of the presence chamber, affecting a confidence she wished she felt. Two huge uniformed men with crossed halberds guarded the door. They glowered, first at Hester, then at her escort, but their expressions changed to perplexity as they read her letter. It appeared she was here on official business and not merely as a royal diversion. The guards separated their weapons and opened the door and let her pass. Hester jumped as the door slammed closed behind her.

oolish, headstrong young woman," said Lady Joyce, but she smoothed her scowl away to smile at yellow-cloaked Sir Edward de Courcy and ear-ringed Sir Henry Asquith.

The latter asked if Lady Joyce and Alice would care to join them in a game of cards.

Lady Joyce agreed. "But pray fetch me more wine and hazelnuts, first."

The two youths bowed and headed toward the sideboard but were intercepted by a black-robed priest. He murmured something to which Sir Edward answered, "Thank you, uncle." Sir Henry frowned, glanced toward Alice, then the three men, together, hastened from the room.

Lady Joyce gasped at their effrontery, and Alice's rosy cheeks blanched in dismay. Sir William, who had been reclining against a mantelpiece, approached.

"Lady Alice, I fear those two young worthies have received information of an unpleasant nature. Is all well at Hartbourne?"

"I believe so, but now I feel anxious to return home." Alice frowned. "The King will not detain Hester long, I hope." She offered up a prayer for her cousin.

Lady Joyce hissed, "Your father is a fool not to take the King's religion."

"Pray, Aunt, do not speak so." Alice's eyes brimmed with tears, but she willed them back.

"See?" continued Lady Joyce. "Fine, eligible young noblemen shun you as if you bore a cloven hoof." She turned to her women. "Bring me more wine," she ordered.

"Lady Joyce, will you permit me to ask your niece to engage in a game of chess?" asked William.

Lady Joyce nodded and Alice gave him a grateful smile. Sir William produced a miniature chess set from his pocket, and Alice arranged the pieces. He moved a pawn and Alice, a knight.

"I do not think I can concentrate," murmured Alice.

"No, but perhaps it will distract you a little." He leaned forward and whispered, "And will spare any need for conversation with your aunt."

※

The light in the presence chamber dazzled Hester's eyes. Jewelled mirrors reflected sunlight shining through the long windows. She stood on a Persian carpet embroidered in green and gold and stared at the rows of Greek marble statues lining the walls. The chamber was empty. Hester felt faint from terror. She tried to regain some kind of control by naming the gods and goddesses to herself: Artemis, or Diana to the Romans, wearing a short dress and bearing a quiver of arrows; Athena, or Minerva, helmeted, holding her shield that bore the head of the gorgon Medusa; Zeus, the king of the gods, holding a thunderbolt in his right hand.

Hester, followed by her awestruck attendants, proceeded to the gilded door that led to the king's privy chambers. She caught sight of her reflection in a mirror. Black rats' tails framed a death mask of a face. With shaking hands she pushed the loose strands inside her hood. She glanced up at a painting of the Annunciation, hanging beside the archway. Ineffable serenity bathed the Virgin's face as she received the angel's salutations.

Oh Lady, succour me, she prayed silently. *I promise to repay you.*

Hester glanced over her shoulder to the door behind, the door that led back to Alice and safety. Again, she produced her parchment for the scrutiny of two guards at the entrance to the king's private chamber. Horrified, she saw the ink had smudged from the perspiration of her hands, blackening her fingers.

The guards wore crimson and black cloaks trimmed with gilded cord and carried gold-plated axes.

"Mistress Vorn, is that it?" queried the first, pretending he could not read her name.

"Vaughan," corrected Hester.

"An uncommon name for a common bawd," jeered the second guard, ripping the parchment in pieces.

Hester's attendants, shocked at the insult, moved closer to her side, but the guards threatened them with their axes, and the youths retreated. The men opened the huge double doors to the King's closet and shoved Hester through. She waited for her escort to join her, but the guards slammed the doors shut in their faces.

Hester hammered on the doors. "I demand you admit my attendants!" But her words fell only upon gilded oak. She panted from terror; for without an escort, her honour was forfeit. An unattended woman entering the King's private chamber could be there for one purpose only.

She tried to straighten her hood, which had fallen askew, but could not because her fingers shook. She wished she could turn into a mouse and vanish in the wainscoting. Even a move to Wales appeared attractive now.

Hester knew if time passed and she did not reappear, Alice would send to Hartbourne for aid. But how disappointed Aunt Maud would be with her, and even worse, Uncle Hugh would know she had lied to him. She surveyed the room. A carved ebony table stood in the centre, and gold-and-scarlet tapestries adorned the walls. In a corner stood a statue of Apollo, holding his lyre, with a cloak draped over one shoulder. The cloak did nothing to hide his nakedness. Hester glanced, almost against her will, at his finely carved genitalia and then immediately averted her gaze.

On the table stood a golden platter of marzipan, a ramekin of custard, and a silver bowl of cherries. There were sweetmeats enough to satisfy twelve, but only one chair. Hester realized this was the King's dining chamber. She noticed a movement behind a tapestry and called out. "Who is there?" A young boy stepped forward. He was a clean-limbed, pretty youth of about twelve years with golden curls spilling out from under a green velvet cap. A guilty blush suffused his face.

He stammered, "It was only the one, lady," although the stains around his mouth gave him the lie. Hester thought he looked how Dickie would have, had he been born with no impairment. She remembered why she had come here—part for power for herself, and part to help her brother. Oh, yes, and to win the King's love.

"I shall not betray you," said Hester, in a low voice, "but you should be ashamed of eating His Majesty's viands."

"Thank you, Your Ladyship."

The little page doffed his cap and made her a flourishing bow.

Hester savoured the title, "Your Ladyship." Yes, she had only to keep her wits about her and soon it would be "Your Majesty."

Hester walked with a firmer step into the King's closet. Never before had she seen so much colour. The walls and ceiling were painted vibrant reds, blues, and golds. She heard the melody of a harp and a man's voice singing from the room next door. *That must be the King in his privy chamber.* She could discern the words:

My mind shall be
Virtue to use
Vice to refuse
Thus shall I use me.

Hester thought, *A king who puts such noble words to music surely cannot be without courtesy.* But then why did her stomach cramp so?

She glanced at a window. Outside, a pair of cawing ravens strutted on the eaves, fighting over a chicken bone. *I am like them. I am raven and shall fight.*

Hester approached the archway of the privy chamber, above which hung a portrait of Mary Magdalene, kneeling at an altar. The penitent whore's pale, smooth breasts were bare, her nipples pink, and her eyes full of tears. With one hand she caressed a skull and with the other, a crucifix bearing the perfect broken body of her Lord.

Two attendants stood guarding the doorway. One looked straight ahead, ignoring Hester. The other stared at her and gave a salacious grin. He opened the door.

"Mistress Vaughan, you are awaited with pleasure."

ester stood in the doorway of the King's bedchamber. The air was redolent with attar of rose and ambergris but also the unmistakable stench of rotting flesh. The King set down his harp and motioned to a groom, who proffered him a pheasant drumstick on a gold platter. Hester made the King a deep curtsey and stayed in that position half a minute as he chewed and swallowed. To her, it seemed like hours.

Henry waved the now bare bone at her. "Get up."

She rose slowly. "If it please Your Majesty, I am—"

"We know very well who you are. Our most learned young apothecary of the dirty fingers."

He turned his head. "Look, Will. What thinkest you of our little bird?"

Will, crouched in the corner, sang out. "A bird with dirty fingers or feathers, to be sure. Let's hope her under feathers are clean!"

The King tossed the bone aside, the groom caught it on the platter.

"Your Majesty, I do heartily apologize for my inky—"

Henry beckoned with his forefinger. "Come here, my little primrose, so I may better inspect you." Terror rooted Hester to the spot.

"So," said Henry, sweetly, "you ignore the command of your King."

Hester stepped one foot in front of the other.

"Shall your remedies have me riding horseback when I set forth next month on my northern progress?" He growled, "Or will I needs be carried in a litter like some beached whale?"

He waved his groom from the chamber.

"I said come here, you saucy wench."

Hester, her knees shaking, reached the bed and looked into the King's eyes. People spoke of Henry's hawk eyes, but the fleshy upper lids made his eyes look more like a pig's. She immediately dropped her gaze.

Henry, leering at her, beckoned her closer yet. Hester obeyed, her heart hammering inside her chest. The King seemed to be looking at her without seeing her. He saw only an object; something that could be of use to him. He did not see her as a person at all.

Hester withdrew her script from her pocket. She spoke in as firm a voice as she could muster. "If it please Your Majesty, I shall commence with examining the lesions on Your Grace's leg."

Henry chuckled. "So this bold poppet wants to see my legs, does she?"

Will sang, "The King's legs, oh the King's legs. The King has three legs, which one shall the poppet see?"

Will's bulbous forehead made him appear more like an ape than a man. Hester tried to reassure herself that he was just a simpleton, like the ones around Hartbourne. Most were harmless, like Dickie, but one or two had been known to—

"Two of my legs do not feel fine today, but do you know what would be fine to feel?" Henry stared at Hester's bosom.

She prayed fervently under her breath, "Oh, Blessed Virgin, help me." Why on earth had she come? Why had she not listened to Sir Hugh? Hester turned to make a rush for the door, but Will saw her intention and scampered over and locked it.

"Feels fine and is fine to feel," echoed the jester.

Hester realized there was no escape for her now. She addressed the King in a low voice, using all her strength to keep her voice steady. "I am here to apply my salves to His Majesty's wounds."

Henry laughed but succumbed to a fit of coughing. He wheezed, "Methinks you have some other cheer for your King."

Hester's mouth was so dry her tongue cleaved to her palate and she could not speak.

Henry laid a greasy hand on her wrist. "Yea, my little mouse, I think you do." He inserted the forefinger of his other hand in his mouth and made sucking noises.

Will straddled a stool and fondled his codpiece. "A good suck for good king Harry."

Hester grasped her script. A dark stain crept along its linen cover from the perspiration of her hands. "Your Majesty, I—"

Henry leaned forward and seized her arms and pulled her onto the bed beside him.

Hester, flinching in reflex from his sour breath, begged, "Please, Your Majesty, forbear!"

"If you find my breath rank, my pretty piece of marchpane, wait until you get a noseful of this."

At the King's signal, Will unlaced the heel of his hose. The smell from the bloody pus exuding from the bandages was so foul, Hester nearly vomited. How could she have ever thought she wanted to marry this rotting hulk?

She turned her head away. Henry slapped her. His fingernails grazed her cheek and cut the corner of her mouth.

"By Saint George, do not dare avert your gaze from God's anointed." Hester felt wetness at the side of her mouth. She licked it—it tasted of salt and rust.

"I know what you are thinking!" cried Henry. "We think it ourselves, don't we, Will?"

Will sang in falsetto, "We think it morning, noon, and night. The King's legs are a monstrous sight."

Henry groaned. "My calves were once the glory of the kingdom. They were far, far superior to those of that popinjay Francis."

Hester was dumbfounded. She swallowed the bile filling her mouth. She thought the smell of the putrid sores, alone, would have been just bearable. But the cloying blend of rotting flesh and perfume heightened her sense of nausea.

She fainted and Will clutched her so she fell forward with her head in the King's lap. Henry stroked her hood. "So you will cure my morbel, will you, chuck?"

"The morbel! The royal morbel!" chanted Will.

Henry pulled Hester up into his arms and covered her mouth with kisses. She struggled and screamed. "By Our Lady, this is not what I expected of the King!"

Henry laughed. "What else should a Howard whore expect?"

"I am no whore. I am not a Howard. My aunt is, but she is as virtuous a dame as ever breathed. I shall tell Sir Hugh how you have treated me!" Hester scrambled from the bed.

"Not if you love your uncle you won't." Henry's eyes narrowed. "That Papist is in trouble enough. I doubt you will say anything that might render him even more noxious to us, will you, now?"

Hester hung her head in acquiescence. Tears coursed down her cheeks. She did not even try to brush them away.

"But I don't want much from you, a pinch here, a thrust there, do you understand me?"

Hester nodded, her eyes still cast down.

"Look at us," he commanded. Hester looked up.

Henry smiled a lewd grimace, revealing his rotten teeth. He motioned Will to pick up Hester's script. "Burn it," he commanded.

Will dropped the linen pouch in the fire and fumes of burning herbs filled the room.

"Now what, pray, might be the purpose of your visit, except to seduce your King? And a woman who calls upon Morgana le Fey, forsooth."

Hester thought longingly of Hartbourne. If only she were with Dickie gathering mint and parsley in the herb garden, or with Aunt Maud in her distillery. Oh, if only she were anywhere but here.

"The Howards will suffer for this. Do they think to make a fool of me, thrice over, in sending you here as marriage bait?"

"A fool! A fool, once, twice, but not thrice a fool!" yodelled Will.

"Hah! They thought they could pawn off that slattern, Catherine, as a pure maid for me to wed. The court laughs behind my back. But they don't know that I know. Fools! I am King. It is our business to know everything that passes in court. Now we give the whipperginnie enough rope to hang herself and then haul her in!" He sobbed, "I loved her. I gave her everything. And this is how she rewards me, by spreading her legs for my chamberer. Ah, but the axe is too swift an end for them. They will be crying out for a sharp blade to end it all by the time my torturers have finished working on them. Or even before I have started. That's what the sight of the rack does to a man."

Henry looked slyly at Hester. "But royalty confers its little pleasures. Come hither, my little pleasure." Again Henry beckoned her with his forefinger, on which glinted a huge ruby ring.

Hester stood stock still and stared at the ring; she could not bear to look at its owner. Will took a red-hot iron from the fire and made circles around her head.

Henry sighed. "It would be such a pity to mar that pure complexion, would it not?"

Hester looked around, prepared to run in any direction. Will brandished the glowing end of the poker inches from her face, nudging her toward the King. She backed into Henry. He grunted with satisfaction as he grasped her breast with one hand and groped for her private part with the other.

Hester turned and tried to hit his face. She missed. "How dare you use me thus, sir?"

Henry guffawed. "By the Mass, a fiery one! Will, hold the wench."

Will dropped the poker beside the bed and leaped up and pulled Hester onto the mattress, pinning her arms above her head. The king lowered himself onto Hester's supine body, plunged his hand down her bodice, and yanked at her chemise, tearing it.

"Ah!" he exclaimed, grabbing her breast. "The pleasure of caressing young flesh."

Hester cried, "Stop! For the love of Our Lady!"

"Hush, wench. It is I who am the outraged one—the innocent victim of treacherous women."

"Poor, poor Harry," consoled Will.

"But they get their comeuppance." The King snorted. "No one gets the better of King Harry and lives to boast of it." He shifted to untie the laces on his codpiece. "All Howard women are Jezebels and should be drowned at birth."

"I tell you, I am not a Howard! God save me!"

Henry pinched her nipple between finger and thumb.

"You are no king, you are an animal!" screamed Hester.

"Nay. It is Howard women who are animals. Bitches in heat, every one of them. First Anne and then her cousin, sweet, sweet Catherine. How could she do this to me? But yet I'll have her head."

"Her head indeed," chorused Will, "if not her maidenhead."

Henry pushed himself semi-upright. He finished unfastening his hose and scowled at its limp occupant. "Look what you have done to me, strumpet!" he snarled. "How dare you come parading your wares before me? Tantalizing me then denying me the pleasure, which is my due. I am the King. You have taken my power away, witch! You are no apothecary but one of Satan's moxies." Henry thrust his right hand up under Hester's skirts.

He squeezed hard. "Little cunt, I've got you now."

Hester pleaded, "Stop, please stop!"

A tiny thread of gold hung from an embroidered rose in the canopy above her head, like spider's gossamer. She focused on that, willing herself to become that tiny thread of gold. From that place she was only mildly surprised to observe herself lying face up on a huge bed. As if in a dream, she saw a man holding her arms above her head. It hurt, but somehow didn't bother her. Another man, a huge fat man, was trying to push something inside her secret place. But it was happening not to her but to someone else.

Henry ranted, "Kate looked just like this one. All seeming pure when I married her, but underneath a scarlet wanton!" So saying, he thrust his finger deep inside Hester.

She screamed, "Blessed Virgin!" and fainted.

※

"Fancy that," said Henry withdrawing his finger, covered with blood. "'Twas a maid indeed, and she a Howard. It surpasses belief."

He wiped his hand on a white damask napkin and stared at the red stain. He scratched his head, bemused.

"She should have stayed away and stayed a maid!" sang Will.

"But dear God! I have never before used a maiden thus," whispered Henry. "It goes against my sacred oath. God knows I have never taken a virgin against her will! Dear Lord, what shall I do?" His voice shook, and then evened out. "But she came here to seduce me, didn't she?"

Henry rocked back and forth, his head in his hands. He looked up through his fingers. "I see you watching me, Mother. And God, you are watching too, aren't you?"

Will echoed in a sing-song voice, "God is watching Harry, oh yes He is!"

Henry gasped, "Oh no! God, please look away, for pity's sake." He roared at Will. "Get out of my sight, fool!" He sobbed, "These women have made a monster of me."

Henry tore at his hair. "Will, come back. Christ's precious body, save me. I am damned. Damned, do you hear? Will?"

The jester peeped out from the curtain, his face distorted with fear.

Neither man noticed wisps of smoke arising from the bedside where the poker had set the bedskirt smoldering.

Henry cried, "What can save me from the eternal flame and the worm that never sleeps?"

Frenzied, he wrenched the ruby ring off his finger. "Who can find a virtuous woman, for her price is far above rubies? I will give her Mother's ruby ring." He held it up to the light. "Elizabeth, Henricus Rex," he whispered as he ran his finger over the engraving inside the gold band. He thrust it in Hester's pocket, as she lay unconscious.

"Your Majesty, please reconsider," protested Will, creeping to the King's side. "That is worth a king's ransom."

Henry groaned. "What profits it a man if he gain the world and lose his soul?"

He stretched his ringless hands in front of him. "My soul is surely worth more than any gem."

"The girl is a nobody, Sire. Give her a few silver pieces instead."

"Keep your tongue guarded behind your teeth, fool. Now wake her up!"

Will poured water from a ewer over Hester's face. She sat up and stared blankly at the King. Henry was fastening his codpiece and did not raise his eyes. His voice was husky. "Don't look at me, witch. Get out, now!"

※

Hester scrambled off the bed, holding her torn chemise together with one hand. She staggered toward the door and Will unlocked it. The guards on the other side straightened themselves. She realized they had been listening all the while. Hester caught sight of a madwoman with livid scratches down her cheeks. She gasped as she realized she was looking into a mirror. The expression in her eyes was animal, not human. Hester turned around and hobbled back toward Henry. Reaching the edge of the bed she leaned forward and spat full in Henry's face. He struck at her, but she ducked away and ran to the door, where the guards caught her.

Will laughed from shock. "A witch has baptized the King for his sins!"

Henry shook his fist. "I am an anointed Christian prince! Do you hear? I shall have no witch's baptism! My sins are forgiven me by my Redeemer! If you ever mention my sins again, I shall have your tongue slit."

Despite the other smells in the room, the pungent odour of smoke became unmistakable and Henry cried out, "Fire!"

The guards released Hester and ran to the King's aid. Hester raced through the closet and on into the dining chamber. The young page pushed his cap back in astonishment. Hester kept running toward the door to the presence chamber. Her shoes clicked a tattoo on the marble floors. Even her footfall seemed to mock her. Hester pounded her fists against the door and the guards opened it. They stared at her, dumfounded by her frenzy. They were accustomed to seeing slightly ruffled-looking young women with red cheeks emerging from the King's privy chambers. But always the little smirk and a musical chink of coin with every step they took. This one was out of her wits. The guards looked at each other and shrugged. Hester ran across the presence chamber and reached the doorway to the watching chamber. Again she hammered on the door. The huge uniformed attendants opened the doors, and Hester stumbled through.

The room fell quiet as its occupants stared at her.

ir William leaped from his chair, "Mistress, you are injured!"

Hester ignored him and seized Alice's arm. "We must leave, at once!"

"By Our Lady, your face, and dress!" Alice rose, knocking over the chess pieces.

Lady Joyce glared at Hester. "Whatever have you done, girl?"

Hester ignored her, also. "Alice, I pray you, now!"

"And where is your escort?" shrieked Lady Joyce.

"I know not."

"You were with the King, unattended?"

Hester shot her a look of such vitriol, that Lady Joyce fell silent, then cried, "Oh, no!" and fainted.

One of her women supported her, while the other turned to Alice. "Lady Joyce will soon recover. Attend to your cousin."

Alice cast Sir William a look of bewilderment. Hester pulled on her sleeve.

"Will you not allow me to assist you?" Sir William asked of Alice.

"Best I do this alone, but thank you, Sir."

"May I beg the honour of being introduced to your parents at Hartbourne?" pleaded Sir William as the two young women sped from the chamber.

"Indeed," replied Alice over her shoulder.

Sir William bowed to her retreating back. Alice's men followed.

"For the love of all the saints, cousin, what happened?" asked Alice.

Hester's voice was hoarse with humiliation and grief. "The King assaulted me! What a fool I have been!"

Alice wanted to comfort her, but this was no time for talking. They reached the courtyard and Alice ordered the carriage. Her men returned with Hester's attendants, dabbing their bloody noses.

One said, "We were set upon by the King's servants."

"This is dreadful," said Alice. "Go fetch your horses. We leave now."

The coachman drove up with the carriage. His face was red and he smelled of liquor. "Well, my lady, what a fine commotion!" he chortled. "One of the King's doxies done set his chamber on fire. Heaven help that woman when they catch her!"

Alice nodded. She helped Hester inside and ordered the coachman to drive on. Hester sat huddled in the corner and winced whenever the wheels hit a hole in the road. Alice knew not what to say. She handed Hester her handkerchief to hold against her cut lip, and she took it. Alice thought, *Poor, poor Hester.* She thought fleetingly of Sir William. Would he come and meet her parents? She was sure they would like him.

Hester's mind was in turmoil. She knew that a violated maid had twenty-four hours in which to make known her wrong and seek redress. But she felt she had sinned in lying to her uncle, plus she could not add her shame to his already heavy burden. Henry was right. She would not tell. And had she been ravished, even? She was nearly certain it was only his finger and not his member inside her. But the King was next to Jesus, and she felt sure Jesus could impregnate a woman just by looking at her, not that He would want to, so the royal finger could easily…But in any case, it was her fault for going there. Her soul had been violated, and the only relief she could find in her unspeakable agony was lacerating herself with blades of guilt.

She could not return to her father's home in Wales, disgraced and possibly pregnant. Death was far preferable than continuing to live, so assoiled, and she knew the means to end it: foxglove.

※

The stench of singed down from the burnt mattress permeated the privy chamber. Attendants opened windows, and a few fluffy white feathers wafted in the breeze.

Henry dismissed the men and groaned. "She has Mother's ring and doesn't even know it."

He caressed the ring's indentation in his finger. "I must have it back."

"Sire," said Will, "give her a few days to recover her wits, then write and send a few gold pieces for its return."

Henry stroked his beard and nodded. "Yes, that will buy her a husband." Then he clenched his fist. "No, by the Mass, she struck me! I should have her hand cut off."

A black-robed priest appeared at the entrance of the chamber and beckoned to Will.

"Sir Hugh has been arrested, Sire," said Will, grinning.

"Hah! Hartbourne will soon be ours. She will surrender the ring without argument. Besides, she will be far too shamed to say how she came by it."

"And Your Majesty will keep his monies where they belong, in the royal coffers." Will chortled. "Mistress Vaughan is not going anywhere with her ill-gotten gem."

"Except to the stews of Southwark with the Grantmire women when I evict them," said Henry. "Those fine ladies can live off their backs in the Bishop of Winchester's brothels. Papists! Damn every one of them."

※

Where can I find foxglove? thought Hester as the carriage trundled along. Lady Maud never grew *digitalis purpurea* in her herb garden, fearing that Dickie might take it into his head to eat it. Ah, but it did grow a mile away at Farmer Bates's cottage. She would go there early tomorrow. She had only to survive this night. Alice would understand, eventually, and she would explain to her aunt and uncle. It would be hard for Dickie, but in any case, she would have been leaving him to go to Wales. And to him that would be practically the same as her dying, since he would likely never see her again.

Hester willed herself to ignore her conscience, which told her suicide was a sin. Likewise she ignored the pain in her body. She remembered Aunt Maud had been preparing physic for Farmer Bates. That would be her excuse to visit.

"Hester, talk to me," implored Alice as the carriage turned into their driveway. She squeezed her cousin's hand. "Your silence frightens me more than anything you could say."

"Do not ask me to speak of this day. It never happened, and if you speak of it to Aunt and Uncle, I shall…" Hester could not finish the sentence, for what could be worse than what she planned to do? Tears welled in her eyes. She told herself not to be a ninny and wiped her eyes roughly with the back of her hand. There might be a time for crying later, but not if she were dead first. That thought comforted her and gave her strength.

Alice helped Hester down from the carriage and handed the coachman two shillings and one to each of the attendants. They took the money and nodded, acknowledging payment for their silence.

Hester said, "Pray tell Lady Maud I am unwell."

"Can I be of help in any way?" beseeched Alice.

"No," replied Hester as she mounted the stairs.

Once inside her room she pulled the curtains tight. The room was dark except for a thin ray of light that shone on the centre of the bed. She lay down and curled into a ball. She rocked back and forth. Her eyes burned and her thoughts raced. She was no longer marriageable, except perhaps to some farmer, one with a stammer and a squint in one eye. He would mock her for her lost virginity and allow her to abide with him only on sufferance that she bear him a dozen brats.

It was inevitable she would die birthing one of them. To die in childbirth was the worst way for a mother to die—it was a mockery of life. For even if her infant lived, it lived blighted, its very soul stamped with responsibility for its mother's death.

Hester arose and stood in front of the mirror. Her lip was swollen but no longer bleeding. The marks of Henry's hand stood out crimson against her white cheek. She surveyed herself with loathing. And she thought of all her prayers to the Virgin. But the Lady had turned her face away.

Her chemise was torn, but the dress was intact. How dare it still look lovely, while she was ruined? Hester managed to unfasten and step out of her skirts but could not untie her bodices.

She flung the dress into the cedar chest. She poured water from a ewer into a bowl and squatted down over it. The coolness came as a relief to the bruised flesh of her perineum. The bleeding was only enough to fill a half walnut shell. But the damage had been done. Her hymen was torn and she was no longer virgin.

Hester climbed back on the bed. Her body convulsed over and over until, finally exhausted, she fell asleep.

In her dream she was walking over a high bridge, and every plank she stepped upon came close to breaking. An abyss yawned below, and she held on to a spear shaft to save herself from plummeting down. The spear turned into a unicorn's horn, then she saw a huge red dragon lurching toward her. The unicorn pierced the dragon through the belly and it bled to death. Then it came to life again as a pig. She felt almost sorry for the dragon, or was it a pig? But it would have killed her had it been able.

Hester woke, gasping for breath, as if she had swum a long ways up from deep under water. She saw Alice standing by the door. She sat up and brushed the hair out of her hot, dry eyes. "I want to be left alone," she whispered.

"I brought you peppermint tea," said Alice.

Hester took it and sipped on it. She hadn't realized how thirsty she was. "Thank you, cousin."

"Let me unlace you," said Alice, unfastening Hester's bodice.

"Oh, if it weren't for your family and Dickie, I would be glad even to go to Wales." She winced as Alice touched a bruise on her shoulder. Alice moved the sleeve of her shift.

"Oh this is all red, and you need something for your swollen lip. I will go fetch some unguent from the distillery."

Hester was left free to shed those tears she could not allow another see. She wished there was someone to whom she could turn for comfort, someone who would not berate her for a fool, as she was berating herself. Aunt Maud would urge confession, but how could she confess such a shameful thing to any priest? And it was not just her body—it felt as if Henry had trampled on her very soul. But in whom else beside her aunt could she confide? Goody's loyalty would be to Lady Maud. As for Sir Hugh, he was a man, and although he would sympathize, he would want justice. And if he accused the King, it would only increase his own danger. Besides, she didn't want to tell a man about this, she wanted a woman. Someone older and wiser than herself.

Hester gasped as it came to her that she wanted her mother. Mother was the only person who might be able to comfort her right now. Her body shook with paroxysms of grief; at the same time she told herself not to be such an imbecile. But the pain of Henry's abuse felt similar to the half-forgotten pain of Mother's death, years ago. Hester sensed that each was a robbery—a robbery of the most intimate part of her being.

lice found her mother in the distillery. Lady Maud stood at a bench staring at a phial of rosewater. She held a jar of beeswax in one hand and in the other, a dish of ground willow bark. Also on the bench lay an opened parchment. Lady Maud heard her daughter's approach and set down the vessels. She turned, and Alice saw tears streaming down her mother's cheeks.

"Oh, is it about Father?" Alice asked, pointing to the letter.

Lady Maud nodded and opened her arms. Alice ran to her embrace.

"He has been charged with treason," said her mother. "A commissioner will come tomorrow, and we shall be expected to leave here by the end of the week."

Despite the shock and her grief, Alice thought fleetingly of Sir William. How would he ever find her? Immediately she felt shame for thinking of romance while her father lay in prison. She shook her head; she must concentrate on the moment. "Are we permitted to visit Father?"

"No, he is held in the Tower and denied visitors. All we can do now is pray." The women bowed their heads for a minute, praying that God and His Mother send comfort to Sir Hugh in the Tower.

"How is Hester?" asked Lady Maud, breaking the silence.

"Hester is unwell. Her stomach gripes and she has a cut lip and bruised shoulder." Alice thought this was close enough to the truth. She yearned to ask her mother's advice about Hester, but she had promised not to.

Lady Maud dried her eyes. "You can take her some of this unguent I am making for Farmer Bates. Will you stir the rosewater into the beeswax?" Alice used a pewter spoon to blend the ingredients. Lady Maud sighed. "There is one little piece of good fortune." Alice paused in her stirring. "Janet, the miller's wife, delivered a son, tiny, but he will survive, God willing. Janet's father has a cottage near Syon and has said we can live there, paying no rent, for the next two months."

"Oh!" exclaimed Alice. "That means that Dickie and John…"

"Yes, there is room for them, too," her mother said. Alice thought how all Hester's troubles to win the King's hand and save Dickie were of no account now. "Trust in the Lord and He will provide," said Lady Maud.

As Alice stirred the unguent, her mind wandered back to Sir William and the way he had made her feel esteemed and protected when those churlish youths insulted her. What if he did visit Hartbourne tomorrow or the next day? She took a deep breath. "I met a young nobleman today in court." She spooned the unguent into a little jar.

"Oh, Alice, what a time to meet a suitor!"

"His name is Sir William of Bayston."

"I know of his parents. They are of the true faith. For what purpose was he in that hornets' nest?"

"His family has been evicted from their lands. Sir William had come to throw himself on the King's mercy."

Lady Maud gave a deep sigh. "I pray he succeeds, although I fear it is unlikely." She looked hard at her daughter. "My dear, you look weary and had best go to bed now."

Alice curtseyed and received her mother's blessing, then returned to her chamber.

"Dear Hester, do not cry anymore," beseeched Alice. She applied the soothing balm to Hester's lip and shoulders.

The softness of Alice's touch aroused feelings in Hester of both pleasure and pain. She could not remember ever having been touched so gently before. Surely Mother would have touched her like that, years ago?

Alice said, "Mother received word today. Father has been arrested. I still cannot believe it."

Hester gasped, remembering that she was not the only one in distress. "Oh, I am sorry. Uncle told me last night he feared this. He made me promise not to tell Aunt Maud."

"Oh!" gasped Alice. "You might have told me." She stood, facing Hester, her eyes angry and her hands on her hips.

"Yes, I should have told you," replied Hester. "I have been very selfish." Tears rolled down her cheeks. "I will find some way to make amends."

Alice frowned. "That will be rather hard when you are in Wales."

Hester sobbed. "I am most sorry."

Alice took her cousin's hand. "Ah, quiet now. You have had griefs enough today."

"Thank you," said Hester in a low voice, dabbing her eyes.

"Now we should pray for Father and get some sleep." Alice yawned.

The cousins knelt by the side of the bed. "Dear Lord, please protect Father in this dark time, and comfort Hester in her grief," prayed Alice.

Hester replied, "Amen," and they crossed themselves and climbed into bed. It was several hours before sleep came to them, each lying awake, wrapped in her own thoughts.

Hester dreamed she was walking along a road when she saw Alice lying in the dirt, writhing in agony. Her belly was swollen. A farmer came with a horse and cart and hauled Alice onto the cart; he was going to bury her. Hester screamed, "Stop! She's not dead!" but the man ignored her. Hester grabbed at Alice's hand. "Please don't leave me!" Alice's hand withered to white bones, and Hester recoiled in horror.

She woke with a start. "Thank the Lord," she thought. "It was just a nightmare." For an instant she felt well, then her stomach contracted as she remembered the previous day's horror. A wave of nausea rose inside her. *Dear God, am I pregnant?*

Hester's heart pounded so hard she was sure it would wake Alice. But even if she were pregnant, in a day or two, she would be on the road to Wales. There she could take foxglove and die. She knew of travellers who had eaten tainted meat at an inn and perished from the flux. Her family need never know she had died by her own hand. Not only was suicide the worst sin, for it precluded redemption, she might also be the murderess of her unborn child.

Hester fell back to sleep and dreamed she awoke in her old house. She climbed down from bed, but the house felt different—it echoed with silence. Hester listened hard and could hear sobbing from the hall downstairs. She knew she must have done something bad but could not remember what. She felt cold inside and like she was about to vomit. An old woman with pointed teeth appeared. She cackled. "Your mother is dead!" Hester shouted out, "No!" and the old woman vanished. Hester picked up her wooden doll, but it turned into a kitten and scratched her hand. It turned back into the doll. "Bad dolly," scolded Hester. The old woman reappeared and shouted, "You are a bad girl!"

Hester screamed back, "I don't care!" As she vanished, the hag shrieked, "No one loves a bad, stupid girl who doesn't care."

ester awoke shaking and sat up in bed. Alice opened her eyes and looked at her. "I had a horrid dream," said Hester.

Alice hugged her and silently helped her into her everyday red woolen dress. When their eyes made contact in the mirror, they both quickly glanced away, their eyes filling with tears.

"I was a fool to go to the King," said Hester.

Alice shook her head. "No, just…misguided."

Hester assisted Alice into her dress.

Downstairs they partook of white bread and small beer from the buttery.

Goody entered and addressed Hester. "Whatever have you done to your face? Gadding about at Hampton Court, I suppose. In any case, Lady Maud requires you in the solar." She abruptly turned and left the room.

Hester caught her breath. *Can Goody see it in my face? Do I look like a whore? Have I sprouted horns?* Hester realized that she was making herself feel guilty, punishing herself for Henry's crime. But if she did not do so, she felt she would disintegrate. A crime had been committed, and someone had to pay. And since it was not to be the King, she would have to pay it herself.

She told herself she did not look any different, at least from the outside. A cut lip and scratched cheek, but there were no horns sprouting from her forehead. Nevertheless, Hester reached up her hand and patted her coif. Just to be sure.

Goody returned with an odd expression on her face. She blushed. "Lady Alice, I would speak with you for a moment."

Hester nodded to her cousin. "We will meet later."

Two attendants admitted Hester to the solar. Her throat tightened; she had known these men since childhood, but this morning they reminded her of Henry's guard.

Lady Maud was leaning on the table but straightened to greet Hester.

When Hester saw the pallor on her aunt's face, her stomach heaved. *She knows what happened! O Blessed Virgin, save me!* Then she recalled Lady Maud had her own grief and ran to embrace her. "Dear Aunt, I am most sorry this has befallen Uncle Hugh."

Lady Maud nodded. "Indeed it is hard, but God will support him." She wiped tears from her eyes. "And the good Lord has seen fit to provide a cottage with room enough for Dickie and John, who I think will come if I ask him." Lady Maud's eyes wandered about the chamber, and it seemed to Hester she was mentally saying goodbye to the tapestries and furniture.

"Oh, Aunt, that is a good piece of news!" replied Hester. She smiled, but it pained her lip.

"I have written to my sister," added Lady Maud, "but she cannot help those attainted for treason without incurring the penalty herself."

Lady Maud glanced at her niece and frowned. "What happened to your lip and your cheek?"

"I tripped and fell against a chimney piece." Hester was shocked at how easily lying came to her now.

"Alice said you had the stomach ache and a sore shoulder, how are they?" Lady Maud gazed out the window at the green expanse of fields surrounding Hartbourne.

"Much better, thank you." Hester stared at the floor. She was grateful for her aunt's distraction, for she feared on closer questioning she would surely break down and tell her all.

"You have been applying the unguent to your lip also?"

Hester nodded.

"Good, it will also help mend the abrasions on your cheek. Now let us make our orisons to the Blessed Virgin and beseech her protection upon your journey."

They crossed to the recessed altar and knelt.

Ave, Regina caelorum,
Ave, Domina Angelorum,
Salve, radix, salve, porta
Ex qua mundo lux est orta.

Hester reflected bitterly, *O, yea, Queen of Heaven and all the angels.* This time yesterday, she had aspired to the queendom of England. *O root and gate by which the light of the world entered.* Little did she care about that, being about to depart from this world.

"You will need for monies for travel." Lady Maud led Hester to a locked coffer by the window. "Take all your books, and remember to read your Bible daily, and the *Republic*, when you are at leisure." She sighed. "I wonder if they have printed Bibles in Wales. I have heard in some villages they are barely Christian." Her eyes brightened. "You must learn to read and write Welsh!" She clasped Hester's hands. "And translate the gospels for those poor people."

Hester marvelled at her aunt's faith. "Alice and I wish to visit Farmer Bates," she said. "You were preparing a salve for him."

"Yes, and take some elderberry wine. They are the oldest couple on the estate. I wish I had time to bid them farewell, but I have much else to attend to."

Lady Maud took a key from her pocket and opened the small, steel-bound chest.

One compartment held a mass of silver shillings, and another Lady Maud's jewels: several emerald brooches, a diamond pendant, and a ruby bracelet.

Hester stepped back when she saw the ruby bracelet. Its finely cut stones reminded her of the ring she had seen on Henry's finger.

"How odd, my pearl necklace is missing," remarked Lady Maud. "Well, that is of little matter—all this will soon belong to the King." She selected a rosary of ivory beads. "This was Sir Hugh's mother's. I know he would like you to have it." Lady Maud fastened the rosary around Hester's neck. Hester touched the crucifix at her throat and her eyes filled.

"Thank you, Aunt, I shall treasure this."

"Always wear it," replied Lady Maud. "It will mark you as a daughter of the true church."

Lady Maud filled a purse with coins and handed it to Hester, who said, "Thank you for all your kindnesses to me."

Lady Maud embraced her niece. "You are kind to think of others at this difficult time. Remember you must pack your belongings, so do not tarry long at the Bateses'."

Hester curtseyed, wiping tears from her eyes. *Surely I am doubly damned. I go to seek my death, and Lady Maud thinks I go to serve others.* "I will see if Dickie is awake, first." Lady Maud nodded.

Dickie's room was beside Sir Hugh's library, facing the front of the house. One wall displayed a painting of the Virgin holding the infant Jesus. In the centre stood Dickie's empty bed with a crucifix nailed above it. Sunlight shone through the bars on the window forming a striped pattern on the rumpled bedclothes. Hester hated those bars, but Dickie had fallen through the window once and cut his arm open. She had held him while Lady Maud stitched the wound.

Dickie was arranging items in a cherry wood cabinet. He paused to hug Hester.

"Hessie what's the matter with your face?"

"I fell and hit it yesterday, but it doesn't hurt much now, and Aunt Maud says I will soon be mended."

"I am glad. Look where I keep all my eggs and feathers." He pointed to a shelf where a black crow's, a red robin's, and a white dove's feathers lay in a row beside their respective eggs.

"John makes a little hole in the bottom of the egg and gets the goop out so they don't stink."

"Where is John?"

"He's gone to fetch stale bread to lure the ducks in the pond. I want a duck egg and a green mallard's feather. See, I have all the others but no green."

Hester nodded. "You need a green, of course." She paused, searching for the right words to tell him she was leaving for Wales.

"Has the cat got your tongue?" asked Dickie, stroking the crow's feather.

"I will come back later." She hugged him.

"Ouch," protested Dickie, "I can't breathe."

She released him. "Goodbye now, and be sure not to fall in the pond."

"I won't, Hessie. You worry too much."

⁂

Alice followed Goody into the buttery. Goody closed the door. "I have a confession to make."

Alice raised her eyebrows. "I am not a priest!"

"I must unburden myself and I could not say this to any priest alive." Goody blushed red as a cockerel's comb.

"Well, then, you may tell me, but surely Mother would be the best—"

"No, for my crime is against her. And against yourself."

Alice took a step backwards. "Goody, you jest."

"Nay. I stole her pearl necklace from her casket last night. I took her keys from her pocket while she slept."

"But why would you do such a thing? And how is it a crime against me?"

"Your blessed mother would have us walk away from Hartbourne penniless. Sure we shall have a roof over our heads, but we will have scant bedding, few kitchen vessels, and not two shillings to rub together for food. These pearls will keep us in vittles for near six months. And yea it is a crime against you, for when your lady mother passes to her eternal reward, they would be yours."

Alice raised her hands to her head and massaged her temples with her fingertips. *It is true, Mother has given no thought to how we will survive in this cottage. But to force Goody to resort to stealth? How dreadful. And what if Mother finds out?* Alice brought her hands down to her sides. She would take care Mother did not find out.

"Where will you hide them? I am sure they will search our clothing." Alice shuddered. A horrid thought, but she knew that is what befell the evicted. *If only Sir William were here.*

Goody kneaded her apron. "I shall hide them where no one will think to look." She stared at Alice, half-defiant and half-shamed. "I have given birth to two babes, big they were, though alas, neither survived. That is how I came to be wet nurse to you. And such a lovely infant you were. And then your poor cousins came. Him just a gawky infant and her speaking not a word of English and squawking to the crows day and—"

Alice interrupted. "You cannot be thinking of hiding a necklace in there? That is…"

She paused, realizing that with no money they would be starving by Whitsuntide. "But Goody, how would you achieve such a thing?"

"Ah, you young ladies know nothing of how country women stop a man's seed from making a baby. They put a little package of moss in there. Likewise I have fashioned a small leather pouch just big enough for the necklace. Once we are safe I shall pull it out, wash the pearls, and drop them behind a bush where your lady mother will find them and call it a miracle." Goody winked at Alice, who stared at her, dumbfounded.

"You will not be telling Lady Maud, or anyone else, now, will you?"

"No, I shall not." Again Alice thought of Sir William coming to their aid, but how could he help, when he too, was nigh penniless?

"Will it not hurt?" asked Alice.

"Not a whit," replied Goody. "A newborn's head is as big as a turnip. What's a little pouch compared with that?"

Goody looked at Alice, as though awaiting her approbation.

"No, Goody," replied Alice. "I am much beholden to you for thinking to help in this way, but it cannot be right."

"But hidden another way might sit well with you?"

"Dear Goody, if you can hide some of mother's pearls another way, that would be a great blessing to us all."

Goody nodded and the women embraced, then Alice, almost in tears, returned to her chamber. Her world was collapsing around her. She sat on the bed, feeling too stunned even to weep.

Hester entered the room, and the cousins looked at each other then glanced away. For a few seconds neither spoke, each lost in her own thoughts.

"So, let us away to the Bateses'," proposed Hester.

Reaching the stables, Hester heard Lady whinny a greeting. She was already saddled and stamping her feet. Hester kissed her nose and stroked her velvet muzzle with the back of her fingers. She inhaled the pony's warm breath and the comforting smell of apple and horse sweat.

Alice placed a satchel with the salve and wine in a saddlebag, then sighed. "I should not think it now, with Father in prison and Mother distracted so, but I do wonder if Sir William will send a message."

"Perchance he will. I could see he favours you…" Hester's voice trailed off. She could not bear to think about yesterday.

Alice blushed. "I told Mother, and I think she and Father

would approve of him." She groaned. "But what if Father is...No, I will not think sad thoughts."

"No sad thoughts," agreed Hester. "Sad thoughts might keep Sir William away."

"I shall go find where Stewart has Mirabel," said Alice.

Hester buried her face in her pony's mane. Paroxysms shook her body. They started in her belly and spread into her chest. Her legs shook. She wrapped her arms around Lady's neck and twisted her fingers into her mane. Once sure that Alice was out of hearing, she howled into Lady's mane like a wolf with its leg caught in a steel trap.

Hester wondered how so great an injury could occur to a woman and there be so little to show for it. Her breast was sore and it hurt when she made water, but otherwise her body was sound. Still she was undone, dishonoured. But a bunch of purple foxgloves would solve it all.

nce mounted, the cousins took the road they had travelled yesterday but in the opposite direction. Birds sang from the hedgerows, and pale yellow primroses blossomed in shady nooks. Briar roses were in bud; veins of deep pink ran along the edge of their folded calyxes. On the sunny side of the road, a few roses had opened their first petals, while one or two were in full bloom. Up in the elm tree branches, baby throstles and linnets called for food. *Food now! And more food!*

A flock of sheep approached, but terrified by sight of the ponies, they ran into the bushes. Their shepherd hallooed and switched at them with a willow wand trying to round them up.

Alice slowed Mirabel and when she smiled at the shepherd, he doffed his cap.

"Good day, milady."

"And to you, Jeremy," replied Alice.

The shepherd merely nodded toward Hester. A flush of anger spread over her face. Then she flushed again, from shame. For it must be shameful to feel anger for so trivial a cause. Especially now, when she was bent upon taking her own life.

Alice pointed to a rose. "Look at that bee inside the petals. It is so drunk on nectar it can barely stand, let alone carry its load of pollen home to its hive."

"Pollen breeches," replied Hester, absently. That had been their nursery term for the fat, yellow legs of pollen-laden honeybees. She watched as bees zigzagged from flower to flower. She mused aloud, "What do you think might happen should a queen bee go home to her hive only to find that hornets had taken it over?"

"The queen never leaves the hive, and besides, why would

hornets want to take over a beehive? They have their own hives, those papery flimsy things. Ugh! I hate hornets." Alice grimaced and tightened the reins. Mirabel shook her head in protest.

"But what if they decided that living in a honeycomb with a queen would be more pleasant than their own ugly hives?" persisted Hester.

"Hornets don't have a queen, do they?" queried Alice. The ponies stopped to nibble the sweet new grass beside the hedgerows.

"No, but if they did, then bees and hornets might live peaceably together."

"Yes, they might, but what matters it how insects thrive?" Alice leaned forward to brush away flies that buzzed around Mirabel's eyes.

"Just that if a queen could make all the difference to them, then maybe a queen would make all the difference to us, in a country where people must either relinquish their faith or die." Hester began to nibble her fingernails but made herself stop.

"I think I understand. You mean if the old religion and the King's new one could get along."

Hester flinched at mention of the King. She felt Lady's flanks quiver beneath her and stroked her neck. "Or at least without people having to die because of it," she said. But how could there be a Queen of England? Edward, Henry's son, would be the next King, but he was sickly and as like to die young. Perhaps Mary, Henry's cancred eldest daughter might become Queen? But if hornets bothered her, she would simply smoke them out. Who could make for a peaceful co-existence? Only someone both very powerful and benevolent, like God. But was God particularly benevolent, considering how many prayers He received and how few He answered? Was there any deity but God? Hester thought of the powerful Greek goddess of war, Athena. Might there be a goddess of England someday who could bless the land? Hester banished the ridiculous thought. There was no such thing as a goddess.

The sound of bells ringing out the noon Angelus brought Hester from her musings. The cousins reined in their ponies and prayed.

Ave Maria, gratia plena,
Dominus tecum.
Benedicta tu in mulieribus, et benedictus fructus ventris tui.

Fruit of her womb. Just like the queen bee, in her hive, thought Hester. She added, under her breath, "And, Blessed Mary Virgin, pray for me, when I die by my own hand."

They turned a corner in the lane and Alice gasped, "What beautiful hawthorn blossoms! We should gather some for Mother Bates." She snapped off a few low-hanging branches.

"Mind you don't prick yourself," warned Hester.

"Ouch!" yelped Alice, sucking at the streak of red on her thumb. "But what is a slight cut, after all."

What indeed, thought Hester, reflecting on the cut inside of her, the one that had ruined her. *If only I had never gone! I wish I were dead. Well…that, at least, is within my reach.*

Alice placed the sweetly pungent flowers in the satchel inside Mirabel's saddlebag.

As they continued on their way, a pair of ravens circled above, their wings flapping in a slow beat.

The Bateses' cottage was a low ramshackle hut with a worn-through thatch. Mother Bates was in the front garden tying up her runner beans with a piece of twine. She wore a brown homespun apron over her grey kirtle.

Anxiety seized Hester. Mother Bates was known as a wise woman. Would she be able to tell by looking at her what had happened? Hester felt as if her forehead was branded with the word "adulteress," but that wasn't the right word. It was not adultery, but what exactly was it? She stared at the profusion of foxgloves along the path. Whatever it was, it did not matter, since very soon she would be dead.

The cousins dismounted and dropped the ponies' reins, leaving them to graze. Alice took out the satchel.

"Saints bless you, my dears," exclaimed Mother Bates. "It is most kind of you to visit."

She curtseyed to Alice then embraced her, exercising her prerogative as the oldest dame for twenty miles around.

"How are your dear parents?"

Alice murmured, "They put their trust in God."

Mother Bates sighed and turned to Hester, who, as was her wont, stiffened at being greeted second. However, when the old dame enfolded her in her arms, Hester felt herself relax almost against her will, and tears pricked her eyes.

Mother Bates leaned back and observed, "You have a cut lip and your cheek is scratched."

"It is nothing. I tripped in the stable and fell against the door." Hester realized she had told Lady Maud something different, but it did not signify now. "I have been applying a salve."

"Good. Your young flesh will heal quickly. And now, how is that poor idiot brother of yours?" asked Mother Bates.

Hester arched away from Mother Bates's embrace and brushed the unshed tears away.

"Now don't get mithered up because a body says truth."

Hester could not help but laugh. "Dickie is well, thank you."

"I am glad to hear it. We all have our trials in this life. The good Lord spares no one, high or low."

The cousins had to duck their heads to pass under the door's lintel. The air inside was stifling. "The Master needs a fire, on account of his rheumatism," explained Mother Bates, shutting the door behind them. "And you know how bad outside air is for an invalid."

In the centre of the room stood a battered pine table. A tiny painting of Saint Anne with the Virgin hung on a wall beside a flitch of bacon and a bunch of onions.

An old man, huddled under a red blanket, sat on a bench beside the hearth.

"Visitors to see you, Goodman!" called his wife.

Alice shouted, "We have brought a salve from Mother's distillery to relieve your pains, and elderberry wine for your good cheer!"

Farmer Bates gave a toothless smile.

Alice opened the satchel. "And we brought hawthorn blossoms to brighten the room."

"What's that you said? Hawthorns?" Quick as a bee sting Mother Bates snatched the flowers. "Out with them!"

Baffled, the cousins followed and watched her throw the blossoms on the midden pile. "Do ye not know it is accursed to bring such into the house in May? A sure harbinger of death, they are." She signed herself with the cross. "And 'tis not myself nor the goodman that minds dying, Heaven knows we have lived long enow. It is one of ye I am afeard for."

Alice frowned. "But the King himself rides out to bring in the May. He and his whole court gather in hawthorn blossoms to celebrate that spring has finally arrived and summer is soon a-coming. There is no harm in it."

"Ah, but that is only newly so." Mother Bates flicked petals from her apron. "Besides, what would you expect from a man who fashions a new religion to suit his lust? In the old days, when there was famine, they would crown and fête a young girl as princess for the day, and at dusk slay her. Only a virgin's blood would ensure the crops thrived. My grandmother told me her grandmother knew a maid who died so. Only it was made to appear an accident."

Alice laughed. "Surely you do not believe such an old wives' tale?"

The goodwife folded her arms over her bosom. "Scything mishaps do occur, but it takes some doing to be sliced right here." Mother Bates gestured with her forefinger against her throat. "The priest buried her right quick, before too many questions were asked. And there was a fine harvest that autumn and the granaries full till the next summer."

Mother Bates looked hard at Alice. "And the maiden held a posy of hawthorn blossoms."

Alice and Hester stepped back. Mother Bates nodded, satisfied. "So sure, I be an old wife, but I shall ne'er have hawthorn under my roof, so long as I be mistress of it."

Hester felt a chill. *The maid was fêted as princess for a day.* She recalled Stewart's words of yesterday: *A right princess is what I would say you were.*

Mother Bates exclaimed, "Why Mistress Hester, you have turned white as that blasted hawthorn. Did someone walk over your grave? Sit ye down and I shall bring us a sup of ale."

Mother Bates produced a pitcher, and the three sat on a bench in the backyard. A couple of chickens pecked around their feet. Mother Bates pointed to the cottage. "You are not used to such sights. Old age, poverty, and loss of your wits make for sad bedfellows. But I suppose three in a bed never did good to any marriage." Hester and Alice smiled. "Although the Lord took six of my babes, he spared me three good 'uns. Our son is a great boon to us, and our daughters too. Although Joan's husband makes merry a tad too often for my liking. Why just the other day, didn't he—"

Hester interrupted. "I will gather some of your foxgloves, by your leave. Lady Maud needs them for a tincture. She says it makes an ailing heart beat stronger."

"I do not recall Mother saying she needed foxgloves," said Alice, in a tone of surprise.

"Oh, it was a few days ago now, when you were in the stable with Mirabel," said Hester, thinking quickly. "She had eaten damp oats and had the colic."

"Oh, yes, I remember that." Alice frowned, and Hester thought she was about to say something else, but Mother Bates was talking on.

"Do mind with the foxglove, now, Mistress Hester, for even a little too much can harm a body. If a fellow gets to seeing yellow lights, he has taken too much."

Ah, thought Hester, *so when I see yellow lights I will know I am nearly there.*

She stood in the pathway looking at the pinkish purple, bell-shaped blossoms. Dark violet spots blotched the snowy white of the inside of the bell. It was as if their Creator had hurled purple paint at His flowers, maybe in a fit of rage. *Did God not care that they were marred forever? Ah, foxgloves are also "Our Lady's gloves," and welcome you are, Lady Mary, to them. I would not put my finger inside one, but I shall drink their juice.* Hester filled the satchel and returned to Mother Bates and Alice.

"…and that woman should be made to wear the bridle and ducked in the village pond on account of the tongue in her," said Mother Bates. "And hanged besides, for she murdered her unborn babe."

Alice startled, her eyes widening. "However do you mean?"

"She was, you know," Mother Bates patted her abdomen. "But it wasn't her husband's so she made a tansy brew. Sick she was for a week, but sure enough her courses came upon her and only a few folks the wiser."

As Hester approached, Alice looked from Mother Bates to Hester and back again.

"I haven't told you the half of it. Wait till I fetch more ale."

Hester spoke. "Mistress Bates, your pardon, but we need to return home, for I leave for Wales very soon."

"Lawks have mercy! So you are off to that land of savages."

Hester glared at her, forgetting those were her very own thoughts.

Mother Bates sighed. "Forgive me, I do remember that your dear father is one of them. But beware, for I hear that some of the Welsh are barely Christian and more like unto the savages across the sea, who sacrifice young ones to their bloodthirsty gods and goddesses. Our parish priest says how a witch gives the child a potion, then it is buried alive." She took a quick in-breath. "This King's grandmother was a witch. I once saw her in London town when I was a little girl. Blond hair and ice-blue eyes. Beautiful. And a serpent if ever there was one."

"Nay," objected Alice. "The old countess was always praying, and she endowed universities and shrines and—"

"Ah, but I mean his mother's mother, and you mean his father's mother. God's truth, Margaret Beaufort was a saint. I do believe she built a shrine up in the north of Wales that still stands. The King is afeard if he allowed Cromwell to tear that down along with all the rest, her spirit would haunt him to the grave and beyond."

A pity then that Cromwell did not tear it down. I wonder if that is the place Uncle Hugh said Mother is buried. I suppose I shall soon find out, thought Hester.

Alice smiled. "Forgive us Mother Bates, but we must be away." She approached Mirabel and took the reins, and Hester followed with Lady.

Mistress Bates bustled after her guests. At the gate she reached out and clasped both to her bosom. "Blessings on you both."

The cousins thanked her and mounted their ponies. They wended their way home in silence. Even the birds seemed to have stopped their singing.

They reached the house and Alice gulped. "By all the angels I shall miss you most dearly."

Hester replied, "And I you." She forced herself not to cry. They might not meet again in this life, and as she would soon be a suicide, neither would they meet in the next.

As the cousins approached the manor house, Goody was standing on the steps watching Stewart and a groom lead five chestnut mares toward the stables. Hester realized her escort had arrived. Grasping the satchel of foxgloves, she disengaged her feet from the saddle and slid down over Lady's flank.

Goody addressed Alice. "The King's man came and put a new padlock on Lady Maud's casket and took an inventory of all the furnishings." She gave Alice a knowing look. Alice returned her a wan smile and led the ponies away. Goody turned to Hester. "Lady Maud and your cousin are in the solar." She sniffed. "I have never seen such a popinjay in all my life."

Hester nodded. "I shall tidy myself first." And she sped to her bedchamber.

She must hide the foxgloves till she had utensils and time wherewith to prepare a brew. She opened the cedar chest and saw her blue dress. She pulled it out and, surveying it with loathing, flung it to the floor. She heard a clunk and gasped as a ruby ring clattered on the floor; it was the one the King was wearing when he violated her. She stared at it as if it were a poisonous toad, then picked it up. Her heart raced as she weighed it in her palm.

Why was it in her dress pocket? Why would the King have given her this precious jewel? She thought for an instant of returning it to him. *No, never!* She ground her teeth. Hester buried the dress at the bottom of the chest. She took out her green dress, thrust the ring into its pocket, and stuffed the foxgloves in after it. She set it on the bed along with her tiny jewellery casket, a half-dozen books, and her medicine cabinet. She gave the room one last look, blinked away her tears, and hurried to the solar.

There she found a young man of about twenty years, dressed in pale purple satin wearing gold chains around his neck, seated beside Aunt Maud. Her aunt looked pale and her eyes were red. "Well, niece," she said. "Here is your cousin, Master Mervyn."

They made the requisite obeisance, but Hester felt embarrassed and knew not what to say to him. She knew Mervyn was her Uncle Llewelyn's bastard, but she could barely remember her own father, let alone her uncle, and she had but the vaguest memories of this cousin. His mother was said to be no Christian, which was why Llewelyn had never married her. Hester glanced down at her nails, bitten to the quick.

Mervyn spoke. "It is a pleasure to meet you again, cousin, after so long." He stared at her swollen lip. "I trust you are well."

Hester blushed, aware of her injured face, and looked down at the floor. She had noted that her cousin had the same hooded eyelids as the King's, and she recalled that she and Henry were related through their Welsh ancestry. She dismissed the horrid thought.

Mervyn added, "I am afraid I am the bearer of sad news." He paused. "Your father, Lord Dafydd, has been smitten by a palsy and may not have long to live."

All Hester's anger toward her father evaporated. "Oh no! Blessed Virgin spare him! Dear Aunt, I can be ready in less than an hour." Then she realized how selfish she sounded and turned to Mervyn. "Oh, but you have just arrived!"

Mervyn shrugged. "'Tis no matter. We spent last night in London, so my men and horses are fresh enough."

Aunt Maud urged, "You must go right away. It would be a terrible pity if you arrived too late."

Hester recovered herself. What was she thinking? She was not going to see her father. She was about to put an end to her life. Mervyn bowed himself out of the room.

Lady Maud's facial muscles worked as she kept charge of her emotions. She held Hester's hands and looked into her eyes. "Do remember to say your prayers."

"Indeed I shall." Hester averted her gaze. There would be very little time for praying. She changed the subject. "Goody said that a commissioner has already been here."

"Indeed. Jenkins was his name and he seemed very anxious to talk with you in particular. He will return on Friday to oversee our departure. I had not realized that you would be leaving so soon." Lady Maud's eyes filled with tears. "We are allowed the clothes on our backs, so long as they be made of cheap stuff, and a cartload of chattels."

Hester's breath caught in her chest. *The King wants his ring back.* Then a surge of anger welled in her gut. *But he will have to find me first!*

There was a rap at the door. "Lady Maud, excuse me," gasped a breathless footman, "Master Dickon fell in the pond."

The women raced to Dickie's chamber where they found him sitting propped up on pillows, a maid towelling his wet hair. Dickie smiled at Hester. "I fell in. I am sorry." He coughed and John caught slimy bits of pondweed in a basin.

"You are too fast for me, Master Dickie," lamented John. "You are quick as a fox."

Lady Maud felt his forehead. "Goody will make a plaster for your chest, but I fear no ill effects."

"Thanks be to Our Lady," murmured Hester, hugging her brother.

Dickie exclaimed, "Look here!" He opened his hand to reveal four iridescent green feathers. "I got them." He laughed and spluttered some more.

Hester hugged him tighter. However could she tell him she was leaving? He would not understand either her leaving for Wales or her death. All he would know was that she was gone, never to return. Lady Maud took John to one side.

Hester could hear fragments of their conversation. She understood that Lady Maud had healed John's mother, twice, of a near-fatal lung infection, and he would be glad to serve her family without wages for as long as he was needed.

Lady Maud turned to Hester. "You must finish your packing, dear, and I must see to ours," and she left the room.

Hester released Dickie, who arranged the feathers in his box. She crossed the room to John.

"I overheard your talking with my lady aunt." She made a curtsey. "I want to thank you with all my heart for…" And then, much to her chagrin, Hester began to cry.

"These are troubled times, Mistress," said John. "I have some little monies put aside, and I would rather stay with a good family than leave for a worser, even if richer, one."

Hester wiped away her tears. "You know I cannot tell my brother that I am leaving him?"

John nodded. "We will fare well, so do not distress yourself." He bowed. "Go with God." Hester turned to Dickie and hugged him once more, then sped from the room.

In her chamber, Hester found a plump, fresh-faced young woman of around the same age as herself inspecting the contents of her medicine cabinet.

"Good morrow, Mistress Vaughan," said she, ducking a curtsey. "I am Nia and shall be attending you." She smiled. "You will want to change into riding garb for the journey."

She assisted Hester out of her red dress and into her riding attire. "You are familiar with healing herbs, I see," said Nia. "And these books and your beautiful green gown and this red dress are coming too?"

"Yes, and thank you for your help," replied Hester. "Your English is far better than my Welsh. I hardly remember any, although it was my first tongue." She smiled then winced from the pain in her lip.

"Mistress Vaughan, you are injured."

"Naught that signifies." Hester changed the subject. "How is it your English is so good?"

"My mother was half-English, so I speak it well enough," explained Nia. "But at home we mostly speak our own language and practice our own ways."

Nia smiled so disarmingly, Hester felt it rude to inquire just what "our own ways" meant. In any case, since she planned to die on the road to Wales, she would never need find out.

Mervyn, his three companions, and Nia were mounted, and a saddled Lady snorted with impatience for her mistress.

Hester lowered her head to receive her aunt's blessing.

"I pray you will be a comfort to your father and a light to those poor heathen peoples."

Hester murmured, "Amen." She and Alice hugged. Alice attempted a smile, but the corners of her mouth turned down. Her face crumpled and tears coursed down her cheeks.

Goody embraced Hester. "Mind you wear flannel shifts, now. There will be all that Welsh dampness to reckon with." Her voice quavered an instant. "And do try not to bite your nails, child. Remember to use dandelion juice on them."

Stewart brought Lady over to Hester and bent down, cupping his hands for her to mount. She retrieved a silver shilling from her purse and handed it to him.

"I do not want your money, Mistress," protested Stewart.

Hester whispered, "Take it, please."

Stewart accepted it, lest Hester be shamed before strangers. He tugged his forelock. "Thankee, Mistress, I am obliged."

Hester looked over at Dickie's room with its barred windows. Guilt roiled inside her. Her eye caught the glimmer of a white face with an open mouth; she imagined she could hear Dickie screaming for her.

Hester wanted to run back to hug him and say goodbye properly. But Aunt Maud fixed her gaze. "I will give him a sleeping draught. You must go."

Hester saw that her escort had already turned the corner and a row of elm trees hid them from view. *Dickie, please forgive me!* she thought, then applied her crop and urged Lady to a canter.

Rooks circled high above, cawing to each other. One swooped down in front of her, its black feathers fanned out. It seemed to

Hester that it glared at her with its sparkling jet eye before flying off to join its relations.

When Hester caught up with Mervyn, he looked at her curiously and commented to the rider beside him, "Just like her mother." The two men laughed. Hester was shocked. *See how they laugh tomorrow, when they wake up to find me dead.*

Hester could not banish the look of anguish on Dickie's face from her mind's eye. She remembered her dream from last night and screaming for Alice not to leave her. That must have been how she had behaved after her mother died, bereft, terrified, and helpless. She could not inflict that unbearable pain upon Dickie, she could not simply vanish from his life. She would not kill herself. She would plead with Father to send for him. They must find a way to be together again.

~⚜~

Alice stood beside the bed that, just a short while ago, she had shared with Hester.

Goody helped her out of her fine silk gown and into a grey linsey-woolsey dress.

"Could be worse," said Goody. "Sometimes womenfolk are evicted wearing naught but their petticoats." But seeing the tears well in Alice's eyes, she added, "I swear you look as fine in drab as the noblest lady in the land decked out in all her finery."

Goody braided Alice's hair and covered it with a plain white linen coif. She kissed the top of Alice's head and left. Alice waited till Goody's footsteps no longer sounded along the hallway then threw herself on the bed and sobbed into the bolster. *It isn't fair. I don't want to live in some stranger's hut. Why must Father be locked in the Tower? Why did Hester have to go?*

She sat up and dried her eyes. Mother needed her help in paying the servants' final wages. Alice found Lady Maud in the solar, kneeling in front of her altar, praying the rosary.

The steady click that accompanied the completion of each ave calmed Alice's mind. The gold beads had been Lady Maud's grandmother's. Alice knelt beside her mother but leaped up at the sound of approaching hooves. Maybe Father had sent word. Perhaps, just perhaps, he had been pardoned.

The women crossed to the window. "I hope this is no new trouble," said Lady Maud, folding the rosary in her pocket.

Alice blushed as she observed a young man rein in his horse at the front steps. "Mother, it is Sir William!"

Alice watched the knight dismount and hand the reins of his black gelding to Stewart. Steps sounded outside the solar and an attendant opened the doors.

"Good day, Lady Alice." Sir William bowed, doffing his white plumed cap. An object glinted at his waist—a sword hilt of wrought silver protruded above a finely tooled leather scabbard.

Alice curtseyed. *Will he think I look a fright in these ugly clothes?* "Mother, allow me to present Sir William of Bayston. Aunt Joyce introduced us at Hampton Court."

He bowed again and addressed Lady Maud. "Pray forgive my intrusion, but I have come to offer my services. I understand your ladyship's esteemed husband has met with trouble for refusing the King's oath, as did my own dear father."

"Yes, he is presently held in the Tower," replied Lady Maud, pursing her lips. "I have not had the pleasure of meeting Lord and Lady Bayston, but I am aware the King appropriated your family's lands."

"It is hard, but they survive with my grandparents' aid."

"We are not so fortunate," said Lady Maud. "Please sit, and Alice, you may offer our guest refreshment."

Alice poured claret and Sir William drank, gazing into her eyes a moment or two. She blushed and looked away. Lady Maud was addressing him and he turned to her.

"We are a small family," said she. "Sir Hugh had but one sister, now deceased, and I have one, Lady Joyce, whom you met, together with our niece, Hester Vaughan."

"Indeed, I had that pleasure. I trust Mistress Vaughan fares well, she seemed rather…"

Alice frowned and Sir William, seeing it, coughed, then continued. "I trust you can find use for an able-bodied male." He grimaced. "I have the greatest respect for your family. Defying the King is not for the weak-stomached."

Alice and her mother smiled. "You are most welcome here at Hartbourne," said Lady Maud.

Sir William bowed. "Thank you, Lady Maud."

"Alice, pray show Sir William to his room." Lady Maud frowned as she turned to the knight. "We shall be leaving Friday at dawn, and I regret we cannot proffer any hospitality in our new abode, a small cottage."

William bowed again, and followed Alice from the room.

"Did you happen to gain your audience with the King?" asked Alice.

"No, I did not." Sir William's brows knitted. "But it came to me, not only was my case hopeless, but there was some other place I would much rather be." He smiled. "That new dress sets off your fair complexion most becomingly," he added.

Alice's heart sang. Walking the corridor, she pointed to his scabbard. "You have come armed, Sir William."

"This sword is the last remnant of my gentle birth. And it can prove helpful when men refuse to listen to reason."

"Do you use it often?"

"No, but I keep the blade honed and polished. Do you have a ribbon to spare?"

Alice ducked into her chamber and emerged with a blue silk ribbon.

"Bid it farewell," said Sir William.

"I will be saying farewell to all my ribbons at the end of the week." Alice gave a wry smile.

Sir William drew his sword and Alice threw the ribbon in the air. Sir William caught it on the blade's edge and made a parrying thrust. Five pieces of blue silk of identical length fell to the floor.

Alice gasped. William smiled and replaced his sword in its scabbard.

Alice showed him into a room with a huge bed with green satin curtains.

"I will send up water for you," said she, closing the door. "Please join us for prayers at six, and supper afterwards."

She put her hand to her cheek and felt it burning.

※

That evening, in the solar, Lady Maud addressed Sir William. "I would ask of you some service."

"Gladly shall I perform it," he replied. Alice looked up from her embroidery and smiled at him. Sir William smiled in return.

"You see the crucifix and the statue of Our Lady before which we just prayed?" asked Lady Maud. "We will not be permitted to take them with us. I ask you to hide them." She sighed. "It would give me pleasure to think that Our Lady and Our Saviour still watched over Hartbourne."

Goody, who was darning a stocking by the window, muttered under her breath, "I should as soon call down the wrath of judgment day on the godless folk who dare to live here after its lawful owners have been driven out."

"You could carve a niche behind the fireplace," continued Lady Maud, ignoring Goody.

Sir William tapped around the stonework. He pulled out a short knife from his doublet.

"A few hours to make a space high and deep enough, then a couple of days for the new mortar to set."

"But, Mother, did not the commissioner see our altar when he visited?" asked Alice.

"He did not look behind the curtain." The corners of Lady

Maud's mouth turned down in disdain. "He was too occupied with numbering the tapestries and silver plate."

John knocked on the door and entered with Dickie. Lady Maud introduced Sir William.

"Do you know where Hessie is?" asked Dickie

"I am sorry, my friend, I do not." William glanced at the box Dickie held. "What do you have in there?"

"John made it to keep my favourite eggs and feathers in." Dickie frowned with concentration and opened it. "You see this blue one, it is a robin's egg. And the red feather is a robin's too. And this green feather, I got that just yesterday, just before, just before Hessie, Hessie…"

Dickie's eyes glazed over and his shoulders slumped. He looked around the room. "Where is she?"

Alice looked at Sir William, mutely pleading with him to somehow intervene.

The knight picked up a black feather. "What bird is this from?"

"Why, a raven of course," replied Dickie, his eyes refocusing.

"Do you have a raven's egg?" asked William.

"Yes, but the box isn't big enough for all my collection. Do you want to come and see the rest?"

"After supper, shall we?"

Goody set the table with a partridge pie, salad with watercress, and pears poached in claret. "This is probably our last good supper," said she. "Cook and the kitchen scullions will be gone tomorrow after they receive their wages."

"Heaven will provide," declared Lady Maud.

Goody caught Alice's eye and grinned.

Alice blushed an even deeper red than the robin's feather. Sir William shot her a quizzical look, but she kept her gaze firmly on her plate.

"Come, you two," declared Dickie, pear juice running down his chin. He sprang up from the table and beckoned to John and Sir William.

"You must wipe your mouth first," said John.

"No I mustn't," retorted Dickie. "We are going to live in a hut and eat acorns. Hessie has gone away and I can do whatever I like now."

"Dickie," said Lady Maud. "We need to remember our manners and be good. Think about Jesus."

"I don't care about Jesus. Is Jesus going to bring Hessie back?"

"Now, now, Master Dickon," said John, taking Dickie by the shoulder. The boy stiffened and fell to the floor, his limbs jerking.

Lady Maud seized a rug from a bench. John and she wrapped Dickie with just his head free. Alice grabbed a wooden spoon from the table and placed the handle in his mouth. Within a few seconds Dickie had calmed and was sitting up on the floor. John helped him stand. Alice turned to Sir William, who had turned rather pale.

"My cousin suffers from the falling sickness. His fits cause no lasting harm, as you can see. But if he were to be riding a horse when one came, then that could be grievous."

"Oh," said Sir William, "and your priest has essayed—"

"It is nothing of the spirit, it is all in the brain," interrupted Lady Maud.

Sir William bowed to her and turned to Alice. "And the spoon handle, for what reason is that…?"

"So he does not bite his tongue," explained Alice. "And we have found that it soothes him to be wrapped up tight when a fit comes on."

She stepped toward Sir William and, smiling, took his hand. The knight, surprised but happy, smiled back.

"Now come see my egg collection," said Dickie, taking his other hand.

ester's party followed Watling Street, the old Roman road that led north from London. They found a hostelry at St. Alban's. After supper Hester visited the garderobe and discarded the foxgloves. *I will see Dickie again, and Aunt Maud and Alice, I swear it.*

Later, sitting on the bed, Nia brushed out Hester's hair.

"Why does my cousin dislike me?" Hester asked her.

"He envies you, 'tis all," replied Nia, untangling a knot with her fingers. "He has no property of his own, and once your father dies, Heaven forbid, you will inherit his land. There's not much left, but even so, Mervyn would give an eye for it."

"Yet he wears gold chains and rings."

Nia put down the brush. "Those were bought from a goldsmith two days ago in London. My lord Llewelyn gives him an allowance, but on his death, that will stop. And because Mervyn is a bastard and your uncle has no legitimate offspring, you will inherit from your uncle, too."

The young women climbed into bed. Hester realized one day she would have wealth enough to bring Dickie to Wales, in a litter, if needs be, and offer a home to Alice and Aunt Maud. She crossed herself against the thought of her father's death. Nonetheless, for the first time since the King's assault, her spirits rose.

She nudged Nia. "It seems I shall be almost a princess in North Wales, then?"

"Yea. Now go to sleep. Tomorrow is a long ride."

"We are close by Hatfield, are we not?"

Nia sighed. "Yes."

Hester continued. "The Lady Elizabeth lives there. Sometimes

I think of her, since both our mothers died when we were very young. I wonder if she remembers her mother, Anne Boleyn, at all." She paused and asked in a softer voice, "Did you ever meet my mother?"

Nia turned to face Hester. "No, but I heard Lady Margaret was kind, though often sad, maybe from homesickness. The old ones still talk about how Lord Dafydd went wild with grief after she died." Nia placed her hand on Hester's arm. "He hacked down their marriage bed with an axe. He burned it, and had his brother not stopped him, he would have burned the whole house down as well. But we must go to sleep now."

Nia turned over in bed, signalling an end to the conversation.

Hester sat up with the blankets bunched around her. "I would like to see Mother's grave in Holywell. I wonder if Elizabeth ever thinks of Anne Boleyn's grave in the Tower of London. What a horrid place to be buried. Even the name of the chapel that holds her body, Saint Peter ad Vincula, sounds sinister, do not you think?"

Nia pulled her half of the bedclothes back. "There's many at home as has no time for saints, good or bad."

"All saints are good," reproved Hester. "Lady Elizabeth was born a princess and was even betrothed to the Dauphin of France. But that ended once she was declared a bastard, and now she is all but forgotten."

Nia touched Hester's shoulder. "Rest you now."

Hester lay back down and fell asleep.

She was in a grove of oak trees near a circle of white-clad men. Their chief held up a toddler with golden red hair and proclaimed, "This is the chosen one." He placed the child on an altar, and she took off her clothes and laughed. The chief held a sickle to her throat. She began to cry, but the sound ended with a gurgle as the priest cut her throat. He incised her abdomen and lifted out the intestines. "So dies the cygnet! The princess's entrails will guide the way." The men grunted their approval.

Hester awoke and realized that the grunting came from the next room.

Nia was shaking with laughter.

"What is it?" demanded Hester.

"Oh dear me, I should not say, but Master Mervyn is ordering his companion to use more goose grease, for the love of God."

"But what can they want with goose grease at this hour of the night?"

"It is so that they can, you know…" Nia thought a moment. "How do you say, copulate."

"What? Mervyn surely cannot be a…a sodomite?"

"Indeed," replied Nia, with her hand over her mouth to still her laughter.

"But is he not afraid of the law and of hanging?"

"Ah, we live in a remote village of but two hundred souls, where laws are more difficult to enforce than in your big city."

Hester wanted to ask more, but Nia had fallen back to sleep, and she did not have the heart to wake her up, yet again. Hester knew that such relationships existed in ancient Greece. After all, Zeus had abducted the pretty youth, Ganymede, to be his lover as well as his cupbearer. The ancient Greeks were excusable, for civilization started with them. An unwelcome thought intruded: were the Greeks civilized? She recalled King Agamemnon sacrificing his daughter, Iphigenia, for a fair wind to carry his ships to the city of Troy. Hester stuck her fingers in her ears to block out the noise from next door and fell asleep.

A crowing cock woke the young women while it was still dark.

Nia lit a stub of candle on the bedside table and climbed out of bed. "The sooner we dress, the earlier we can start," she said, and pulled her woolen gown over her head.

Hester felt her stomach clench. She did not want to move. How could she face Mervyn now she knew about his vice? "How long has Mervyn been a…?"

"Sodomite?" said Nia, pulling a brush through Hester's hair. "As long as I can recall. My mother said it was his father made him so from all the beating."

"How so?"

"Llewelyn was married once and had a son, Arthur, born the same month as Mervyn," said Nia, now braiding Hester's hair. "Which was the same month as the King's bastard, Henry Fitzroy, who died a few years ago." Nia fastened Hester's bodices. "Llewelyn wanted everything for his son the same as for the King's. So when Arthur began his lessons, he had to have a whipping boy, just as had Henry Fitzroy. And Arthur, I understand, hated Mervyn and always misbehaved so Mervyn would be punished for it."

"Oh, that is horrible!" exclaimed Hester. Her hand flew to cover her mouth.

"But it is a long time ago now," said Nia, attaching the sleeves to Hester's gown.

"What happened to Arthur and his mother?"

"They died soon after your own dear mother, from what cause, I know not."

Nia fastened Hester's kirtle and started to braid her own hair. "You go down to breakfast, Mistress, while I repack."

Hester entered a small chamber with dingy, smoke-stained walls. The landlady, her forehead etched in a habitual scowl, set a tankard of small ale and slices of rye bread on a table. She cast a look of disdain at the four unshaven men lounging in their rumpled linen, then left the room.

Mervyn stood beside the fireplace, where a few damp sticks spluttered, picking his teeth with the point of a knife. Hester looked at him and for a moment saw in his eyes the traces of a sad, bewildered little boy. She looked away but not before Mervyn had noticed her softened expression. His lips turned downward in a sneer. Hester sat at the table and reached for a piece of bread. Mervyn sauntered over to her and squeezed her shoulder. The pain made her gasp and she dropped the bread on the table; it was stale and fell with a thunk. "So my cousin has heard tell of my noble childhood," hissed Mervyn.

"I do not understand you," said Hester, blushing. She took a sip of the ale. It was sour, and she pushed it away. Mervyn grabbed her chin and forced her to look at him.

"Ow, my lip!" said Hester. Mervyn released her.

"Your lying needs some practise, Hester Vaughan."

"You are right. Nia did tell me. It is one of the most awful things I have ever heard of. But it gives you no right to bully me." Scorn flashed in her eyes. "And it is disgusting, what you—" Mervyn squeezed her shoulder again. "That hurts!" she cried as she tried to wriggle out of his grasp. He tightened it further and Hester's eyes watered.

"Oh, so my cousin disapproves of love between men," said Mervyn, stepping back. "Perhaps she is not the scholar we have been led to believe. Methought she had studied Plato and would know that only love between noble-minded persons, in other words, men, deserves the name love."

"Indeed I have read the *Symposium*, but the participants were drunk and hence their discourse worthy only of the besotted."

Mervyn's eyes opened wide, but he forced a laugh."A woman always has the last word, but she is forgiven because her body is so soft and yielding."

He stepped close and squeezed her breast. Hester cried out from pain as well as from the affront. Tears coursed down her cheeks.

"Look at her cry, just like her mother."

"Do not dare to mention my mother, you foul caitiff!"

Hester grabbed Mervyn's hand and bit into it hard. She felt her teeth meet through the skin and she tasted blood. For a moment Mervyn was paralyzed by shock, then he leaped back.

His men laughed. Mervyn, enraged, clenched his fist to hit Hester in the face, but the man closest seized his arm and hissed something in Welsh.

Not understanding what had been said, Hester looked at the man, but he would not meet her eye.

Mervyn called for the landlady and ordered her to fetch linen to bind his hand. She returned with strips and cast Hester a glance of fear mingled with admiration. The landlady dressed the wound. Silence hung in the air like a drip refusing to fall from a spigot.

Nia entered and saw the proceedings and Hester's face. "Ah, do not let him provoke you."

Mervyn nursed his injured hand. "The bitch has fangs like a she-wolf! She should be muzzled."

He called for their horses, and the party continued on their way.

Mervyn and two men travelled in front and Hester and Nia behind, with one rider bringing up the rear. Once Hester was sure they would not be overheard, she asked, "Nia, why am I recalled home?"

"I would think it is because your father lies ill, and before he passes, wants to see you suitably married."

Hester let the subject rest.

They continued north. The second night they passed in Dunstable and the third in Towcester, where Boadicea, the leader of the Iceni, fought her last battle.

Before Hester fell asleep in the inn, she wondered what it might be like to lead troops in battle. She had read that the Empress Maud had led her men in a civil war four hundred years ago. People still spoke of it with horror, and no one forgot that a woman was its cause. There had been no reigning queen in England since, nor was there likely to be, ever.

Thursday night they passed at Kenilworth, close to the castle. Ravens cawed from the battlements and Hester felt comforted; it was a sound from home.

Friday morning, while the women rode abreast, Hester asked Nia, "How will I understand what people are saying in the village?"

"It will depend on who you are talking to, now, won't it," replied Nia, smiling.

"What do you mean?" Hester frowned.

"Well, your dear departed lady mother started a school for

the children and adults, so everyone your age and older knows some English." Nia grinned. "People attended because you can get more money out of the English on market day if you speak their language."

Hester felt her heart flutter as she wondered how someone from the oppressive nation would be received in Dinas Emrys.

riday morning came only too soon for the inhabitants of Hartbourne manor. The women had said farewell to as many tenants as possible in the past few days; they had taken brews and salves to the sick, whom Lady Maud had assured would remain in her prayers.

Lady Maud, Goody, and Alice stood on the steps watching the approach of five riders—the commissioner and his men. The women shivered in the dawn air and pulled their thin cloaks tighter.

"The Devil's hind hoof take them," muttered Goody.

Lady Maud began to offer a gentle rebuke but stopped herself.

Below, Stewart held Mirabel's bridle; she flicked her ears in annoyance. She was harnessed to a cart piled with an old straw mattress, a kettle, two iron skillets, a couple of blankets, a package of clean clothing, and a half-dozen pewter mugs.

Lady Maud descended to Stewart. "I regret you cannot come abide with us, but we will have very little room in the cottage."

"Pray do not concern yourself on my account, my lady. I have a married sister down south and shall head off tomorrow."

Alice saw swallows carrying clumps of mud to make their nests in the eaves. She envied them for they were staying at Hartbourne. Her upward gaze was caught by a shadow moving in the window of the solar. It must be William applying soot over the fireplace where he had hidden the crucifix and statuette of the Virgin.

The commissioner dismounted, as did his companions. He was a scrawny man of middle years, balding with a grizzled beard and downturned mouth. He motioned to two of his men. "Start with the jewellery chest and silver plate."

He turned to Lady Maud. "You remember me? Edward Jenkins?" He nodded toward Alice. "This is Mistress Vaughan, I presume?"

"No, Master Jenkins, this is my daughter, Lady Alice."

His eyes narrowed. "Then where is Mistress Vaughan? I have particular orders to find her."

"I do not know," replied Lady Maud. "She is travelling to North Wales." She turned to the cart to better secure the iron skillets between the mattress and blankets.

Jenkins's face turned white, then red, and his beard wobbled. "When will she return?"

"She has gone to stay with her father. She will not be returning."

Jenkins tugged at his beard. "When did she leave?"

"Four days ago."

"God's cock!" exclaimed Jenkins. Lady Maud shot him a glance of pure disdain.

He thumped his forehead with his clenched fist.

"Where in North Wales are they headed?"

Lady Maud stared into his eyes. "I forget the name of the village. It is near Snowdonia."

"You men," he pointed to two of his companions, "follow the road north and find them. Change horses every three hours if needs be. It is the King's express command that she be found."

The men remounted, whipped their horses, and galloped off.

"A four-day start." Jenkins near sobbed with frustration. "They will never find her."

He spat on the ground, his face contorted with rage. Lady Maud turned from him, back to the cart.

"You there," ordered Jenkins, pointing at his other two companions, "search out any forbidden articles."

The younger of the pair, a youth with a purple birthmark covering one cheek, found Lady Maud's New Testament and missal. He cast a sorrowful glance toward their owner and handed them to the commissioner.

"I saw that look, Martin, my lad. You are going to have to harden your stomach if you want to prosper in this line of work."

"Pray, sir, can they not keep these harmless items?"

Lady Maud echoed his plea. "That missal has been in my family for near a hundred years."

"The missal is a tool of the papists, and only gentlewomen are allowed to own a copy of the scriptures now." Jenkins gave a mock bow. "You are no longer a gentlewoman. You are soon to be widow of a traitor to His most Gracious Majesty King Henry the Eighth, King of England, France, and Lord of Ireland."

The commissioner, grinning, looked at his chief henchman, a hunchback with bulging eyes, awaiting his approbation; the man chuckled, but Martin only stared at the ground.

"You are in error, Master Jenkins," said Lady Maud in a quiet but firm voice. "His Majesty has not forbidden ordinary women to read the Bible, it is simply that his conscience troubles him about it."

Jenkins snorted. "When the King's conscience is troubled it is as good as law, and which of you fine dames is going to argue that?"

Lady Maud and Goody bowed their heads, but Alice stared at him, defiance in her eyes.

"A spirited maid, this one, a filly in need of taming, I would say." Jenkins leered at Alice, and guffawed. He continued. "So, we are agreed that these books are to be destroyed." He turned to the lad and handed him the books. "Martin, do it. Rip the covers off and tear the pages."

Martin took them, still staring at the ground. Jenkins shook the lad by the shoulders.

The Bible and missal fell to the ground, and Lady Maud bent down and retrieved them.

"Look at you, milk instead of red blood in your veins," shouted Jenkins, spittle flying from his mouth. "I have only taken you on for your mother's sake. Do you want to be sent home to be, again, the twelfth mouth she has to feed?" The commissioner scowled. "How are we to put hairs on your cockles, or...?"

Jenkins halted in his diatribe as John and Dickie, holding his prize box, approached.

"Who and what have we here?"

"I am Dickon and this is my egg collection. Do you want to see it, sir?"

"Pray do not mind him, Master Jenkins," implored Lady Maud. "Dickie is an innocent."

"An idiot, rather. An idiot holding the family jewels." He laughed and the hunchback guffawed.

Martin attempted to laugh but the sound came out more like a kitten's mewling.

The commissioner's eyes narrowed and he gave a sly grin. "Alright, Martin, you have a choice." He shoved him toward Dickie. "You are to destroy one or the other. Which is it to be, the books or the idiot's eggs?"

"Not my eggs!" cried Dickie, holding the box tight.

"No sir, I co – couldn't do either."

"You stuttering fool. So you prefer to be sent home in disgrace?"

Martin's forehead creased in the centre, then relaxed.

Alice noticed a gleam in Martin's eye. He walked with a determined step to Lady Maud. "Pray, my lady, let me have them." He winked several times, but she did not seem to realize he was conveying a message. Alice, however, understood.

Lady Maud looked in horror as Alice tugged the books away from her and handed them to Martin.

"Daughter, how could you…?"

Alice leaned in and whispered, "It will mend well. Trust me."

"Now lad," ordered Jenkins, "rip them to shreds."

"Do you know that it is against church law to destroy a consecrated book, except by fire?" said Alice, looking the commissioner in the eye. Her heart pounded like galloping horses, but she kept her voice firm. "This missal was consecrated by the Archbishop of Canterbury a century ago, and the Bible just last year by the Bishop of London."

"You would be excommunicated for such a sin," said Lady Maud, a tight smile on her lips.

Jenkins gasped and made the sign of the cross. Excommunication meant he would go straight to hell when he died. He gave a nervous laugh and tugged at his beard. "Very well, Martin, lad, keep them until we can get a fire going." The lad tucked them inside his jerkin. "Check to see what else they might be taking with them that they oughtn't." He turned to Dickie. "Yes, boy, now show me your egg collection."

Martin shuffled through the cart's contents, and, noticed only by Lady Maud and Alice, shoved the books under the mattress.

Jenkins threw Dickie's box on the ground. The eggs smashed. The commissioner laughed and stomped on the shards. Dickie screamed and pummelled him in the chest. Jenkins sneered and swatted him away. Dickie dived for the wooden box, its lid broken, and held it in his arms. He wailed like a calf taken from its mother and fell writhing to the ground.

The men stood back and blessed themselves.

Lady Maud leaned over him. "Dickie, Dickie, listen to me. There will be more eggs."

The fit lasted but a few seconds.

"Phew! What is that stink?" asked the commissioner. He snorted. "The idiot has shat himself."

"Come into the house and we will clean you up," said John. "Let us see if there are any comfits, or perhaps some raisins left in the kitchen."

"No, you don't," snarled Jenkins. "Unless you want to be charged with trespass. That is no longer your home."

"Let's go to the barn then." John gently took Dickie's elbow. "After you are cleaned we can search for a mouse in the hayloft."

Dickie sniffed. "Alright, a mouseling would be nice, but I would rather have my eggs." He hugged the broken box to his chest.

The commissioner leered at the women. "I have orders to search your persons also." He advanced on them. "I know where women keep their jewels." He noticed Goody's face flush. "I would wager the Devil's balls she has them in her cunny." He advanced on her, wiping spittle from his chin.

Lady Maud and Alice stepped between Jenkins and Goody, but he thrust them aside. Goody screamed.

"Hold her," he shouted. The hunchback pinioned Goody's arms behind her back.

"How dare you, sirrah?" cried Alice, seizing Jenkin's arm. Again he shoved her away.

"Patience, sweetling, you must await your turn."

"Sir, pray do not…" Martin stepped forward, beads of sweat on his brow.

"Go and fetch hay for our horses if you are not man enough to help here." Head down, Martin walked away to the stable. The commissioner grunted and thrust his hand up under Goody's kirtle. Goody made a mewling sound then stood stock still. Her eyes glazed over. Jenkins withdrew his hand and scowled. Goody, regaining her senses, yanked herself free. Two dozen opalescent orbs, each the size of a large pea, flew into the air and landed on the gravel.

Jenkins laughed. "She must have had them tied around her dugs." He and the hunchback went down on all fours scrabbling for the pearls. Three landed by Alice's feet. She could not stoop to pick them up as the men would notice her movement. She stepped forward a few inches so the hem of her dress hid the pearls from sight.

She looked up at the window. Surely Sir William had heard the commotion. *Please God he comes to our aid.*

Lady Maud was holding Goody. "Was that one of my necklaces?" she asked.

Goody nodded, unable to answer. She stared at the ground, her face as white as the pearls.

"Thank you," whispered Lady Maud.

A piercing yell sounded from the direction of the stables.

"You disgusting churl!" yelled Stewart, running, as Old Shep limped behind him. The horses whinnied in fright. Stewart wielded a pitchfork in front of him. "Ye cravens, molesting unarmed women!"

Stewart jabbed at Jenkins but caught him only a glancing blow on the chest. Jenkins and the hunchback rushed at Stewart and knocked him to the ground. Jenkins sliced at his throat and cut through the artery beside the windpipe. Blood spurted from the severed vessel. Goody rushed to him and supported his head in her lap, and Lady Maud pressed on the artery with her kerchief, but it was soaked within seconds. Shep whimpered and moulded his body against her legs.

Alice, horrified, wanted to help Stewart, but that would mean revealing the hidden pearls. They were all that stood between them and the agony of slow starvation. Alice felt it wicked to stand idly by as Stewart's blood poured onto the ground but assuaged her conscience with the knowledge that there was nothing she could do to help him.

The commissioner unfastened his jerkin and saw that he had sustained but a shallow cut. Only Alice noticed William bounding down the steps wielding his drawn sword. Jenkins turned to Alice. "If the old hag had pearls in her duckies, I expect you have diamonds in your quim." He stooped to lift her dress. Alice felt an icy grip in her bowels and her legs shook; she was just about to kick at his hand, when she heard William shout.

"Stop, sirrah!" he commanded, brandishing his sword.

The commissioner rose on hearing the voice of authority. William leaped forward and held the tip of his sword to Jenkins's throat. The hunchback approached with a hunting knife.

"One step nearer and your master's windpipe is slit open," said William to the hunchback.

William leaned lightly on the blade and two crimson drops

of blood appeared over Jenkins's Adam's apple. The hunchback stepped away.

"I am the King's man. Kill me at your peril," hissed the commissioner through clenched teeth.

"I have no intention of sullying my weapon with your blood." William began to sheathe his sword and turned to Alice. "What happened here?"

Jenkins, in a flash, thrust a dagger toward William's back.

The knight, seeing Alice's eyes widen in horror, ducked and, turning, sliced a fist-sized gash in the man's cheek. Jenkins howled. Lady Maud and Goody looked up for a moment, then returned their attention to Stewart. The horror of the past few minutes overcame Alice. She uttered a high-pitched cry like the shriek of an eagle. Then she collapsed on the ground, weeping. William raised her and supported her with his free arm.

The commissioner tore off the sleeve of his shirt and crumpled it against the cut. Martin, white as a new weaned lamb, ran from the stables to offer help, but Jenkins waved him away. Blood trickling down the side of his face, Jenkins mounted his horse, as did Martin and the hunchback. "My men will return by sunset," Jenkins shouted at Lady Maud. "Make sure you draggletails are gone by then."

He glared at Alice. "You will be sorry when next we meet." He addressed William. "And you, sir, will be rotting in Newgate Prison this time next week."

nce they had departed, Alice dried her eyes on her apron and lifted the hem of her dress to reveal the pearls still hidden there. William picked them up, and she placed them in her pocket. "Thank you for being here," she said.

"There is no place on earth I would sooner be," replied the knight.

The pair turned their attention to Stewart. He was making choking sounds. Goody supported his head while Lady Maud offered him water from a cup. "We shall light a candle for Saint Christopher and have a Mass said for you," said she, "in the old way."

"Oh, Stewart, bless you for your courtesy," said Goody, between sobs. "I shall never forget you."

"Stewart, say the prayer," entreated Lady Maud.

"*In manus tuas, Domine, commendo spiritum meum,*" he whispered.

A gurgling sound came from his windpipe, then his body jerked and he lay still.

"Into your hands, Lord, I commend my soul," murmured Alice, echoing the words.

"*Requiescat in pace,*" said William, reaching down to close his eyes.

"Amen," responded the women in unison, weeping, as they blessed themselves.

Three men who had been working in the field approached. Lady Maud recovered herself.

"Godfrey, Simon, Adam," she addressed them. "Stewart died defending us women."

They doffed their caps. "A terrible business this," said the oldest, crossing himself.

"And no redress, I would hazard, under the law," said another, scowling.

"Pray see Stewart well buried," said Lady Maud. "I am afraid all our monies have gone to paying off the servants. I have nothing left for the mass…" Her words trailed off.

Alice fingered the pearls in her pocket. She felt she should offer one, but a pall of fear descended upon her. The idea of a quick death she could bear, but the horror of wasting away for want of bread was well-nigh unthinkable. She realized she did not even know the price of a loaf of bread, even cheap rye bread. She clutched the pearls till they were slippery with her sweat.

Lady Maud turned to the cart and pulled out a pair of pewter cups. "Perhaps you could sell these?"

"No, my lady, pray do not fret yourself," said Godfrey. "Stewart was one of ours. We will see him right." He and his companions fetched a pallet from the stable. When they returned, Godfrey said, "My mother and aunt will ready him for burial." He shook his head as his companions lifted Stewart's body onto the pallet. "This king is a rogue and a tyrant, yet every day they thank God for him and peace. They remember the war of near sixty years ago when they learned to lay out the dead as surely as to skin rabbits."

"I will take Shep," said the youngest of the three. He pulled the whimpering dog away from Lady Maud's side.

"Thank you, Simon," said Lady Maud. "Sir Hugh would be most grateful. He was very fond of that hound."

Goody staggered to standing, her apron and kirtle drenched with blood. Flies settled on Stewart's open wound and she shooed them away. She took a blanket from the cart and covered the body.

"Mother, Goody," said Alice, taking a package of clothing from the cart, "come to the stables and change your dress."

Goody appeared not to hear her; she was watching the puddle on the ground change from red to brown.

"We heard the clamour. I could keep him away no longer," called John coming from the direction of the barn. Dickie ran ahead of him.

"Who was that?" Dickie asked.

"Stewart. He was very brave and died fighting for us," said Lady Maud. She opened her arms to him, then noticing the blood on her dress, let them hang limp.

Dickie's face turned white. "Bad men killed him. Did they kill Hessie, too?"

"No, no," said Alice. "Hessie is safe." Dickie seemed not to hear and fell to the ground.

"Nay, Master Dickon, don't be doing that now," said John.

The men gasped, put down the makeshift bier, and blessed themselves.

"Do not be afeard, he has only fainted," said Lady Maud. "I have hartshorn." She drew a phial from her pocket and wafted it under Dickie's nostrils. He sat up and rubbed his head.

"Oh, poor Stewart," moaned Goody. "He did it to save me."

Sir William murmured to Alice, "He did not touch you did he?"

"Only my dress. You were too quick." Alice gave a timid smile and William brushed a strand of hair from her face.

"Just quick enough." Sir William frowned. "For otherwise he would have lost his life rather than just his pure complexion."

"I wish we could stay and see Stewart well buried," said Lady Maud to the labourers. "But we must leave now, else face arrest." The men bowed their heads and departed with the body.

"God's blessings upon you all," she called out. They responded with a muted "Amen."

John fetched a pail of water and sluiced away the blood from the path.

Dickie sat on the steps watching him and quietly sang, "Jack and Jill went up the hill to fetch a pail of water, Jack fell down and broke his crown and Jill came tumbling after."

A rider approached. "What new mischief is this?" muttered Goody as he reined his horse at the steps.

He looked askance at the women in their bloodied garments. Lady Maud stepped forward and received a rolled parchment from him, then he turned his horse and galloped away

"It is from the constable in the Tower," said Lady Maud.

Alice hovered over her shoulder. Lady Maud broke the red wax seal releasing a faint smell of honey. She studied the letter, her hands shaking. "I cannot read it. William, will you?" She handed him the scroll.

"'Honourable Lady Maud Grantmire, I have great sadness in informing you that Sir Hugh will be executed on the eve of the feast of Saints Peter and Paul,'" read William. He calculated, "That is three weeks hence." He continued to read. "'I, too, am of the old faith and would not have Sir Hugh die without the consolation of a true priest and the rites of Holy Mother Church.'" William gulped and took a deep breath before he read on. "'I can secure the offices of a Roman priest, but it will be costly on account of the need for secrecy. I hazard three sovereigns would suffice. Pray inform me of your will in this matter, Your Humble Servant, Gregory Chambers, Constable of the Tower of London.'"

"My poor husband!" Lady Maud staggered, but Goody supported her on one side and Alice on the other. "Three sovereigns," she gasped. "It might as well be three hundred."

Alice could not bear the look of desolation on her mother's face. She fingered the pearls. She knew they were worth more than three sovereigns. *What am I to do?* She racked herself for an answer. A sudden rage overtook her. Why all this bloodshed and agony over an oath consisting of two sentences? Why must it be her parents and herself who died or starved for their faith? Could a person eat words, or a Bible? The bindings were leather. Maybe they could be boiled to make a stew? Alice clenched her teeth as she felt revulsion tighten inside her. Then she looked over at William gazing at her with affection, and the feeling passed. She felt only terrible regret. *Please, Blessed Virgin, succour Father in his cell*, she prayed.

Alice helped her mother and Goody wash themselves clean of Stewart's blood and into fresh clothing. John and Dickie waited beside Mirabel and the loaded cart. Before long, the little party was ready to set out. Alice felt she could not give all three pearls to help her father, but she must offer two, come what may. She held out two in her palm to Sir William. "For Father," she said.

"These will fetch three sovereigns, I am sure of it," said he, taking them and smiling.

With no one noticing, William kissed her outstretched palm "You do still have one left with which to provide for yourselves?"

Alice blushed and nodded.

William, a smile lingering on his lips, turned to Lady Maud. "With your permission, I will accompany you to the cottage and set off for London town at first light tomorrow. Lady Alice saved a couple of pearls that I can sell to help Sir Hugh."

Lady Maud sighed. "Thank you, you are most kind." She turned to Alice. "Did I not say the Lord would provide?" Alice knitted her brows, but William winked at her and she could not help but smile in return. Lady Maud looked up at the sun. "It is midmorning already, let us be on our way."

Goody was seated on the bottom step of the house, sipping on a mug of ale one of the workers had brought her. "I cannot believe it! Stewart, who never hurt anybody." She cried and sniffled into a handkerchief. "Murdered by that dreadful man."

"It is absolutely terrible," said Alice, helping her rise. Goody staggered but steadied herself. Alice looked at her nurse with concern. "Will you be able to walk the six miles to Syon?"

"I do not know," replied Goody. Alice looked at Lady Maud, whose haggard visage made Alice wonder if her mother could make the journey, either.

Alice supported Lady Maud, and John took Goody's arm. They

walked along the tow path by the river, encouraging Mirabel, who was unused to pulling a loaded wagon.

William rode his horse, holding Dickie in the saddle in front, who sobbed as he clutched his empty box. "Come back birdies, come back Hessie," he called, between gasping breaths.

The sun shone warmly upon them, but a cool breeze blew from the river and made their journey easier. The path underfoot was softened by pine needles and last autumn's leaves. The air was suffused with the sweet smell of river grass, and a throstle sang its lilting tune from a nearby elm. *It should be dark and drear*, thought Alice. *It isn't right that such a perfect day should bear witness to our misery.*

Alice caught fragments of her mother speaking to her. She asked her to repeat herself.

"I wish I could visit him in the Tower," said Lady Maud. She released her daughter's arm and continued to walk, holding herself erect. Alice could sense the tautness in her mother's frame and feared that she was close to collapse.

"Of course you do," agreed Alice. "But I do not think I could bear to be alone in a strange place with Dickie fragile and Goody not herself." She continued, "William can find a jeweller and fetch a good price for the pearls. I doubt you could do that, Mother dear."

"It is true I would find myself lost in under two minutes in London town," admitted Lady Maud.

At noon they halted beneath a tree to eat the remains of last night's partridge pie.

Dickie looked up at a branch. "I see a bird's nest. Can you reach it, John?" It was about twelve feet above their heads.

"I think I can," replied John. "Sir William, can you give me a leg up?" John ascended into the branches and retrieved the nest. "We are in luck. It's an abandoned magpie's."

He climbed back down and handed the nest to Dickie. "Oh, my!" Dickie cradled one of the pale blue eggs with brown-black speckles. "Beautiful. And look at these shiny black-and-white feathers." He stroked them. "This is a sure sign of good fortune." Dickie threw his shoulders back and marched to each of the women in turn, showing off his prize.

Lady Maud and Alice smiled.

"Very fine, providing we don't see the bird that laid them," declared Goody. "You know how the old rhyme goes. 'One for sorrow...'" She paused. "And if we do see the magpie, what must we do?"

"I don't know," replied Dickie.

"Bow to it and greet it as if it were the King's own sergeant." Goody gave a wry laugh. "Although I think we have seen enough of the King's men for a lifetime."

Alice gave a prayer of thanksgiving that Goody seemed recovered from the shock of Stewart's terrible death. She felt a chill run down her spine and prayed God keep their little group safe.

Late afternoon they saw the chimneys of Syon House. They passed by the great house, and beyond a coppice stood a hut. The weary group made their way along a path littered with acorns. Dickie stopped to pick them up. "Look! Just like eggs, only smaller." No one had energy to respond.

The air was infused with the sweet scent of honeysuckle. A vine, intertwined with wisteria, climbed the front wall of the tiny cottage. Heavy purple blossoms draped over the handleless door, which, missing a hinge, swayed with the breeze. The thatch was bare around the chimney, and grey bird droppings streaked the space beneath the eaves. Two crows, perched above the lintel, squawked at the travellers before flying away.

"Here we are." Lady Maud pushed open the door. The walls had been freshly whitewashed and the acrid smell remained. New rushes, strewn with herbs, lay on the packed dirt floor, and their sweetness offset the pungent smell of lime. Sir William set to lighting a fire in the grate.

"I'm hungry," said Dickie.

"Soon," replied his aunt.

A scrubbed pine table held a loaf of rye bread and a wheel of hard cheese. Beside it stood a pottery vase filled with bluebells. The women set out their shabby eating utensils. Next to the table stood two rickety chairs and three stools. Lady Maud sank onto one of the chairs and Goody on the other.

John was first to spy the flagon of beer in the corner and he poured some into each of the six pewter cups. He passed the first to Lady Maud. Dickie lunged for the loaf of bread.

"First we give thanks that the Lord has seen fit to provide us with a roof over our heads and this food for our bodily sustenance," said Lady Maud.

"Amen," responded all.

That's the shortest prayer Mother has ever made, thought Alice.

Under the cheese a note in an almost illegible hand read, *In gratitude for all your ministrations. I wish we could have left the cottage in better repair, and left you choicer vittles, but these are hard times. Dorcas and Alison*

Lady Maud leaned forward, her head in her hands, her shoulders shaking. She sobbed. "Oh, they have remembered."

"Who, Mother?" asked Alice.

"Two women whose children I had dosed with physic against the croup last winter. Dorcas and Alison are the miller's sisters, aunts of the babe I delivered last week."

"Mother, this is no need for crying," said Alice, her brow furrowed.

"You are young and have not yet learned it is kindness that breaks the heart open." She wiped her eyes.

Goody cut the bread and cheese and handed it around the table. Dickie filled his mouth. "Why isn't Hessie here, waiting for us?"

"Hessie is safe with your father," replied Lady Maud. "Now swallow your food before talking again."

Dickie obeyed. "Father? Do I have a father?"

"Yes, he was unwell, that is why you and Hester came to live at Hartbourne."

"Oh," said Dickie. "Am I going to go and live with him, too?"

"It is a long way to Wales." Lady Maud shook her head. "You cannot ride that far, you are not strong enough."

Dickie scowled. "Help me with my new eggs, John." The pair sat on the floor by the fireplace and arranged the magpie eggs in the centre of the box with the acorns around it. Dickie reverently placed the feathers on top.

Lady Maud retrieved her hidden missal from the cart and began to read, "Today is the feast of…" then sighed and shut the book.

Alice stole a furtive glance at Sir William to find him beaming at her. His hair was dishevelled and his doublet was soiled, but to her eyes he had never looked more handsome.

John and William hauled in the mattress. "Take it to the loft," said Lady Maud, motioning to a ladder against a wall. "We women will sleep up there and you men will keep the fire company."

The men tried to get the mattress up the ladder, but it was bulky, so Alice lent a shoulder. They had just hoisted it up when Dickie called, "John! John! There is something in the garden! I think it's a hedgehog." John groaned and went back down.

William and Alice sank onto the mattress. Alice wanted nothing more than to lie down and sleep forever, but modesty forbade. She forced herself to stand. William took her hand and looked into her eyes. "I shall do my utmost to obtain a true priest for Sir Hugh, but there is also something I need to ask of him. I need to ask his permission."

"Oh?" said Alice, her heart skipping a beat.

"It is true we have but recently met, yet what we have encountered in this brief time is more than many married couples do in a lifetime."

Alice nodded. William went down on one knee before her.

"So, will you, sweet Alice, do me the great honour of giving me your hand in marriage?"

"Oh, dear William, I would," she said, reaching down and placing her hand on his cheek, "but now is not the time to ask, with Father soon to die and our family's fortune in ruins."

William stood. "You are correct, of course, but that is of little comfort to me."

Alice placed her hand over his heart, and William put both his hands over hers.

lice woke with the dawn to see Sir William off. They embraced, but just briefly before Alice pulled away. She withdrew a piece of blue silk ribbon from her bosom, and they both blushed as she handed it to him.

"Is this the same ribbon?" asked the knight, arching an eyebrow.

"The very same that you dealt with so mercilessly at Hartbourne."

Sir William placed it in his doublet over his heart. He took Alice's hand and kissed it. "I shall take this as pledge of our betrothal."

"Nay, do not say those words, yet. Ask Father, and when you return we will tell Mother."

William mounted his horse. He leaned down and Alice stood on tiptoes and kissed him lightly on the cheek.

"God bless you, my dear, and keep you safe under His wing," said William.

"And God keep you, even as the apple of His eye," replied Alice. William nudged his horse as Alice waved goodbye. He turned around five times to ensure she was still there, waving. Alice felt tears prick her eyes, but there was much work to be done—water to fetch from the river, wood to be gathered for the fire, and linen to be washed. There would be time to cry, later. She offered up a prayer for William's Godspeed and her father's welfare.

Alice saw Lady Maud and Goody walking around the overgrown kitchen garden and overheard Lady Maud say, "Look, blue hyssop for the cough, and here is purple comfrey for healing wounds, and lettuce too. Lettuce will be good for our gums and teeth." She continued her perambulation.

"Aye," muttered Goody, "surely we will be dead of starvation before the week is out."

"But with good teeth," added Alice, approaching them. She permitted herself the smallest smile, realizing that her mother's mind was, at least for the moment, occupied with thoughts other than Father's… Alice could not finish the dreadful thought.

"It is very good of William to ride to London," said Lady Maud to Alice. "What a courteous young man." Alice blushed with pleasure. "I feel he is an angel, sent by God to comfort my dear Hugh."

Alice felt anxious. She bit on her lower lip. Was Mother's mind wandering? She pushed away the worrisome thought. Lady Maud continued, "Here is rosemary, which I have heard is good for the complexion, and sage for whitening teeth." She inhaled with satisfaction. "And we have chamomile, and, oh, this is tansy." Her lips pursed in disapproval. "But we have no need of that. I must ask John to pull it up."

"Why, Mother?" Alice recalled hearing something about tansy quite recently.

"We shall not talk about it, Alice. The angels will have naught to do with tansy, only devils grow it." Lady Maud turned and walked toward the cottage.

Alice, puzzled, looked toward Goody.

"It is the shock," said Goody. "It will take a little time for her to get used to all the newness here."

Alice nodded and brought the pearl out from her dress pocket. "The nearest village is Brentford; we can sell this at the market."

"So one survived!" remarked Goody. "Out of two dozen. But you have never set foot in a village market—folks do not trade pearls in such places."

"Well then," said Alice, "let's ask Mother what to do."

Inside, they posed their question to Lady Maud. "The mistress of Syon House may buy it," said Lady Maud. "The King has leased the house to a man who works in steel, or is a shipbuilder, I forget which. It used to be the Bridgettine sisters', and they had a wonderful library." Lady Maud frowned. "I doubt the present family uses it. I do not expect they will remain long." She sniffed and opened her missal.

Alice and Goody washed their faces in the rain bucket, combed each other's hair, and after breakfast of bread, cheese, and lettuce, set off for the big house. Dew lay on the grass, sparkling in the early sunlight. Ewes in the field were kicking away the near-grown lambs who still wanted to suckle. Larks swooped low over the fields, and the air smelled of hawthorn and newly turned earth.

Hawthorn reminded Alice of being with Hester at the Bateses' cottage. *I wonder how she fares. I do wish she were here*, but with a pang she realized her cousin would prove yet another mouth to feed. She recalled it was Mother Bates who had spoken of tansy but could not remember in what context.

"Goody," asked Alice, "what is tansy used for?"

"Why, for the kidneys and to aid digestion."

"Then why does Mother view it askance?"

"Some women use it to prevent their getting with child, which is a sin, as you well know." Goody flicked away a ladybird climbing up her sleeve and grimaced. "And some wicked ones take it to rid themselves of an unwanted babe."

A peacock stood in front of the gates to the great house, its tail feathers fanned out in a full display of sky blue, forest green, and bright orange. The women stopped to admire it. It lowered its iridescent sapphire neck and hissed at them then ran toward Goody, its black beak open and ready to bite. Alice shouted, "Get away!" and flapped her skirts, and it ran off into some bushes. It emitted a piercing squawk as it ran, and reminded Alice of a tenant's child who had made a similar sound while struggling against the barber to pull his tooth. It was a gut-wrenching cry of anguish and protest.

"What a horrid creature!" exclaimed Goody. "I hope there aren't any more." They met with a few drab peahens, feathered in beige, which hurried away from them.

"The sultan's wives, I suppose," said Alice.

"He's like our King, just Henry doesn't have them all at the same time," replied Goody. "He was handsome as the sun when he was young, but now, ugh." She spat behind her. "Vain as that peacock and nasty to boot."

They mounted the steps of the great front entrance of Syon House. Alice knocked and a footman in none too clean livery opened it. "Tradespeople to the back entrance," he said, looking down on them.

"I am Lady Alice Grantmire," began Alice. A slight aroma of roast pork met her nostrils, and she felt and heard her stomach rumble. She hoped the sound wasn't loud enough for the servant to hear. He glowered at them.

"No hawkers or peddlers. Begone!" He tried to close the door, but Goody already had her foot there.

There was shouting from the top of the stairs. "I wish I were back in Sheffield," cried a young woman in a strong Midlands accent.

"You ungrateful girl!" replied an older woman. "All this is so you can make an advantageous marriage."

"And all I want is a necklace or bracelet or brooch to enliven these mournful clothes."

"Jewels are works of the Devil, and blue silk is hardly mourning wear."

"Just what Father says, and where is he? How am I to meet any lords or dukes when he is busy overseeing his precious steelworks?" The young woman plopped herself down on a step halfway down the winding staircase.

"Abigail, you cannot sit on the stairs, get up." The older woman, realizing there were people at the door, addressed the footman. "Arthur, who are these women?"

"I am telling them to be off, Mistress Smith."

"Excuse me, madam," said Alice through the half-closed door.

The woman responded to Alice's cultured tones, and smiled.

"Admit them, Arthur."

But Mistress Smith's smile faded when she saw how meanly dressed were her visitors. She fingered her navy blue silk with white Brussels lace edging.

Her daughter joined her in the entrance. She was tall and thin and her face covered in tiny red pustules. Her mouth, half-open, revealed yellow buck teeth.

"What is your business?" demanded Mistress Smith of Alice.

Alice introduced herself again, making a slight curtsey.

The mother gave a mere incline of her head, and Abigail made a slight bow.

Alice felt herself blush at their rudeness. She took a deep breath. "And this is my nurse and friend, Goody."

Alice sensed Goody was about to snarl at mother and daughter for their discourtesy, but instead Goody smiled, which served only to make her look more ferocious.

Alice cast her a sympathetic glance then turned back to Mistress Smith. "My mother is Lady Maud Grantmire."

"Oh, you are the family new to the cottage with a boy possessed of a demon." Abigail shuddered.

"My cousin, Dickon, has the falling sickness," said Alice. "Moreover, we find ourselves in straitened circumstances. I have this pearl." She took out a crumpled handkerchief and revealed the white sphere nestled inside. It had been the largest in the necklace.

"It is magnificent!" Abigail reached for the pearl. "Look, Mother, it is the size of a rosehip." She paused, her hand about to grasp it, but then dropped her hand to her side. "Father doesn't believe a woman should wear jewels." Her eyes glazed over and she recited, as if by rote, "A woman has only one jewel of any worth, and that is her virtue."

"And needs no further adornment," added her mother. She looked askance at Alice. "Only Papists adore jewels, as if God cared how many baubles dangle from a body."

"Yes, but Mother, I have monies," said Abigail, lifting the

pearl from Alice's palm, "and I would dearly love to have this bauble dangling—"

"Monies with which Father intends to buy fur-lined sleeves for your good velvet dress," interrupted Mistress Smith.

"It is nearly summer. What needs I of fur-lined sleeves?" replied Abigail, caressing the pearl. "This will make an exquisite pendant, and I shall not speak to you all week if I cannot have it."

Mistress Smith glared at her daughter, but Abigail rummaged at her waist and brought forth a purse.

"Here is a sovereign."

Alice looked at Goody, who winked and extended two fingers from the hand clasped in front of her.

"It will be two sovereigns," said Alice.

"One sovereign and ten shillings," replied Abigail, picking at a pimple on her cheek.

Alice caught Goody's approving nod and also a gesture like she was shaking a bag. "In crowns, pray."

Abigail nodded and counted out seven pieces of silver into Goody's palm. She then looked closely at Alice. "What a beautiful complexion you have. Your skin is perfect, like my pearl."

Alice dipped her head, acknowledging the compliment.

"Yes, the lemon juice worked wonders on her freckles," murmured Goody. Then she gave a little startle and said aloud, "Lady Alice owes her fine complexion to washing twice daily in water of rosemary, and," she added, "the whiteness of her teeth is entirely due to a sage compound." She looked hard at Mistress Smith. "Lady Grantmire is skilled in the preparation of such remedies."

"Oh!" exclaimed Abigail. "Does she have any of either at the present? I will come with you." She turned to the attendant. "Arthur, fetch my cloak."

Arthur gave an almost imperceptible scowl. It was not his domain to fetch and carry articles of clothing. Alice smiled, it was as if she read his mind and he was thinking, *These low-born people with their new-made money and no idea of etiquette.* Exactly her own thoughts.

"Abigail, Abigail," chided her mother. "You cannot be seen traipsing over to that peasants' cottage. Let them bring their remedies here, and to the back door."

Alice and Goody took their leave.

"Whatever did you mean?" asked Alice as they descended the steps. "I have only ever washed my face in rosewater."

"Yes, but I have heard tell that rosemary is also excellent," replied Goody. "And as you may have noticed, we have rosemary growing in the garden and no roses."

Alice smiled. "And, thanks to Our Lady, we also happen to have sage."

"I be thinking," said Goody, jangling the coins in her pocket, "this will keep us but two weeks, after John has bought all we need for the garden, but if these rich folk purchase our remedies, then the whole village will flock to our door and we will have vittles forever."

"We have no phials or jars," said Alice, not at all happy about living in their cottage "forever."

"So we make a visit to the apothecary in Brentford."

They walked with caution toward the gates, but there was no sign of their gloriously plumaged attacker.

"Maybe he will be on the dinner table tonight," said Goody with a cackle.

"But he was so beautiful," replied Alice, the corners of her mouth turning down.

"Not as much meat on one of them as on a pheasant, at least from what I have heard."

"Stop," said Alice, "my mouth is watering."

"A little patience, Lady Alice," said Goody, smiling. "A crown will get us two loaves of bread, two pounds of mutton for today, and everything we need to set up as herbalists." She paused. "I forget what day is it. I pray it's not Friday, fish day."

"Saturday," replied Alice.

"Fine, mutton it is, and a roundel of cheese and even a pound of butter," said Goody.

The spire of Brentford church came into view. "Mother will want to go to church and hear Mass tomorrow for Whitsunday," said Alice.

"Not if she doesn't remember it is Whitsunday," said Goody. "I had forgotten what day of the week it was, and I dare say your poor lady mother won't remember either, after all she has endured." Goody sniffed. "And I, for one, will surely not be reminding her. Heaven knows how we would be looked upon, a parcel of vagrants traipsing into the parish church."

Alice reflected to herself, *It would be one of King Henry's new priests in the pulpit. What if Mother pronounced that all present had turned to heresy and damned their immortal souls?* Alice smiled grimly. *We should be turned out and one of the King's men would come to arrest us. Maybe that horrid man Jenkins would take us to prison... And William not here. Sweet Lady Mary, help us.*

She asked herself, *What do I believe? Could a king be head of a church?* The idea was ridiculous, but near everyone in the kingdom had conformed to the notion, and left to herself, so would she. Alice clenched her fists. She felt angry at God for allowing this to happen. But she was glad there was God to feel angry at, otherwise she would have to be angry with her mother and father, and that would be nigh unbearable. Her dress caught on a bramble and she stopped to untangle it.

Goody remarked on Alice's silence. "Penny for your thoughts," said she.

Alice laughed. "No, they are not worth so much." She disliked concealing Whitsunday Mass from her mother, but she assuaged her conscience by telling herself that the Virgin Mary, at least, would approve. Our Lady would not want them to imperil their mortal lives by attending a service at an unfamiliar church with a potentially hostile congregation.

Brentford village consisted of a single street lined with houses and shops. In the centre the marketplace still hummed with activity, even though it was gone ten in the morning. The lie-a-bed housewives were picking over the last of the produce—tattered onions, cabbages, and parsnips.

Alice and Goody navigated around deep puddles in the unpaved street—their dresses were dingy enough already, and they did not need, in addition, mud-splattered hems.

They found the baker, the butcher, and were able to buy butter and cheese from a dairy. They were also able to obtain yeast and a few handfuls of barley for brewing ale.

"We want a pestle and mortar if we are to make liniments, and also beeswax," said Alice as they rested a moment with their heavy packages.

In a back alleyway, they found the apothecary's shop, with its neat array of bottles and jars lined up on window shelves.

"We had best knock and go in," said Alice, hesitating. She felt a sudden unaccountable nervousness.

"Wait," said Goody. "I should go alone. Your voice and carriage would betray you as high born. It would look odd for such a one to be purchasing the necessaries for concocting unguents and potions and so on. We do not want him to suspect he may have a rival in the village."

Alice nodded agreement.

"Whereas I," continued Goody, "am staying with my daughter who is expecting her first baby any day now, God willing, and I wish to make herbal teas and liniments for her and her newborn."

"Will he not know everyone in the village?" objected Alice.

"They have just moved here from Nottingham. Her husband has recently been appointed a royal forester and they know no one as yet."

"Goody," said Alice, "you should be writing tales like Geoffrey Chaucer."

Goody beamed under her mistress's praise. "You wait for me outside the chandler's on the main street."

Just as Goody rapped on the front door, a smartly dressed woman of middle age stepped out from a side entrance. A strong smell of lavender wafted behind her. *That must be the apothecary's wife*, thought Alice.

She found the chandlery and bought a pound of beeswax. To hide her cultured accent Alice spoke in monosyllables. She imagined the chandler, a tall stooped man with a hare lip, must take her for a half-wit.

Afterwards, Alice stood outside the store waiting for Goody. She was pushed aside by a group of young boys.

"Make way, make way for the scold!" they cried.

Soon a handcart came into view. On a seat at the back of the cart sat a scowling woman with tangled grey hair whose dress was in disarray. Her face was lined and wrinkled. A leather belt secured her to the chair, but when the cart hit a pothole she rocked so wildly she was nearly flung off. The boys pelted the woman with black, rotten vegetables: turnips and slimy cabbage leaves.

At first, the woman attempted to wipe the garbage from her face, but the barrage was so intense she surrendered the effort and sat, slumped forward, seemingly insensible of her persecutors.

A seamstress came out to watch, as did the other householders on the street.

"What has that poor woman done to be treated so?" asked Alice.

"She is a scold," replied the seamstress. "She nags her husband for money. True she has six children to feed and himself, a tanner, spends all his money on beer, but she should not harangue him so. It is a wife's duty to accept the lot God has given her and to obey her husband meekly and in silence."

A youth lounged over toward them. "Aye, and betimes she won't open her legs when her lord and master bids her." He leered at Alice, who blushed and turned her head. Goody arrived just then and they wended their way home.

"Fairly done," pronounced Goody. "Two shillings for pestle and mortar and a dozen of those little glass bottles and a half-dozen jars." She patted the contents of her sack. "How much for the beeswax, mistress? And here, you take charge of our privy purse." Goody handed over the remaining silver.

"A shilling," replied Alice and fingered the coins in her pocket.

The women spent the afternoon cooking, and in the early evening they, together with John and Dickie, began weeding out the cottage garden. Parsley added to the mutton made for a savoury broth, and after Lady Maud gave thanks, everyone, exhausted, ate in silence. Afterwards, John and Dickie gave Mirabel a good rubdown and took her into a field to graze on new grass.

Although it was still light at nine o'clock, the women dragged themselves up the ladder to bed. Alice kept touching the remaining coins in her pocket. Most of the money gained by the sale of the pearl had been spent on necessities: a spade, a hoe, a water bucket, paying the blacksmith for a new hinge for the door, and cloth for new breeches and shirt for Dickie, for his old ones were tattered beyond repair. Alice thought, *If we sacrifice cheese and butter, we could keep ourselves for maybe a couple of months, but what then?* She felt the coins gave her strength; she could feel their metal infusing her frame. Is this how a miser began? Avarice was the name of that sin. She decided she would sin while asleep. She would place the coins under her side of the mattress and absorb their power while she slumbered. Thankfully there was hay aplenty for Mirabel, and so long as Alice had hope of Sir William's return, she felt she could survive.

Next morning, Alice climbed down the ladder, fatigued from strange dreams in which her father was drowning in rosemary water. She found Lady Maud in the kitchen reading her missal, while Goody set the barley to malt, in preparation for their first batch of ale.

"Alice, dear, it is Whitsunday and we should attend Mass in Brentford," said Lady Maud.

"Mother, it will not be at all the same as when Father Thomas said Mass in our chapel at Hartbourne."

"I wonder where he is now?" murmured Lady Maud. "Oh, how I miss your father." She closed her missal. "But let us avail of what spiritual sustenance is available to us in the parish church. Alice, dear, will you fetch our cloaks?" She tried to stand but collapsed back on the chair. "My legs are weak," she said. "I do not think I can walk to the village."

"You worked too hard yesterday," said Alice. "Go back to bed and I will bring you some bread and ale."

"I am not hungry and I would prefer chamomile tea." There was a querulous edge to Lady Maud's voice that Alice had never heard before. She looked at Goody who nodded and set the kettle on to boil. Alice helped her mother upstairs and into bed where Lady Maud picked at the blanket edge and unravelled a thread. She hummed an old hymn and wound the thread around her finger.

Alice's relief at avoiding a likely altercation in church was replaced by worry. *Is mother's mind giving way?*

"I have been thinking," said Goody, on Alice's descent. "If we don't go to Mass, someone will become suspicious. They may realize we are of the true faith but prefer to think of us as witches."

Both women crossed themselves. Goody poured hot water over the chamomile blossoms.

"Goody, we must set our minds to our livelihood, and if the wardens come to ask why we are not in church, we will think of some excuse." Alice cut the bread and stopped to brush a tendril of hair from her cheek. "But we must find buyers for our herbal remedies," she continued. "Otherwise we will starve and it will matter no whit what religion we profess."

Goody picked up the rough earthenware mug containing the brew and climbed up the ladder, cursing under her breath as the hot liquid sloshed out onto her hand. "The pox take that King Henry. Nary a fortnight ago my lady was drinking her tea from fine porcelain and her wine from Italian crystal." She muttered, "I hope God appreciates what she has done for Him."

ester's party spent Friday night in Dudley and Saturday night in Shrewsbury, close upon the Welsh border. Hester awoke to find herself covered in red, itchy lumps. Nia was likewise smitten. The pair removed their shifts and looked at each other and laughed, then Hester broke down and cried.

"I miss Dickie and Aunt Maud. I miss Alice and Uncle Hugh," she sobbed. "I wish I could go home. Why do I even want to see my father? He is a stranger to me." She wiped her eyes on the hem of her shift. "And now I am covered in flea bites!"

"Do not cry, Mistress fach," comforted Nia, "for it will all be as the gods and goddesses will it."

Hester had not heard the word "fach" for many years—it meant "little one" or "darling." She was too overwrought to ask Nia about her "gods and goddesses."

Nia added, "Today is Whitsunday and we will go hear Mass. Master Mervyn is keen to attend a particular church, but I must warn you, it may not be what you are used to."

Hester and Mervyn had not spoken for several days. But even his unwelcome presence could not detract from the comforting familiarity of the Mass.

As they rode to St. Lawrence's church, cows lowed in the fields and larks circled above. Mervyn opened the gate for Hester and she preceded him up the yew-lined path to the church door. She nearly fainted from mortification when she saw the sculpture poised above the entrance. It was of a broad, squatting woman with her hands inserted in her secret place. She held her introitus open for all to see. The expression on her face was both cheerful and salacious. Her eyes were wide open and her eyebrows arched with pleasure.

Hester blushed and stammered, "What in the name of all the saints is that?"

Mervyn and his men keeled over, laughing.

Nia explained, "That is a sheela na gig, and she is welcoming worshippers to her church."

"Surely it is some devil," protested Hester.

"Nay. There is no devil but what the Romans have conjured to terrify folks with." Nia gestured up at the carving. "She is all that remains of the great goddess. Men laugh at her, but that is only to cover their fear she will steal their cocks away. The Mothers give and the Mothers take."

Hester, attempting to cover her confusion, spoke sternly. "Nia, the Lord giveth and the Lord taketh away. And the Romans and the Roman Church are not the same thing."

Nia shook her head. "No? They share a name, so 'tis sure they go hand in hand together."

Hester resolved to explain the True Faith to Nia, later.

Inside, Hester was glad an aisle separated the men and women. A tapestry depicting the battle between St. George and the dragon hung behind the altar. Hester remembered making Alice swear on St. Margaret's dragon; St. George's dragon was different. This dragon lay on its back, impaled by the saint's spear. The gaping red wound in the dragon's belly resembled the spread open vulva of the sheela na gig. A brood of tiny serpents scurried around their dying dragon mother. Could it be a female Welsh dragon? No, St. George must have fought this dragon in the holy land. But could a Welsh dragoness arise and, and, what? Save the country from this pitting of the new faith against the old? Hester dismissed the ridiculous idea.

To begin the service, the priest said, "Who shall find a valiant woman? Far and from the uttermost coasts is the price of her."

Hester tried to pay attention and forced herself not to bite her fingernails.

"Strength and beauty are her clothing, and she shall laugh in the latter day," he continued. "She hath opened her mouth to wisdom, and the law of clemency is on her tongue. Surely her price is above rubies." Hester remembered the ruby lying inside the pocket of her packed dress. *Have I cursed my gown by putting the ring there? What if it creeps inside of me and grows, like Cancer the crab?*

Hester sat rigid for the remainder of the Mass. When it ended, the priest sped to the porch to receive his visitors. He was of small stature and squinted; his rusty black vestments were patched at elbow and darned at hem.

"Welcome to the Church of Saint Lawrence, patron saint of librarians and cooks," he chirruped. "Our martyr beseeched the men as they roasted him over the slow fire, 'Turn me over, for this side is well cooked.' Such was his love for our Lord he could jest even with his torturers."

Hester smiled and slid a few pennies into a padlocked wooden box. She stared straight ahead while passing under the lintel of the porch. Mervyn was not going to enjoy her discomfiture again, but she could not rid her mind of the image of the smiling woman and her gaping stone vulva. Every tree she passed seemed to have at least one knot in its trunk, with a central depression surrounded by a smooth rolled edge of bark.

As they journeyed onwards into Wales, the few inhabitants they encountered were thin and meanly clad.

"Why are they so poor?" asked Hester, pointing to a group of labourers in a field.

"The harvests are never so plentiful up here as in the south," replied Nia, "and the price of corn has doubled since this Henry's father usurped the throne—that Henry, who brought the sweat with him." Nia's horse snorted and Lady nickered in response. "Only the pestilence is more feared."

Hester blessed herself, and Nia inscribed a circle in the air before her.

"What was that sign you just made?" asked Hester.

"Why, to ward off the evil eye, of course."

Hester felt too weary to remonstrate.

"Your uncle hates Henry and cares for no church," said Nia, with satisfaction.

Hester wondered, was her uncle then a heretic? Or maybe he was just a pagan and for some reason had not been converted to the True Faith. Pagans were simply ignorant, but a heretic was evil—someone who had heard the truth of the Church and rejected it. But there were a lot of heretics in the country now. Before Henry, anyone who disagreed with Rome was a heretic; now anyone who disagreed with Henry was one. But even in Wales, surely they had been Christian for over a thousand years now? Hester prayed for the souls of all pagans and heretics and especially her own soul. After a few minutes she developed a bad headache and had to leave off praying.

During the journey, Nia helped Hester remember her native tongue. It was hard to become accustomed to Welsh again with its double consonants, the *ll*'s and the *dd*'s, but she was glad of something to occupy her mind. It stopped her thinking about Hartbourne and worrying about her family there. If Nia spoke slowly, Hester could converse with her in Welsh about the weather and the food set in front of them at mealtime, but it was beyond her to understand what Mervyn's men said amongst themselves.

That night the party stayed at an inn in Caerhun. Hester sat in a wooden tub while Nia scrubbed her down with lavender soap.

"By Our Lady, that feels good," Hester exclaimed. She realized the cut inside her must have healed as she felt no pain there as she lay half-submerged in the warm water.

"You have a bruise here, on your shoulder," said Nia

"It is a week old now and doesn't hurt. And thank the Lord the flea bites don't itch so much now."

Afterwards Nia helped her into a clean shift then dried her hair, rubbing the strands in a piece of flannel.

"We will not see any more of those horrid statues, like the one above the church, will we?"

"You mean the sheela na gig, the image of the Mother? No, there are not many statues left of her, now."

"Nia," reproved Hester, "you must not speak of that grotesque image as Mother. The only mother is the Blessed Virgin, our Mother Mary. Ouch! You are tugging."

"Sorry, Mistress. But true it is there are better-looking goddesses than the sheela na gig." Nia chuckled.

"There are no goddesses. I will dry the rest of my hair myself." Hester frowned and took the flannel from Nia.

"Well, I have heard there is a statue by a shrine hereabouts," said Nia, "and I don't believe it is the Virgin Mary."

"Then it must be one of the saints," replied Hester.

"How many women saints wear a helmet, a breast plate, a shield, and carry a spear?"

"Then she must be the Roman goddess, Minerva."

Nia snorted. "Why, and isn't that exactly what I've been saying, a goddess, just like Mother Mary?"

Hester sighed. "No, you do not understand. The Romans were pagans, so they erected statues to their own gods and goddesses. But that ended with Christianity."

"Is that so?" quizzed Nia.

"Indeed," retorted Hester.

"Well, but a body can't help but be confused. Gods, goddesses, saints, angels, and so on. The old goddesses are there, if only you look for them."

"Good Christians do not go looking for old gods or goddesses."

Nia brushed and braided Hester's hair. "There now, you look mighty fine. It is good your face is all healed up as we will be home tomorrow night, please God and His mothers."

"I cannot believe that I will see Father again after all this time," said Hester. "I wish Dickie could be here too." She bit on her fingernails. "Will you find me a mirror so I can see myself?"

Nia left and returned a few minutes later.

"Our landlady said this is what she uses."

It was a piece of glass the size of Nia's palm, with a tarnished silver back. Only a square inch was clear enough to cast a reflection.

Hester looked at her image. *At least I look alright from the outside*, she thought.

The next day they travelled on, westwards, and the white hawthorn in the hedgerows gave way to yellow gorse with its sharp green thorns and warm buttery fragrance.

"I will surely be glad to get home," said Nia, from behind Hester on the bridle path. "I hope Twgardan has missed me as much as I have missed him."

"Twgardan is your sweetheart?" asked Hester, turning in her saddle and trying to pronounce the unfamiliar name.

"Yes, and he is a fine archer withal. He hunts wild boar and deer, and we never go hungry, thanks to him. But he will be off and away soon with Lord Llewelyn on his great hunting party."

"Where are they going?"

"Down south near London town."

"Why does Lord Llewelyn go a-hunting there? Surely game is plentiful close to home."

"I never said they were hunting boar, Mistress. King Henry starts soon upon his northern progress, and he is the boar. Our men have practised for months shooting at their butts. I wish one of them would get Master Mervyn in his." Both girls laughed.

But Hester was perplexed. Did her uncle really intend to shoot down Henry outside London? He must be deranged. Such a mad plan could never succeed.

A drizzling mist set in midafternoon. The party had climbed to higher ground where a few scraggly sheep grazed in rock-strewn fields. As they rounded a hillside, they came across a peasant family sheltering under a tree. The children lay listless, their scalps and faces covered with open sores, their bare arms no wider than alder twigs. Their blank-eyed mother stared into the distance. A baby sucked at one breast and a toddler tugged at the other. The father approached Mervyn and begged a few coins.

Mervyn slashed at him with his riding whip, forgetting his injured hand. "God's wounds, varlet, let me pass!"

The man ducked away from the blow, then reached up in supplication to grasp Mervyn's foot. Mervyn hit him across the face. The man staggered backwards, and a wide gash appeared, red and glistening through the dirt on his cheek. His wife shrieked an imprecation at Mervyn.

Mervyn's face turned white and his cheeks sagged.

Hester asked Nia, "What did she say?"

"That he will die a slow and agonizing death and shall leave no heirs. And Modron will feast on him in the underworld, forever."

"Who is Modron?"

"The Great Mother."

Hester crossed herself. Mervyn spoke a few words to the wife. She shrank back.

Nia whispered, "Master has threatened to charge her with witchcraft."

The man threw himself on his knees before Mervyn's horse, begging him to reconsider.

"But surely Mervyn could not be bothered to arraign her before the assizes?" asked Hester.

"No, but these peasants are not to know that."

Mervyn barked an order and the man and woman stepped forward and kissed the toe of his boot. He gestured to the younger children, and their father lifted them so they could also kiss Mervyn's foot. But the eldest boy, a child of perhaps ten years with flaxen hair, refused to move from under the tree. He stood stock still glaring at Mervyn as his father shouted at him. The boy reminded Hester of Dickie—there was an air of innocence around him, and his shock of fair hair, although full of twigs, made him look angelic. She watched Mervyn, horrified and fascinated at the same time.

Nia translated. "The man is telling his son his mother will be burned for a witch if he does not kiss the master's foot."

Mervyn licked his lips and his eyes glittered. The peasant assured his son that he would come to no harm. He hauled the boy forward so that his lips touched Mervyn's boot. Mervyn stared into the child's stubborn eyes and drew back his foot. He lunged it straight into the boy's face. There was a sickening crack as the child's jaw broke. The lad screamed, and the mother's shrieks tore through the air. The father crumpled, holding his son against his chest. Blood streamed down his jerkin. Ravens circled overhead, cawing at the disturbance.

Hester opened her purse and flung a handful of silver shillings toward the man. Mervyn's companions gasped and dismounted to gather them up.

"For shame!" cried Nia. "What would your mothers think of you?"

The men remounted empty-handed.

Thank goodness Aunt Maud gave me monies, thought Hester. *And I shall not need much once I am…home.* She could barely bring herself to think the word.

Mervyn, grinning at his companions' discomfiture, gestured for them to ride on.

Nia turned to Hester. "Mistress, that was well done, but you must not be flinging your money at every pauper you meet."

Hester glared at her and hissed, "Do not tell me what to do!"

Nia opened her mouth as if to speak again but instead applied her crop to her pony and cantered ahead.

Hester could not afford to lose her only friend. She urged Lady on till she was abreast of Nia. "I am sorry for being angry. That poor lad reminded me of my brother, Dickie. You didn't meet him. He is a simpleton. The idea of someone hurting him…oh, it breaks my heart. And how I would like to hurt the person who does it." Hester clenched the reins.

"Ah, Mistress, I understand," said Nia, and they rode on side by side.

The mountains of Snowdonia appeared ahead of them, but Hester was too tired to admire the magnificent views—she was nearly asleep in the saddle. The horses, however, scented home and picked up the pace. Hester was jolted awake as Lady broke into a canter, and she had to cling to the reins not to be thrown.

Late afternoon, the sun broke through the clouds; the men complained of the heat and wanted to stop to rest.

"We must reach the village by nightfall," Mervyn declared. "Otherwise…" His voice trailed off. He ducked his head and Hester thought she saw him signing the cross, but he might just have been swatting away a fly, and the travellers continued on their way.

Nia whispered over to Hester. "Even in summer, travellers go a-missing, for the Tylwyth Teg, our fairy folk, snatch them away."

Hester was too fatigued to correct Nia about the non-existence of fairies. But as the evening shadows lengthened, she saw flickering shapes darting through the stunted, wind-whipped trees. Hester wondered if fairies lived in Wales but not in England. With relief she heard a raven caw—even a Welsh fairy couldn't caw.

After another few miles, the riders veered off the road and followed a rock-strewn sheep track upwards.

Nia smiled at her. "Nearly there now. I hope there is boiled tripe with leeks for supper."

Hester thought she would rather not have to eat sheep's stomach on her first evening home. "Home" was such a little word, yet it meant the world to her. Her father was waiting there, and she felt a surge of excitement to see him. It was he who had first taught her to sit on a pony. Hester felt a pang of regret that she had so little memory of him, either good or bad.

Lady's strength was flagging—her hooves slipped on loose shale and her breathing came hard. Hester urged her on with a promise of an apple and a nose-bag of oats once they reached the village. *Will they have apples?* she wondered. *But there will surely be oats.*

The sun was setting as they passed through a grove of ancient oak trees. Hester gasped, "How beautiful!"

"They are a thousand years old," replied Nia. "They were planted after the Romans destroyed the first grove. As if tearing down their trees could break the power of the old ones."

"The old ones?" queried Hester, her heart inexplicably racing. But then something else caught her eye. "What is that shining up there?" She pointed toward a hillock.

"The tomb of Dinas Emrys, the dragons for whom the village is named."

"But there are no dragons," protested Hester. She realized how feeble her voice sounded.

"As you like, Mistress, but the old ones put that stone slab there, and the fairy folk dance around it at Beltane."

"You mean Saint Joseph's Day?" stammered Hester, grasping for something familiar in a twilight where she felt anything might happen.

"That is what the Christians call May Day. This Beltane just past there was blood splattered all over the stone. Mayhap it was only an animal's." Disappointment tinged Nia's voice.

Hester watched the fading sunbeams gild the tips of the oak trees. She could almost imagine tiny sprites dancing on their leaves. Hester could not escape the sense that she had crossed a threshold into a strange and terrible world—one that civilization had passed by. She stroked Lady's mane to reassure herself that her pony was still solid beneath her.

She recalled Mother Bates's abhorrence of hawthorn. The old dame had been trying to keep magic out of her home; now she, Hester, was travelling in the land where magic had been born. This was the land of Merlin, the magician who had brought the infant King Arthur to Wales to be raised, the same King Arthur Henry claimed for his ancestor. Thinking of Henry sent a dart of shame and terror through her. She focused on a tuft of grey hair behind Lady's ear, but that reminded her of Henry's hair, so she shifted her gaze ahead to a strangely shaped tree branch. Once she had passed under it, she listened to the cries of the ravens. She counted them, up to ten. Then she counted to ten in Welsh, over and over, trying to exorcise the King from her mind.

here was barely light to see by when the rough palisade of Dinas Emrys came into view. *So this is home*, thought Hester. A group of peasants sat huddled at its base, their shapes just visible in the encroaching darkness. The women's ragged blankets barely covered their shoulders. None wore shoes, and the sight of their bare, callused feet sent a chill through Hester's own body. A little girl, hardly more than a toddler, struggled to hold a baby in her arms. Hester threw two pennies toward her, but the child just stared at the coins. Her mother, or at least Hester hoped it was her mother, rushed forward and picked them up from the dirt. She shouted her thanks to Hester, who felt a score of eyes focused upon her. She threw a dozen more pennies and a fight broke out over them between two men and a woman. Hester reproached herself for her foolishness. Nia shook her head.

Mervyn shouted, "Halloo there!"

An old man came out of a hut. He hawked a covert spit to one side when he saw who hailed him, and unbolted the gate. He addressed Mervyn in wheedling tones. "A fair welcome home to you, Master."

The man was missing one ear—he stroked his good one as he spoke.

"As well that you heard me call this time, Evan. 'Twould be pity to lose your one remaining ear."

"Indeed, Master, indeed."

Hester looked around her. Scattered braziers cast enough light that she could make out the dim outline of a square, some fifty yards across, flanked on three sides by timber buildings; a stone church occupied the fourth. Hester could hear, but not see, people passing by, their wooden clogs ringing on the cobblestones. A smithy by his forge shoed a destrier that snorted with every nail hammered into its hoof. A cooper was closing his store for the night; several barrels were lined up behind the door, all in different stages of completion.

A short, round man bearing a rush light bustled forward to greet the party. He had small eyes and a crooked nose and springy black hair—his tonsure had long grown over. A wooden rosary hung at the waist of his brown fustian robe.

"Greetings, Master Mervyn," said the cleric.

Mervyn dismounted and the man kissed him hard on the lips. Mervyn averted his face, making no effort to hide his disgust.

The cleric appeared not the least discomfited and cheerfully called out to Hester, in English, "How fares m'lady?"

Hester dipped her head in acknowledgement and inwardly swelled with pride at being addressed as "m'lady."

He helped her dismount. "I am Friar Gwylim. I take good care of matters both corporeal and spiritual." He gestured to his rotund belly then waved to a stableboy. "Take m'lady's mount."

Hester flinched as Lady, her only connection with Hartbourne, receded into the darkness. "Where will I find Lord Dafydd?" she asked.

"In that hall, there." Gwylim pointed across the courtyard. Hester was startled to see that the "hall" was no bigger than one of Sir Hugh's stables at home. No, not at home. This was home now.

Nia called out a greeting to a woman; their ensuing brief conversation in Welsh held a sing-song lilt to it and sounded to Hester more like a melody than a string of words. After they had bid each other good night, Nia turned to Hester. "Do you not wish to change your garb, first?"

"Father won't mind a little dust."

Nia brushed down Hester's riding dress with the palm of her hand.

"Indeed, my dearest cousin," agreed Mervyn, appearing by her side, "you can be sure a warm welcome awaits within."

Hester, surprised by his kind words, saw the friar wince. Gwylim scowled and marched off toward the church.

Mervyn and Nia escorted Hester up the steps of the hall. Mervyn opened the door, letting out sounds of laughter and the scraping of benches. Mervyn looked at his travel-stained doublet. He smiled at Hester and said, "I shall exchange my attire and join you forthwith."

The women walked along a centre aisle between rows of men sitting at tables. Each man cradled a tankard of ale. Tallow candles set on shelves cast a dim light, and smoke thickened the air. The rafters were finely carved with dragons and mermaids, but the ragged wall hangings were spotted with mould.

Two men sat on a raised dais behind which burned a log fire. The larger of the pair reclined on a huge mahogany armchair. On his left sat a frail, darkly visaged man. It took Hester a few moments to recognize her father in the latter, and when she did, she had to quell her impulse to run to him. Because others were present, she walked sedately with Nia by her side.

Hester ascended the dais, while Nia took a seat at a nearby table.

The big man stood. He was in middle age and looked to have once been athletic before indolence set to thickening him. Strands of thin chestnut hair framed his face. He opened thick red lips and drawled in English, "Dear niece, welcome. We hear you are an accomplished herbalist. I am Llewelyn Vaughan and this, of course, is Lord Dafydd, your father."

Hester made a deep curtsey and answered Llewelyn in Welsh. "Thank you for your kind welcome, Uncle." She wanted to add that she was also a Classics scholar but could not think of how to say that in Welsh, and besides, she was most anxious to greet her father.

Hester turned to embrace Dafydd. "Oh, Father, I am most glad to see you! How fare you?" She had rehearsed these two sentences and only wished she could say more to him in his native tongue; additional words eluded her.

She could barely see his face, for he was bundled up in a fur cloak.

Dafydd raised his hands toward her, but it cost him great effort and they fell back in his lap. His face was expressionless. Hester kissed him and found his cheek cold as glass.

Bewildered, she turned to her uncle and reverted to English. "My lord, my father is not well. Where are his physicians?"

Llewelyn's paunch protruded over the table as he leaned forward and replied, "There are no physicians here."

"But Master Mervyn told me—"

Llewelyn interrupted her. "In the old days we had enough of them, but not now. Your father has the palsy; it came on him a fortnight ago."

"Oh, why did you not call for my return earlier, Father?"

She received the same blank stare.

Llewelyn stared at a ring on his finger. "We sent for you two ays after it struck him." He scowled. "One must endure that which cannot be cured. But niece, we have matters to discuss, you and I."

Hester wanted only to tend to her father but remembered she was a guest here. The slow rise and fall of the cloak over Dafydd's chest proclaimed him already asleep. Llewelyn gestured for two men to carry his brother down from the dais and out of the hall.

Then, turning from Hester, Llewelyn addressed the crowd in rapidly spoken Welsh, of which she could discern but the occasional word. She knew he was speaking about the King and with such vitriol that spittle formed in the corners of his mouth.

A rumbling sound swelled the hall, and tankards slammed on the tables. People were shouting, "Freedom for Wales!"

Llewelyn glanced toward her as he spoke to the assembly, and she made out the word for "English."

The crowd quieted, and her uncle turned to her and said, "You are wearied after your travels. Good night, niece. We will talk more tomorrow."

Hester wondered what any of this had to do with her. She curtseyed and left the hall with Nia. She asked her companion, "Why did you not tell me that my uncle despises the English so?"

"I am afraid nearly every Welshman despises the English," replied Nia.

Hester brushed tears from her eyes. She had come this far, only to find her father so close to death he barely recognized her and that her next nearest kinsman viewed her as his enemy. She wished she had never left Hartbourne, for that was her home, not this remote mountainous village, miles from civilization.

"Now don't you cry, for weeping never helps," said Nia.

The young woman conducted Hester up the stairs of a house adjacent to the hall. They entered a small chamber divided by an arras. A pair of rush lights lit the room, and a fire flickered low in the grate. Hester's two dresses lay on the four-poster bed with her jewellery case beside it. Her package of books and box of medicaments stood on a table by the window.

"Oh, I see Gwendolyn has been settling you in," remarked Nia. "I will go fetch a third bolster for our bed. I am so ravenous I could eat an entire mountain goat. I must see what I can find in the kitchen."

As Nia left, there was a rustling from behind the arras and a young woman emerged. She was dressed in loose folds of pale purple silk and wore her long blond hair in a single braid. Hester was shocked to see her mother's pendant at the girl's throat and one of her handkerchiefs in her hand.

The girl dropped the slightest of curtseys. She straightened, stroking the handkerchief. "I am Gwendolyn." She grinned, revealing even teeth white as lily of the valley blossoms. "And, yes, I speak English, for where is the pleasure in insulting you if you cannot understand me?"

"How dare you steal my possessions?" gasped Hester, her eyes wide with disbelief and anger. "Give them back!"

But then she remembered she was alone here, and practically friendless. She choked back her rage. "Keep the handkerchief if you like, but I must have the necklace."

Gwendolyn stared at her with pale blue eyes. "Why thank you, that is most kind, and you an English lady. But what about this which is worth more than all the jewels in Lord Llewelyn's coffers?" She opened her hand and revealed Henry's ring.

Hester's mind swam. This girl, who was to be her companion, obviously hated her. She thought for a moment of Alice and Dickie. Her throat tightened. Her father was dying, her cousin Mervyn loathed her, and now there was this one who hated her too. Hester knew now that she had fallen among vipers. Gwendolyn's blond eyelashes made her eyes look enormous. They held power, and for a second, Hester wondered if the girl could read her mind.

Hester coloured, despite her best efforts. "That ring was a gift."

"How strange. It is clearly engraved 'Henricus Rex,' and beside it, in smaller letters, 'Elizabeth.' It was in the pocket of your dress. Did you steal it?"

Hester felt faint but forced herself to stand erect. She held out her palm and spoke softly. "Give me back my necklace and ring."

Gwendolyn continued to stare into Hester's eyes, but in the face of such controlled rage, her gaze wavered. Nevertheless she tried once more.

"And if I don't care to part with either?"

"Then you shall not see Saint John's Day. For I shall scratch out your eyes while you sleep. That pendant means the world to me."

Gwendolyn took a step back, alarmed. Then she grinned. "But are you not afeard I might harm you first?" she said, her boldness returning.

Hester felt as if an abyss had opened up before her, but she kept her voice steady. "No. My father is not long for this world, then I shall be entirely among strangers. I cannot see I have much to lose."

Gwendolyn unclasped the necklace from her throat. "Come and get them then." She waved the ring and necklace in front of Hester's face then jumped aside as Hester reached for them. "Go grovel for them, you southern cow!" She threw the jewels under the bed and Hester dived for them.

Hester placed the pendant and ring in her jewellery casket then turned to the young woman.

"That necklace was my mother's, you witch! What have I ever done to you?" Hester tugged at Gwendolyn's braid and Gwendolyn clawed at Hester's face.

Nia returned, carrying a tray of food. She called out, "Mistresses! Stop this caterwauling. Be friends now."

Gwendolyn ignored her and shrieked at Hester, "How dare you come here with your finery and books and herbs and be lauded as some kind of princess!"

Nia stepped between the girls. Gwendolyn scratched at her hand with her nails, and Nia gasped as blood oozed from her cut skin.

"You should not have interfered," snarled Gwendolyn.

Nia took a handkerchief from her pocket and wrapped the wound. She scolded, "This is no way for cousins to behave." She sat down on the bed and ate.

"Cousins?" echoed Hester, staring at Gwendolyn. "Does that mean you are…?"

"Yes, I am Llewelyn's natural daughter. I am Mervyn's sister, and we should be our father's heirs." She scowled. "Only our mother, Maryse, mislikes priests. And the priests told our dear father that his prick will fall off if he marries her, so she goes unwed, and we, her children, suffer for it." She turned and flounced out the door.

Nia tapped the bed beside her and ordered Hester, "Now eat!"

Hester obeyed, then murmured, "Mm, Nia, you are right. This tripe is delicious."

Afterwards, Nia cleared the dishes and placed Hester's dresses in a wooden chest.

"Your green dress is beautiful," she said, stroking the velvet fabric with her fingers.

Hester placed her jewellery casket on the window ledge. She hesitated over it.

"Do not worry," assured Nia, "Gwendolyn will not make off with your jewels. Everyone would know she had stolen them."

Hester unpacked her books: Homer's *Odyssey* and *Iliad*, Plato's *Symposium* and *Republic*, and her Bible.

A thought occurred to her. "Why did Lord Llewelyn not marry again?"

Nia snorted. "After his wife and son died, he took up more with Maryse. I believe he was injured soon after Gwendolyn was born and lost the use of his manhood. Or Maryse cursed him when he refused to marry her. I know not which."

Their backs were to the door, so they did not hear Gwendolyn enter.

"Yes, but he is still man enough to slay Henry."

Hester paled at the King's name.

"What is it?' demanded Gwendolyn. "You and Henry." She stared into Hester's face and hissed, "I see desperation in your eyes." Hester looked away. "And envy bordering on hatred. The envy of the motherless, who hungers no matter how full her belly or how many rings she steals."

"How dare you!" shouted Hester. She leaped forward, raising her hand to strike, but Gwendolyn turned and ran back out the door.

"Don't mind her," soothed Nia. "That one always acts like she has a gripe in her bowels." She absently rubbed her wounded hand. The blood had soaked through her handkerchief.

Hester said, "I have tincture of calendula in my medicine box." She opened a small glass phial, poured a few drops on a linen bandage, and rewrapped the cut. She sighed. "If only there were something in here for Father's palsy. But I fear he is beyond even the most skilled physicians' help."

Nia replied, "Still you are here, now, and your presence will cheer him. But it is late, we must go to bed."

ester opened her eyes to see the first rays of the sun shining through a cluster of pink clouds. *Where am I?* Then she remembered Gwendolyn. *I am hated here.* With this thought, she was struck with panic. She did what she always did to calm herself, think about the ancient Greeks and bite her nails. Hester gazed at the pink clouds and murmured "*rhododendros*" to herself. It was Homer's description for Eos, the goddess of dawn, "she of the rosy fingers." There was silver-ankled Thetis, the mother of Achilles, and ox-eyed Hera, the wife of Zeus, king of the gods. Whoever would have taken being called "ox-eyed" as a compliment? No wonder Hera was such a shrew.

Hester heard rustling from the other side of the room. She looked over and saw Nia shaking out her green velvet dress. "Mistress, pray stop chewing on your fingernails and get up for we do not want to be late for Mass."

Hester climbed out of bed. "I would like that." Then she remembered the last time she had thought it would be pleasant to attend Mass. She blushed thinking of that dreadful female creature crouched over the porch door.

"But it is Tuesday and not a saint's day, so wherefore Mass?" Hester stepped into a clean shift.

"You will see soon enough," replied Nia.

"And where is Gwendolyn?" asked Hester, a frown creasing her forehead.

"With her mother, I expect," replied Nia with a grimace. "I am glad for your sake that Mass is in Latin," she continued. "Father Ignatius can speak some English but no Welsh." Nia fastened

Hester's bodices. "He is a Spanish émigré priest. They say he was in the New World converting those heathen folks."

"So why did he come here?"

"By the Pope's special command."

"Well at least Father Ignatius is of the old faith," declared Hester. "Aunt Maud would approve." She murmured prayers for her family at Hartbourne and for her father, here.

"Mistress, don't talk of old and new faiths. The Christ faith is not old. The goddess Arianrhod's reef is but a few miles down the coast, and we are barely more than a stone's throw from the island of Anglesey." Nia helped Hester into her dress and tied the sleeves.

Hester remembered learning that the druids' stronghold was on Anglesey. "But we are Christians now. How can a goddess or Anglesey matter to anyone?" she asked. Her heart raced, yet she could fathom no reason for it.

Nia fastened Hester's rosary beads around her neck and straightened the crucifix at her throat.

"Did not the Romans vanquish the druids over a thousand years ago?" asked Hester. Her hands shook. "Nia, pray explain the goddesses."

"Pray do not ask so many questions, Mistress. That way you will not be told things you have no wish to hear. The mountains and valleys hold secrets," cautioned Nia, "and the wise do not pry into them."

Nia brushed Hester's hair, braided it, and set her coif in place. "You will be the best-dressed lady that ever entered the chapel, as the Blessed Mother herself only knows."

Indeed, there was much staring as Hester advanced up the aisle. Only women were present, and several moved aside in deference while casting her a mixture of admiring and envious looks. This attention was what Hester had always craved, but worry for her father robbed most of the pleasure.

The priest had his back to them. "Why is he wearing a black

chasuble and stole?" whispered Hester to Nia. "Does Father Ignatius think it is Good Friday or All Souls' Day?"

"Sh." Nia put her finger to her lips. "You shall see."

The chapel was adorned with black hangings emblazoned with the red dragon of Wales—Henry's dragon.

The priest intoned, "*Dies irae, dies illa, Solvet saeclum in favilla: Teste David cum Sybilla.*"

The day of wrath, foretold by the Sybil long before David ruled Israel, translated Hester silently. She felt dizzy. She saw the Sybil prophesying at her sacred oracle at Delphi, ages before the sun god, Apollo, destroyed her shrine. Apollo robbed the Sybil of her serpent and then, goading her to frenzy, entered and rode her, compelling her to spew forth the sacred oak leaves, on which were written her soothsaying words. Only now it was Apollo who placed the words in her mouth and his priests who interpreted them. The Sybil, herself, was nowhere in this charade, her divinity dragged down into whoredom. Hester tried to blank out the image. Apollo had degraded the Sybil, just as Henry had humiliated her.

Hester fingered the crucifix at her throat and whispered to Nia, "This is Mass for the Dead. Who has died?"

Again, Nia held a finger to her lips.

In a mocking tone the priest declared, "Henry, King of England, but never King of Wales. Anti-Christ of the Apocalypse. *Requiescat in Pace.*"

Hester gasped. "But it is forbidden to say Mass for the Dead for someone still living. This is black magic."

"Perhaps," replied Nia, "but it is said never to fail."

The priest consecrated the host and turned to face his congregation. His aquiline nose bespoke a Roman patrimony, and his carriage was that of an aristocrat.

Nia nudged Hester, who led the line of women to the altar rail where they knelt.

At the words *Corpus Christi*, Hester opened her mouth and received the host on her tongue. She closed her mouth, but instead of moving to the next communicant, the priest stood in front of her and stared at her neck. The muscles around his eyes flickered in anger.

Hester felt confused. She touched the crucifix. What was wrong with it?

Nia hissed in her ear, "Swallow." Hester obeyed.

Disappointment hovered at the corners of the priest's mouth as he moved to the next communicant. Hester was puzzled.

"He is afraid you may spit it out and take it home in your handkerchief," whispered Nia. "You might sell it to Farmer Jones who will sprinkle it on his cabbages to keep the caterpillars away."

Hester giggled a moment but stopped herself from laughing aloud.

Mass over, she and Nia stood outside the chapel. The courtyard rang with the hammering of anvils.

Hester quizzed Nia, "What was that service about?"

"Every Tuesday, the day sacred to Mawrth, Mass for the Dead is said for Henry."

"Mawrth? Do you mean Mars, the Roman god of war? But why?"

"Because Llewelyn is planning to strike at the King in the coming weeks. He will take every able-bodied man in the village with him, all twenty-four of them."

"That explains this," Hester waved her hand toward a pile of arrowheads heaped outside the smithy's hut. "But the king has a vast army, and Llewelyn's men would be slaughtered long before they reached London."

"With the gods on his side, he will surely succeed. But I am famished, let's go break our fast." Nia nudged Hester toward the hall.

"Maybe afterwards I will find Father a little recovered." Hester looked down at her nails, but there was not a single one left for her to bite. They were all nibbled down to the quick.

Following breakfast, Nia pointed out Dafydd's chamber. Hester ascended the staircase, knocked lightly on the door, and entered. A four-poster bed occupied the centre, beside which stood a hard-backed chair and a low table. The windows were draped with red damask curtains; in the dimness it was hard to make out the wasted form lying in the bed. She tiptoed over to her sleeping father and kissed him on the forehead—his brow was sweat-dampened. Seeing her father so helpless touched her deeply, and she knelt beside the bed and wept. Not wishing to disturb him, she returned to her chamber and leafed through her books.

Toward noon, Nia entered. "It is dinnertime, and you shall meet Twgardan."

"Gladly," replied Hester, "but only if I do not have to greet him by name."

Nia chuckled.

"Will Gwendolyn dine in hall?" asked Hester.

"No, she is with her mother. They are become like a canker in Lord Llewelyn's eyes now that the priest is here, telling him how he has imperilled his soul by fornicating with the heathen. Llewelyn mislikes seeing them yet dare not banish them, for Maryse is learned in the old ways."

The pair crossed to the hall. "Father Ignatius told him Maryse was like Delilah and she was robbing him, Samson, of his hair. Llewelyn listened because he is afeard of going bald."

Hester tried to explain. "Nia, it wasn't about Samson's hair. Delilah was a non-believer and she robbed him of his strength by cutting his hair. Losing his hair was nothing. Hair grows back."

"That may be so, but Lord Llewelyn would like what little he has to stay on his head."

They walked between the tables toward the dais. Only a few tiny windows, set high in the walls, provided light, but their eyes soon acclimatized to the dimness. There was great clanging as scullery boys placed huge iron pots of stew and loaves of bread on tables. Dogs, snoozing in the front porch, came to life as savoury smells wafted toward them.

Nia took her place at the end of the table. Hester sat between her uncle and a white-bearded man with one good and one dull, blind eye. A flagon of ale was set before her. She took a sip and belched, and a youth on the other side of the older man smiled impishly at her. He had dark curly hair and his eyes were the merriest blue Hester had ever seen.

The young man leaned over. "Takes some getting used to, our Welsh ale. I am Gareth." He had even, white teeth, and the corners of his eyes crinkled. She blushed furiously. How dare this youth address her in such a familiar way? She glared at him then looked down at her dinner—a quarter loaf of barley bread and a dollop of venison stew.

Llewelyn stood and addressed the hall. "I shall speak in English as my niece has yet to relearn our tongue. I present to you Lady Hester, daughter to Lord Dafydd. She has been raised by Sir Hugh Grantmire, near London town, since the death of her mother, Lady Margaret. But now my niece has returned to grace us with her presence, and just in time, what say ye?"

The men guffawed into their tankards.

Hester felt uneasy. This was not regular laughter, more an outpouring of communal relief. She stood and bowed to the assembly.

She heard a murmuring in English from the lower tables. "Ah, but she is so young, surely 'tis a pity."

Another man spoke in Welsh while gazing at Hester with something like sadness in his eyes. He was shushed by his neighbour.

Llewelyn glanced at Hester then called out, "Peredur, noble bard, give us a tune in celebration."

The old man pushed back his chair, and the youth reached under the table and drew out a wooden chest. From it he lifted a harp, intricately carved with vines. The scroll on top was in the form of a woman with large breasts. The old bard stroked them and said something that made the men laugh and the women make expostulatory sounds. Hester blushed at his actions and noticed that the youth stared down at his tankard, as if also embarrassed.

Peredur's hands fumbled over the strings; he passed the harp to Gareth and nodded.

Gareth took the harp and made minor adjustments to the pegs. He stood up. He was a little above the average height and slender and lithe about the chest and hips. He plucked a few notes, and Hester felt the seat beneath her vibrate in sympathy with the lower strings.

In deference to Hester, Gareth sang in English, softly at first, of the perfidy of Ceridwen, the sorceress who made her servant boy, Gwion Bach, stir her cauldron for a year. There was a raucous laugh when a man shouted he wouldn't mind stirring his doxy's cauldron for a year, but when Gareth dropped to a diminuendo, every ear strained to catch his words. Three magic drops from the cauldron fell on Gwion Bach, and he could understand all the language of the birds and beasts and take their form at will. Ceridwen waxed wroth, for this gift was designed for her own son. Gareth's voice rose to a crescendo as he sang of her pursuit of Gwion Bach. He turned into a hare and she into a greyhound. He ran to the river and turned into a fish, but she changed into an otter, and finally he changed into a grain of wheat, and Ceridwen became a hen and ate him. Nine months later she gave birth to a beautiful baby boy. He was so lovely she could not find it in herself to kill him, so she wrapped him in a leather bag and threw him in the sea. Gareth paused for effect. "By Caernarfon, near where we live, in that place sacred to the goddess Arianrhod." The notes shimmered away as if departing to another world, leaving but their ghosts behind.

Hester took a sharp in-breath. The goddess again! She touched the crucifix at her throat.

The hall was silent, save for a pair of dogs crunching bones at the back of the room.

"And, thus," continued Gareth, "was born Taliesin, the greatest bard of all."

Peredur interrupted him in Welsh. Hester was able to discern most of what he said.

"Do not forget Merlin, who set King Arthur to rule over all these lands!" So saying, the old man stood and took the harp from his apprentice. "Arthur who was born under the sign of Pendragon."

"Sir, do not strain yourself," implored the youth.

Peredur sang, and Gareth simultaneously translated for Hester. The bard told of how their village was named for the ancient tomb of Dinas Emrys, where a red dragon and a white dragon had once battled. The red Pendragon won. Then Peredur fell to murmuring that in olden times, the bard was considered second in importance only to the High King of Wales. A bard's raiment was spun so fine he would be mistaken for the king, were it not for his harp. "But," he concluded, "that was in the time of the druids, long before Christianity came and turned our people to sheep." Peredur's fingers hovered over the harp strings and he stared into space.

Gareth whispered to Hester, "The awen is come upon him. The muse often shares with him a vision fortelling the future."

After a few moments, Peredur blinked and looked around. Llewelyn grabbed him by the shoulders, and from the intensity with which he spoke, Hester gathered he wanted to know what the bard had seen in his vision.

"I see an old dragon falling palsied from the sky," declared Peredur. "The she-dragon rises and swirls in triumph. The sun shines on her red-gold wings. The goddess will smile on Wales again." The bard's head sank on his chest, and he began to snore.

Llewelyn, his face ruddy with exultation, announced, "The seer has spoken! The Tudor princeling will fall, and I, the rightful lord of Wales, will rule in his stead."

Gareth, seeing Hester's perplexity, translated Peredur's vision and Llewelyn's reaction. She gave him a nod of appreciation and understanding, then took a cautious sip of ale. How strange that her uncle identified with a she-dragon. But determined people saw signs of their success everywhere. She recalled the seers declaring the planets aligned for Anne Boleyn to birth a son. Lost in thought, Hester did not notice Gareth leave the hall.

A tall, weather-beaten man entered and, striding up to Llewelyn's chair, bowed.

"Welcome, Iolo! What news from the coast?"

"A dozen of Henry's men were in Caernarfon early this morning, my lord, searching for your niece. I told them she was with you in Anglesey. They took a boat over, and the boat unaccountably sank." He spoke slowly and enunciated clearly.

Hester felt ice prickle her stomach. *Oh, no!* she thought. *Henry wants his ring back.* But how had he known where to look for her? Then she remembered that most everyone at Hartbourne knew she was leaving for North Wales.

"Lady Hester, this is my captain, Iolo Williams," said Llewelyn. "Iolo, my niece, Lady Hester Vaughan."

Iolo bowed. Llewelyn dismissed him and he took a seat at the end of the table.

To Hester Llewelyn said, "Know you why Henry's men are in search of you?"

Hester thought fast. She whispered, so only her uncle could hear, "The King saw me at court recently while I was with Aunt Maud and he…he—"

"Say no more," interrupted her uncle. "The King took a fancy to you, and because you did not yield your virtue to him, he pursues you. We know about his insatiable lusts and are glad the Grantmires have kept you safe."

Hester blushed and gave a faint nod.

"Henry won't find you here." Llewelyn grinned at her, a big wolf-like smile. He raised his voice. "Niece, you are safe among us."

"Aye, safe enough until—" came a cry from the back of the hall. There was scuffling and the sound of a man being shoved outdoors.

Llewelyn scowled. The vein at his temple throbbed purple. "Our father aided Henry Tudor and was rewarded with great lands. His son, this Henry, has stolen them, suppressed our customs, and forbade any Welshman to set foot in town, save he goes in, grovelling, to sell his produce on market day."

Cries of anger rose from the men, and tankards crashed on wood.

Hester felt an overwhelming urge to flee. But flee where? Alone into the mountains where she might not survive even one night? She forced herself to stay seated and glanced down the table toward Nia, but she was deep in conversation with a smiling young, red-haired man. *That must be Twgardan*, Hester thought. *He doesn't look as if he hates anyone, not even the English.* Hester spoke sternly to herself: her uncle was probably just of a choleric disposition and given to outbursts that soon blew over. No cause for alarm. She needed to become more familiar with the ways of her kinsman, that was all.

Llewelyn's spleen continued its torrent but in Welsh, and Hester could not follow its meaning. All of a sudden he stopped and turned to her. It was strange, she thought, how he was looking at her exactly as Henry had, as if she were not a person but an object with some particular use.

She shook herself in an attempt to cast off the pall of fear she felt.

"So welcome, and doubly welcome, niece, for without you—"

A middle-aged man wearing a black gown lined with rabbit fur approached the dais, and said, "Caution, my lord, lest—"

Llewelyn gestured him to silence. "Both the King and I descend from Ednyfed Fychan, seneschal of the princes of Wales, but Arthur Pendragon is my ancestor alone. The auguries declare I shall prevail."

A cheer resounded in the hall, and Llewelyn sank back in his chair, breathless. His smooth face was flushed and his hair, sweat-darkened, clung to his brow.

The noise woke the old bard, who stared at Hester with his one good eye. "Ah, Margaret," he said in English, "it is good to look on your face again. Do you still play the melodies I taught you?"

At that moment, Gareth returned, carrying a small leather pouch. He sprinkled its contents into Peredur's goblet.

"Drink this, master. It will ease you back from the other world."

"Wait!" cried Hester. "Your master has just mistaken me for my mother. I must know more."

"Do not heed him, my lady," replied Gareth. "After the awen leaves him he is wont to ramble awhile."

"You mean that trance he went into?" asked Hester.

Gareth nodded. "The goddess comes to him and bids him speak."

Hester, not understanding him, turned to Peredur. "Margaret was my mother, bard. How did you know her?"

"It was many years ago," murmured Peredur.

"Perhaps you might visit our apartments tomorrow?" suggested Gareth. "My master will, please the gods, be recovered by then."

"Thank you, I will come." Hester was close to tears. "My mother has been dead these thirteen years."

"And it is but seven since I apprenticed to Peredur. But you are distressed. Let me call your waiting woman." He went to fetch Nia.

Perhaps if the bard taught my mother the harp, he could teach me, thought Hester.

She composed herself and Nia came to her side, blushing with happiness from her conversation with Twgardan.

Gareth assisted Peredur to his feet. The old man addressed Hester. "Remember, Margaret, your soul is a flame from the goddess. Fan it. Do not let any sad Christian priest persuade you otherwise."

Hester gasped—the old man must be quite demented. Turning to her uncle, she asked to be to be excused, but Llewelyn was sunk in his own thoughts.

Hester and Nia followed the bard and his pupil down the hall. The assembly rose as Hester passed. At the entrance she encountered Father Ignatius. His black Dominican robes swept over the wooden floor, causing little piles of dirt to eddy around his sandals. Passing Hester, he cast her a look of rage that made her heart seize.

The priest shouted at Llewelyn in Latin. "You swore she would be a heretic like all Henry's nobles! But she is a daughter of the true church." Ignatius snarled, "I, even more than you, wish to dispatch Henry back to his master, Beelzebub! But you must find another, for she will not do."

Llewelyn's face took on a dusky hue. "I say she will," he growled.

"She wears the rosary," insisted the priest. "She is a Roman Catholic."

Llewelyn snarled as he spoke. "You have secured us an ally, in that priest at Saint Alban's, but if you balk now, you will be forced to slink back to Rome with your tail between your legs." He gave a short laugh. "And surely, as an Inquisitor, you can sniff out the taint of heresy anywhere, even if it means planting it yourself. Remember, you have only until the solstice."

Father Ignatius's sallow face turned brick-red and he spun around. The gleam of the fanatic burned in his eyes as he pushed past Hester and the others.

Hester felt dazed. She understood only a few of the Latin words the pair had spoken. *Does Father Ignatius think I am not a good Catholic?* Maybe she wasn't. She had not been to confession since Henry's assault. But how to confess what someone else had done to her? A voice at the back of her mind insisted it was her fault. She should never have gone to court. Perhaps she should confess to Father Ignatius? But he was obviously angry with her, and she remembered Peredur's words about not trusting sad priests. Maybe angry ones were not to be trusted either.

Outside, Hester paused in the bright sunlight and watched Gareth lead Peredur to his rooms. The noise from the smith hammering arrowheads outside his shop was deafening. Next door, a fletcher whittled ash boughs for their shafts.

"Nia, why were Father Ignatius and Uncle arguing about me?"

"There is no love lost between them, 'tis sure. Lord Llewelyn never hears Mass. He goes to the tomb of Dinas Emrys to pray to one of the gods or goddesses."

"Then why does Father Ignatius stay?"

"Have you not heard it said, 'the enemy of my enemy is my friend'? And there is no doubt who their enemy is." Changing the subject, Nia asked, "But what think you of my sweetheart? Is he not fine?" She frowned. "I wish he were not leaving tomorrow, but he will be back soon."

Hester smiled and reflected she was glad Gareth was absent when Iolo told Llewelyn about Henry's men pursuing her. But she told herself crossly that Gareth was just a pleasant-looking youth with a beautiful voice and soulful eyes.

Nia nudged her. "Look who it is."

Mervyn crossed the courtyard and addressed Hester. "I understand you brawled with my sister. I wish I had been there to witness it."

Hester said nothing.

"Well, my little sparrow hawk, I expect I will be able to make you sing for me, soon enough." Mervyn chuckled and sauntered away.

Hester smoothed her skirts, as if ridding herself of contamination. "I will go to Father now."

ester found a veiled woman sitting beside her father's bed. The woman held a quill in one hand and a parchment in the other. She had been trying to coax Dafydd to write, for drops of ink stained the coverlet. But he was asleep and his fingers clean—the woman had not succeeded.

"I did not expect to find anyone here," said Hester, and, feeling herself an intruder, a flush rose to her cheeks. The woman made no response so she continued, "I am Hester, daughter to Dafydd Vaughan."

"In that case, I shall be on my way, Hester fach." The woman lifted her veil to reveal almond-shaped black eyes set in a face pale and withered as an old marrow. "I am Maryse. You have met my son and daughter already."

"Oh, you are Gwendolyn's mother."

"And Mervyn's too, of course." She stared at Hester. "How like you my son?"

Hester frowned and glanced away.

"He was greatly wronged as a child, but you can help justice prevail by marrying him. That will restore him to his rightful inheritance."

Hester pretended she had not heard and stared at her sleeping father.

Maryse gave a low chuckle. "I see how it is, then. Well, that is sad for you, for he goes soon to prepare a home for his fortunate bride."

Hester wanted to protest that she would never marry Mervyn. But this village was Maryse's home, and she, Hester, was the stranger here. Maryse arose from the chair with difficulty. Hester moved to assist her but was waved away. The woman left the room. She walked like a raven, with her head jutting out with every step. Dafydd woke and saw Hester. He groaned, "No, no!" then fell back asleep.

Hester sat beside him and took his hand. It had shrunk and was now no bigger than hers, its blue veins standing out against a background of brown, mottled spots. She remembered how this hand had pointed out the constellations in the night sky. Ursa Major was named for Callisto, the nymph beloved by Zeus. And there was Ursa Minor. Big bear and little bear; like mother and… no, she wasn't going to think of Mother, not now. Father and daughter, yes, that thought was bearable. But, no, it was not, for he was about to enter the next world.

She sobbed, "Father, don't die, please don't leave me here alone."

Dafydd woke. Frantic, he clawed at the bedsheet. When Hester tried to soothe him, he became more agitated. She took a taste from a little phial on the bedside table and identified valerian root. She coaxed a spoonful into his mouth and his limbs slackened. Within a few minutes, he was fast asleep. Hester kissed his brow and left.

In the sunlit yard, dairy maids crossed back and forth carrying pails of milk; men laden with rushes jostled with boys sweeping the cobbles. And always the hammering of the anvil.

Hester hoped prayer might assuage her grief. She entered the church and was thankful for the dimness and quiet. Praying in front of the altar were four elderly women, each wearing a red woolen cloak. They turned as they heard the door open and stared at Hester. Hester bid them good morrow, but they glared at her as if she were their enemy.

Hester remembered herself and repeated the greeting in Welsh, and the women, in unison, smiled and returned the salutation. Hester, seeking solitude, entered a side archway to the Lady Chapel, where stood a marble statue of the Blessed Virgin. It was a great relief to her to have someone tangible to whom to pray. She gave thanks that Henry had not yet extended his wrecking arm into Wales. Hester knelt and, having recited her Ave Marias, was about to rise when she heard the ringing of footsteps followed by a familiar voice in the chancel, the breathless tone of Friar Gwylim. Then she identified Mervyn's mocking twang as he whispered, "Speak in English, you fool! Do you want those crones yonder to know our business?"

Not wanting to give Mervyn the pleasure of seeing her tear-stained face, Hester remained still.

"Please, Mervyn, how can our love mean so little to you?"

"I must think to my stomach first. However would we live—you a defrocked cleric and I an impoverished bastard?"

"But tell me you love me, and not her."

"Love that mewling chit? God's eyes, no, but her property, once her Da dies, yes."

Dear God, thought Hester. *They are talking about me.*

"I shall not allow this! You have racked my heart, Mervyn."

"Saint Dewi's prick, man, see sense. A house and land!"

"I shall tell Father Ignatius! You know she has not been brought here for you."

"My poor addle-pated friar, jealousy has unhinged your noggin. Besides, you have not the ballocks to tell. You want to see us both hanged?"

"Sweet Jesu, let this not be happening," murmured Gwylim in an anguished tone.

Hester heard two sets of men's footsteps sounding in the aisle, then the door creaking open and slamming shut. She waited a minute. There was the shuffling of several pairs of wooden clogs and women's soft conversation; the door opened again but this time closed quietly.

Hester realized she was alone in the church. Her breath came rapidly, and when she rose she felt faint. She leaned against a pillar and tried to calm herself. She reasoned that Father would never give his consent to such a marriage; moreover, in his condition, he could not. Having regained her composure, she left the Lady Chapel.

She would have to find out more about Mervyn's plans, but whom to ask? Perhaps Nia could tell her something.

She found Nia in their room, sewing the last stitches into the heel of a pair of woolen hose.

Nia leaped up. "Twgardan came by, and what do you suppose?" Without waiting for a response, she continued, "We are to be married come Lammas Day."

"What wonderful news! That is just two months hence," responded Hester.

Nia bit through a thread.

"Nia," started Hester, "Mervyn's mother expects me to marry him."

"That cannot be," replied Nia. "For your lord father would surely object." She waved the stockings in the air. "I must go visit Twgardan's mother now and take these to him. I do not want him to catch cold on the road to London."

"But, it is June!" replied Hester.

"Ah now, if you had a sweetheart you would understand." Nia gave her a sly glance from the doorway. "And were you not planning to visit Gareth today? I mean, Peredur."

"Yes, but I don't think I shall," replied Hester, primly.

"Did not you think Peredur's good eye looked rheumy this morning?" Nia pointed to Hester's medicine cabinet. "You will have something to help him in there, I am sure."

"I do have eyebright, *Euphrasia*," agreed Hester.

"How do you know which herb will cure which ailment?" asked Nia.

"Eyebright's purple- and yellow-striped flower looks like a bloodshot eye and, of course, like cures like. Yes, I will brew some. Can you make a fire?"

"Very well. Twgardan's feet can wait another few minutes." Nia grinned and struck a flint to the hearth.

Hester searched the chest, reciting, "Peppermint for the bowel, blessed thistle for digestion, juniper for the dropsy, feverfew for the headache, and eyebright for the eyes."

"How do you remember all that physic?" asked Nia, setting the kettle to boil.

Hester shook out a few dried leaves into an earthenware vessel.

"Aunt Maud had us gather the herbs and prepare the decoctions, so we would recognize them by sight, taste, and smell. And as a further aid to memory, as you see, the bottles are labelled!"

The young women laughed. *Oh*, thought Hester, *I wonder how Aunt Maud fares, and Dickie and Alice, and Uncle Hugh*. She murmured a prayer for them as she steeped the eyebright.

Nia accompanied Hester to Peredur's quarters but left as soon as Gareth opened the door. The room was of middling size, furnished with a fine oak table and chairs, and woolen carpets lay upon the stone floor. Parchment-covered windows admitted a soft light that cast a glow on furniture and wainscoting. Gareth pointed Hester to a cushioned chair, beside which stood a harp.

He smiled, saying, "I will fetch my master."

A minute later Peredur entered, leaning on Gareth's arm. He sat and greeted her in Welsh.

"Lady Margaret, welcome. Alas, I see not so well these days, for my good eye is always tearing."

"Master Peredur," said Hester, offering her hand, which he took and raised to his lips. "I pray your indulgence. May we speak in English? I have not yet regained full command of my native tongue."

"It will come, my dear, give it time." Peredur said in English and chuckled. "Have you visited the sacred oak grove yet?"

"Not yet. But pray take my handkerchief." A scent of lavender wafted through the room. Peredur dabbed his eye with a corner.

"And these drops will help. Instill two in the morning and two in the evening for a week."

"Thank you, Lady Margaret, you are most kind."

"How is it you knew my mother?" asked Hester, but Peredur seemed not to hear her.

"Now," said he, "Gareth, pass me my harp, and my lady will sing, not in English but in Welsh."

The bard played a melody Hester remembered from childhood, and although her voice faltered over the longer words, Peredur's face glowed with pleasure. As the final chord faded, he sighed.

"I grow weary, but I have taught Gareth all I know, and he will teach you the harp." He stared at Hester. "Remember the old ways. I say to you, again, your soul is a flame from the goddess." The old man's hands trembled. "And remember to visit the oak grove and the altar of Dinas Emrys."

Gareth loosed the harp from the old man's hands and led him from the room.

"What ails him?" inquired Hester on Gareth's return.

"It is a slight palsy," replied Gareth, "and, betimes, as you see, his memory fails him. Nonetheless he is still the greatest bard in all the county. So, Mistress Vaughan, would you like your first lesson?"

Hester was curious. With raised eyebrows she asked, "What does he mean, talking about goddesses? Is it because his mind wanders? And why is the altar of Dinas Emrys important?"

Gareth strummed the harp strings. "Peredur's mind crosses time and place. And Mother Ane has received many a beast sacrificed on that altar." He handed the harp to Hester.

"Why would Saint Anne want the blood of an animal?"

"Not Saint Anne, Ane. Ane is the mother of all. She is the Great Goddess whom all of Wales, aye, and most of France worshipped, before ever a saint put foot on our soil. We honour her in Dinas Emrys together with her two sons, God and Jesus."

"By Our Lady!" exclaimed Hester, signing herself with the cross. "What is this place?"

Gareth smiled. "The last stronghold of the old faith."

Hester shook her head in disbelief and wondered what Aunt Maud would think of all this. She ran her fingers over the strings, which trilled in harmony. "What a beautiful sound! I wonder what tunes Mother knew."

"I will happily teach you some melodies, Mistress." He laughed. "Long ago, we used a raven's claw to pluck the strings, but now we use our fingernails. Oh, but you don't have any!"

Hester flushed and hid her hands behind her back. She drew herself erect. "I am Hester Vaughan, niece to Lord Llewelyn, and as for you, Gareth, do you even have a surname?"

Gareth's laugh froze. His jaw worked as if he had been struck. "Thank you for honouring us with your presence today," he murmured, then bowed and escorted her to the door.

Hester found herself speechless with rage in the courtyard, furious that an apprentice should dismiss her so, but mostly furious with herself for letting her vanity get the better of her sense. For who, now, was to teach her to play the harp?

he inhabitants of the little cottage by Syon had spent Whitsunday in prayer and reading, instead of attending Mass. John and Dickie had pleaded exemption from prayers to be allowed to dig in the garden. Lady Maud, aware that without their exertions there would not even be cabbage in the pot for dinner, had assented.

The past couple of days, the women had worked from dawn to dusk, brewing teas and preparing salves. Lady Maud had forbidden Alice to return to Syon House, not wanting her to form an acquaintance with heretics. Lady Maud also insisted on giving remedies, free of charge, to anyone who knocked on the door stating a need, despite the entreaties of Alice and Goody.

Early Tuesday morning, John and Dickie went to the river to fish. Lady Maud knelt on the floor beside Goody and Alice beseeching God and the Blessed Virgin to comfort Sir Hugh. Alice prayed for him and for William's swift return. They were thus absorbed when Goody rose from her knees. She had to hold on to the table edge to straighten herself. "Lady Maud, I hear folks galumphing up the path. From the chatter I am sure it is Mistress Abigail and her mother. Alleluia, we are saved!"

Lady Maud sighed and closed her missal. She beckoned to Alice, who helped her to her feet.

"Nourishment for the spirit will have to wait, I do suppose," said Lady Maud, passing her hand over her forehead.

Abigail knocked but without waiting for a response, barged through the door.

Mistress Smith stood stiff as a bean pole under the lintel, staring around the tiny room.

"It has been four days, counting today, since you said you would visit us, and I could not wait any longer, so we have come to you," said Abigail, embracing Alice.

Mistress Smith uttered a "tut tut" and Abigail released her new friend.

Alice introduced the visitors to Lady Maud. Mistress Smith ducked a curtsey, and Lady Maud inclined her head in acknowledgement.

Mistress Smith flushed and Alice realized she was annoyed with herself for curtseying. After all, she was mistress of Syon House, and the hovel dwellers but penniless Papists.

Alice took down a jar from the shelf. "We have rosemary brew for the complexion but have not yet prepared sage for the teeth," said she, pouring Abigail a phial of the liquid.

Abigail handed over a sixpence, and the women went outside.

"This reminds me of my little garden in Sheffield," said Mistress Smith. "I hardly know where to turn in the huge grounds of Syon."

"Even Hartbourne was not so extensive a property," said Lady Maud.

"Have you heard?" asked Mistress Smith. "A London brewer has taken your old manor."

Lady Maud gasped. "A brewer!"

Mistress Smith's head nodded up and down. "A friend of the King's."

The tenants of Syon House took their leave, Abigail promising to revisit soon.

Over breakfast Alice listened for hoofbeats, knowing that William should return soon. Afterwards she went into the garden, where the scent of warm herbs—rosemary, dill, sage, and thyme—filled the air. Alice gathered rosemary in a wicker basket, using a knife to cut through the woody stalk.

She had to concentrate, knowing if she allowed herself to become distracted she could well slice off a fingertip. William should have returned by now, but perhaps he was having difficulty finding a buyer for the pearl. At least that is what Alice told herself. She could not permit herself to think the terrifying thought that he, too, had been arrested.

Goody was tending the vegetable patch. "Enough slugs on this here lettuce to sink one of King Henry's ships," she muttered under her breath.

Lady Maud, wearing her cloak, appeared at the front door and stood, hesitating, under the lintel. "Pray find John," she said to Goody.

"Hope he's caught something, this time," said Goody, and she set off, muttering, "Dickie cries if John uses live worms on his hook, and no self-respecting fish will be tricked by a dead one."

Lady Maud turned to Alice. "I have prayed, and God tells me I needs must travel to London myself." She tugged on the cloak strings. "I do not know why William tarries so long, but he may be occupied helping your father tidy his affairs, and of course he cannot afford to send a messenger." Lady Maud stooped to pluck a leaf of sage and crushed it between her shaking fingers; she sniffed at it and gazed into the distance. "I must know if Sir Hugh has been shriven by a true priest before he leaves this earth."

Alice looked at her mother's yellow-tinged face and trembling hands. "Mother, you have an ague, you cannot go."

"I shall take John with me," said Lady Maud, ignoring her.

Alice felt a tremor of earth and heard the stamp of hooves. Five riders pulled up their steeds outside the cottage. Alice recognized her aunt among them.

"I had hoped this day would never come," said Lady Joyce, as an attendant assisted her from her saddle.

"Joyce, I did not expect to see you," said Lady Maud, moving to greet her sister.

Alice dropped her basket and stepped to her mother's side. A sense of foreboding made her want to protect her.

The sisters embraced and then stood, looking at each other. "You are unwell," declared Lady Joyce.

"I live in terror for the state of my husband's soul," replied Lady Maud, plucking another leaf of sage.

Lady Joyce proffered her cheek to Alice, who gave her a brief kiss.

"Look at you, you are dressed as a pauper!" exclaimed Lady Joyce as she surveyed Alice's cheap linsey-woolsey dress and soiled linen apron. Alice ignored her and tugged on her mother's sleeve to remind her of her duty to her guests.

Lady Maud straightened. "Will you enter and partake of some refreshment?"

"No, I thank you. This will take but a minute." Lady Joyce turned to her gentlewoman. "Jane, bring my purse."

Jane, avoiding any eye contact with Alice or her mother, obeyed.

Goody returned from the river with John and Dickie. Dickie was reciting the magpie song, "One for sorrow, two for joy, three for a girl, and four for a boy." He stared at Lady Joyce. "And five, for the Devil's spawn."

"Hush," said John. Dickie unfastened the points of his hose and, still staring at Lady Joyce, began to pass water against the side of the cottage.

"Come around the back, Master Dickon." John guided him away. "Remember, we do not piss in front of others. Then we will go catch frogs. I found a net especially made for it."

Lady Maud kept silent, so Alice spoke. "Please forgive him. My cousin's mind is scattered betimes."

Lady Joyce fondled a blue velvet purse and appeared not to hear her. "I bring sad news."

"Concerning Sir Hugh?" asked Lady Maud. Her eyes closed a moment then re-opened.

Joyce nodded. "He was executed yesterday morning."

Alice's hands flew to her mouth and smothered a cry. Goody gasped and reached for Lady Maud.

"No, that cannot be!" Lady Maud covered her face with her hands. She mumbled, "His execution was set for the eve of the feast of Saint Peter and Saint Paul, which is yet three weeks hence." Alice embraced her mother, who stood motionless as a dead tree trunk, Goody's hand on her back.

"Poor, poor Father," sobbed Alice, her head pressed against her mother's bosom.

"The King sets out on his great progress to the north at the end of the month," said Lady Joyce. She rushed on. "His Majesty is taking five thousand horses, there has been nothing like this since he came to the throne." Lady Joyce paused for breath. "The King has executed any who might garner sympathy while he is away— that is anyone prepared to die for the old faith." She gabbled on, "Sir Thomas More, God rest his soul, is already considered a saint by many; the King wants no more saints of that ilk." She beckoned to Jane to fetch a parchment from her saddlebag.

"This is a letter from the constable of the Tower addressed to you," said Lady Joyce.

Lady Maud tore her hands from her face to take the letter. She broke the wax seal and read aloud, "Honourable Lady Maud Grantmire, greetings and salutations. I am entrusting this letter to your lady sister, not knowing your new abode. Yesterday morning, your husband, Sir Hugh, was assoiled of his sins by a true priest and went to his death in perfect countenance."

Lady Maud wiped her eyes. "I cannot read any more. Alice, pray continue."

Alice read: "I admired the devotion with which Sir Hugh addressed the bill, soon to be introduced to parliament that will protect wise women who succour the indigent sick. This matter touches me, because I had a beloved aunt who was hanged for ministering physic to our parish poor."

Alice paused. "Oh, Father! This is too sad. Oh, Mother, what will we do without him?"

"Continue, dear," said Lady Maud.

Alice rubbed at her eyes and read on: "At Sir Hugh's request, I have conveyed his drafts to parliament and, next spring, God willing, his bill shall become law. I am most sorry to trouble you again for the monies for the priest, which I have not yet received. I beg you, my lady, pray for me, a sinner. Your humble servant, Gregory Chambers, Constable of the Tower."

Lady Maud placed the letter in her pocket. Her face went pale as lamb's fleece and her eyes shifted from Lady Joyce to Alice and back. She opened her mouth but uttered no word; her body began to sway, and Alice held out her arms to support her. Goody hurried into the cottage and brought out a stool. Once Lady Maud was seated, Alice, tears running down her cheeks, fetched seats for Lady Joyce and Jane. Goody poured ale for all, including the mounted riders, intermittently dabbing at her eyes with her sleeve. For a few seconds the only sounds were the breathing of the horses, their riders gulping their drinks, and bees buzzing among the herbs.

Lady Maud waited until her visitors had refreshed themselves. "Was he given a trial?" She choked out the words.

"No, sister, for he was attainted for treason and so…"

"And his body?" Lady Maud picked at a thread from her apron.

"Buried in the Tower chapel," replied her sister.

"All of his body?"

"Indeed. There was no time to place his head on a pike on Tower Bridge. The King, in the midst of plans for his great progress, could not trouble himself with it."

"Could not trouble himself," mouthed Lady Maud, staring at Alice.

Lady Maud clutched her chest and bent double. Alice knelt in front of her mother and clasped her arms around her.

Goody screamed, "That no-good, bastard, Mouldwarp king! Pray the Tudor line ends with him."

"Treasonous speech! Silence, you fool!" cried Lady Joyce.

Jane and the riders shifted their mugs of ale to their left hand, so they could bless themselves with their right.

Lady Maud, after a few moments, recovered herself. Alice

rose and stood behind her mother, a hand on her shoulder. Lady Maud clasped her hands in her lap and offered a prayer under her breath. "Thank you, Lord, for that mercy." She addressed Lady Joyce. "My worst fear is dispelled. My husband's soul is not damned." Lady Maud took a deep breath. "And how is your health, sister?"

"Poor, for I have no rest day or night." Lady Joyce wiped a hand across her brow. "Queen Catherine behaves most strangely. At midnight she will call for her dresses and jewels to try on. She demands a different gown, embroidered in shades of silver, to wear each day." She fanned her face with a glove. "It seems they will visit every town in the north. The King demands tribute from all those who aided the rebels in the Pilgrimage of Grace three years ago. Henry demands also that his wife shine beside him. Catherine is the moon to his Majesty's sun." She took a gulp of ale.

"If her Majesty were pregnant she, too, would wear gold and would be crowned Queen in York," added Jane. "But alas, there is no sign, yet." She brushed away a bee that had landed on her sleeve.

"It is said she cannot conceive," continued Lady Joyce, "which troubles the King greatly, with his having but one son, barely out of infancy, and two bastard daughters." Lady Joyce's face took on a haunted expression. Her florid cheeks grew pale and her eyes darted around her. She waved Jane away. "You may remount."

Alice stayed in position behind her mother. Once beyond the initial shock of knowing that Father was dead, she realized that William had not reached the Tower, or else the constable would not be asking for monies. So where was William? This question was uppermost in her mind; she saw her aunt lean in toward her mother but absorbed only fragments the speech.

"The queen acts like a woman possessed," said Lady Joyce. "One minute she laughs and dances, as her ladies play the lute and virginals, but the next she is collapsed, weeping on the floor, whispering words of love to a letter she keeps in her bosom. And, betimes, she encircles her neck with her hands. It is pitiful to watch. Rumour has it the ghost of her cousin, our cousin, Anne Boleyn, haunts her." Lady Joyce fussed with the folds of her gown.

"That sounds most difficult," agreed Lady Maud, wrapping her hands in her apron. She brought a hand to her cheek to wipe away a tear. "Oh, my dearest Hugh, I am so sorry." She gazed around as if she did not know where she was. Alice squeezed her mother's shoulder, and Lady Maud reached up and stroked her daughter's hand. Lady Maud gulped and focused on her sister. "But we have discussed the likelihood that Catherine has been unchaste and, when she is discovered, the King will put her away."

"I would hazard by Christmas he will know all, and I fear he will call it treason. She will burn and her family be imprisoned," replied Lady Joyce.

"Let us hope not," said Lady Maud. "But now, sister, you must leave us. I have been trying to prepare myself, but Hugh's death has still come as a shock."

"I am sorry," said Lady Joyce, finishing her ale. "And you will forget all I have said about the queen, yes?" She handed the blue velvet purse to her sister. "And pray accept this."

Lady Maud looked inside the purse. "We owe this to the constable and the coffin maker, and Masses will need to be said. I expect the priest who attended Hugh can arrange that." She handed the purse back to her sister. "Can you see this is done, pray?"

Lady Joyce took it and frowned. "Very well, if that is your wish."

"You have my thanks," said Lady Maud. She kissed her sister on the cheek and turned back to the cottage.

Lady Joyce reached into the purse. "But take these few shillings at least, for you and Alice for mourning clothes. You could purchase several yards of fine black wool…"

Alice stepped forward and accepted the coins. "Thank you, Aunt." *This will buy us food for two weeks*, she thought.

Lady Maud turned to her daughter. "Alice, return those coins to your aunt. What profits it, your wearing fine clothes when your father lies dead in his grave?"

"Mother," pleaded Alice, near to tears, "we need it for food, not new clothes. Do you think Father would want us to starve?"

"We pass most swiftly through this vale of tears," said Lady Maud. The expression on her face was so stricken that Alice returned the coins to her aunt. But she had felt the weight of them and could almost sense their power seeping into her soul. She clenched her fists as an attendant assisted Lady Joyce to mount. Alice knew she could only survive if William did.

"Have you heard any news of Sir William of Bayston?" she asked her aunt.

Lady Joyce looked down at her from the saddle, a blank expression on her face.

"The young knight from Hampton court," Alice explained.

"I do remember. What of him?"

"Sir William helped us settle into this cottage and then went to aid Father, but it is clear from that letter he never reached the Tower." Alice felt her cheeks flush but cared not that she had revealed her heart to her aunt. "We have heard no news of him. Might you make inquiries?"

"I shall do what I can," promised Lady Joyce.

"Thank you," said Alice.

Lady Joyce bent down and kissed Alice's cheek then signalled her party to depart. Goody gathered their empty mugs, which she took to wash in the rain barrel, and the riders galloped away. The thud of retreating hooves sounding in her ears, Alice joined her mother, who sat by the empty hearth, staring at her hands.

"It is too hard," said she, lifting her head to Alice.

"It is," agreed Alice. Her jaw clenched and she rubbed her cheeks to try to relieve the spasm. "And it is not made any easier on an empty stomach." Alice hated herself for her anger toward her mother, but she could not suppress it. "I do not have your faith!" she cried, clenching her hands by her sides. "I no longer give tuppence for the next world. I want this one to be at least bearable, and it isn't."

Lady Maud's face crumpled. "Oh, Alice, I am sorry." Tears welled again in Lady Maud's already reddened eyes.

"I still have nightmares about Stewart and that nasty man, Jenkins."

"My dear child, it will get better, for God is looking after us." Lady Maud extended her arms to her daughter. Alice wanted to shout that she did not give tuppence for God, either, but she ground her teeth and said nothing. She ran from the room.

he month of June wore on, and only a handful of men remained in the village. Mervyn was away and Llewelyn kept to his chambers, encloseted there with his counsellors. Hester spent her time between visiting her father's bedside and walking Lady around the perimeter of the village. She feared to go much beyond the gates, lest they become lost.

Hester brought her *Republic* to read to Dafydd, and occasionally he seemed to derive pleasure from it, but mostly she read to herself. The ancient language absorbed her. She enjoyed the shapes of the Greek letters, with their hint of the esoteric. Sometimes she imagined she was in the agora at Athens, engaging in discourse with Socrates. She pretended she was one of the elect, someone who mattered. Someone who was mothered. Both words derived from the same root. *Mater, matter.* Socrates was as unlike a mother as anybody could be, but that made him easier, or at least safer, to love. He was not going to suddenly vanish from her life. She had his book to hold. It was not going to grow wings and fly away to heaven and become an angel, like Mother had done. Hester could breathe in the smell of its leather bindings and caress its smooth vellum pages, almost as if it were a living creature.

Hester worked on a cambric nightgown for her father. At least, she told herself it was a nightgown, but she knew it was his shroud. Tears fell with the stitches, and she sewed into the twilit evenings. Nia kept her company, spinning woolen thread on her spindle.

The women ate their meals in their chamber. Nia was in low spirits because of Twgardan's absence, and Hester saw nothing of Gareth and was too proud to apologize for her previous rudeness toward him. She was trying hard not to bite her nails, just in case she had another chance to learn the harp from him. Gwendolyn spent her days with her mother and also, it was rumoured, with her suitor.

One morning, Hester declared, "My head is pounding, I will brew some feverfew for myself and then go visit Father. I cannot understand why he is never happy to see me."

Nia looked up from her spinning. "It is surely because of his illness."

Hester sighed. "I know what I shall do. I will offer up Mother's sapphire pendant to Our Lady and pray she restores his health."

Hester placed her jewellery casket and *Republic* in a satchel. She thought, *Maybe I should sacrifice my* Republic, *as well as the necklace. But what would Our Lady want with that?* Hester smiled. She could not imagine the Mother of God approving Socrates's idea that women should participate in gymnastics naked, just as the men did.

She pushed open the heavy door of the church and knelt before the Virgin's altar.

"Please heal Father. I give you Mother's pendant. It is all I have of hers, but take it, and beg God spare him." Sobbing, she draped the necklace over the Virgin's clasped hands. She prayed also for her family at Hartbourne.

Hester did not hear footsteps behind her and was startled to see Father Ignatius frowning down at her.

He addressed her in English, his Spanish accent lending his words a mellifluence that Hester found soothing to her ears. "My daughter, I overheard your supplications. Since it seems to be God's will to take your father ere long, you must rather pray to school your heart in submission to His holy ways."

Hester, lulled by the cadence of his speech, was half inclined to agree with Ignatius. But then her heart, grief-sore, moved her to stand. "I do not see how it can be God's will that we are given more pain than we can bear," she replied, tears welling in her eyes. "First my mother, whom I barely knew, and now my father, whom I can never know."

Father Ignatius drew his robe tight around his lean body. "It is not for us to question the Almighty." Then, more gently, "Do you question the Almighty, my child?"

Hester responded to the priest's sympathetic tone. "Sometimes I do, Father."

Ignatius's glance fell on the open satchel. "What is that book?"

Hester handed the *Republic* to him.

The priest's pale nostrils quivered with shock and indignation. "This is the work of the Devil! Did not Tertullian, that most venerable Church Father, condemn the works of Plato, as leading even wise men astray? How much worse, when they fall into the hands of susceptible young women?" He glared at her. "Who taught you to read Greek?"

"My Aunt Maud, Father. She learned it with Sir Thomas More's daughters."

"'Tis enough that a woman learn humility and obedience. My teacher, Tomás de Torquemada, considered More a fool for inflaming his daughters' minds."

Hester shuddered at the name of the founder of the Inquisition. How much blood had been shed under Torquemada's direction? No, not blood—the Church was forbidden to draw blood. Rather, it was how many joints crushed, how many limbs racked, and how many screams rent from the throats of burning men and women? Yet Peredur's words sounded in her ears: *Your soul is a flame from the goddess, fan it.*

"Aunt Maud saw nothing wrong in Plato's writings," replied Hester, "and she is the most Christian woman I know."

Father Ignatius's mouth creased in a slow smile and his eyes blazed with the flame of the pyre. He thrust the book back into Hester's hands and prostrated himself before the altar. He sang in a mixture of Spanish and Latin. Hester could not make out the words, and although she told herself a deranged Spanish priest was none of her concern, her heart raced as she left the church.

Clutching her book, Hester crossed to Dafydd's chamber. The damask curtains were closed tight, but new rushes strewed the floor and the smell of sweet woodruff scented the air. Dafydd was asleep, his cheeks sunken and his mouth agape.

Hester saw ink stains on his fingers and thought, "Oh, Father can write, even if he cannot speak. When he wakes I will ask him to write for me."

Dafydd stirred, but when he opened his eyes and saw Hester, he moaned and turned his head away.

"Why will you not look at me?" she pleaded.

She set a piece of parchment before him and placed a quill in his hand. Dafydd scratched the letter *I* and beside it a circle with a line through it—the Greek letter *phi*. Then his hand shook. He sobbed in frustration and fell back into a fitful doze. Hester stared at the two letters; *I* and *phi*. They must mean something; were they someone's initials? But who did she know with Greek initals? It made no sense. She brought her thumb to her mouth and bit on the nail then stopped herself. She kissed her father on the cheek and left.

That night she dreamed that her mother was in the Lady Chapel, standing beside the statue of the Virgin. "Where have you been?" cried Hester. Her mother opened her arms. "Why, waiting here, for you to find me." Hester ran to her embrace, but her mother changed into a witch, and bony fingers clutched Hester's throat. The witch became Henry. He exulted, "Now my navy will conquer the Spanish fleet!"

※

That same evening, Peredur lay in bed listening to Gareth recite poetry. Suddenly he sat up. "I see her, the King's daughter. Her golden red hair flames around her head. She is young and dreadfully wounded; her heart is turning to stone." He leaped up, scurrying the bedclothes to the floor. "No, this must not happen to the chosen of the Welsh dragon. Elizabeth cannot let her heart become cancred like her father's, for she is to rule in wisdom and charity."

Gareth fetched him a goblet of wine, but Peredur brushed it aside.

Then he sighed with relief. "Margaret will warm the young dragon's heart."

"Do you mean Mistress Vaughan is to aid the King's younger daughter, Lady Elizabeth?" asked Gareth, puzzled.

Peredur rubbed his eyes. "Ah, yes, Taliesin's poem. Pray continue."

Reluctantly, Gareth obeyed.

What is the seat of the breath?
What is the best that has been?
Why do the cattle have horns?
Why is a woman fond?

He paused.

"You are thinking of Margaret, aren't you?" asked Peredur.

Gareth blushed. Peredur chuckled. "I'm not totally blind. I see her handkerchief peeking from your pocket. I would wager there's something else in your pocket that would like to be peeking at her too."

"You must not say such things, sir!" exclaimed Gareth, aghast. "Mistress Vaughan is a fine lady."

"The goddess gave us passion in our hearts and loins. Don't let the Christians make you ashamed of the salmon leaping. And you must stay by her side, lest her heart fail without you."

"But I am only a bard, sir."

"Only a bard!" roared Peredur. "The druids, the vates, and the bards always advised the King in times past, and now we are all that remain. Does the goddess visit the Church's pale-bellied priests? Never!" Peredur raised his arms. "What is the function of the bard?"

Gareth recited, "To know the history of the kings of Britain, her language and genealogies."

Peredur, satisfied, lowered his hands.

Gareth chuckled. "But printing presses now make books that hold that knowledge."

"Printing presses! Books!" roared Peredur. "As if scratches on a page could replace hearing the old stories sung by the fire." Peredur laughed. "Ah, you have served me well for my slight on your love. But I meant it not as such. Our bodies are instruments that we must play as best we can. Soon you must leave me, for without your help Margaret cannot hope to succour the goddess returned."

"I cannot imagine Lady Elizabeth as the goddess returned, Master, but I have never before seen such beauty and fire in a woman as in Lady Hester. If I could make her love me, I would surely ask her to be my wife."

Gareth sat on the bed beside his teacher and lowered his head. Peredur lightly kissed the top of it. "An old man with a good son is not afraid to die."

"You are not—"

"Sh, lad, bards tell the truth. Now finish the poem."

Gareth recited:

There is a song in their going
A song from a hundred minstrels
And it is this they speak of,
The slaughter of the daughter of Lliant.

Hester woke to hear Nia humming a tune Peredur had played.

"Nia," she exclaimed, "I am determined to learn to play the harp." She blushed, realizing how much she wanted to see Gareth again, and added, "For it might cheer Father." She clambered out of bed, slipped into her red woolen dress, and covered her hair with a white linen coif.

"Do you wish me to come with you?" asked Nia. She hesitated. "Twgardan and a few of the men returned late last night."

"No, you go meet him."

"They are only here for two days to collect more barrels of arrows. When the King leaves London on his progress next week, our men will be lying in wait."

"But the King will have hundreds of guards about him."

"It takes but one arrow to kill any man, and there will be scores of them raining down on him."

"From where?"

Nia chuckled. "Father Ignatius and the priest of Saint Alban's have sorted it between them so that when Henry passes by, a dozen of our men shall be up in the church tower."

"And how will they escape afterwards?"

Nia hummed again and Hester thought how obstinate people were when they wanted something, and how they refused to see the most glaring pitfalls. *Oh, like when I was sure I could cure the King.*

Hester gazed at the nightgown she had sewn for her father. She could start another, but then no man needed two shrouds. She made herself think of something cheerful: the harp and Gareth with his eyes as blue as periwinkles.

The sweet smell of fresh bread wafted from the bakery. A pair of crows pecked at the cobblestones outside Peredur's door. Hester stood outside, thinking she had come too early, but hearing music within, she knocked.

"Come in!" called Gareth.

She entered and he set down the harp and bowed.

Hester dipped a curtsey. "I came because…" She stared at her handkerchief in his pocket and blushed.

Gareth stammered, "I wish to apologize for commenting on… And you lent this to Peredur on your last visit. Your first visit, that is." He handed her the little square of cambric.

"Pray keep the handkerchief; I do have others." Their eyes met, then both looked away at once.

Peredur entered and greeted Hester. A muffled croaking sound came from the far end of the room.

Gareth remarked, "Corwen is awake."

"Who is Corwen?"

"Our third musician."

"I see no one, and what an odd sound he makes."

Gareth smiled. "Corwen is an old crow with a broken wing. He can still fly, but only short distances."

Hester smiled too. "Can I see him?"

"Very well, but do not go too closely to his cage. He may try to bite you." Gareth grinned mischievously. "He will nibble your nails down even farther."

Hester laughed and followed him to a corner, where stood a wicker cage covered with a blanket. Gareth removed it to reveal a bedraggled crow.

"Your hair is the same colour as Corwen's feathers," remarked Gareth, blushing. "I mean, not his feathers as they are now, all ruffled, but as a crow's usually are—shiny and black."

Hester felt her face flush and tucked a loose tendril of hair back under her coif.

Peredur stood by the front door. "Mind you tell no one of our feathered friend, my dear. A covert messenger can be most useful."

"It will be our secret," promised Hester.

"I shall leave you to your lesson and sit outside a while. The morning rays are comfort for a man in the sunset of his age."

Peredur leaned on Gareth's arm but tripped passing through the door. He did not fall, thanks to Gareth steadying him and lowering him to a bench. Gareth returned and shut the door, which blocked out the new-risen sound of hammer on anvil.

"That dreadful noise!" groaned Hester, seating herself beside a little table on which stood a vase of pink briar roses. "And how does Lord Llewelyn think he will best Henry's army?"

"The prowess of our Welsh archers is unequalled," declared Gareth with pride. "They can hit a target from two hundred yards. It was they who won Agincourt and France for Henry the Fifth."

"But why attack the King so close to London? Why not wait until he comes closer on his progress?"

"He will be expecting trouble in the north; he will not be on guard near to home."

"Yes, I heard they have not accepted the new faith in the north." Hester sniffed at the roses, and the sweet scent reminded her of Hartbourne. She said a silent prayer for her family there, and also one for her father.

Gareth scowled. "His reforms press the people very hard." He looked at Hester and his brow cleared. "They cannot tie a rosary around the feet of Saint Blaise to relieve their sore throat or give a penny for a candle to Saint Austin to preserve the health of their hogs."

Hester laughed and covered her mouth. Gareth lifted the harp to her lap and adjusted the pegs.

"How did you become Peredur's apprentice?" she asked.

"My mother had seven of us. When I turned nine I was sent to work in the kitchen of an English lord who owned property in South Wales." Gareth smiled at Hester. "Because I was a seventh child, the lord expected my presence would bring good fortune, so I received a good education. There I learned to read, write, and sing in both English and Welsh."

Hester sighed with pleasure at the rippling sound the strings produced as she strummed across them.

"When Peredur visited and heard me sing, he persuaded my lord to part with me. My new master sent a purse of silver to my family, and I have travelled with him ever since."

"That is a happy story," remarked Hester.

"We sing the old songs and warm our people's hearts. Our ancestors were first to dwell on this island. We remind them that once we worshipped in woods and by rivers, and not, as now, in stone huts."

Hester stilled the harp strings. "Peredur mentioned the oak grove. We passed by it on our way here. I would love to visit a place where my mother had been. I know it sounds foolish, but because Wales was the last place I ever saw her, I had this fond hope that she might be waiting here for me."

For some reason, she felt safe in this young bard's company, and the sense of relief brought tears to her eyes. Two drops fell on the scroll of the harp.

Gareth handed her the handkerchief. "It is your turn now. Peredur and I have each had use of it."

Hester laughed and dried her eyes. Gareth took one of her hands in his own. Hester tried to pull hers away, but then sighed and left it in his.

"You look such an elegant lady, except for these," said Gareth taking her bitten index and middle finger tips to his mouth and kissing them. A shiver sparkled down Hester's spine.

She protested. "No one has ever kissed them before. I hate them. I wish I could stop biting them."

"Let me hold them; then you will have no choice in the matter."

They laughed and Corwen squawked from his cage.

Hester announced, "I should go visit Father." They both rose.

"But you will return tomorrow for another lesson, will you not?" asked Gareth, a smile on his lips but an anxious frown on his forehead.

"Indeed I shall."

⁕

Hester crossed to her father's chamber and thought, *I must not let myself become fond of Gareth. But oh, his music, and the touch of him…*

She nearly collided with Maryse, who was leaving the room. Maryse held a parchment clutched to her bosom and was humming to herself. Her broad smile reminded Hester of the sheela na gig at St. Lawrence's church.

Dafydd was awake, but he shut his eyes when he saw Hester.

"Please, Father, look at me. Will you not try to write something more for me today? You have written for Maryse." Hester cried, "What have I done to distress you?"

Tears pooled in the corners of Dafydd's eyes.

"Perhaps it is that your spirits are disordered." She touched his shoulder. "Do not despair, for I know the remedy. I will prepare a decoction of St. John's wort, *hypericum*, for you."

The most efficacious brew was made from flowers gathered on St. John's Eve, which she realized was the next day.

Hester returned to her room to find Nia at her spindle. "Will you come with me the morrow and help me gather St. John's wort for Father?"

"I have promised to help my aunt in the bake house, but why not ask Gareth? I am sure Peredur can spare him for a few hours." She added, "Bronwyn, my cousin, can wait on you. She is still spry enough even though her first is due on Calan Awst."

"Which is when?" asked Hester.

"August first, so…," Nia counted on her fingers, "she is nearly eight months gone, so you and Gareth can give her the slip should you have a mind to it."

Hester blushed and murmured to herself, "Well, I was going to see him for another lesson tomorrow. Father might not approve, but…but, this is to heal him." She spoke louder. "The ancients believed those flowers were blessed by Helios, the sun god, and I am sure a decoction will lift Father's melancholy. You know, Nia, they are called *Hypericum perforatum* because the little golden flowers are…" She stopped, realizing she was babbling.

Nia smiled. "And Saint John's Eve is always charged with magic. I will go and make Gareth aware of the change in plans."

ronwyn, a fair young woman of some twenty-five years, escorted Hester to Peredur's rooms just after dawn on St. John's Eve.

Gareth bowed first to Hester, who ducked her head to hide her blush as she curtseyed, then to Bronwyn.

"You are blooming like a ship in full sail," said he. "How long now?"

"A little over one full moon and I shall be delivered, God and His mother willing." Bronwyn made the sign with finger and thumb to ward off evil.

Evan the Ear opened the gates for the trio. He grinned and touched his brow as Gareth handed him a silver groat.

The party started uphill through the woodlands, tramping last autumn's dead leaves underfoot. They entered a meadow studded with fragrant yellow gorse bushes, a few strands of sheep's wool clinging to their spiny leaves. Bronwyn trailed behind Hester and Gareth, and the couple paused at the top of a hillock, staring out to sea.

Hester inhaled deeply. "I have never seen the ocean before. How alive it looks with the waves rolling, and what a fresh scent there is to the air." She glanced behind. "We should wait here for Bronwyn."

Gareth spread his cloak on the ground and Hester sat, careful not to look at him. Staring ahead at the sea, she asked, "Where is Arianrhod's reef?"

Gareth made a vague gesture. "No one is certain, but 'tis said that what was once the castle of the goddess can be seen at low tide and that mermaids comb their hair and sing among the ruins."

Hester turned to face him. "Do you believe that? Not in mermaids, but in a goddess?"

Gareth nodded just as Bronwyn arrived, a little out of breath.

"By the mothers, you two lope along like young wolves."

Hester made room for her on the cloak. Bronwyn stretched out in the warm sun and covered her face with her handkerchief.

Hester mused, "I wish Peredur could have told me something about Mother, since Father cannot, and Uncle Llewelyn has been closeted away since I arrived. And back home, I mean at Hartbourne, I could never ask Uncle Hugh."

Gareth moved his hand toward Hester's.

"Why could you not?"

"He was heartbroken, for she was his younger sister."

"Ah, so there was guilt as well as grief."

Hester stared at him. "How do you mean?"

"The older should not be survivor in the race against time."

"How know you this?"

Gareth looked at Hester, engaging her eyes. She blushed and turned her head away.

"A bard must know what moves the heart strings, as well as the harp's."

"I would love to know what music Mother liked, and...and...oh anything at all about her." She brushed tears from her eyes. "I miss my family at Hartbourne." She told Gareth how Dickie had fallen into the pond the day she left but how thrilled he was because he held onto the duck feathers he wanted. Gareth took her hand. His fingertips were calloused from the harp strings, but his skin was warm. Hester rested her hand in his for a few seconds before withdrawing it.

"No, you will only bite your fingernails," protested Gareth. "Grant me at least brief custody."

Hester smiled and replaced her hand in his. Gareth traced a circle on her palm, and she felt a tingling course up her arm and down to her toes.

Two crows lighted a few yards from where they sat. Gareth made a sound that was half-warble and half-cackle. He released Hester's hand and held out both of his. A crow alighted on each, their toes curling around the base of his middle fingers. Hester stared in amazement.

"I called them," explained Gareth. "We speak a common tongue. You can stroke them."

Hester hesitated.

"They will not bite, I promise."

She reached out her hand and stroked the head of one. The bird preened its feathers under her touch. It made a gravelly sound, and she could feel its throat rumble. Then it jumped aside, as if saying, "One touch is enough."

"You are one of theirs," said Gareth. "Crows do not permit just anyone to caress them."

"I remember talking to crows when Sir Hugh took Dickie and me into his home. I could not understand a word anyone said, for Welsh was all I knew. Mother was English but she spoke Welsh at home to please Father, I suppose." Hester frowned and plucked a blade of grass and nibbled on it. "She must have thought there would be plenty of time to teach me English. Anyway, I was terrified at Hartbourne, for no one could understand me. Uncle Hugh told me, later, that I cawed like a crow for many months. He was very kind to me."

"They were hard losses," said Gareth. "Your mother to death, your father to grief, and then your country and your language, too."

"I have never quite considered them as such, before." The crow approached again and gently nibbled on Hester's fingernail. She smiled. "So I am not the only one who does that."

Gareth smiled in return. "And did the crows converse with you?"

"Yes, or at least I imagined they did." Hester ran two fingers over the bird's head and neck. "If I were outside and cawed, all the rookery cawed too. But after Aunt Maud taught me English, I stopped talking to crows."

"You came by the crow tongue the hard way," observed Gareth.

"And did you not?"

"No, just like singing. I remember—"

The crows cawed in unison and Bronwyn awoke. "Holy Mary and the mothers, save us," she gasped, as she struggled to sit upright. She lay both hands protectively over her large belly. "Know you not that only Ceridwen has power over carrion crows?"

"Ah, we are among friends, Bronwyn," said Gareth. "There is no need for worry, and I think it is time for refreshments." He nodded to the crows and they flew away. Gareth reached into a satchel and produced a loaf of fresh bread, a goat's cheese, and a small flagon of ale.

Hester recalled the story of the sorceress. "I remember your saying how Ceridwen pursued Taliesin, the bard," remarked Hester.

"Ceridwen is our goddess of death and rebirth," said Gareth.

"She holds formidable power, then," mused Hester. "Yet men object to powerful women." She nibbled a crust of bread. "There has been no ruling queen of England since…"

Gareth laughed. "The last one who well-nigh destroyed England."

"You mean the Empress Matilda," replied Hester. Uncle Hugh had once explained Henry's desperation for a male heir was because no Englishman would submit to female rule on account of Matilda. Thinking of Henry made Hester raise her fingernails to her mouth, but she stopped and plucked another stem of grass to nibble on instead. "But that was a long time ago. Perhaps, now, England is ready for a true queen."

"Any queen or king would be better than this tyrant Henry," remarked Bronwyn, her mouth full of bread and cheese. She swallowed then lay down again, covering her face with her kerchief against the sun's rays

Gareth offered Hester the ale, and she took a sip. Hester saw that he noted where her lips had touched the flagon's edge and that he turned the flagon in order to drink from that same spot. He looked at her and smiled, his blue eyes shining as he watched for her response. Hester developed a sudden interest in a ladybird climbing along the hem of her dress.

She liked Gareth, but could this become love? Besides, how was she ever to love someone, to trust them not to leave her when she most depended upon them? Like with Mother, years ago, and now, with Father. *Play it safe*, said her mind to her heart. *Don't risk loving and losing again.* To cover her confusion, she leaped up. "Look over there! That field is full of St. John's wort. Let us gather some."

"You two go ahead, I will stay right here," murmured Bronwyn from beneath her handkerchief.

Gareth sang in Welsh as they picked the tiny yellow flowers, and Hester was delighted she understood all the words. She plucked some purple borage, too, as its blossoms were also said to be efficacious against melancholy.

They deposited the full basket beside Bronwyn. Gareth gestured toward a little wood. "We are only half a mile from the sacred grove, would you like to see it?"

"Yes, indeed."

Bronwyn sat up. "I have had enough traipsing around the country for one day, so I shall wait for ye here." She gave a toothy smile. "And you needn't hurry back, either."

The pair walked through a copse of beech trees until they reached the denser foliage of the oak grove. In the centre stood a clearing where late bluebells spangled the grass. The smell of last year's leaves mingled with the scent of new growth, and a thrush warbled in the still air.

Hester twirled in the dappled light. "It is beautiful here!" She smiled at Gareth and looked straight into his eyes. "I told Nia I don't believe in fairies, but in this place, I would not be so sure."

Gareth's grin broadened at the hint of archness in her

expression. He pointed. "Dinas Emrys, the stone slab that Peredur talked of, is atop that hill."

It was a steep climb to the granite slab, which stood in a cleared circle about twenty yards across. Hester declared, "The stone has been polished recently. I can see my reflection in it."

"And a most winsome reflection it is, too."

Hester blushed. "Nia said, when we passed here a few weeks ago, that there was blood on it, just after Saint Joseph's Day."

"Ah, you mean May Day." Gareth frowned. "That would have been the deer's that was sacrificed to the god and goddess of the woods."

Hester pointed to a pile of freshly cut wood beside the slab. "I wonder what that is for."

"There is always a bonfire on Saint John's Day, our solstice. Another deer will die."

Hester felt sad for the animal, but there was something more. In what Greek myth was a deer sacrificed instead of a maiden?

Two ravens, shrieking, swooped down from a tree and circled Hester's head, close enough to ruffle her coif. Gareth shooed them away.

Hester stood trembling. "Why did they do that?"

"I don't know." Gareth opened his arms and Hester entered his embrace. Gareth held her to him, and she rested her cheek against his chest, feeling his heartbeat. She allowed the warmth of him to comfort her, and when she looked up she saw tenderness and concern in his eyes. She panicked, feeling she had let him in too close. Leaning back, but careful not to fully disengage herself, she took a sly tone and quizzed him. "Are you sure you didn't arrange that little altercation, so that…"

Gareth gasped. "I am as shocked as you are, Hester. I did not call them." He blushed, for it was the first time he had called her by her Christian name. "I would never hurt you!"

Hester smiled. "I know, I was teasing." She gazed into his eyes.

"Naughty damsel," murmured Gareth. Then, grasping her around the waist, he leaned his face down, and she tilted hers up. His lips brushed against hers, and she instinctively opened her mouth. His tongue moved between her lips, beyond her teeth, and softly yet firmly swept the inside of her mouth. Hester felt he was claiming her for his own, and an aching warmth, ember-like, swelled deep inside her.

It was too much pleasure. She stepped back and brought her fingers to her mouth as if she could not believe what had just taken place there.

Gareth's voice was husky with desire. "I love you, please marry me."

Hester did not know if she truly loved him; she did not know if she could truly love anyone outside her family at Hartbourne. She wasn't sure she loved her father, she hardly knew him. And Gareth, did she know him at all? She felt she could trust him, yet he was just a person, someone who might suddenly die and leave her. But she sensed a danger she could not identify drawing around her. Gareth was a port of safety, so she replied, "Yes."

"I am nearing the end of my apprenticeship, and then we shall be wed."

"Yes, we must wait till then," agreed Hester, relieved that she had time in which to recant her word, if necessary. Gareth noticed her change of countenance and his smile faded.

They sat down on the grass, holding hands.

Hester murmured, "This must be the magic Nia talked of on Saint John's Eve."

Gareth stroked the inside of her wrist and lifted it to his lips and kissed it. The softness of his lips against her skin made her want to cry.

A cloud crossed the sun. Hester rose. "We had best rejoin Bronwyn."

"Not yet, or are you afeard the fairies have taken her?"

Anxiety hardened Hester's voice. "There are no fairies, and

who in their right mind could believe in bloodthirsty old gods and goddesses?" Yet she felt if such existed, then it was among these ancient mountains that they dwelled.

"I do, as does Peredur. And your uncle when it suits him."

"Peredur's ripe age and poetry excuse him, somehow. As for my uncle, I understand him not at all. But what do you mean by it?"

"A pagan worships the god of the place he is in. It is common courtesy. If you were invited to a banquet, would you bring your own dinner with you? Christians always carry their god with them."

"But the one God is everywhere! And what about us, if we—I mean, when we get married?"

Gareth joked, "Then I shall be whatever my lady wishes. If you desire to marry a Muslim I shall prostrate myself before Allah at your command."

Hester was so shocked, she laughed aloud. Gareth continued, "It is because Llewelyn is devoted to the old religion that he invited Peredur and me here." His voice grew more animated. "Bards are the closest he can get to a druid. And the Romans, even with their huge armies, still feared the druids."

"Yes, and the Romans worshipped many gods, but now we know there is only one." Hester bit on her fingernails, and Gareth took both her hands in his.

"Perhaps. Yet it is Mary, the mother, whom the people worship in their hearts, for all they say their *Pater Nosters* to God. This is how it has always been. The goddess brings life and the goddess takes it away." He kissed her fingertips. "For who else dances in summer's breeze and bids the barley ripen on the stalk?"

Hester could not answer. Why could she not defend the God in whom she had believed since infancy? She changed the subject. "Llewelyn will never approach close enough to kill Henry."

"He needs but a fair wind behind his arrows. And tonight he will sacrifice to Modron and Ane, the Great Mothers."

The pair walked, hand in hand, in silence.

Gareth sought to distract her from her sombre mood. "Have you read the tales of King Arthur?"

"Yes, I think they are marvellous!"

Gareth supported her arm as they descended an incline. "And who is your favourite knight, my lady?"

"Tristan," replied Hester. They were nearing the grove, and Hester, embarrassed to be seen holding Gareth's hand, released it. He nodded, as if he understood, but his mouth tightened. Hester, aware she had hurt him, spoke faster to gloss over the injury. "'Twas not Tristan's fault that his uncle, King Mark of Cornwall, sent him to fetch the king's bride. It was the nurse who administered the love potion to the ill-starred pair."

They found Bronwyn drinking the remains of the ale. She wiped her mouth on her handkerchief. "It wasn't the nurse's fault at all! Everyone always blames Branwen."

Hester laughed. "You defend her because your names are practically the same."

"Not at all. Branwen was nowise in the wrong. I blame King Mark for sending Tristan as a messenger." Bronwyn gave a loud burp and patted her belly. She stood and rubbed the small of her back. "Look at Launcelot and Guinevere and that great to-do, all because King Arthur sent his best knight to escort her to Camelot rather than going himself. But oh, I do love hearing Gareth and Peredur tell those stories."

Gareth addressed Hester. "It was fortunate for your religion, then, that the Virgin Mary did not become enamoured of the angel Gabriel."

The women were shocked and amused at the same time. Bronwyn commented that it was already near evening, so the women tidied their coifs and brushed strands of grass and gorse from their skirts in preparation to leave.

"Did you enjoy your ramble?" asked Bronwyn, looking first at Gareth, whose face beamed, then at Hester, whose cheeks flushed rosy pink. "Ah, so a good day's work, thanks to Saint John the Baptist and his friends, the Tylwyth Teg."

Bronwyn's broad smile reminded Hester of Maryse's satisfied grin. Then she was reminded again of the sheela na gig and blushed even deeper.

Gareth addressed Bronwyn. "Mistress Vaughan doesn't believe in the old gods and goddesses."

"Ah, Mistress, there's many around here won't take their cows to market unless they have first been blessed by a god, be it the saint of the well or the fairies of the hill."

Gareth picked up the basket of flowers, and the trio set off back to the village. Bronwyn proceeded to regale Hester with stories of the fairy folk, while Gareth hummed tunes under his breath.

On their return, Evan the Ear opened the gate for them. Gareth handed him a silver shilling.

"Much obliged, Master Gareth. Most kind of you, sir."

"My pleasure, Evan. After all, a man does not betroth himself a wife every day of the week."

"Ah, my congratulations to you. Good day to you too, ladies."

To Bronwyn, Hester said, "Thank you for accompanying us."

"You are welcome. It was the perfect day to be up on the hillside and away from all the noise in the village." She laughed and rubbed her belly. "I shall not be able to do that again for a while. Now I had best go home and make sure Dewi has a fine supper in him, for he will be off at first light to fight that tyrant king." Her eyes moistened. "Dewi is a good husband. I hope fortune smiles upon him and all our men."

"They are well prepared and cannot fail," said Gareth.

Bronwyn nodded and walked off toward her dwelling.

Gareth accompanied Hester to her door. He took her hands in his and inspected her fingernails. "I swear they have grown a full hair's breadth since yesterday and by Lammastide will be longer than a Chinaman's."

Hester laughed and curtseyed. "Kind sir, my nails are most appreciative of your efforts."

Gareth hesitated a moment. "Will I see you tomorrow?"

"I shall return for another lesson on the harp. Now I must pray Our Lady to bless these flowers then go prepare a brew for Father."

A pair of crows perched on the gates cawed in unison.

ave for a pair of old women reciting their beads near the altar, the church was empty. Hester entered the Lady Chapel and placed the basket of flowers before the statue of the Virgin. She prayed, looking up longingly at her sapphire necklace. *Better to lose that than Father*.

Hester picked up the basket and as she left the chapel, she passed Gwylim, in tears, kneeling in front of a painting of St. Sebastian. The saint's slender body was pierced with arrows and his exquisitely youthful features contorted in agony. His loin cloth had fallen low enough to reveal that smoothest part of a man's torso, the hollow where belly gives way to flank. The cloth, of course, concealed the zone below.

Hester's gown rustled as she passed by Gwylim. He looked over at her, and to Hester's eyes, the expression of anguish on his face was that of a soul in Hell.

As Hester walked on, Father Ignatius entered the chapel. Gwylim rushed past Hester and tugged on the priest's sleeve. Ignatius, his face twisted in disgust, stepped back.

Pointing at Hester, Gwylim hissed in Latin, "Mervyn is determined to marry her and elopes with her tonight. And I have my scant possessions packed and shall leave now, never to return."

Father Ignatius raised his hand as if to strike the friar and shouted at him in Latin, interspersed with Spanish. Hester, shaken both by Gwylim's words and the priest's rage, hurried to the door and left.

She must tell Father that she would never wed Mervyn. She hoped the herbal brew would revive him enough so he could understand.

Hester was straining the potion into a flask when Gwendolyn entered, humming. The girl held a swath of pale yellow silk against her bosom and, ignoring Hester, preened before the polished steel mirror.

"Look at you!" said Hester. "Smug as a cat with cream."

Gwendolyn smiled. "I am going to marry Bedwor as soon as you…" She gasped and covered her mouth with her hand.

Hester grabbed the fabric and Gwendolyn shrieked, "Give it back! It is for my wedding dress. I promised Mother I would not tell."

"Promised you would not tell what? And wherefore is your wedding of concern to me?" When Gwendolyn did not answer, Hester tore a rip in the silk.

Gwendolyn choked. "Stop! Pray stop! Mother said when you wed Mervyn, he will bestow a handsome dowry upon me." Hester threw the shimmering bolt of material to the floor. "Why are you so angry?" asked Gwendolyn, bending to retrieve it. "Mervyn is handsome. Many women think so. Aye, and men too."

"Where is Nia?" demanded Hester, her mind in turmoil. On whom else could she rely for the truth?

"With the old bard. He fell and broke his leg while you were out gadding. Is Gareth your sweetheart?" Gwendolyn gave a sly grin. "All that will have to end once you are Mervyn's wife. Or again, maybe not."

Disgusted, Hester left, carrying the brew. She needed to see Nia and wanted to help her with Peredur, but she must see Father first.

The room was stifling hot with a fire burning in the grate. Hester opened a window overlooking the courtyard. It was quiet, not a soul in sight. Dafydd was asleep so she shook him by the shoulder. "Father, I cannot marry that vile man." She held the flask to his lips; most of the liquid spilled over his chin, but a little entered his mouth. Dafydd circled his hand in a writing motion. Hester brought parchment and a quill and ink from the desk. He wrote shakily, *Iphigenia, or wed M.*

Dafydd sank back with the pallor of the corpse already upon his face. Hester sat beside him, her mind racing, trying to puzzle out her father's writings. She heard footsteps and voices in the courtyard, and recognizing Ignatius's voice and Maryse's, she drew closer to the window. They were speaking in English.

In a low voice, Ignatius said, "I have wind of your treachery. Give me that parchment."

"No. Dafydd has signed and they will marry this evening."

Hester smothered a cry. She felt her legs give way and leaned against the windowsill for support. She looked down; the pair had not noticed her above them.

"You know this cannot pass. The maiden has a higher purpose."

Maryse spoke in a wheedling tone. "But it is not fair. Mervyn will have nothing unless he marries her."

The priest said, "My bargain is with Llewelyn. His niece dies, I witness Henry's death and take the news to Rome. You are not to meddle in this."

Maryse hissed, "And you get a cardinal's hat!"

"Curb your tongue, woman. Be thankful it is not your daughter."

Maryse groaned. "I am. I know a bastard's death would not please the gods."

Ignatius droned, like a schoolboy reciting his lines, "Better that one die, than thousands suffer Hellfire for eternity."

Hester gasped. *Oh! I am Iphigenia and Llewelyn is Agamemnon. Just as the Greek king sacrificed his daughter in return for a fair wind for his fleet, Llewelyn will kill me so his arrows fly true.* Her stomach clenched and her breath quickened. She was paralyzed by terror, but her eyes darted around the room, seeking a means of escape. She must flee, but how and to where? Her mind spun until it rested upon Gareth. He would help her; he knew the countryside and where to find a safe hiding place.

The priest continued, "These are hard times, and Mother Church must make shift with strange bedfellows. But at least the sacrifice will take place on Saint John the Baptist's Day, and not your solstice."

"Call it what you will," replied Maryse. "Your Christ religion is just a flicker—it will fade away and it will be the solstice again, as it always was."

Ignatius's voice quivered in ecstasy. "As Saint John gave his life for the church, so will the maid. Henry must not live to sire a son on his new young queen. Once sickly Edward dies, Mary will inherit England and marry Spain. She will bear a Catholic son, and save this country." He cleared his throat. "But how did you persuade Dafydd to consent to his daughter's marrying a sodomite?"

"I promised to find some orphan girl to take his daughter's place and physic her to keep her quiet. One veiled maiden burning in the pre-dawn shadows looks no different from another." Hester felt bile rise in her throat, but forced herself to swallow it down. Maryse continued, "And after Llewelyn has struck down Henry, I bring the happy couple back from Dafydd's house in the valley, and Llewelyn embraces them and gives thanks that his hands are clean of his kinswoman's blood."

Hester felt faint. She willed her knees to stop shaking.

"But listen, Maryse, once Llewelyn has reclaimed his father's stolen lands, he will surely grant his natural son a fair share in them."

Maryse murmured, "Yes, that is probable."

Hester was shocked that Maryse could be both so ruthless and so gullible.

Having wafted a carrot, Ignatius now brandished the stick. "And mind, I can have you brought before the bishop's court for witchcraft, for I know about your brews."

Maryse gasped. "You would not do that!"

"You doubt the word of an Inquisitor?"

Maryse hurried off, and the priest's heavier footsteps followed. Hester wondered if she had heard aright. True, women burned for heresy, but to be sacrificed? The ancient Celts had practised human sacrifice, but long, long ago. Then she remembered Mother Bates saying how the May Queen's death ensured the harvest. To flee Dinas Emrys would cost money, of which she had very little. But she had Henry's ring to sell, once she reached a market town and found a buyer. She thought it more likely, though, that she would be arrested under suspicion of having stolen such a fine jewel. Hester thought fleetingly of her necklace draped over the Virgin's hands, but she would not commit an act of desecration and take it back. Not now, when she needed Our Lady's help more than ever.

Hester stumbled to the bed and whispered, "Father, I will return soon. I shall not leave you to die alone." She kissed his damp forehead. "I understand why you agreed I should wed Mervyn, for better that than death."

It was dusk by the time she entered her chamber. She wrapped Henry's ring in a cambric handkerchief, crossed the courtyard, and rapped on Peredur's door.

Gareth answered. He shot Hester a look of anguish. "Peredur has broken his leg. Nia is tending to him."

"I am sorry! Thank heaven he has you both. I wish I could stay, but Father is at death's door. Something else goes very wrong here. Llewelyn's sacrifice is not a deer, it is I."

Gareth's eyes widened in shock. He clasped Hester in his arms. "I cannot believe this! Is Llewelyn demented?" He released her and his eyes narrowed. "Dear heart, we must leave here at once."

"I cannot abandon Father now, when he is dying," replied Hester. She handed Gareth the knotted handkerchief. "Pray keep this safe. It may be our only means of escape. I must return to Father, now."

He placed it in his doublet. "Your life is more important. We should be away at first light."

Hester stared forlornly into Gareth's hollowed eyes. "You cannot leave Peredur now."

"You have my heart, and Peredur would say it is right to follow your heart. Nia will nurse him. He will not be alone." Hester tilted her face upwards and he stroked her cheek. "We can reach the shrine at Holywell, on the border, the day after tomorrow. If we are pursued, we can claim sanctuary and there be wed."

Hester thought, *Holywell, where Mother is buried*. She nodded assent.

Neither heard the two men approach. One grabbed Hester and clamped his hand over her mouth, and she heard an ugly thud. *Gareth!* She tried desperately to release herself, but the man's hand clamped even tighter, and he half-lifted, half-dragged her away.

"That has put paid to your fine suitor, my lady," mocked the man. His hand still over her mouth, he shoved her into a side entrance of the hall and thence into a small chamber lit by a single tallow candle. A lanky youth, one eye covered by a patch, joined them. He held a length of rope in one hand and wielded a club in the other; Hester, to her horror, saw a smear of crimson blood at its end.

Once the door was firmly shut behind them, the man removed his hand from her mouth, and Hester cried out, "You savages! What have you done to him?"

Her captor was a short wiry man with a pockmarked face. "Don't be afeard. My young friend gave him only a tap on the head. What with Peredur about to meet his maker, Lord Llewelyn wouldn't want both his bards playing their music for the angels, would he now?"

"What do you want with me?" demanded Hester. The men pushed her into a chair and stood beside her, pinning her arms down. The youth bound her hands together with the rope.

Father Ignatius entered carrying her *Republic*.

Hester cried, "How dare you take my possessions?"

He approached her and leaned down, breathing into her face. "Did I not warn you it is a sin to read heretical writing? You should burn, but if you confess your heresy and repent, you will receive mercy and your throat will be slit before you are cast on the pyre. If you prove recalcitrant, well, I do not have to describe the agony you will endure." He gave a thin-lipped smile and his eyes glazed over.

"I am a faithful daughter of the Church," retorted Hester, "and it is nonsense to say reading the ancients is heresy." She glared at him, though shaking with terror. "I demand to speak to Lord Llewelyn."

"I doubt that will profit your cause," replied Ignatius. He blinked. "Where is the soul of Socrates?"

Hester was taken aback. "I would think he is in Purgatory."

Ignatius's smile broadened. "Wrong. He is in Hell. It would seem you believe sinners may achieve grace without the sacraments of Holy Mother Church."

"You care not what I say. You wish to condemn me, so I am condemned."

She felt her stomach seize with panic but was determined not to give Ignatius the satisfaction of seeing her cry.

"Tonight is the eve of the feast of Saint John the Baptist," said the priest. "The pagans call it the summer solstice. But we Christians celebrate Saint John, who was decapitated by King Herod at the request of a dancing maiden. Only this time, the maiden dies."

Ignatius looked up at the ceiling. "Soul of Wales, hear me! We have been trying to stamp out the old religion for over a thousand years." He raised his arms. "We have taken wells and springs from their wanton goddesses and named them for our saints. We have replaced their wicked festivals with Christian holy days. Yet what have we gained? A people who love Mary, the mother, above God and His son. And now, England is fallen to the whore of Babylon and her whoreson Henry." He wiped spittle from his mouth, and, his eyes radiant, addressed Hester. "Llewelyn needs only to be convinced that his gods favour him and he strikes." A rabid smile distorted the priest's lips.

Hester shut her eyes and tried to pray. *Blessed Virgin, succour me in my hour of need.* The words sounded as pitiful to her now as when she was molested by Henry. *Should I then pray to the goddesses of this land? Ane, Modron, Arianrhod, great and powerful ones, come to my aid.*

An idea flickered in her mind. Llewelyn wanted a maiden sacrifice. Was she a maiden?

s June progressed the little garden flourished under the care of the cottage's new inhabitants. A currant bush put forth purple fruit, still sour, but in another week it would be ready to eat. In the burgeoning herb section the parsley's fronded leaves expanded, and borage blossoms, pink and blue on their short stalks, rose from their white-and-green-mottled leaves. What had originally looked to be two bare sticks in the earth proved to be blackberry and raspberry canes. Fresh carrots and parsnips made welcome additions to the paltry shreds of meat from the oft-stewed mutton bone that simmered over the cooking fire. Fortunately, worms thrived in the alluvial soil, and so John and Dickie caught enough fish for Friday suppers. Dickie was stronger physically, having developed upper arm and chest muscles from the work of digging and carrying water, and his fits came less frequently, but every night he called out in his sleep for his sister's return. Alice could hear him from the barn where he slept with John. But John, who would sleep through the trumpets of the Resurrection, did not complain.

A deep sadness permeated the cottage. The women cried quietly, but each in her own time and alone—Lady Maud for her deceased husband, Goody from worry over her mistress's declining health, and Alice from grief for her father, fear for her mother who appeared more cadaverous every day, and anxiety over William.

The women prepared possets and liniments; however, as yet, their sole customer was Abigail of the great house. Her silver groats and occasional shilling afforded the family only the most meagre fare, and more times than not, they went to bed hungry. Alice's anger toward her mother for refusing Lady Joyce's present was replaced by anxiety for her health. Lady Maud scarcely ate, and her wasted form gave Alice to believe that she was already half in the next world. Meanwhile Alice kept pushing to the back of her mind the question, why had William not returned?

A week after Lady Joyce's visit, Alice opened the door to find a package on the top step. An attached letter said it had been delivered it to Syon House and a servant had brought it to the cottage. He had not tarried to speak to the cottage's inhabitants, who were considered unlucky. What could be more unlucky than the head of a noble household executed for treason and his family banished to eke a subsistence in a hovel? The parcel contained two fine, black, woolen dresses.

Alice read the enclosed letter aloud. "To my beloved sister, Lady Maud, and niece, Lady Alice, God's blessings on you both. Pray accept these mourning garments. Next week I depart on the royal progress. As concerns Sir William of Bayston, I as yet know naught, but I am making inquiries in the gaols and hospitals. Pray for me, your loving sister and aunt, Joyce."

Gaols and hospitals, thought Alice. *Please not either, but better than if he were dead; I couldn't bear that. He could be drowned in the river, or fallen beneath a cart and crushed.* Alice refused to allow her mind to dwell on these thoughts. She held up the dresses. One was exactly her size, and the other, slightly longer, was for Lady Maud.

"God will protect Sir William," said Lady Maud, as if she had read her daughter's mind. "Have no concern. Now go don your new dress." She looked up from grinding the mutton bone from yesterday's meal in the pestle and mortar. She coughed and spat into an old cloth, which she quickly put in her pocket.

Alice ascended the ladder and changed her gown. She felt a spasm of guilt. These were mourning clothes for Father, but it was such a pleasure to wear good, black, smooth cloth against her skin, so unlike the scratchy, coarse woolen dress she had worn since leaving Hartbourne. The folds of material were plentiful, and fine stitching ran along the neckline and cuffs. It was the dress of a gentlewoman.

Alice wished William could see her now and felt shame for the sin of vanity with Father so newly dead. But still she wished she had a mirror. She thought back to the day she had last seen her reflection. It must have been the day she and Hester visited Hampton Court Palace. Thinking of her cousin, Alice offered a prayer that she, at least, was safe and content with her family in Wales. She glanced over to her mother's side of the bed, where the bolster was stained brown from the blood-streaked sputum her mother coughed up. Alice and Goody had brewed willow bark for when Lady Maud had fever, but until mullein and hyssop bloomed in the garden there was no remedy for the cough.

Alice descended from the loft. "Let us see how your new dress suits you, Mother." But Alice could tell, just by looking, that it was far too big for her mother's shrivelled body. Alice was seized by a moment of terror; in her mind's eye she saw her mother as a corpse wearing grave clothes, and with shaking hands, she draped the gown over a stool. Lady Maud wiped perspiration from her brow with the edge of her apron. "Once the seams have been…," she began but then coughed too hard to talk. The spasm passed and Alice offered her a mug of ale; Lady Maud waved it away and returned to her task of grinding the mutton bone.

Alice tugged down a bunch of sage hanging from a hook above the hearth and began chopping the stalks. Tears pooled in her eyes. *Poor Mother, and poor Father, to have died alone.* And where was William? The grey leaves crumbled between her fingers. She sniffed the fragrance and dried her eyes on the back of her hand, then added the sage to the crushed bone in the mortar, making a paste.

"Who would have thought yesterday's supper would provide for tomorrow's?" said Goody, entering with a basket of peas. "For indeed, whitening Mistress Abigail's teeth means our bellies do not go quite empty." Goody laughed at her own witticism; Alice forced a smile and spooned the paste into little jars.

"Ah, speak of the devil!" said Goody.

Abigail stood in the lintel, smiling, and her teeth, while not yet white, were already a less distinct shade of yellow. She had also been using rosemary water for the past week, resulting in fewer pustules on her face.

"Is that for me?" she asked Alice in her broad Midlands accent.

Alice nodded and handed a jar to her mother who wrote on a piece of parchment, "Sage (Salvia) for whitening teeth. Use b.i.d."

"Lady Maud, you did not write on the previous ones. Is this different?" asked Abigail.

Lady Maud looked blank. "Oh, I forgot until now. At home when I prepared physic I always wrote the name in Latin." She paused. "You do read Latin, do you not?"

Abigail stared at the label, then blushed and smoothed down her skirts.

"*Bis in die* means twice a day," said Lady Maud.

"That will be a shilling, thank you kindly, madam," said Goody.

Abigail handed over her coin then looked over at Alice. "Lady Alice," she said, her eyes widening, "you do look splendid in that black gown."

"Thank you," said Alice.

Abigail stepped closer. "My courses are dreadful," she whispered. "I am in bed for five days…"

"We have raspberry bushes in the garden," said Goody, overhearing her. "We need but the leaves, which is as well seeing as the fruit won't ripen till next month."

"I shall brew a tea for you, dear," said Lady Maud. "Come back tomorrow."

"It will be another sixpence," said Goody.

Abigail nodded, then handed a little package to Alice. "This is for your cousin. Raisins," she said.

Alice thanked her and gave an inward sigh. She had been planning on taking Mirabel for a ride later, but now she would be chopping raspberry leaves till dusk. She was thankful that Mirabel had plentiful new grass to graze on. Her pony, alone of the family, was getting plump. Alice changed back into her workaday dress, ready to gather the leaves.

Goody poked her head out of the doorway. "Master Dickon has cut off the dandelion heads and scattered them on the path. We have to get it through his noggin that we need them for our brews." She paused, then exclaimed, "Oh, it appears we have a patient."

A stooped, balding man, wearing an apron over a baggy tunic, approached the door. He was covered in white powder—his hair, face, and arms, all white.

"It is the miller!" whispered Goody, rubbing her hands in anticipation.

Lady Maud began to cough again and sat, her breathing rapid. Alice brought her ale, which, this time, she accepted.

The man stood in the doorway.

Once the spasm passed, Lady Maud said to Alice, "Ask what ails him."

"Good afternoon," said Alice.

"Good day to you, Mistress, and what a fine, sober-looking wench you are."

Alice narrowed her eyes. No one had ever called her a wench before. "How may we assist, Master Miller?" she asked.

"My ankles," he said. "They swell to the size of mutton legs. They start off fine in the morning, but by evening I can barely get my shoes off, they are that bad."

Alice knew that the dropsy was common enough in the middle-aged and elderly and was worse in warmer weather. No one knew what caused it. The physicians said it was an imbalance of the humours. But then the physicians claimed all illness was due to imbalance of the humours.

"We have a brew that will help. Dandelion, yarrow, and parsley," said Lady Maud. "Alice, it is on the top shelf. One of those phials with the yellow liquid." Alice handed it to the man.

"How much do I owe you?" he asked.

"Nothing," said Lady Maud. "Take a thimbleful first thing in the morning, and God be with you."

Alice and Goody, nonplussed, stared at each other. "Mother," said Alice, in a low voice, "we need the money."

"Do we, dear?" Lady Maud frowned and gazed around the tiny room, a look of puzzlement clouding her face. "Where am I? Whose cottage is this?" she whispered. Alice stood between her and the miller, so he could not witness that her mother had, for the moment, lost her wits. Alice's heart pounded in her chest. Then Lady Maud looked at Alice. "Now I remember," she passed a hand across her forehead. "Something came over me, but I am recovered, thanks be to God."

Alice exhaled and Goody crossed herself, murmuring, "God bless her," then turned to their patient.

"Four pence, please," said she.

"Gladly, for the apothecary charges sixpence for his cures, and I swear they are no more than foul-tasting, cloudy water. I suspect he grinds up newts' eyes and adds horse piss for flavouring." The man pulled out his purse and counted a few pennies. "Besides, who can afford that kind of money? I surely cannot, when I earn but a shilling on my busiest days."

He bowed and made ready to leave but stood lingering in the entrance, his hand resting on the broken doorknob. "My daughter has a morbel on her cheek that won't mend."

"Send her here. We can prepare a comfrey liniment that will help," said Lady Maud, in her usual kind, authoritative voice.

The miller went his way, whistling under his breath.

Lady Maud coughed. "I am very cold," she said. Alice could see she was shivering.

"There is no wood chopped for a fire yet," said her daughter, "but we could help you into your new woolen gown on top of the dress you have on, and then you would be warmer."

The fine black dress fit easily over the thin, cheap one Lady

Maud already wore. "I feel better now, thank you," said she, resuming her seat.

Goody called from the door, "Another! A young woman carrying a babe."

"Come in," said Goody, gesturing the young mother to a stool.

The woman sat and unwrapped the baby, who was a week old, pale and scrawny and mewling like a kitten.

"My milk is too scant." She looked down at her infant. "He sucks and sucks but nothing gets into him. And what affrights me most is he does not even cry any more, just moans like this."

"We have goat's rue," said Lady Maud. "It will make your milk plentiful." She stood, turning to Alice. "There is a patch on the west side of the garden. Look for a tall flower, like foxglove, only with paler and smaller flowers. Also pray gather sticks for a fire." Lady Maud filled the kettle. "Goody, you may give this woman some ale," said she.

As Alice went in search of goat's rue, she saw that a single stalk of mullein was in flower. It stood like a furry poker with a few yellow blossoms protruding from the very tip.

At last, she thought. *Mother's cough will clear, please God.* As she plucked the stalks of goat's rue and mullein, she prayed for the health of her mother, the young woman, and her babe. And, of course, for William, and, with a guilty start at the afterthought, for her father's soul. She placed the herbs gently in her apron pocket and gathered an armful of sticks.

Alice brought the herbs and fuel in to Goody, who lit a fire and boiled the goat's rue in water and strained the liquid. Alice brewed the mullein and returned to the garden while the teas cooled. The blossoming herbs attracted tiny iridescent blue butterflies that reminded Alice of a silk dress she had owned but a month ago. She buried her head in her hands and forced herself not to cry. Alice noticed her dirty fingernails and the torn cuffs of her dress. She felt a tendril of loose hair and removed her coif to rebraid her hair. A fistful of dull copper hair came away in her hand. William might still love her in her ragged dress, but how could he love her if all her hair fell out? Alice felt a terrible urge to scream. She opened her mouth but uttered no sound, knowing how it would upset her mother and Goody. Instead, she bit down, hard, on the inside of her cheek. Once she drew blood she felt satisfied and stopped.

Alice threw the hank of hair on the midden. She returned inside where Goody was handing the young woman the brew. "That will be two pence."

Alice almost added, "And a penny for the ale" but stopped herself and inwardly blushed for shame. With great concentration the woman counted out four half pennies. Her purse was now empty. Her dress was of the cheapest stuff and threadbare in the elbows, and the baby was wrapped in an old sack that from the smell of it, had once held parsnips.

Alice went up to the loft and pulled the sheet off the bed. She tried to rip the bottom quarter off, but the fabric was too strong, so she bit into it and rent off a piece, which she folded into a square. She came down to find Goody returning three half pennies to the young woman. Alice handed the piece of clean linen to the young mother, who, with tears in her eyes, wrapped her baby in it. "God bless you all!" she said and walked away humming a lullaby to her infant.

Dickie and John returned, each dangling a trout over his shoulder.

"Well done!" exclaimed Goody. "Grilled in a little butter with a sprig of thyme and—"

"No! A witch! Get away!" shrieked Dickie, seeing Lady Maud. "A black witch! What have you done with Aunt Maud?" He flew at his aunt, but John caught him. Dickie pummelled on John's chest. "A witch, oh no! Hessie! Hessie, has a witch gotten you? Are they going to kill you?"

He fell to the floor, limbs jerking and spittle flying from his mouth.

gnatius chanted to the ceiling in his excitement. "With Henry dead, our Spanish priests will whip the heretic to the pyre with chains, and this land shall again submit to Rome."

Three cowled women entered the room. Hester recognized Maryse and Gwendolyn, despite their veils. The third she did not.

The priest exhorted Hester, "So, maiden, recant, or it will go hard with you."

Maiden, thought Hester, and again that question, *But am I a maiden?* She understood that a groom took his bride's maidenhead on their wedding night, and her bleeding proved she had been virgin at the altar. Like the bleeding she noticed after Henry had molested her.

"Rejoice!" exulted Ignatius. "Your death will ensure the salvation of myriad souls. The English and Welsh peoples, regenerate, will be your people."

Not long ago, Hester would have given her life for a sense of belonging. She had, at times, imagined that sacrificing her life might mean Mother would return. Also, in her despair, she had thought that since her life was worthless to her, she could dispose of it in saving others. Like Jesus had given his life for the world. All these thoughts flashed through her mind. But now, faced with death, she was determined to live.

Ignatius signalled the men to leave. The women drew closer, and the one unfamiliar to Hester placed a bony hand on her shoulder.

Her hands bound, Hester kicked her. "Don't touch me, hag."

The woman slapped her.

Ignatius remonstrated, "Nay, daughter, she must go to the pyre unblemished."

"Be not affrighted, for the bruise will not show for several hours, and by then she will be but a pile of ashes," cackled the crone. Her voice was similar to Maryse's. Was she Maryse's mother, then?

Father Ignatius demanded, "What sins have you to confess?"

"This is no confessional," retorted Hester.

"Have you lain with a man?"

"No."

"Have you cast any spells to secure the affections of a man?"

"No."

"Do you recant the works of the Devil?"

Hester wanted to spit in Ignatius's face and call him the Devil, but her courage fled and she replied, "I do."

Ignatius looked almost disappointed. "Very well. You shall have the quick end I promised." He marched out of the room.

Hester felt immobilized by terror. *This cannot be happening.* She willed her legs to lift her and race her to the door, but they would not.

The old woman leaned toward her to wrap a linen bandage around Hester's mouth. "No one wants to hear your screaming afore your throat is slit."

Hester drew back and twisted her head from side to side. *Who are you? Who am I?* she thought. *I am someone who is not going to die on a pyre tonight.* She bit the old woman's finger.

"Ouch! English whore!" The old woman gave a powerful blow to the side of Hester's head, which drooped like a snowdrop. She half-sat, half-lay while the old woman completed her task and the other two undressed her down to her shift. They clothed her in a white robe of sarsenet, draped a lace veil over her face, and removed her shoes. There came a rapping at the door. Two men entered and carried Hester outside, where a closed litter awaited. The men placed Hester inside then lifted the litter. One of the bearers tripped and the jerking motion brought Hester back to consciousness. She remembered what was happening and her insides froze. In the mottled glow of burning rush lights, she could see villagers in the courtyard. All was silent. She heard the rustle of people following behind. An owl hooted in the distance. Hester gnawed on the bandage in her mouth, determined to chew through it.

They walked for some distance, then up a hill. When they set her down, she shrank against the side of the litter, but a huge man lifted her out as easily as he would have lifted a calf. In the faint pre-dawn light, she saw a pyre on the stone slab of Dinas Emrys. With linen strands still caught between her teeth, Hester screamed at the man to release her and kicked out as he carried her to the slab. He propped her against the pyre, and the youth with the eye patch stepped forward; he clamped one hand over Hester's mouth and used the other to hold her legs down. Her captor withdrew a knife from his boot and examined its blade.

Llewelyn approached her, his eyes averted. He ordered another man, "Quick. Light the fire. The sacrifice must be made before sunrise."

A pink glow in the east announced its imminence. Llewelyn called to a tall woman with long grey hair, dressed in black. She placed a hawthorn branch thick with white blossoms between Hester's bound hands. The thorns tore at her skin, and drops of blood fell on her white dress.

Father Ignatius spoke. "We beseech thee, O Lord, to save this country from the wickedness of—"

Llewelyn grunted. "Enough! Now let the priestess of Ane speak."

Ignatius scowled and walked away. "I wash my hands of you."

Llewelyn pleaded, "Priestess of Ane, make haste, for sunrise is upon us."

The tall woman in black sang in a lilting voice,

Gods of our people hearken to our prayer.
Goddess, lark of the morning, Goddess, queen of hives at noon,
Goddess, raven of dusk, Goddess, tomb of us all, accept this sacrifice.

"Faster, Lady," beseeched Llewelyn, "the sun is halfway up."

The priestess continued, "Behold a royal maid, pure and unspotted as the lily. The fire god will enter the virgin in holy marriage, and Ceridwen will smile upon our land."

Llewelyn signalled the huge man to slit Hester's throat.

Hester used all her strength to kick at the youth holding her. Startled, he withdrew his hand from her mouth, and she cried out, "I am no virgin!"

"No, this cannot be! The maid has lost her wits. Lady, continue!" cried Llewellyn.

"Halt," commanded the priestess, "we must not risk making an impure sacrifice."

Llewelyn railed at Hester. "You have been closeted with one of the most upright families in England. How could you have played the whore?" He turned to the priestess. "The girl is lying to save herself."

"Aye, but Llewelyn Vaughan, if she speaks sooth, to spill her blood on this altar would be foul desecration. The old gods are jealous of their prizes. And the goddesses, too. A tainted sacrifice would bring down ruin upon our people. I shall examine the maid, and if she be intact and these are just the shriekings of a terrified girl, the sacrifice can continue. Otherwise…"

The priestess raised her arms. "People, turn your backs. If she be virgin, the gods must not have their sacrifice sullied by human gaze." The crowd murmured and obeyed. She ordered Hester to step back from the pyre and to spread her legs. She thrust her hand up Hester's shift and inserted two fingers inside her introitus. Hester wanted to kick her but knew her life depended upon the woman's declaring she was not *virgo intacta*.

The priestess cried, "She is no virgin!"

Llewelyn stammered, "Cast her aside. She will die by stoning, later."

Hester choked. She had escaped one hideous fate, only to be facing a worse.

Llewelyn roared, "We need a maid of the royal blood. Fetch Gwendolyn."

Hearing her name, Gwendolyn fled but two of Llewelyn's guards caught her. Two others pinned down Maryse and her mother. The priestess tore the sacrificial robes from Hester's frame and draped them over Gwendolyn's flailing body. Hester was thrown, her hands still bound, against the base of an oak tree. She felt the roots pressing into her back and thighs. *I shall take strength from this tree. They will not chop me down on this day nor any other, God and the goddesses of this land willing.*

"I have a lover!" screamed Gwendolyn.

Llewelyn replied, "You lie. But, Priestess of Ane, make sure of it."

Again the crowd turned their backs and the woman pronounced, "This one is a maid!"

"No!" cried out Maryse. "The goddess curse you! Epona, the mare that gives suck to her foal, Modron the Lady mother and Rigantona—"

"Silence her!" ordered Llewelyn as he thrust Gwendolyn upon the pyre. The girl struggled to get down, but the hem of her dress caught between the logs. Llewelyn lit the fire. His henchman reached across to slit the girl's throat before her clothes took light but could make only a small cut in her neck before he was forced to leap back, flames lapping at his feet. Blood trickled down the side of Gwendolyn's throat and she screamed as her dress caught fire. A trio of ravens perched in an oak tree echoed her cries. Gwendolyn convulsed in a fit of coughing. Then the only sounds were crackling of the logs and the sizzling of burning flesh.

The stench was unbearable.

Llewelyn muffled his face in his cloak and tried to call out,

"Gods and goddesses of Wales, guide my men's arrows. Death to the tyrant!"

"Freedom for Wales," responded the men, but their cry was muted—most had known Gwendolyn since she was an infant. It was one thing that an English stranger die, quite another when it was one of their own.

Llewelyn wept with frustration. "This is a botched affair. The gods have been ill-served."

A breeze picked up and blew black, greasy smoke in all directions. The crowd dispersed, coughing and deploring the horrible smell. Several of them held pieces of cloth to their mouths and noses, muttering that they had witnessed an ill-done deed.

For a few blessed moments, Hester thought she might have been forgotten. Her face hurt from the earlier blow, and the stench from the fire curdled her stomach, but she was alive. Then Maryse and her mother hauled her to her feet. Maryse was silent, but the older woman slapped Hester.

"You will wish it was yourself on that pyre by the time we have done with you." Hester half-walked and was half-dragged back to the village.

They reached the gates and Maryse hissed, "The last woman who died by stoning took her sweet time. By the fourth day, rats were chewing on her face, but it wasn't till the seventh that she died."

Evan the Ear was warming his hands over a brazier. He admitted the women and, glancing at Hester, muttered, "And this be the maid betrothed to Gareth." He blessed himself with one hand and fondled his good ear with the other.

The women thrust Hester across the courtyard toward a low building. They opened a door and shoved her down a flight of stairs. "May she rot in there!" screamed Maryse. "The draggle-tail has murdered my Gwendolyn."

Hester raised her arms to protect her head from the blow as she landed—it never came, she fell on a pile of mouldy straw. The door thudded shut, leaving her in total darkness. The only sound was of water dripping. Taking shallow breaths to avoid inhaling the stench, she stood and stretched her bound hands in front of her and groped around the cellar walls. She needed to know the physical confines of her prison, to grant herself even the illusion of having some kind of control over her environment. She jerked away on touching something slimy and tried to rub the stuff off on her shift. It felt like congealing blood. She had Gwendolyn's blood on her hands.

"Oh, Gwendolyn, I am sorry!" She curled up in a ball on the rancid straw and, exhausted, fell asleep.

areth woke and groaned, "Where is Hester?"

He saw Nia asleep on a pallet by the door. From the slant of the light coming through the window, he knew it was late morning.

Peredur coughed and asked him, "How is your head?"

"It throbs like the Devil, but I must go to Hester. I dreamed last night she was pregnant with a dragon."

"Ah, the goddess came to you." Peredur tried to sit up, but a fit of wheezing overtook him. He continued, "Of course, you have to go," he paused to catch his breath, "but it doesn't take two good eyes to see you've been badly mauled."

Gareth stood up. He staggered but managed to remain upright.

Corwen croaked from his cage in the corner.

There was a hammering on the door and a bass voice proclaimed, "Nia, your mistress is imprisoned, charged with harlotry. You must come with us."

"That's a lie!" cried Gareth.

"It cannot be!" mumbled Nia, awakening.

The guard entered. "And Lord Dafydd passed away at dawn; you must inform Mistress Vaughan. And Gwendolyn is dead."

Nia gasped and Peredur asked, "How came Gwendolyn to die?"

Gareth helped him sit up.

"I was not there," replied the guard. "I heard Lord Llewelyn needed a virgin sacrifice. Since his niece was none, Gwendolyn burned on the pyre instead."

"That is nonsense. Of course Mistress Vaughan is a maid. But how dreadful!" exclaimed Gareth. "Poor Gwendolyn!"

Nia choked, "How could her own father be so cruel?"

Gareth leaned against the wall. "Nia, you stay here and I shall go to Hester. There has been a grave mistake."

The guard snorted. "You can barely stand." He escorted Nia from the chamber.

Gareth arranged the bolsters behind Peredur, but the old man's chest barely moved, and a blue tinge coloured his lips. Gareth felt a warm trickle down his cheek. He touched his head—his fingers came away bloody. He stumbled to the dresser and found a linen rag to wrap around his head.

He mulled over the slur upon Hester's honour, but right now Peredur needed his attention.

He sat down beside his master and took his hand in his own. Peredur smiled at him, and Gareth, brushing tears from his eyes, smiled back.

Hester was wakened by a scurrying sound and felt something with a long tail scamper over her bare feet. She cried, "Oh God! Rats!" and the sound echoed off the walls. She buried her head in her arms and wept. She was being left here to die. But had they not said they were going to stone her to death? Even that was better than slow starvation in this cellar. What had she become, to wish for death by stoning? She laughed out loud at the ridiculous thought. A cackle ricocheted from the walls. She gasped. How could the witch from her nightmare have found her here? But then she realized that it was her own voice she heard. *Mother of God, save me! Am I turning into a witch?*

The door creaked open and Nia entered bearing a candlestick in one hand and a basket in the other. The door closed again behind her. She stuttered, "D–did you make that d–dreadful sound?"

Hester nodded. Nia set the basket and candle on the ground and embraced her. "Look at your poor bound hands! I have brought food and drink and some herbs against this foul cellar air."

In the glow of the single candle, the women's shadows danced an eerie pattern on the wall. Nia unbound the ropes and Hester sobbed with relief. She asked, "Do you know what happened last night?"

"Yes, the talk is all through the village how Llewelyn wanted to kill you. It is said he needed a pure sacrifice of his own kin to win the gods to his side for his attack on Henry."

"So you know about poor Gwendolyn?"

"I do. She was no saint, but no one deserves that death."

They bowed their heads and murmured a prayer for the repose of her soul.

"I have more sad news. Your father passed away at dawn."

"I knew last night he was dying. May he rest in peace."

Nia responded, "May Lady Mary, Ane, and Modron, the three Great Mothers, take him to their bosom." She sighed. "I have been all this time with Peredur and Gareth."

Forgetting her own woes, Hester exclaimed, "Oh, how do they fare?"

"Gareth's head was nigh broken but will mend. Peredur, though, bless him, is near unto death."

Hester groaned. "I am sorry for it all. But why have they let you come to me?"

"To tell you your father died and that you are to stand trial today, for Llewelyn joins his men down south this evening." Nia added, "Had Twgardan known of Llewelyn's plan, he would have acted on both your and Gwendolyn's defence." She peered at Hester's face in the candlelight. "Your face is bruised." Then she looked down. "And your feet are bleeding. I will fetch some liniment and bandages."

"No wait…do not go," pleaded Hester.

Nia paused by the door.

"I will be quick. But, Mistress, is it true you did not die on the altar because…? Was it Gareth, who…um, deflowered you, so?"

The thought of Gareth moved Hester to tears. "No, it was not Gareth, it was…" A thought came to her. *The King's ring robbed me of my maidenhead, and it can save me now.* "Bring me the ruby ring I gave him. Pray tell him disbelieve any word said against me today. Including any I say against myself."

Nia's brows knit in puzzlement, but she nodded. "Yes, now do eat something. You need to keep your strength up."

Hester had no appetite, but to please Nia, she took a few bites of mutton pie and drank some ale. She looked down at her ragged petticoat. "And bring me a dress."

Nia pursed her lips. "I doubt that will be permitted. A woman on trial for harlotry appears only in her shift. I pray you are convicted only of that and not the other—treason."

"Treason?" gasped Hester.

"Aye. Llewelyn claims that losing your maidenhead has thwarted his attack on Henry."

"The man is a lunatic!"

"Yea, and you are permitted a trial solely because council would not allow him, alone, to pass sentence, now that you hold your poor father's lands, and—"

Hester snarled, "And the priest?"

"Father Ignatius left this morning, for he sees the wind gone from Llewelyn's sails and has no faith he can kill Henry now."

"An ill wind to them all. Now pray fetch the ring," her voice faltered, "but do not be gone long."

"You will surely not be allowed to appear clothed and bejewelled like a fine lady," murmured Nia.

Hester gave a bitter laugh. "I look not to wear the ring for adornment." Her voice softened. "Tell Gareth that I am safe."

"He will be glad, for he is half-frantic right now, between your arrest and Peredur about to die, and that bash on his head." She picked up the basket and candlestick.

"Do not leave me in the dark!" beseeched Hester.

Nia set the half-spent candle down. "This bunch of rosemary will stave off the stench, and I will be back soon. Him at the door is Twgardan's cousin and shall not deny me."

Hester heard the key turn in the door. She sank down on the heap of straw and shredded the stalks of rosemary. She crushed the tiny pointed leaves then bit her nails to the quick. The rusty taste of her own blood comforted as well as disgusted her. Hester thought of her father and began to weep. She fell asleep seconds before the candle gutted out.

⁂

"See that my body is burned near the oak grove," gasped Peredur. "Let no Christian prayers be mumbled over me. My spirit rises to the wind, not to their bare heaven."

"It shall be as you wish, Master," assured Gareth, stroking the old man's hand.

Nia entered.

Peredur's breathing became erratic—a few shallow breaths followed a deep one.

"How is she?" inquired Gareth.

"Sadly worn out, but she says do not fret, for she is out of danger. I am to take her the ring, for what reason I do not know."

Gareth fingered the edges of the handkerchief containing the gem, and handed it to Nia.

"Tell her I do not believe that vile accusation," his voice cracked. "Say I love her and I am sure she will explain…"

Peredur's breathing ceased and the death rattle sounded in his windpipe.

Gareth and Nia both uttered a low wail, and the crow squawked from its corner.

"He is gone," said Gareth, his voice choking, "and you must go back to Hester."

"I shall return to help lay him out," said Nia, tears streaming down her cheeks.

"No, I shall do that, and besides, Hester needs you. Once I know she is released I shall see to burning Peredur's body. Tell her I shall send Corwen to her and she can send a message through him."

Gareth closed his teacher's eyes.

he women were up with first light. But before she rose from her bed, Alice mentally counted the tiny pile of pennies she kept beneath her side of the pillow. She got up, dressed, and rubbed some lard over her hands. It smelled foul, but it meant that the skin of her fingers, worn from all the digging up and chopping of herbs, at least did not fissure and bleed.

As they sat at table, Lady Maud spoke. "Today we celebrate the feast of Saint John the Baptist." She withdrew her missal from her pocket. There was a clinking sound.

"Are those your rosary beads?" asked Alice, setting down a jug of ale.

"I forgot to put them under the mattress before I arose this morning."

Goody took a knife to the heel of a loaf of bread. The knife skidded and clattered on the floor. "There is no blade in Christendom can cut this," she muttered.

"Those beads are worth at least two sovereigns," said Alice, her voice husky with anguish. "We are near starving, and you have kept them hidden!" She scowled and clenched her fists by her sides.

"I will get some water from the barrel to soften the loaf," said Goody, leaving the room.

"Even a shilling would buy us soap made from rosewater and I would not have to scrub my hands with lye to clean them." Alice thrust her blistered palms in front of her mother.

Lady Maud showed her palms. The centres were raw and oozing yellow pus.

"Mercy, just like Christ's stigmata!" shouted Alice. "I hope they make you happy!"

Lady Maud reached out as if to strike Alice but started coughing and fell back on her chair. "I shall not tolerate blasphemy," she uttered, between coughs.

Alice, affrighted by her mother's anger, stepped back, but when Lady Maud continued to cough, she offered her a mug of ale.

Recovered from her coughing spell, Lady Maud said, "Ah, so you want food better than rock hard bread and vegetable broth, twice a day, with a fish thrown in if the boys are fortunate down at the river? Then why not look under your side of the bolster?" She frowned and banged down her mug of ale.

"I am saving money so we can all have horses, to escape, when William returns." Alice stood facing her mother, hands on her hips.

"And where will we escape to?"

"I do not know. Anywhere other than here. That is why William must come back."

Lady Maud sat and slumped forward, her face in her hands and her elbows on her knees. "I am sorry. It is hard for you, for you are not yet accustomed to this life."

"I do not ever want to become accustomed to this life. I hate bartering our remedies for pennies. I hate even worse when you accept the laces and stockings of dead relatives if the patient has not a half-pence to spare." Tears of rage poured down Alice's cheeks. "Why can't we sell the beads?"

"Alice, dear," said Lady Maud, with severity as well as gentleness in her voice, "you cannot place a price on everything. You know these beads are a family heirloom."

Alice, avoiding her mother's gaze, placed twigs in the fireplace.

John and Dickie came in, and John looked from mother to daughter. "Master Dickon, let's go find a field mouse for you to pet."

"But I'm hungry," protested Dickie. "I want my breakfast."

"We will come back in a few minutes, do not fret." John steered Dickie away.

Alice lit the fire. "How did you manage to hide your beads from that horrid commissioner the day we left Hartbourne?"

"I did not hide them, they were in my pocket." Lady Maud turned the page of her missal, mouthing the words as she read.

"But what if he had searched you?" Alice faltered, her face paling. Neither one had ever spoken of the horror of that day.

"But he did not, did he?" replied her mother. "The Lord kept them safe."

Alice gave a grunt of exasperation. "Mother, I am worried for you. You know that you cough blood at night?" She stood behind her mother and put her hands on her shoulders.

Lady Maud nodded but did not take her eyes off her book. "Sit and read with me," and Alice obeyed.

A half-hour later, the boys returned. "I caught a field mouse," announced Dickie.

"You must be gentle with it," cautioned his aunt, "and make sure you keep it where it cannot get into our stores."

Dickie held out his hands and the little creature snuffled around his palms, its little black eyes aglow and its whiskers vibrating. "It tickles!" Dickie laughed.

Goody returned carrying a basket of vegetables and the dampened loaf. She handed out pieces of bread. Alice filled the kettle and put it on the fire to boil.

Goody chopped parsnips and carrots for their noon pottage. She swept them into the kettle and added a handful of oats; she kept a few back, which she gave to Dickie. The field mouse sat up, took the oats in its tiny paws, and nibbled on them. Dickie giggled and tried to kiss it on the nose and sang to it.

Several sick villagers were already waiting outside the cottage door, although the sun had barely risen. To Alice, the red-golden orb seemed to suspend itself on the horizon a moment, as if considering whether to rise or sink back into darkness.

The women handed out possets and liniments and received their patients' half-pennies in return. By midmorning there remained only a girl of about fifteen years. She stood in the doorway, head bent, tugging her sleeve down over a lurid purple bruise on her wrist.

She looked at each woman in turn, then at the floor. "I don't want to bear a child," she said.

"Are you with child now?" asked Lady Maud.

"I do not know, Lady, for we are but new married." She gave a high-pitched laugh that sounded more like a squeak.

Dickie looked up from playing with his new pet. "That is a mouse but looks like a girl," he remarked.

"Sh," said Alice. She motioned to John, who was stacking wood by the fire, to take Dickie away.

"Let's go fishing, Master Dickon." The boy stuffed the field mouse in his pocket and followed John out the door.

"And wherefore do you not wish to bear a child?" Lady Maud spoke with asperity.

"Because he is sixty years old and is a brute. His bowels move whether he will or no, and I must wash his linen from dawn into the night to keep him from stinking up to Heaven, or down to the other place." She looked at Lady Maud with dull eyes, kneading her apron. "He has money enough to pay for a dozen nurses but says why should he, when he has a wife. He walks with a cane, and that's not all he uses his cane for." She pushed up her sleeve. Her entire arm was a mass of yellow and purple.

"Alice, fetch the comfrey liniment," said Lady Maud.

"I love another who loves me," continued the girl, crying, "but he has nothing save his good name." She dabbed her eyes with her apron. "I know my husband cannot be long for this world." Her words came out gasping. "Please give me a brew, in case he gets me with child."

Lady Maud frowned. "We cannot help you."

Alice had never heard her mother speak in so harsh a tone.

"But, Mother," interjected Alice, "she is so young." She thought, *How dreadful, to be married to a cruel man and be in love with a good one.* "And we do have tansy growing."

"However did you learn of such?" asked Lady Maud, her voice quivering.

Alice looked toward Goody, who busied herself with sweeping the floor.

"Alice," repeated Lady Maud, "I asked you a question."

The girl stood in the doorway looking from one speaker to the other.

"He beats her," pleaded Alice. "He will probably beat any child she bears."

"That is his right as her husband and the child's father."

Alice stared at her mother a few seconds, her mouth open in disbelief.

The girl dipped a curtsey to Lady Maud and turned to leave.

"I am sorry for your trouble," said Alice, pressing the jar of liniment into her hands.

Alice excused herself to her mother, then ran down to the river, needing to be alone. When she reached the bank, she saw John and Dickie fishing, so she walked along the bank and found a dry patch beneath a weeping willow. She sat and gazed at the flowing water. Tears pooled in her eyes. *Why do Mother and I argue so much?* She forced herself not to cry, for what good came of that? Just a red nose and redder eyes. *Dear William, where are you?* After a few minutes she felt composed enough to return to the cottage. As she passed the garden she was hailed by Mistress Smith, with Abigail in tow.

"Ah, Mistress Alice," called the mother. "We are come to see you. Pray tarry a minute."

Alice paused to tidy her coif. She wished the hem of her skirt was not sodden and besmirched with mud.

"Tell her, Abigail," ordered Mistress Smith.

"No," replied her daughter, reddening.

Mistress Smith clucked in exasperation. "Abigail here can barely read, and her writing is atrocious. These matters must be rectified. And Father believes a smattering of Latin would not come amiss."

Abigail groaned. "For what reason must I learn such useless

things? Queen Catherine can barely read, and her writing is atrocious too, I hear."

Mistress Smith boxed her daughter's ears. "None of that from you, missy." Tears ran down Abigail's face. "Do you think I enjoy traipsing in the mud to ask favours in a peasant's hovel?" continued Mistress Smith. "Look at the state of my new satin slippers." She glowered at her footwear. "The village priest said he could learn you, but your father distrusts clerics so."

Mistress Smith looked up at Alice. Her voice softened. "Please, Lady Alice, I shall pay you well for your pains."

Alice looked back at the woman. It seemed a lifetime ago since she had been addressed as Lady Alice. And oh! The prospect of earning easy money and being spared grubbing in the dirt all day long.

Mistress Smith read Alice's eyes. "Good, that is settled," said she, a sheen of perspiration on her brow.

"I will have to consult Mother, and if she can spare me, then—"

"A shilling a morning," interrupted Mistress Smith. "Just the scriptures, mind, in English first and then a bit of the gospels in Latin. And learn her to write a fair hand. After all, she may be marrying a duke someday, or at least an earl." She paused for breath and fanned her face with a glove. "And you will take your dinners with us. Today we are having pheasant stuffed with quail stuffed with chestnuts, then marchpane and pineapple, with plenty left over to bring home to your family."

"Pineapple," repeated Alice, in a soft voice. She could smell it, even though she had only ever eaten pineapple once—it had been a gift to her father from a wealthy nobleman. Alice became aware of her stomach rumbling and hoped the Smiths could not hear it.

John and Dickie, returning from the river, approached the women. John carried a fish net full of writhing smelts.

"Bow to us, ladies," commanded Dickie, "for we are Jesus Christ and his good friend Saint Andrew, bloody fine fishers of men."

Mother and daughter stepped back, appalled.

"Dickie mistrues his lessons," explained Alice. "Pray forgive him." She noticed something dangling from Dickie's belt. The field mouse, dead.

"Wherefore come ye hither, fat dame with your speckled chick?" asked Dickie, making clucking sounds.

"Dickie, you zany, beg pardon this instant!" ordered Alice, her cheeks burning. Her palms tingled and for the first time ever, she wanted to smack her cousin's head. *What is happening to him? To me? To Mother?*

"I like the chick. Sorry chick." Dickie bowed to Abigail. "You brought me raisins last time. This time I would like candied ginger. Thank you, Mistress Chick." He bowed again.

Abigail smiled and made a slight curtsey in return, but her mother stood stiff, her mouth wide open.

"Mother, do not mind what Master Dickon says," advised Abigail. "Remember, we had plenty of such simple folk when we lived in Sheffield."

Alice felt a surge of gratitude toward the young woman.

"Come, Master Dickon, Goody is waiting for our fish," said John, trying to suppress a grin. "Then we will go search for heron feathers and maybe find an egg or two."

"John," said Alice, "pray tell Lady Maud I am with Mistress Smith and her daughter and shall return soon."

"Yes, Mistress Alice." John bowed and steered Dickie toward the cottage.

"I understand you have a new good black dress," said Mistress Smith, glaring at Alice's dirty skirt.

So you will not be ashamed of my dining with you in your hall, thought Alice. She gave a slight curtsey, and spoke with coolness. "If Mother permits, I shall come tomorrow."

Entering the cottage, Alice watched Goody take the dead field mouse from an unresisting Dickie and dump it on the midden pile. She wondered for a second what boiled field mouse tasted like and shuddered. *We will have money again soon, thank God.*

Alice told her mother of Mistress Smith's proposition and Dickie's rude behaviour.

Maud prepared a borage infusion. "This, I hope, will soothe Dickie's mind, and yes, I can spare you for the present, dear," said Lady Maud. "It would be an act of charity to teach an unschooled young woman like Mistress Abigail to read the scriptures."

There was a knock on the door and a stout woman in a fine blue wool dress peered inside. Alice thought she looked familiar.

"Do you have anything for the headache?" asked the woman.

"I am sorry, we do not have feverfew planted yet in our garden," replied Lady Maud.

"Never mind. I saw you have lettuce and I would give three pence for a half-dozen."

As Goody went to gather them, Alice noticed the woman scanning the shelves, and a waft of lavender scented the room. She had seen their visitor before, leaving the apothecary's shop, and had wondered if she might be the apothecary's wife. But why would an apothecary's wife need to buy feverfew from them, when surely they had it in their own shop?

Goody set the lettuce on the table, and John and Dickie trundled in carrying bunches of carrots. Dickie wore a long feather in his cap. He pointed to it. "But no eggs, alas," said he. Dickie sniffed the air. "Something smells sweet," he squinted at the woman, "but I would hazard her nether regions do not. Sulphurous stench! Burning. Hessie! No, not Hessie!"

Lady Maud moved to quieten Dickie but tripped over her stool, and Goody had to steady her.

"Stop that, Dickie!" cried Alice. "This good woman has come only to buy lettuce." She wrestled with Dickie and tried to get him out the door, but Dickie pushed her away and she fell to the floor. John went to help Alice, but she cried out, "I am fine, take Dickie away."

John seized Dickie by the arm, but Dickie threw him off and prostrated himself at the woman's feet. His face was white with terror. "My aunt is harmless. She looks like a black witch but is none." He groaned. "It was I who chopped off the heads of the dandelions, not she." Dickie pawed at the woman's skirt. "Off they came. Lickety spit. They are not John the Baptists with their heads chopped off by the maiden."

Alice rose and ran to assist John. Between them they grappled with Dickie and separated him from the woman. Dickie panted, "King Henry the Eighth is the greatest of head-choppers. Uncle Hugh had a head too, until the king said he mayn't have one anymore."

The woman gaped, her breathing was rapid and her face pale with shock.

Goody, having seated Lady Maud on her stool by the hearth, stepped over to the woman and eased her onto a seat. Goody knelt down before her and chafed her hands. "He is simple," said Goody, "touched in the head, and means not a word he says."

"He should be locked away," said the woman, her colour returning, "so he cannot spew his madness at good Christian folk."

Dickie's limbs stiffened, then his whole body relaxed and he fell from Alice and John's grip. His eyes rolled to the back of his head, and his arms and legs began to shake.

Goody fetched the wooden spoon and placed it between Dickie's teeth.

"Master Dickon, no, no," entreated John, laying him on the ground and holding him down.

Alice raced to the loft to fetch a blanket.

Their visitor crossed herself. "He must be the Devil's own!" she gasped. "*Pater noster qui es in—*"

"Not at all," interrupted Lady Maud, her face white as a snowdrift. "Dickie is not possessed, he is an innocent and will soon be recovered." Her forehead creased. "I am most sorry for your distress in seeing him this way."

Only Alice, bringing down the blanket, saw their visitor give a fleeting smile.

"Of course he is, just as you say, an innocent," said the woman. "Bless him, poor soul. I shall leave you to tend to him," and she stood and left the cottage.

Dickie returned to his senses and sat up. "Where has she gone? That woman who tried to hurt Hessie?"

"She has gone home to her own house. No one is hurting your sister. She is safe with your father in Wales," said Lady Maud.

Dickie shook his head back and forth. "No! You are wrong!"

"Goody, give him some borage tea to sooth his spirits," said Lady Maud.

"What about my jangled spirits?" asked Goody, massaging her temples. "Whatever will that woman think of us here?" She shook her head. "And she forgot to take her lettuces."

ester tossed on her bed of mouldy straw. She dreamed she was a Roman vestal virgin who had broken her vow of chastity and was condemned to death. She was dressed in her finest robes and placed in a closed litter. Then, as if a corpse on a funeral bier, she was carried through streets lined with silent people. She was set down deep inside a cave, then its entrance blocked with a huge stone. Her lamp held enough oil for twelve hours, and she had bread and water for two days. Hester cried out for her mother, who had also been buried alive in that same cave, only long ago. Her mother's corpse appeared and came to life. But it was not her mother, it was the witch, who stretched out her bony fingers and cackled, "Welcome home, daughter."

Hester awoke in terror. The door creaked open.

"Nia, thank God it is you!"

"I have the ring and a clean shift for you. Peredur passed but a few minutes ago."

"God rest his soul."

Nia helped her dress, brushed out her hair, and tended to the cuts on her feet. "You must wear my cloak, for there will be a gaggle of folk come to stare at you."

Guards escorted the pair to the entrance of the great hall. As they crossed the courtyard, Hester, clutching the ring in her hand, gulped deep breaths of fresh air. When they arrived at the porch, a guard removed the cloak from her shoulders. "Lord Llewelyn's orders are that on account of your harlotry, you are to appear before him bare-headed and clad only in your shift."

Nia began to protest. "It is cold as gun metal in here, my mistress will—"

"Do not worry," Hester said to Nia. "I shall leave this hall better dressed than anyone in it."

Nia nodded. "I shall wait for you here, by the door."

Hester walked slowly up to the dais, where Llewelyn sat in the centre of half a dozen men, with Mervyn at one end. The fire grate lay empty, and dampness hung in the air. She felt goosebumps rise over her arms and legs. As Hester passed through the rows of tables, she became aware of the translucency of her shift. She watched as the collective gaze drifted downwards from her bosom until it focused over the dark triangle of her *mons veneris*. The men's jaws fell open in salacious delectation. *Sate yourselves while you can*, she thought.

Hester made the briefest of curtseys to Llewellyn. She felt a sudden relief that Father was dead and not present to witness her disgrace. Her eyes filled with tears and she hoped the assembled lords did not notice, but she need not have been concerned—their attention was focused on her half-naked body. When she stepped onto the dais, the men, almost in unison, coughed and bent their heads over their parchments.

Llewelyn spoke. "You stand self-condemned of a foul crime. As punishment, you will die by stoning. You, of course, will gather the stones over the forthcoming days." He paused for breath, then resumed, his voice rising with each word. "After your death, which I promise you will be a protracted one, you will be buried in an unmarked grave, as befits a cheap and common whore." He shrieked, "You, a princess of royal Welsh blood! You have snatched victory from me. The gods know you were their intended sacrifice. Do you understand? Harlot!"

Llewelyn's face crumpled in rage and self-pity. "Who was your paramour? Or have there been too many for your remembrance? I would hazard the bard's apprentice was one…"

Hester hesitated a moment, taken aback. *Dear gods, what if they arrest Gareth? Sore injured as he is, would he survive even one night in that dank cellar?* For a moment she feared she might pass out from this new terror, but she squeezed the ring tighter, and the pain kept her upright.

"It was not Gareth," said Hester.

"You lie! I know you and he have spent time together, and under Peredur's blind eye, the youth could easily have slipped himself into your quim."

Hester felt her entire body tighten, both from the disgust she felt for this man and from the cold. She took a deep breath. "Henry, King of England, is my betrothed."

Silence filled the hall. A second later came the outburst. "No! Surely not!" and "She has lain with the enemy—she must die!"

After the ruckus had subsided to a hum, Hester stared at her uncle. "And I am with child by him."

The men's jaws dropped simultaneously and their jowls wobbled. Their hands flapped useless as birds' broken wings above the table. Hester wanted to laugh aloud but clenched her jaws instead.

"Have you any proof of this?" demanded Llewellyn.

"My courses have not come upon me this month." Hester blushed at speaking of so intimate a matter before an assembly of men. She made herself think of her father, and the sadness whitened her face.

"For how long have you been betrothed?"

"Since Christmas." Hester's teeth chattered.

"You are an abhorrence to my country." Llewelyn ordered the guards, "Take her back to prison."

An aged counsellor in a black robe stood. "Stay, my lord. Suppose she is delivered of a son? Henry would nigh worship him, fearful as he is that Catherine is barren and that his only true son, Edward, will die young."

Another man scraped back his chair. "Before Edward, he planned to crown his bastard, Henry Fitzroy, King of Ireland. The next step was the English throne."

Llewelyn sprang to his feet and slammed his fist on the table. "So, we have an heir to the crown amongst us!"

A young man stood up at the back of the hall. "My lord, if the King cares aught for your niece, why has he not pursued her?"

Llewelyn hummed a moment. "Those men that Iolo waylaid in Caernarfon were looking for her." He demanded of Hester, "What proof have you of his esteem?"

"Henry bestowed this ring upon me as token of his enduring love." Hester forced herself to smile and placed the jewel on the table. "Once I tell him I am with child, he will find cause to put away Catherine, and we shall be wed before my belly shows."

"By the mothers!" exclaimed Llewelyn. He picked up the ring, examined the engraving in the band, and placed it on his index finger. It was too big so it fell off, landing on the table with a clunk. His counsellors pretended not to notice.

"You can bargain with the King, my lord," said the old one, rubbing the back of his neck. "You will permit your niece to wed Henry, and hence legitimize his son, but only on condition he returns your lands." He clasped his hands in front of him. "And not a drop of Welsh blood risks being shed."

Llewelyn nodded. He stared at Hester's middle. "Niece, you must not catch a chill. The golden goose needs golden feathers." He undid his belt and removed his velvet robe, trimmed with ermine. He draped it around Hester's shoulders and fastened the belt around her waist. The robe trailed on the floor, but at least she could feel her body growing warm.

Hester did not hear Mervyn's soft-soled shoes as he walked up behind her.

"What a magnificent gem." He smirked. "Surely someone should guard it for my dear cousin! It is far too great a responsibility for a woman who is already bearing a great responsibility." He bowed, with an air of the gravest respect, toward Hester, but his eyes glinted.

Hester felt chilled, despite the furred robe. She had thwarted Mervyn's plan to marry her and gain her property. His anger must be seething like a cornered boar's when facing the hounds.

Mervyn picked up the ring and it winked, bloodshot, in his palm.

Panic-stricken but trying to keep her voice even, Hester said, "Take it, but no man wearing it has ever again enjoyed good health. Think of the King, hag-ridden by pain."

Mervyn set down the ring, and Hester rewrapped it in the handkerchief. She inclined her head toward Llewelyn, then turned to make her way back down the hall.

"Stay, cousin, not quite so fast," murmured Mervyn.

Hester stopped to look at him, willing her heart to stop hammering inside her chest.

Mervyn addressed Llewelyn. "My lord, would it not be wise to consult the midwife, just in case our dear kinswoman is mistaken?"

Llewelyn scowled. "That can wait till the morrow. For the present, my niece will rest, guarded, in her own rooms."

The assembly rose while Hester walked down the aisle. She felt a savage pleasure at having fooled all these men. As she exited the hall, she could make out various mutterings.

"This one will surely bring forth a man child. Look how she carries herself."

"We gain the victory with no lives risked."

"I would rather a fight and skewer that bastard Henry on the end of my arrow."

"Think of your sweetheart, happy on the end of your weapon, instead." A grunt of laugher followed.

Nia waited in the porch. She shook her head. "Certainly you spoke aright earlier, for you are the best dressed person leaving this hall."

ester sat on the bed in her chamber, facing Nia. "I learned a little about childbearing from Aunt Maud. No midwife can say if a woman be pregnant or no until she has missed two of her courses."

"And are you pregnant with the King's son?"

"No more than you are. And even if I have to be poked and prodded again, I am safe until…"

"Until your courses come upon you. When was your last bleeding?"

"Late last month, on Trinity Sunday. I remember, because Alice was too, and we went to the distillery and got tipsy, drinking elderberry wine."

Nia hugged her. "It has been hard for you, coming here."

All the grief Hester had held in check escaped and overran her. As long as she had an enemy to oppose she could be strong. But like Gareth's gentle touch, Nia's compassion undid her, and she sobbed into her friend's arms. She sank down on the bed, then sprang up. "Gwendolyn slept here but two nights ago."

They offered up prayers for her, then although it was but midafternoon, being exhausted, they fell asleep.

Toward evening, a tapping at the window wakened them.

Nia exclaimed, "It is Corwen. I forgot to say Gareth said to send messages through him."

Hester took a sliver of parchment from his beak and read, "Dearest, I have heard strange reports, but I understand you are safe. At dusk, I take Peredur's body to his pyre. I shall wait upon you tomorrow morning."

Hester groaned. "Whatever can he think of me? But I must return the ring to him for safekeeping, as I know Mervyn covets it."

She scratched on a fresh piece of parchment, *I am most sorry for Peredur's death. I hope your head is mending. Pray take care of this again. Your own Hester.*

She rewrapped the ring and placed it before the crow. Corwen cocked his head from side to side, picked it up in his beak, and flew off.

Hester fell back asleep and dreamed of a child, around eight years old, with red-gold hair and eyes black as obsidian. She held a sceptre in her right hand and an orb in her left. The sceptre became a serpent and wound itself around the child's neck. Hester woke with the dawn light. Who was that child in her dream? But she was distracted by the dull pain in her lower belly. *No,* she thought. *Please, Blessed Virgin, my courses should not be upon me for another week.*

There was hammering on the door, and Mervyn forced himself into the room, despite the guards' protests.

"Good morning, cousin. You know why I am here. I want that ring." He smirked. "Oh yes, and condolences on your loss."

Hester pulled the sheets up to her neck. "How dare you come in here?" she demanded, her cheeks flushing.

"Ah, sweet coz, you may have fooled Llewelyn, but let us see what the midwife says."

Hester gripped the bedclothes. "I do not have the ring." Her confidence declared she told the truth.

"Then I wonder if Gareth has it."

The colour faded from her face.

Mervyn laughed and sauntered from the room.

"What have I done?" cried Hester.

"Do not be afeard for Gareth," replied Nia. "Llewelyn will not permit his bastard harm him." She nearly spat as she said, "The shame of Mervyn coming here, and his poor sister's bones not even cold yet. Now, you stay abed, and eat something. Llewelyn had vittles sent over for ye." She pointed to the sideboard where lay a quartered pheasant, a loaf of the finest manchet bread, and a decanter of claret.

Hester nodded and ate a piece of bread. "I must get dressed and attend Father's funeral."

"Llewelyn will not want you getting upset and risking a miscarriage."

"Pray you go, then, instead. But I wonder who will say Mass for him now Father Ignatius has left."

"With Friar Gwylim gone too, it will be up to our village priest, old dodderer that he is. But so long as he has not drunk too much, he will do it well enough."

The guards opened the door for Nia, where she encountered a short woman carrying a basket.

"Well, now, Nia, how are you dear?" inquired the woman.

"I am well, Mistress Price, thank you. Are you bringing dinner to your great husband here?" Nia pointed to the older guard, a tall man with a black beard and a scar over his forehead.

Through the half-opened door, Hester saw the man make a playful grab at his wife's bottom.

"Thomas, not here!" She smiled and turned to Nia. The corners of her mouth turned down. "Wasn't it terrible about poor Mistress Gwendolyn?"

Nia shook her head. "I still cannot believe it." She left, leaving the door a few inches ajar.

"I must be off home," said Mistress Price to Thomas. "Gwyneth is minding little Pwyll, and heaven knows what mischief he will be up to."

She glanced through the partly open door and saw Hester watching their conversation and, dropping a curtsey, whispered to her husband, "So that English is carrying another of Henry's bastards, is she?"

"Goodwife, do not speak so," said Thomas, closing the door. "She is barely more than a child herself and is but newly made an orphan."

Mistress Price harrumphed and clumped down the stairs.

The guard's kind words touched Hester. She stared out the

window at a group of ravens pecking on the ground. The young ones had compact glossy feathers, black as anthracite. The older ravens' plumage was bedraggled and greying. Hester wondered why a flock of ravens was called an "unkindness." She realized she had not thought of her family at Hartbourne in days, and then remembered she had not seen Lady for nearly a week. And with a guilty start, she recalled that her father had died but this morning. She murmured prayers for them all, including, and especially, Gareth.

***

Corwen half-flew, half-glided to the bards' windowsill and dropped his burden. Gareth read the message and, placing the ring in his doublet, smiled despite his grief.

Peredur's corpse, wrapped in fine linen, lay on the bed.

Gareth sang Peredur's soul on the first part of its journey. "Farewell, dear teacher. Your great spirit will repose by the clear running stream, beside the oak tree and the alder, the poplar and the willow, until—"

There came banging on the door.

"We have orders to search your rooms," announced a bass voice.

They want the ring, thought Gareth. He whispered, "I am sorry, dear master." He opened Peredur's mouth, dropped in the jewel, and covered his face with a cloth.

Two men barged in. "Sorry, Master Gareth. Mervyn's orders," said the elder of the pair. He glanced over at the corpse and crossed himself. After searching the room, he said, "And your person also."

The men, satisfied after their examination, left. Murmuring apologies to his master, Gareth withdrew the ring and replaced it in his doublet. His head wound still throbbed and oozed blood, so he changed the bandage. Soon after, six men arrived and lifted

Peredur onto a bier. Gareth, stumbling, followed them, carrying the old bard's harp.

Evan the Ear opened the gates and wiped his eyes on his sleeve. "I am sorry, Master Gareth. I loved Peredur's songs. Take care of yourself now, for you look more dead than alive."

Gareth touched his head and winced.

Corwen half-flew and half-hopped behind the pallbearers. Every few yards he fluttered up to the bier and pecked at his old master's shoulder, trying to awaken him.

On reaching the oak grove, the men proceeded to cut down several dead branches. They hewed them into logs and built a pyre. Two men lifted the body to the top.

Gareth knelt at one corner of the pyre and struck a spark with a flint. He sprinkled tinder over it and blew gently until the flame caught, then added dry leaves and twigs. He waited till the lowest log was alight then stood and raised his hands. "Peredur, great bard, you slept on the mountainside of Cader Idris, where the goddess's silver tongue lapped upon yours. She told you her secrets and bade you sing to rouse the dragon's spirit and inspire the peoples of Wales."

The men made the sign with finger and thumb against the evil eye, then crossed themselves.

Gareth lit the three remaining corners of the pyre. He said, "I shall stay here alone," and the men left.

He played Peredur's harp and sang:

I was a spark in the fire,
I was wood in a bonfire;
I am not one who does not sing,
I have sung since I was small,
I sang in the army of the tree's branches…

Gareth watched while the flames consumed Peredur's remains,

then, exhausted, he stretched out on the grass and fell asleep. Corwen hopped close and clucked mournfully in his ear.

Master Thomas knocked. "Mistress Lydwin and the midwife are here."

"Let them enter," replied Hester. She stood up and felt a warmth between her thighs; looking down she saw the hem of her shift streaked with blood. Maryse's mother entered, followed by a middle-aged dame. Hester realized she had not known the old woman's name.

Mistress Lydwin shrieked, "You have destroyed the hopes of my family. Maryse, my darling daughter, is gathering Gwendolyn's bones for…" She paused, aware of the midwife's stare, fixed upon Hester's shift. "Ah," she gave a sigh of malevolent satisfaction. "Find Master Mervyn and tell him he shall be wed tonight." She handed the midwife a shilling. "Tell only him."

Lydwin turned to Hester. A black mole bobbed on her chin. "So we're not pregnant. What a mischievous liar! But, if you agree to marry my grandson, you will live." She stroked Hester's cheek with long fingernails, and Hester shrank back in revulsion.

"Ah, my touch was once coveted, as I am sure yours now is," murmured Lydwin. "My rough hands and shrivelled dugs were not always thus." She hissed, "You will continue my lineage. Mervyn will do his duty!" The crone laughed. "So what is it to be—marry him tonight, or perish by stoning and have the crows peck out your still-living eyes while you lie, broken-armed, helpless to fend them off?"

"I will marry him." *Saying so buys me time until Gareth returns.*

Lydwin smiled. "Now to tell Llewelyn."

She left and Hester curled up on the bed and wept.

An hour later, Nia returned. "It was a small service but done well." Then she cried, "Whatever is amiss?"

"My courses came early."

Nia groaned. "Oh, dear. I will fetch some linen clouts."

"Mervyn's grandmother came. She wants us to marry."

Nia scowled. "Mervyn always schemed after your land and the fine house on it."

"Is it nearby?"

"Maybe a few leagues to the east. I am not sure, but as soon as Gareth hears of this, he will find you."

"Oh, Nia, what will he think of me?"

Nia stroked Hester's shoulder. "He would understand 'tis terror of a more hideous fate that compels you to do this."

Hester shrugged her off. "I can't bear it. I can't bear any of it."

Nia left and Hester pulled the coverlet over her head. She called out in the dark, "Mother, help me! But how can you? Oh, why did you bear me at all? Mother, I hate you. I wish I were dead." Her body convulsed. Surely only a monster would hate the woman who had given her life.

When she fell asleep, in her dream the witch jeered, "Never fear, for I, unlike your mother, will never leave you!"

Hester woke to see Mervyn and one of his cronies sauntering into the room. His hair was slicked back with oil and droplets pooled in the creases of his forehead.

"Quite a stir on account of a little blood," mused Mervyn. "Llewelyn is furious. But he has left for the south, because the old bard had foretold his triumph." He grinned at Hester. "Your uncle has consented to our marriage, because he considers it a worse punishment for you than death by stoning. Fancy that. So, my dear, where is the ring? For I know Gareth does not have it."

"I do not know." Hester moved as far back in the bed as she could.

Mervyn hoisted her out and forced her into a chair. "Huw, hold her fast."

Hester struggled but was easily overpowered. She did not call out for help; shame at agreeing to wed this creature stilled her tongue.

Mervyn reached into his sleeve and withdrew a silver instrument the size of a candle snuffer.

"Do you know what this is?"

"No," replied Hester, her voice quivering, despite her attempts to steady it.

"This dainty little apparatus is a thumbscrew. Father Ignatius left it with me, saying it might prove useful, during any…conversations that might arise between us." The thumbscrew glinted in the sunlight. "An Inquisitor's tool, as it draws no blood." Mervyn sighed. "Blood, ah yes." His voice lowered to a near whisper. "One day I may show you my back. Your hand would near fit in some of the scars."

"You would not dare use that," whispered Hester, in shock.

"The good priest found it lubricated the tongues of witches and heretics most satisfactorily."

Hester blanched. "Guards, pray help me!" she cried out.

"They are in my service now, and since in a few hours you will become my property, why not answer the question? Where is the ring?"

Huw secured Hester's wrist and Mervyn forced her thumb into the instrument's aperture. He tightened the screw.

Hester screamed, "Dear God, make it stop!"

Another half turn and she gasped, "Gareth has it."

"Liar. I had both him and his rooms searched. If you co-operate you may be able to hold a pen again one day. Whereas if you do not…"

Perspiration poured down Hester's brow. She fought back waves of nausea. "Then I know not where it is. Stop, please!"

"Gently does it. Wondrous how it takes minimal force to operate, yet in return for so little effort, yields so much pain. The ancient Greeks invented the screw; I am sure you know that, my sweet."

"Mother, help me!" Her eyes watered; she did not want to give Mervyn the pleasure of seeing her cry but knew she could not hold out much longer.

"Mother," echoed Mervyn. "You do not know how it feels to have your very existence a reproach to your mother, do you?" He shouted, "So that simply for bearing you, she is held in contempt by all men and women. But it is women who are the cruellest. My mother has been shunned and pecked by all the hens in this village!"

"Please stop!" The pain seared through her hand and tears poured down her cheeks.

The door opened and Thomas and his companion marched in.

Thomas exclaimed, "We have no orders to stand for mistreatment of our charge!"

"Get out," hissed Mervyn. "I shall see you lose your posts!"

Thomas aimed his staff at Mervyn's midriff. "Leave now, sirrah. You are hardly a man, and to call you a woman would be to insult half of humankind."

He prodded Mervyn and Huw out the door.

"Let us get rid of this tool of Satan," said Thomas, unfastening the screw and handing it to his companion. "Rowan, hold this," he said.

"Thank God you came just now!" gasped Hester. She looked at her thumb, white from the pressure and starting to swell. Tears coursed down her face, and Thomas handed her a linen kerchief. He stood behind her with a hand on her shoulder as she wiped her eyes.

"There, there, you are safe now," he said.

Rowan stared in amazement at the thumbscrew in his hand.

"Why, have you never seen one of these before?" asked Thomas. "A terrible wound it inflicts. 'Tis like being beaten with a blackthorn stick, so the flesh rots from inside. The midden pile is the place for that." He took Hester's thumb in his hand. "I don't believe the joint is crushed, but the tendons are sore bruised. Can you bend it at all?" Hester could not. Thomas shook his head. "I am afraid that is an ill sign." He fetched his basket and took out a flagon of ale. "Now drink you some of this."

Hester spluttered as the sharp taste revived her. She said, "Bring me my cabinet!" pointing to her medicine chest. She withdrew a glass phial the size of her little finger. "This is tincture of poppy seed and henbane; it deadens pain." The men blessed themselves.

"Nay, it is not witchcraft but a remedy the Lord has provided for our pains." Hester drank half the phial's contents and immediately regretted it, remembering the normal dose was two or three drops. She restoppered the phial and placed it in her pocket.

Thomas stroked Hester's good hand, but awkwardly, as if it were made of thistledown and might crumple beneath his own fingers.

Nia entered and set down her pile of linen. "Mistress, what has happened?"

Hester was too drowsy to answer.

"Mervyn was here," explained Thomas, "and used the torture on her."

Nia ran to Hester's side. "Is she very sick?"

"No. Her thumb is injured. 'Tis but physic that makes her sleep."

Two armed men ascended the stairs. "Both you men," one said, addressing Thomas and Rowan, "come with me and report for duty in the courtyard. We are to follow Lord Llewelyn south without delay."

Nia frowned. "My Twgardan must be already at Saint Alban's. The tyrant will kill him! Mistress, what am I to do?"

Hester heard her friend as if from the bottom of a well. "Find him and tell him to come home."

"Thank you. I will return when I have brought him back, hothead that he is. And I know Gareth will be by your side soon." She embraced Hester and followed the guards downstairs. Hester fell into a drugged slumber.

She woke to find two girls standing beside her bed. She lifted her head from the bolster and could not understand why she felt woozy, but then she remembered, she had taken too much poppyseed juice.

The pair bobbed their curtseys. "Good evening, Mistress Vaughan."

The taller girl set down a basket. "I am Bessie, Twgardan's older sister."

"And I am Maire, his younger sister." Maire had red hair and reminded Hester of Alice. The girl held a dress draped over her arm; the bodice and overskirt were of red velvet and the sleeves trimmed with ermine. The underskirt was ivory damask, embroidered with silver flowers in interweaving spirals.

Bessie said, "This wedding gown has been worn by royal brides for…," she faltered, "for, well, for a very long time."

Hester wondered why they had brought it to her. Her head ached and her entire hand throbbed. She got out of bed and held onto the post to steady herself.

Bessie added, "I heard that the last time it was worn was by your mother at her marriage."

All the horror of the previous few hours cascaded upon Hester. She had agreed to marry Mervyn and would be wearing the same wedding dress in which her mother had married for love. Tears began to fall, but she told herself, *not now*. She took the dress and hugged it. Underneath the slight musty odour there was a trace of rose perfume, and beneath that, she imagined another scent—the smell of her mother's skin.

"Be careful," implored Maire. "The gown cannot withstand your crushing it, so."

Hester felt near mesmerized by holding for the first time a dress her mother had worn. Bessie helped her into a chemise of fine lawn, intricately embroidered around the yoke. *Mother must have sewn this chemise, as a young girl. Oh, how I wish I had learned embroidery from her.* But then again, she had learned much from Aunt Maud. She could identify those plants that healed a man, and, because physic and poison are bedmates, which could kill him.

Hester's thumb throbbed and she thought of brewing monk's hood or foxglove for Mervyn. Her heart froze a second, and she prayed silently, *Dear God, let Gareth come, and prevent me from slaying this hateful man.* She knew a man who killed his wife was simply guilty of murder and would be hanged, but a woman who murdered her husband was guilty of treason—she was a vassal who had struck against her liege lord and was hence a traitor to divine order. Hanging was not sufficient punishment for such an abhorrent crime, and so she would be burned or, if a poisoner, boiled alive.

"Oh, mistress," said Bessie, "it is such a shame that your flowers are upon you on your wedding day. Here, let me pleat the folds of your shift so you do not bleed through and mire the beautiful gown."

Hester stepped into the embroidered underskirt, then the over gown. Bessie and Maire fastened the pearl buttons down the back. Hester ran her hands over the soft red velvet and thought of her mother making the same gesture; she could feel the warmth of her mother's touch in the material.

Bessie attached the sleeves and stood back. "Your mother must have been two or three inches shorter than you, for the hem doesn't reach the floor."

Hester looked down and thought, *How strange that I never knew how tall she was.*

Despite her terror of Mervyn, Hester wanted to see how she looked in her mother's bridal gown. She looked in the mirror and saw a white face with red-rimmed eyes staring back at her. The bruise on her cheek, where the old woman had slapped her, was violet with yellow edging.

Maire consoled her, saying, "There is always the veil."

Hester smiled, despite herself.

Bessie inquired, hesitantly, "And about your hair, mistress?"

Hester knew that a bride on her wedding day wore her hair long, in token of her virginity. The only other time a woman wore her hair down was at her coronation, as had Anne Boleyn. Hester recalled that Anne was crowned when she was five months pregnant and newly married to the King. *Just like I told Llewelyn I would be when Henry and I wed.* If only her courses had not come upon her early!

"I will wear my hair up," replied Hester, with a shrug of her shoulders. "There is not one villager who believes me a maid." *One day soon, Gareth will, and he is the only person who counts.*

A man poked his head inside the room. "Mistress Vaughan is awaited in the chapel."

Hester thought of the phial of poppy juice. If Gareth did not come, she might need it, as a last resort. Death was far preferable to life with Mervyn. She withdrew it from her discarded dress pocket.

Maire asked, "What is that?"

"It is a love philter," lied Hester "I will tuck it here inside my bodice."

The girls blushed and Bessie wafted a veil of Brussels lace over Hester's hair and pinned it in place with two silver combs.

Hester was thankful for a barrier between her and the world, especially between her and Mervyn. Then she chided herself for relying on something so fragile the gentlest breeze could cast it away.

She prayed under her breath to Stella Maris, the patroness of shipwrecked sailors, just as Alice had prayed the evening before they went to Hampton Court. But the Blessed Virgin had turned her face from her, with Henry and with her father's death. A gush of blood exited from her and caught in the pleats of her shift. Even her body had betrayed her.

The church was dark, save for a pair of candles burning at the altar, where Mervyn stood beside a scarecrow of a priest. Hester walked slowly down the aisle with Maire and Bessie on either side.

Mervyn called out, "I must join Llewelyn tomorrow and have but a few hours to consummate our marriage, so make haste, my sweet!"

Hester and her bridesmaids arrived at the altar. The priest's speech was slurred. "Do you, Hester Vaughan, take this man for your husband?"

She murmured, "I do."

Mervyn snarled, "I do" and dragged Hester away.

"And the exchange of rings?" protested the cleric.

"My bride has injured her hand, and, alas cannot receive mine. But she is going to give me hers, very soon." He turned to Hester, "Aren't you, dear wife?"

She pretended she had not heard.

Outside, Mervyn's horse was ready saddled.

Hester removed her veil and handed it to Bessie. "And take these, as well," she said, handing each girl a silver comb.

"Thank you, mistress," they chorused, making a deep curtsey.

Mervyn mounted and pulled Hester up behind him. She secured her good hand under his belt.

"Pray for me," she beseeched the girls, as Mervyn's horse trotted away.

"Indeed we shall!" replied Bessie.

A month ago, thought Hester, *I would not have stooped to ask strangers for their prayers. I was going to be queen and everyone would beg me for favours. Please, Gareth, make haste.*

Mervyn snarled at Evan, who opened the gates. Once through, Mervyn urged his horse to a canter. Exhaustion befriended Hester and she fell asleep to the rhythm of the horse's hooves.

A full moon, pallid as a sightless eye, had risen by the time they reached the house. Hester knew not how far they had come, but the mountains of Snowdonia appeared close.

A climbing rose wended its way up the door frame of the two-storeyed, timbered building. Its leaves quivered in the cool evening breeze.

"This was your parents' cottage when they wanted to be alone," jeered Mervyn. "But your father abandoned it after your mother died."

Hester closed her eyes and groaned inwardly but kept silent.

Mervyn kicked open the door and dragged her through it. "Over the lintel with you, and you will only being going back over it in your coffin."

An old man carrying a bumper of claret appeared. "Welcome home, Master Mervyn, and your bride." A little terrier ran between the man's legs. "Get away, Blackie!" He kicked the dog, which yelped and ran away.

"That dog," murmured Hester, "has only three legs."

Mervyn snorted. He drained the claret and dismissed the servant. "Now, about the ring?" He gently squeezed Hester's injured thumb. "If it were not for you, Llewelyn would have made me his heir, so the least you can do is give me the jewel."

The numbing effect of the potion had worn off and she screamed.

Mervyn chuckled. "Iestyn is deaf as a hammer and sleeps in a shed out back. Shriek away." Hester struggled against him as he carried her upstairs to the bedchamber. He set her down on a chair and she quickly scanned the room. Candlelight revealed a bed hung with green damask curtains; a posy of wild pink roses lay on the bolster. A bedside table held a decanter of wine and a single goblet, and against the far wall stood a large wardrobe. Hester inhaled the scent of roses. Mother was here; she must be hiding somewhere, playing their old game of hide-and-go-seek.

The wardrobe, of course! She ran and flung the doors open. A large bolster stood upright in a corner. For one moment, the bolster was her mother, but in the next, it was just a bolster. To be sure, Hester touched it. Only then was she convinced; she dropped to her knees and wept.

Mervyn scowled. "Are you gone quite mad? Where is my ring?"

"If Gareth has it not, I do not know where it is."

Mervyn dragged her upright. "Well," he drawled, "I suggest you try to remember." He drew a slender knife from his boot. "I may as well get something for my pains. I am pressed for time, so shall cut you out of the dress and make our marriage legal."

"No!" gasped Hester, her eyes dilating with shock. If he chose to rape her, she would simply repeat what she had done with Henry; imagine she was someplace else, until it was over. But she could not bear to have her mother's dress destroyed.

A crow alighted on the windowsill and she pointed at it. "The crow took the ring."

"How could a crow—?"

"Corwen, Peredur's crow, is trained to carry messages."

Hester coloured, feeling a surge of shame; she had betrayed Gareth for a dress. She knew Mervyn needed to join Llewelyn as soon as possible in order to retain his father's goodwill. However, only consummation of the marriage would render him legal possessor of her property. She watched expressions of triumph and anxiety flicker over Mervyn's face. On the verge of hysteria, Hester giggled, then immediately wished she had not.

Mervyn slashed her skirt and ripped it from her waist. He threw her on the bed face down and pushed her chemise up around her hips. With one hand, he pressed down on her back, pinning her to the bed. Hester looked behind and watched as he undid the points on his codpiece with his other hand and pulled out his yard. He rubbed some stiffness into it. For a split second Hester wondered why a man's member was called a yard; Mervyn's could only measure a few inches. She wanted to turn away yet felt compelled to watch Mervyn's performance, horrified and fascinated at the same time. She was reminded of when she had tripped over an adder's nest and disturbed its occupants. She had run away but once safe, turned to watch the baby snakes writhe in angry protest.

Mervyn looked at her and noticed the blood on her chemise. "You disgusting cow!" he snarled. "I can't go in that filthy hole." Limpness set in. "I want that ruby!" he cried. His member stiffened, momentarily, at the thought of the gem, but at the sight in front of him his rod drooped, and Hester could not suppress a smile.

"Damn you, witch!" He slapped her face. Hester cried out and Mervyn snarled, "I shall pretend you are Huw! Now where is the goose grease?" He left the room.

Hester gathered up the slashed skirt and held it to her breast. She plucked the phial from her bodice, poured its contents into the goblet on the table, and added wine from the decanter. She thrust the empty phial under the bed. *That should preserve me this one night*, she thought. *Gareth, pray make haste!*

Mervyn returned with a small silver cup. He placed it on the bedside table and drank off the goblet of wine in one swallow. "Ugh! This is sour. Devil take that Iestyn. I shall have to fetch another bottle." He stomped downstairs. Hester prayed he would lose consciousness in the cellar, but a minute later she heard his footsteps returning. Her heart sank.

There was barking and a "God damn you, dog!" then a tremendous crash and silence.

Hester thanked God and His mother. Then she was terrified. What if Mervyn was dead and it was discovered she had given him physic? She forced herself go to the landing. In the moonlight she could see Mervyn lying against the stair rail on the bottom step. His left leg was twisted under him and he did not move, but his chest rose and fell.

Hester fell asleep on the bed holding the torn dress. She dreamed she was little, climbing a staircase, looking for Mother's hiding place. The witch appeared in front of her and chortled. "At last, I have made you mine!" Hester ran down the stairs, but the steps kept breaking beneath her. Then she was in a meadow and a cow was licking her face. She woke to find something warm and wet against her mouth. She screamed, thinking it was Mervyn's yard come up against her. She shielded her face with her arms, but it was only the little dog. She winced as Blackie wriggled against her injured thumb.

The lightening sky told her it was but an hour before dawn and Mervyn must soon awaken. Maybe Gareth believed she was pregnant with Henry's child and would never come. She hid her face in Blackie's soft, furry coat and cried. After some time, exhausted, she fell back asleep.

lice entered the hall of Syon House, where Mistress Smith and Abigail were awaiting her. New-dyed tapestries that still smelled of sheep hung on the walls, and gleaming silver plates stood exhibited on a railing that ran beneath the rafters.

"Father only refuses to permit adornment of the female person," whispered Abigail, noting Alice's curious glance.

"Show Lady Alice into the library," said Mistress Smith. She spoke in a loud voice for the benefit of servants who peered around doors wondering who their mistress's very first guest might be. "Father wishes you to be well versed in the scriptures," continued Mistress Smith, following the young women. "We have the Holy Bible there." She pointed to a huge volume on a table in the centre of the room. "Master Smith expects to be elevated to the peerage in the New Year and is determined to become well-read." She waved her hand around the room.

Hundreds of glittering spines of books lined each of the four walls; they appeared never to have been opened. Most were theological works, but on a top shelf Alice spied Chaucer's *Canterbury Tales* and Plato's *Republic*. She was reminded of her father's library, the few times she had been in there. His tomes, however, were well worn, and always there had been Shep lying beside the hearth. *What could have happened to Shep?* Alice had managed to rid her mind of most of that horrid morning's events. *Oh, one of the labourers who carried poor Stewart away had taken Shep.* Alice offered a prayer for Stewart and her father; she wondered if Hester had found her father still alive in Wales. She prayed for William that he be well and return to her soon.

Mistress Smith was still speaking. "The King does love his ships, and what's a ship without cannons? And Master Smith is the best ironmonger in England, and I dare say in the world." She smoothed her skirts. "Abigail will be presented at court, and His Majesty may ask her to read to him." She read the look of surprise in Alice's face. "Ah, you thought that because we are newly made rich from our steelworks, the King's favour would stop at renting us this fine house. But my husband was a friend of Thomas Cromwell, a mere blacksmith's son, who rose to become Lord Privy Seal." Mistress Smith, pouting, clasped and unclasped her hands. "Sad that he ended on the block last year."

Alice frowned, thinking of the man who, almost single-handedly, had destroyed England's shrines and monasteries to pander to Henry's avarice. Then she remembered the argument with her mother over the rosary beads. *Is money now everything to me, also?*

"Once she has mastered reading and writing English," continued Mistress Smith, "you may teach her Latin. The King favours educated young women. The Lady Elizabeth, even if she is merely his bastard, knows Latin." She twiddled her thumbs. "She probably knows French and Spanish, but we will leave those for now."

"You forget German, Portuguese, and ancient Egyptian," said Abigail, grinning.

Her mother scowled and boxed her on the ear. "None of your insolence, now."

"Ow!" exclaimed the daughter, her eyes watering. "That hurt!"

"It is all for your own good. You want to marry well, do you not?"

Abigail rubbed her ear and nodded.

Mistress Smith harrumphed, and turned and left the library.

Alice and Abigail sat on carved, hard-backed chairs by the table, and Alice opened the Bible. It was Coverdale's English translation. Half an hour later, Alice wished she was in the garden weeding, even if it meant sore knees and dirt wedged under her fingernails. Abigail had sounded out every letter in the first verse of the Epistle of Saint Paul to the Corinthians. Abigail slumped over the table, her forehead resting on the open page.

Alice rolled her eyes. "This is hopeless! You are not going to learn to read unless we find something that holds your interest." She stood on a chair and reached down the Chaucer.

"No," said Abigail, her brow furrowed; she looked around, as if being spied upon. "Father would never permit it."

"Well, perhaps this," said Alice, with a determined set to her chin. She handed a volume of Apuleius to her pupil.

"*The Golden Ass*," chuckled Abigail on deciphering the title. Alice pointed to the lines and translated the tale of bandits who capture a girl on her wedding night. An old woman, attempting to assuage the bride's misery, tells her the myth of Psyche and Amor. Psyche is a young princess and Amor the god of love, who becomes enraptured of her.

Engrossed in the story, the young women did not hear footsteps in the hall. The library door flung open, and Abigail and Alice, both blushing, leaped to their feet.

Abigail curtseyed and greeted a stout, balding, middle-aged man with bushy eyebrows. He wore tan breeches and a pale-blue velvet doublet besmirched by dust from the road.

"Father, this is my friend, Lady Alice Grantmire." Abigail looked down at her feet.

The man glared at Alice. She dipped a slight curtsey and he bowed with some effort.

"Good day, Master Smith," said Alice, a smile on her lips. He ignored her greeting and stared at the open book on the table. His face reddened. "I have grammar school Latin enough to know this is no fit reading for gentlewomen. I work day and night to give you a grand roof over your head, and this is my reward?" Scowling, he raged on. "I come home to find you gawping over lewd stuff fit only for sailors and their doxies." He swiped the book to the floor and stomped from the room.

Alice, her eyes wide as sovereigns, stared at Abigail. Then

Master Smith, his face red from exertion, returned, pulling his wife by the arm with one hand and brandishing a riding whip in the other.

"Husband, you are hurting me!" wailed Mistress Smith. He threw her into a chair, where she covered her head with her hands and wept. Abigail attempted to embrace her mother but was brushed away. "Look what you have gone and done now!" Mistress Smith moaned. "Made the master angry. We will never hear the end of it."

Her father seized Abigail and, flailing the whip, slashed her across the back. "This will learn you to behave, you baggage!" Abigail's face contorted with pain and she screamed. "Stop! Please stop!"

Alice drew back in horror. She wanted to go to her friend's aid, but her legs felt paralyzed and would not move. She tried to shout in protest, but her mouth was dry and no words came. Mistress Smith leaped from the chair and reached up to stay her husband's arm, but he threw her off.

"You are hurting her and you will tear her new dress!" cried Mistress Smith. "It cost ten pounds." Master Smith struck Abigail another few blows, then flung the whip down.

"She is fortunate I do not rip it from her back. I return from business to find my house a den of base-living and vice."

Abigail fell on the floor. "It was only a book," she sobbed.

"A book filled with wanton goddesses and their wicked lusts."

Master Smith, his cheeks purple, turned to Alice. "Go, you, and do not return." He was panting for breath. "We are good Christians in this household and want no papists breathing their idolatry into innocent minds."

Abigail howled. "Lady Alice is my only friend. I hate it here and I want to go home." She lay curled up on the thick carpet and banged her fists on the floor.

Alice felt queasy and feared she might vomit. She wanted only to disappear from this place but could not leave just yet, knowing she was the cause of Master Smith's rage. He leaned against the chimney piece, glaring at his daughter. Alice's throat tightened as she watched Abigail thrash on the floor. Seeing that her mother made no move to comfort her, Alice knelt down beside her. Abigail ignored her and continued to sob and writhe face down on the carpet. "Will she soon recover from this?" asked Alice, looking over at Mistress Smith.

"Sure she has had worse beatings many times over," said the mother, rubbing her forehead with her hand, as if to dispel a headache. "Hush now, Abigail, and stand up."

Mistress Smith turned to her husband. "I have promised Lady Alice a good dinner. I have ordered up chine of beef and cheese tart, then raspberries and custard with—"

"Madam!" said Master Smith, smacking the whip against his own leg. "You both will eat nothing but bread and small ale for the next three days. Abigail, you will remain in your chamber and repent of polluting your immortal soul with this vile book." He stopped, again having run out of breath.

"Husband, pray do not be so harsh," begged Mistress Smith, with furrowed brow and clasped hands. "It was only so—"

"Silence, wife," ordered Master Smith, puffing out his cheeks. "I am fatigued." He sat on a chair and slumped back. "Bring me refreshment. No, by Saint Christopher, wherefore do I keep all these servants? Call for one of 'em."

Mistress Smith followed Alice to the front door and sent the footman for claret and biscuits for the master. Alice watched the man smirking; no doubt he had seen and enjoyed the altercation in the library. He went off, humming an ale-house song.

"Pray excuse the master," pleaded Mistress Smith. "When he gets his dander up, he is like a raging bull, and there's no stopping him."

Alice was halfway down the front steps; Mistress Smith followed her. "I will find a way to make it up to you, I promise. He will be gone again in a few days."

She pressed a shilling into Alice's hand. At first, Alice refused to take it but then thought better of it and accepted the coin before Mistress Smith could return it to her purse.

Alice sped home to the cottage, stopping once to catch her breath. She felt her cheeks hot against her cold fingers. She was burning with shame at having been expelled from an ironmonger's house. How would she explain to Mother?

Something gave way inside Alice's mind. A surge of anger rose in her. *Why had Mother and Father needed to be so obstinate? They had forfeited manor, fortune, and fair name, when a quick lie, a stroke of the pen, could have kept them comfortably at Hartbourne forever. Just like everyone they knew had done.* Alice chided herself for these ungrateful thoughts. They were her parents…well, her mother was her only parent now.

Alice took the path to the river and sat by its edge; her feet were hot and itchy. She kicked off her clogs, tugged off the rough woolen stockings that had belonged to a woman who died in childbirth, and paddled her feet in the water. She watched a pair of herons, some twenty yards away, straighten their long necks, spread their grey wings, and fly upwards. Alice noted the sun was at its zenith. *I must go back and confess to Mother what happened.* She dried off her feet with the hem of her dress and guided one then the other into her stockings; they felt a little cooler now.

Inside the cottage, Alice found her mother holding a parchment. Lady Maud's hands shook, but then it seemed to Alice that her mother's hands always shook now. Alice felt a surge of protectiveness toward her and ran to embrace her.

"Oh, Alice," cried Lady Maud. "Yet another cross to bear for Our Lord." She flapped the parchment in front of Alice's eyes. "This came from your Aunt Joyce." She faltered. "I cannot believe it."

"Is it about William?" asked Alice, tightness gripping her throat.

"He has been arrested and is held in Newgate Prison," replied Lady Maud.

"No," whispered Alice. Her eyes grew round, and her stomach sank.

"That dreadful man, Jenkins, sought him out and has accused him of attempted murder."

"Nonsense," replied Alice, trying to keep the tremor out of her voice. "The man received a cut to his cheek, but he killed poor Stewart…"

Dickie and John came through the door. "Nonsense, nonsense, murder, murder," echoed Dickie. He pulled the poker from beside the grate and flourished it above his head.

"Now, Master Dickon," entreated John, "give me that."

Dickie held John at bay with the poker. "Nonsense means no brains. A poker to the head and John will have no brains, then his head will be full of nonsense."

John managed to wrestle the poker away from him and nudged him out the door, saying, "I need you to help me make a bonfire, to get rid of all the weeds we have been digging up."

"A bonfire," echoed Dickie. "A bone fire. I would like that."

Alice, desolate, stared at her mother. "I must go to Sir William," she said.

"Alice, you cannot," protested Lady Maud, her eyes wide with horror. "Do you think you would be accorded the scantest respect, a poor, young, unmarried woman visiting a gaol cell? Any man you met could misuse you…"

"John could come," Alice began, but she stopped mid-sentence. She knew Goody and her mother could not, between them, cope with Dickie.

Alice noted how sharply her mother's cheekbones showed beneath the skin of her face. Lady Maud gave a deep rattling cough.

I will find a way to see you again, my own William. Aloud, Alice said, "Let me brew a decoction of hyssop for you."

"I have tried that, and also a mullein brew, but my catarrh seems not to want to mend." Lady Maud smiled, almost apologetically.

She opened her arms and Alice entered her mother's embrace.

What am I to do? thought Alice. *Mother is dying, but what if they hang William without our being able, at least, to say goodbye to each other?*

A horrid thought came to her and she collapsed onto the stool behind her. She felt the blood drain from her face, and her hands shook in her lap. If it were discovered William was a papist and a dispossessed knight, he would not be beheaded as a nobleman but burned at the stake as a commoner. She knew that a merciful gaoler would sometimes tie a pouch of gunpowder around the victim's head so that when she or he was half-burned it would explode. Alice clenched her hands to stop them shaking, but they still shook. Her stomach churned at the thought that the best she could pray for was that William's skull exploded to save him the excruciating agony of burning alive. In her mind, she could almost hear his screams.

Alice looked at her mother. She could tell from her eyes that she was aware of the full import of William's sentence.

Lady Maud fell to the floor.

he chill in the pre-dawn air woke Gareth. He stretched, waking Corwen, who croaked and glared at him. The flames on Peredur's pyre had died down, and Gareth had one more duty to perform—to cast his master's harp onto the glowing embers. He was loath to destroy such a beautiful instrument, and, with reverence, moved his hands over the harp's carved breasts. Remembering the last night Peredur had played in hall, he thought of Hester. She could not be pregnant by the King, as people said, but yet she was not virgin, else she would have died on the pyre. Gareth held his head in his hands a minute. The wound throbbed and he could not think straight.

He took the ring from his pocket. The engraving, "Henricus Rex," was plain, but he could not decipher the worn inscription beside it. The sun rose and in its light he read "Elizabeth." How did Hester come to have this ring? Gareth reassured himself she said she was safe and would explain all later. He strummed the harp strings, but the sound was discordant, no matter how he adjusted the pegs. It was a sign. Taking a deep in-breath, Gareth cast the harp upon the glowing remains of the fire. The wood took flame and the strings snapped.

Peredur's voice spoke. "Hester is in danger. Go now! Only she can minister to the goddess's daughter."

Gareth, shocked, half-expected to see his master rise from the flames. He collected himself and staggered back to the village, with Corwen perched on his shoulder.

Evan the Ear greeted him. "Master Gareth, you look like a new-buried corpse."

Gareth grimaced. "Yea, but I must find Mistress Vaughan."

"I'm sorry to tell you, she is newly wed and gone with Mervyn."

Gareth choked. "She would never have married that weasel of her own accord. Where are they?"

"Lord Dafydd's old house. Go past the tomb of Dinas Emrys, turn inland for a mile, then follow the river uphill for another ten. You will see it, for it is the only dwelling for miles around."

"Thank you, my friend," replied Gareth.

Gareth and Corwen entered their old rooms. Gareth brushed away tears as he collected his harp and, rummaging at the bottom of an old chest, found a small bag of silver. He packed a loaf of barley bread and a jug of ale then fetched his pony and Lady from the stables. With Corwen clucking in his ear, he gave a shilling to Evan and rode out through the gates into the rising sun.

◈

Hester dreamed she was lying in a coffin with the witch hammering the lid shut. She shouted, "But I am alive!"

She woke to the thudding of horses' hooves. Blackie hid under the bed while Hester ran to the window and waved to Gareth. "Bless him, and he has brought Lady!" Blackie followed her downstairs. Hester could open only one eye. The other throbbed and she remembered Mervyn hitting her. But when she went to the landing, she could see that Mervyn still lay sprawled at the foot of the stairs, his leg twisted under him.

Hester and Gareth embraced, and Hester sobbed with relief. But when Gareth took her hands in his she drew back in pain.

He looked at her thumb. "This redness looks ill, indeed." He felt the joint. "It is hot, too." He looked at her face. "Your eye is bruised, also."

"Mervyn did it," she mumbled.

Blackie ran over to Mervyn and barked. Mervyn opened his eyes and muttered, "Devil take you, dog!" then lost consciousness again.

"He's alive," observed Gareth. "Did he…force himself on you?"

Hester bit her lip. "No, he only tried."

Gareth scowled and the veins on his forehead stood out. "He is fortunate then. Otherwise I would kill him as he lies there."

Hester had never seen Gareth angry before; she felt frightened and happy at the same time. "I physicked his wine and then Blackie tripped him on the stairs and he fell."

"Let us pray he never discovers the truth." Gareth took her good hand. "Now let us go."

Hester snatched her hand away to run upstairs. When she returned she said, "This is all that is left to me of my mother. It was her wedding dress." She clutched the damaged skirt against her chest.

"Have you nothing else to wear other than your petticoat?" asked Gareth, perplexed.

Hester shook her head, so he took off his cloak and draped it over her shoulders. "Who else lives here?"

"Only a deaf servant in the back."

Gareth stuffed the ruined dress into one saddle bag and Blackie, yipping with excitement, into the other. Hester greeted her pony, "Oh, Lady, it is good to see you again," and Lady snickered in recognition. As Gareth helped her mount, he murmured, "My love is sore injured and can barely ride, Corwen has his broken wing, and now I have a pup missing a leg."

Mid-morning, they rested near a rocky outcrop in a gorse-strewn field.

"Where are we going?" asked Hester, chewing on a crust of bread.

"To Holywell, on the English border. Remember I was telling you before those brutes came?"

"Yes, then one hit you on the head."

"If we travel hard, we will reach the shrine of Saint Winifred tomorrow evening."

Hester whispered, "Where lie Mother's remains." She spoke a

little louder. "Gareth, I must needs tell you about what befell me before ever we met."

Unless she told him about Henry now, she might never again find it in herself to do so.

Gareth took her bruised face between his hands and kissed her gently on the forehead. "Yes, dear heart, but we can talk tomorrow. All that matters is that you are safe and we are together."

They passed the night in an abandoned barn; Hester slept up in the loft with Blackie curled in her arms, and Gareth lay himself down on a pile of straw below. Corwen cawed several times before settling on a stunted apple tree close by.

Next morning Gareth asked, "Dear heart, will you say how you came to marry that wretch?"

Hester turned her face away. Only the moment of their meeting had held force enough to break down the barrier of her shame. Now, she felt as if a stone wall had gone up that she was unable to bring down. She felt feverish and her hand throbbed, and she could not bend her wrist. She drank a little ale.

Gareth tried again. "Hester, please talk to me."

"When we get to Holywell, where Mother is buried." Her eyes glazed over.

"Ah," said Gareth, sensing her distance. He changed the subject. "I heard Peredur speak from the flames of his pyre. He said you will aid the goddess when she returns. I did not, I do not understand…"

Without thinking, Hester touched his arm with her injured hand. She moaned and drew it back.

"Oh, my dear, your whole wrist is red and swollen now, and to me it looks poisoned. The nuns will know how to heal it, but we must make haste."

Gareth helped her mount. It took all of Hester's strength to sit upright. When Lady moved forward, she uttered a cry of pain as the reins jolted her hand.

It was a cool, bright morning. The sun shone against the highest crags of the mountains, and dew sparkled on the grass as they set out along the Roman road to Holywell. Lady settled into a canter, and the regular rhythm soothed Hester and she was able, for a time, to ignore the pain in her hand. She tried to banish Mervyn from her mind. She worried whether Gareth still loved her and berated herself. *I should have told him about Henry when he asked me to marry him.*

At noon they dismounted in a copse to eat and rest. Hester could not look directly at Gareth. She sat against a tree, hunched forward; she had no appetite and picked at her bread. Blackie scampered for the crumbs she dropped for him.

Corwen flew down for his share, and Blackie hid under Hester's cloak.

"I love you," said Gareth, "and shall not love you any the less for things that might have happened in the past. But it is hard for me to imagine that you and Henry..." He did not finish the sentence. "Hester, it took me some trouble to come to you, though it matters not a whit, if only you will talk to me."

Hester looked up and saw that his wound had reopened. She pulled out her mother's crumpled dress, kissed it, and tore off a strip. She bandaged Gareth's head, but awkwardly, using just the one hand. When her fingers touched his skin, Gareth startled; he felt her forehead and she cringed away.

"Hester, you are hot as burning coals. Drink this," he urged.

She took the flask, gulped down half its contents, and soon fell asleep. She moaned and ground her teeth while she slept.

Gareth knew it was not simply physical pain, or delirium that caused Hester to flinch from his touch. It was because he was a man, and Hester could not distinguish between him and those who had hurt her. He drew a little comfort in that she had sacrificed her mother's dress to bind his broken head.

They reached the shrine at dusk, when the larks were swooping low in the fields. Crows called from tree to tree, and Corwen joined in the fracas.

Gareth slammed the rapper on the door of the main building. Footsteps approached and he called into the iron grill. "I bring Hester Vaughan, who is ill and in need of the good sisters' aid."

A fair-haired girl with a small purple birthmark on her forehead undid the door bolts. She beckoned them in, and Gareth carried Hester, unconscious, into a spacious parlour and set her down on a wide, cushioned bench. A writing desk stood by a curtained window, a fine book cabinet took up one wall, and two armchairs and stools were grouped around a stone fireplace.

The girl stood in the doorway, wrapping and unwrapping her hands in her apron. "I am Myfanwy, please you, sir." At first Gareth thought she was a child of ten, but on second glance realized she must be about fourteen.

"Pray fetch the sister in charge of the infirmary." Gareth's voice rasped with desperation.

While he waited, he looked up at a painting above the hearth. Mary was holding the infant Jesus, who was blowing into a dandelion puffball, scattering its seeds in all directions, to the obvious delight of His mother.

Myfanwy returned, accompanied by a slender woman dressed in a grey habit, with a carved boxwood rosary hanging from her waist.

"I am Sister Agnes, and is this Hester Vaughan? By Our Lady, this must be the daughter of Margaret Vaughan, our late benefactress."

Hester groaned and tried to sit up but could not.

"Her mother's name was Margaret, but Sister, she is very sick." Gareth was exhausted, he could barely stay awake. "It started with a crushed thumb, but now it is her entire arm, and she is fevered and cannot eat."

"Our infirmary is full to overflowing, but we have one empty cell. Follow me." She said to the maid, "Myfanwy, you, too."

Gareth carried Hester and placed her on a cot in a tiny room, which contained a stool and a rough-hewn table, on which stood a wooden crucifix.

Sister Agnes examined Hester's hand. "This looks ill, but she is young and will mend, God willing."

Hester screamed, "Get away, don't touch me! Mother, where are you? Please come out now!"

The nun ordered Myfanwy, "Tell Sister Dorothy to prepare a comfrey poultice and a decoction of valerian." The little maid ran down the hallway.

Gareth sank down on the stool, his head in his hands.

Blackie appeared in the doorway and leaped up and licked Hester's face.

"Get down!" shouted Gareth.

"So you have brought another supplicant to Holywell." Sister Agnes stroked Blackie's head. "I misdoubt even the miraculous waters of Saint Winifred can do aught for his missing leg."

She looked at Gareth's head. "We will change that bandage tomorrow, but right now, you need rest."

"Thank you, Sister." Gareth's eyes were already closed. "And our horses?"

"They will be tended to."

Myfanwy returned with Sister Dorothy, a short, dark young woman, smelling of peppermint. She curtseyed to Sister Agnes and gave Gareth a quizzical glance, then applied a poultice to Hester's hand.

Hester moaned but was too weak to struggle. Sister Agnes gave her a draught of valerian to ensure she slept well.

"May the good Lord and His Blessed Mother watch over and heal this young woman. Keep her safe under the roof of Saint

Winifred's, and when her days upon this earth are done, in accordance with thy will, bring her to everlasting life. "

Gareth, Myfanwy, and Sister Dorothy responded, "Amen." Sister Dorothy stayed to keep watch over the patient, and Sister Agnes, after telling Myfanwy to take Blackie to the kitchen, led Gareth back to her parlour.

"Oh," exclaimed Gareth, "I have forgotten Corwen."

"Your groom?" inquired Sister Agnes.

"No, my master's lame crow."

"It will be fine with the horses," she assured him. "Now, pray tell, are you kin to Mistress Vaughan?"

Gareth smiled through his fatigue. "Sister, my name is Gareth ap Fychan, recently apprenticed to a great bard, who died just two days ago." He brushed away tears. "Mistress Vaughan and I are betrothed." He sighed. "But it is complicated, for she was recently married to another, against her will. That man crushed her thumb, but fortunately the marriage was not…" Gareth could not bring himself to say the word *consummated*.

Sister Agnes nodded. "It is good you brought her here. The Vaughans were great benefactors of the shrine before King Henry took their lands." She gazed up at the painting of Mary and Jesus with the dandelion puffball. "Much grief has accompanied the adoption of the King's new religion, with no hope of its being assuaged."

"My master foretold the coming of a goddess for that very purpose." Gareth stared into the empty grate, realizing how odd he must sound, especially in a Christian shrine. "Not the goddess herself, exactly, but the Lady Elizabeth, as the personification…" He was too tired to explain. He could feel the wound on his head throbbing, and he put up his hand to it.

Sister Agnes nodded. "That cannot wait. I shall re-dress it now."

She withdrew scissors and a linen bandage from a leather pouch at her waist and set to work.

"It is bleeding only a little," she said. "I shall look at it again in the morning."

"Thank you for your care," said Gareth. "We have some monies…"

"Keep your silver. Later you may look at our roof. Henry's men removed part of the lead, so it leaks."

"Willingly."

"Although we were fortunate compared to some of our neighbouring monasteries." Sister Agnes clenched her hands. "Compared to the atrocities suffered by…"

Gareth's eyes had closed and he was snoring. The nun gently roused him. "I will send for bedding. You may sleep here by the hearth tonight."

Gareth bid Sister Agnes goodnight. Myfanwy came with blankets, and as he lay down he felt the ruby ring digging into his side. He threw it beside the grate, where it glared malevolently at him, or so he imagined, then a few moments later he was asleep.

※

Sister Agnes entered Hester's cell early the next morning. Sister Dorothy told her she had woken twice in the night with fever, so she had given her powdered willow bark.

"Well done. You may go," said Sister Agnes, with a nod of approval.

Hester woke. "Where am I?" she mumbled. "I have to leave; he mustn't find me."

"You are at the shrine of Saint Winifred," replied the nun. "You have a bruised eye and your hand is badly wounded. You need rest."

"Where is Blackie?"

"Cook is taking care of him."

Hester's eyes darted around the room. "Where is he?"

"Master Gareth is—"

Hester interrupted, "No, my—oh God forbid—my husband! He will come after me. But he may not be my husband because he did not…" Hester clutched Sister Agnes's robe with her good hand. "He will track me down so he can do it, then he...but no, his leg is broken, he cannot..."

Sister Agnes soothed her. "You are in sanctuary now. Not even King Henry can harm you here."

"Henry!" moaned Hester. "Oh, dear God, will he come after me too? Mother! Where are you? You are here, under the ground, hiding from me! Why do you send the witch in your place?" She writhed in delirium and tears poured down her cheeks.

Sister Agnes urged a draught of black henbane between Hester's lips. It felled her into unconsciousness. The nun murmured, "If I could only get my hands on the man who did this to her."

She looked up and saw Sister Dorothy in the doorway and gave a wry laugh. "Three days on bread and water for me, as penance for uncharitable thoughts. I will see to her friend now. Pray inform me when Mistress Vaughan wakes."

Sister Agnes headed to her parlour, her wooden clogs sounding on the stone floor, and her rosary swishing against the skirts of her habit.

Gareth was stirring awake beside the hearth.

"How fares your head?" asked Sister Agnes.

He rose and yawned. "Well enough, thank you, Sister. How is Mistress Vaughan?" then realizing his rudeness, added, "Oh, and how are you?"

"I am well, but I fear our patient's spirit is equally damaged with her hand."

Gareth sat in despair with his head between his hands.

Sister Agnes removed the bandage. "Your head is mending well."

Gareth looked at the fabric she had removed. "That was not on my head before."

"No, there was a piece of old silk binding your wound."

Gareth leaped up. "I must get the dress for her!" He explained that Hester had clung to the remnants of her mother's old wedding gown as if her life depended upon it. "She tore off a piece to make a bandage. The dress is still in my saddlebag."

"Sit you still, while I rebind your head," ordered Sister Agnes. "The dress can wait. Another day on the road and Mistress Vaughan's hand would have gone to gangrene. It is fortunate you arrived when you did. Dresses can be replaced, limbs cannot." The nun completed her task and turned her attention to the ring lying in the grate. "That is a very fine gem." She picked it up and read aloud the band's inscription. "'Henricus Rex,' and beside it, quite faded away, 'Elizabeth.'" She frowned. "I would hazard this once belonged to the King's mother, Elizabeth of York. How came you by it?"

"Hester gave it to me, to mind," said Gareth, placing it in his pocket. "We planned to sell it so we could reach London and find her family." He told her about Dafyyd's death, Sir Hugh's arrest, and how Lady Maud, Alice, and Dickie were sheltering in the remains of a convent outside London.

"But how came Mistress Vaughan by this ring?"

"I wish I knew," groaned Gareth. "Rumour was that she and Henry…" He reddened.

Sister Agnes interposed, "Many troubled young women seek counsel here, and I have learned to distinguish, over time, those who have enjoyed a man's embrace from those who have not. I doubt Mistress Vaughan is one of the first category." She spoke more briskly. "And now, you may attend Matins, then after breakfast, make yourself useful."

Gareth's countenance cleared. "Thank you, Sister, for your words, but surely I may sit outside her door and play my harp, at least for today. The music will lift her spirits."

"Later, for an hour this evening." Sister Agnes nodded. "I mentioned our roof is in sore need of repairs. Your head is near healed, and you are strong and agile enough to work up there without risk of falling and breaking your neck." She laughed. "We have no need of more invalids requiring Saint Winifred's miraculous cures."

lice and Goody carried Lady Maud upstairs. Her cough was worse; she ate nothing and could barely drink the teas Alice made. Two days later she was still confined to bed.

The sun beat down on Alice's back as she weeded out daisies from among the parsley and chamomile. The herb beds flowed over the edges of the garden. Purple-flowered lavender vied for precedence over yellow calendula and grey sage. The scent in the warm air served as a temporary balm to Alice's spirits, but much of the time now, she felt close to despair. She did not sleep at night because of Mother's cough and also from worry over William. She fretted about how long they could live on the few coppers she had stowed under the bolster, since only the rare patient could afford to part with more than a half-penny for their physick. Alice forcefully averted her eyes from a pile of rocks near the barn door. If life became unbearable, she would sew some into the hem of her dress and walk into the river. Alice had identified which rocks she would use. The Church deemed suicide the worst sin, as it was the only one which could not be repented of, but she did not care. She felt there should be a limit to the amount of suffering in this life.

The steady hack-hack of Lady Maud's cough coming through the unshuttered bedroom window jangled Alice's nerves. She glared at the weeds as she ripped them up by the roots. Then the cough became a laboured wheeze.

Alice straightened. *Poor Mother, her pillow must have fallen.* Alice grunted. *Not a pillow, an old sack stuffed with straw. Why has Goody not gone to see to her?* She remembered; her old nurse had gone to market to try to sell bunches of their lavender.

Up in the loft, Alice retrieved the pillow from the floor and propped her mother upright, and Lady Maud's breathing eased. Alice sat and caressed her mother's dirt-grimed hand, noticing how loosely her gold wedding ring sat on her finger.

Lady Maud frowned. "I am very cold, dear."

"Mother, I am sorry, but I do not know what can be done. You are wearing your two dresses, and we have but the one blanket." In frustration, Alice bit down on the inside of her cheek.

"Read to me," said Lady Maud. She pointed to the psalter beside her. Alice picked it up, glancing at her broken nails and callused fingers. She looked at the Latin text. Oh, if only she had never touched that volume of *The Golden Ass*, she would have earned enough from tutoring Abigail to buy Mother a feather pillow and three woolen blankets.

Alice opened the book to an antiphon of Our Lady, inscribed beneath a picture of the Virgin enthroned in Heaven. She wore a crown of stars and smiled upon the world, while angels blew on trumpets and played string instruments around her.

Alice began, *"Alma Redemptoris Mater—"*

She was interrupted by a rap at the door and someone shouting. "I am Master Simon Black with a warrant for the arrest of Maud Grantmire. Open up in the King's name."

Lady Maud sank back on her pillow, her face whiter than a snowdrop petal.

"Have no fear, there must be some mistake," Alice told her mother, stooping to kiss her cheek. She descended the ladder to find a heavy-set man standing in the entrance. His head was tiny in comparison to the bulk of his body. *Like a turnip balanced on a sack of flour*, thought Alice. She gripped the railing in both hands and prayed she would not giggle. *I am coming undone*, she thought, in terror. *Please God, no more imprisonments, no more deaths.* Alice took a deep breath to steady herself.

"I am Alice, Lady Maud Grantmire's daughter. What is the charge against my mother, Master Black?" she asked.

The man opened the paper and peered at the words. He scowled. "Witchcraft." He crossed himself, as did Alice.

"That cannot be," she declared. "Look around you. We brew herbal teas, remedies for simple ailments, like the pleurisy and the fever and the strangury. There are no grimoires or poppets here."

The man's eyes travelled the room. He frowned and nodded. "I had the strangury myself, a few months ago, and mightily glad I was of the wise woman's brew. By the Devil's hind hoof, without it, the pain would nigh have killed me."

"Yes, Master Black," said Alice, "and you visited a wise woman when you had the kidney stone and not a physician, and why, sir, was that?" *Perhaps he can be made to see sense*, thought Alice, *and he will leave us in peace.*

"He would have charged six shillings. Who can afford a physician at that price, except rich folks?"

"Indeed," agreed Alice. "So my lady mother, together with my nurse and myself, treat the poor at a price they can afford."

Master Black heaved a sigh. "The wise woman I consulted died in a snowdrift two years ago. They evicted her from her hut because she owned a black cat, and that was proof she consorted with Satan."

Alice clenched her jaw and strangled a gasp of terror. "Who accuses us?"

The man looked with an uncertain glance at the paper again. "It says here that the apothecary's wife's lettuces have all shrivelled and died, that her sister-in-law miscarried, and that her neighbour's cow has gone dry. All this is all laid to your charge."

The apothecary's wife. Alice remembered the day she had come looking for a remedy and how Dickie had said she smelled of sulphur. Alice felt dizzy and sat on a stool. *Of course, they must have lost customers, and so this charge.*

"I am merely carrying out my duties," said Black. "The warrant names you also, Alice Grantmire, in addition to one Goody… there is no surname for her."

Alice heard her mother descending the rungs of the ladder. She held the missal in one hand, still open to the page showing Mary, as Queen of Heaven. Alice helped her mother down the last step and from the corner of her eye saw Master Black bow to the picture of the Virgin, then straighten himself. His face flushed and he shifted his feet in embarrassment.

"So you are Maud Grantmire," said he. Lady Maud nodded. "You had best hide that popish work. You do not want to be charged with heresy in addition to witchcraft."

"I am glad to see you retain respect for the Blessed Virgin," said Lady Maud. "I imagine it is hard to become accustomed to the new ways."

Master Black made a slight bow then scratched his head. "Truly it is, my lady. The statues of the saints gone from church, and their candles too. But worst of all is the Mother of God taken from us."

"I understand, sir," said Lady Maud. A fit of coughing overtook her and she steadied herself against the table. Alice rubbed her back.

Goody entered carrying a basket of bread.

"What is this now?" she demanded of Master Black.

"I suppose you are Goody," said the man, "also accused of witchcraft."

Goody shrieked and dropped the basket on the floor. She tore off her linen coif and wailed. "No! Not that!"

"Hush now, Goody, all will be well," admonished Lady Maud. "The Lord has told me so." She helped Goody replace her coif. Goody sat and buried her face in her apron, sobbing.

"Where are you taking us, Master Black?" asked Lady Maud.

"The inn at Brentford has a cellar. You will be imprisoned there until an escort can conduct you to Newgate, where you will await trial. Mayhap the escort will be assembled by the time we reach Brentford and can take you direct to Newgate."

Newgate. I will see William before we both die, thought Alice.

But then she realized, how would she ever find him among the hundreds of prisoners?

Lady Maud wheezed and could not catch her breath.

"Sit down, Mother," implored Alice. "Master Black can allow us a few minutes." She took her mother's shaking hands in her own.

"We are being sorely tried indeed, daughter, but we shall keep faith. God sees our plight and will deliver us." Lady Maud sat upright, dry-eyed, and offered her handkerchief to Alice, as tears rolled down her daughter's cheeks. "However, I doubt I can walk to Brentford," said Lady Maud, between coughs.

Black sighed. "I shall have to send for the cart."

"No!" cried Alice. She recalled seeing the poor woman in Brentford tied into a cart. Alice thought being transported in a cart would be tantamount to an admission of their guilt for a crime they had not committed. "Goody and I can support you, Mother. Let us try to walk…"

"What is this?" cried Dickie, stepping through the doorway. "Who is this giant? How dare he distress you ladies?" He lifted a shovel resting on the doorpost.

John arrived behind him carrying a barrel of water on his shoulder. He set it down and ran to Dickie, just as he lunged at Master Black's chest with the blade of the shovel.

"Go back to your lord Satan, I bid thee!" shouted Dickie. "Leave these innocent women in peace."

John wrenched the shovel from Dickie's grip as Master Black pulled out his musket.

Dickie fell, convulsing, to the floor. Black crossed himself. "He is possessed by a demon. Surely this is, indeed, a house of witch-craft." His hands shook as he replaced his weapon in his belt.

John placed the wooden spoon between Dickie's teeth.

"Why doest thou that?" demanded Master Black. "Surely you should rather use a crucifix."

John looked up, frowning. "It is so he does not bite his tongue."

"He has the falling sickness," said Alice.

"He needs a priest to cast out the demon," retorted Black. "But I have no warrant for him. So come on, you women, for we have a journey to make."

Alice insisted she be allowed upstairs to change into her good black dress; she swept up her little pile of copper coins and thrust them in her pocket. She checked under her mother's side of the mattress. Nothing, so she must have her rosary beads with her. Alice descended to find Black peering into jars of herbs, while Lady Maud and Goody stood hugging each other.

Dickie had not fully regained consciousness as the women departed, but John was there on the floor beside him, holding his hand.

Lady Maud, Goody, and Alice each grasped John's free hand in turn.

"God bless you, John. Do not be afraid for us," said Lady Maud.

"God bless you too, ladies." He swiped a tear from his eyes.

Master Black escorted the women from the cottage.

"I would have liked to say goodbye to Dickie," said Lady Maud.

"I also," said Alice, but she felt that saying goodbye aloud might mean they would never meet again. She mentally said goodbye to Mirabel, whom she had planned to spend time with that afternoon, but added *just for now*. Until she knew for a fact that William was dead, she would not give up hope.

As they set off on the path to Brentford, Alice wondered how her mother would ever survive a night in prison and sent up prayers for Mother, for Goody, for Father, for William, and for herself. But uppermost in her mind was: *We shall be dead and buried before the week's end.* Her knees shook and she nearly made both herself and her mother stumble. Goody kept her eyes down; she prayed and sobbed quietly. Lady Maud's steps faltered, yet she insisted on walking unaided. She, too, prayed under her breath.

Master Black sidled up to Alice. "Well, my sweet," he whispered, "you be good to me and maybe we save you from hanging." He stroked her cheek with his finger. "You understand me, honey?

I could tell them you were a good girl, not Satan's consort, like the other two."

Alice shot him a look of pure loathing. Then she rolled her eyes and fell to the ground. She shook her arms and legs and, jerking her head, ground her teeth.

Black jumped back from her and crossed himself.

Lady Maud rushed to her daughter's side while Goody broke off a twig from a nearby tree to place between Alice's teeth. As she kneeled to do so, Alice whispered, "He shall not have his way of me."

Goody and Lady Maud nodded in understanding.

Goody wailed, "Oh my poor young mistress, afflicted just like her cousin. This terrible curse on the family!"

Lady Maud stood by, weeping and praying silently over Alice.

Black stood several feet away, reciting the Lord's Prayer aloud. After a minute, Alice left off shaking her body and spat out the twig. Lady Maud and Goody helped her up, then Alice looked around her, pretending to be dazed, brushed the dust from her dress, and addressed her mother. "Oh, I must have taken a fit. But I am fine now, so I suppose we must continue on."

Black's face was haggard. He looked at Alice with horror-filled eyes, and when they resumed their journey he made sure that Goody and Lady Maud walked between him and Alice.

Alice's mouth was dry and her stomach cramped, but she knew she was safe. Master Black's fear of madness outweighed his lust. Lady Maud, leaning on Alice, prayed her Ave Marias, while Goody, her head down, walked on. Her lips moved, but not a word escaped them.

A pelting rain began as they entered Brentford. Alice shivered as her dress became soaked through. Water ran down both Goody's and her mother's backs, and their hands were trembling. *Perhaps we will die of pleurisy before they hang us*, thought Alice.

They passed the apothecary's shop and the goodwife stepped outside. "See the witches!" she cried. "To the pond, neighbours, to swim them!" Then every door on the street was flung open to shouts of "Damn the witches!" "Death to the Devil's own!" with the occasional plea, "But those wise women helped us, don't harm them!"

A group of boys hurled refuse, horse dung, and rotted vegetables at the three of them. From one window the contents of a piss pot just missed Alice's head. As they turned a corner a gang of men with pitchforks charged at them, and Master Black fled into an alleyway. Their leader, a tall man with an eye patch, laughed. "A fine guard he is." He turned to the women. "We hear that two of you are high-born ladies, no doubt with friends among the London judges." He spat in the street. "Here in Brentford we like to see justice done proper-like to witches, even if they be rich ones."

His cronies jabbed at the women, and Goody fell to the ground. A man kicked her in the ribs. "Get up, crone!" he shouted, but she could not rise, even with Alice and Lady Maud's help.

"A swim will do you good, witch! Wash the Devil from you before you hang," said he, yanking her upright.

The men forced the three women around the corner to the village pond. On its banks stood the apothecary's wife, with several women on either side of her. Alice stopped, her heart racing and her stomach frozen.

"On you go," said the leader. Alice turned to look at him.

"Don't look at me, witch," he said, shielding his face with his arm.

He jabbed at Alice, and she moved out of reach. Lady Maud put her arm around her shoulders, and they walked together to the edge of the pond.

Alice focused her gaze on a pair of ducks that flew off, outraged by the noise.

"Take your hex off my lettuces," cried the apothecary's wife.

"They never attend Mass!" shouted another woman. "They would choke if they ate the host."

"Papists! Heretics! Burn them, hanging's too good for the Devil's spawn!"

"My cow won't give milk!" cried one. "You cast the evil eye upon her!"

"My grandson was stillborn. Roast in hell, you foul witches!"

Her mind frozen, Alice stared at the rain making pockmarks in the water's surface. Two of the men lifted Goody and threw her into the pond; she landed on her back and her dress ballooned outward.

"She floats! The witch floats!" yelled a boy.

Two other men with long poles, to which metal hooks were attached, reached toward Goody. "No!" Alice cried, thinking they planned to rip Goody's flesh apart. "What are they doing?" she asked her mother.

"I am afraid they are hauling her in," replied Lady Maud. "Goody didn't sink, which proves, in their eyes, she is a witch."

Alice groaned and covered her face with her hands. Her mother held her tight.

The youth she had encountered outside the chandler's a few weeks ago called to one of his companions and pointed at her. "This pretty witch looks worth swyving."

"God's balls!" exclaimed his companion. "Would you tup a woman who has been fubbed by a goat?"

The youth's jaw dropped open.

"That's how Satan comes to them," explained the man with the eye patch.

"No, maybe not," replied the youth, his face reddening. The men laughed.

"Your cock would drop off, most like," added his crony, making the sign of the cross.

The man with the eye patch told Alice and her mother to remove their shoes. The men with pitchforks prodded them along, through the long grass and into the water. Alice felt the ooze of mud between her toes and tiny darting movements around her ankles. She told herself it was only mud and fish, but she stopped, paralyzed by terror.

"Swim the witches, hang the witches," chorused the crowd.

"Be quicker about it," said a man behind her, jabbing her in the shoulder with a pitchfork.

Lady Maud, beside her, stumbled, and when she tried to regain her footing, found she was out of her depth. She cast a loving look toward Alice and wrapped her arms tight around herself. The weight of her sodden garments pulled her skeletal frame underwater.

"No, Mother!" shrieked Alice, trying to thrash her way to Lady Maud. But although Alice's woolen dress was heavy, air had gotten trapped under it and buoyed her up. She felt a jab in her neck and saw a red cloud swirl in the water.

"I have her," said a man holding a hooked pole. "In you come, my floating darling. The noose awaits you, provided you don't burn for a papist."

A minute later, Alice stood dripping on the grass with Goody beside her. Both vomited pond water mixed with bile. Alice heard the approach of a cart and marching men. She looked up to see a white-haired gentleman garbed in a black, fur-trimmed gown striding toward them, followed by six sergeants-at-arms.

The elderly official addressed the man with the eye patch. "According to the King's law, the accused must be tried before sentencing." Two sergeants seized him. His men fled and were pursued by another pair of officers. Most of the villagers, grumbling, returned to their homes.

The remaining two sergeants escorted Alice and Goody to a cart. Its driver was a middle-aged man with a bald pate and wearing a brown leather jerkin, sitting hunched over in the rain. Alice stared toward the pond, willing her mother to walk out of it. It was unbelievable that Mother should have been alive five minutes ago, and now she was dead.

Alice heard the apothecary's wife, her voice shrill with self-importance. "Your Excellency, I have a niece who went to see those women with a sore foot. The old one asked her if she was with child, and when my niece said no, the old one gave her a posset that would dislodge the babe if ever she should be wanting rid of one."

Alice gasped in disbelief. "That woman lies!" she shouted. "She seeks our destruction because her husband, the apothecary, was losing custom to us."

The official frowned and his eyebrows met in the centre of his forehead. He looked at Alice. "She shall be questioned. At present, you are the ones under arrest."

He handed the driver of the cart a parchment with an official seal. "Give this to the gaoler at Newgate. It has the names and charges. You will need to say that the woman Maud Grantmire has died."

The driver touched his cap. "It shall be done, master."

Alice climbed into the cart, but she could not leave her mother's body sunk in this pond with not a single prayer said over her. "My mother is drowned," she said to the driver, "and I must lay out her body for burial." She wondered out loud where she would find the money to pay the coffin-maker, the sexton, and the priest. Alice's thoughts became muddled. She realized she would need to sell Mother's rosary to pay for the burial. But the rosary was still in Mother's pocket and would probably be stolen by the men who pulled her corpse ashore. The rosary that had caused cruel words between them, words she very much regretted now.

"Others will attend to that," the cart driver said, "but she will be buried outside the church yard."

"Outside?" faltered Alice. "Why outside?"

The driver looked at her and sighed. He rubbed his bald patch. "A witch cannot be buried in sanctified ground."

"But she was not a witch, for she did not float." *Like Goody and I did*, Alice thought. She felt that, by floating herself, she had somehow betrayed her mother. But her teeth chattered from the cold, and she could not talk anymore. She heard a horse galloping toward them. *It is William, come to rescue us.* But her hope was dashed when a female voice called out, "Stop! What is happening here?"

"These women are witches," said a sergeant. "They were swam and they floated."

Abigail gasped when she saw Alice and Goody in the cart. "Mother and I heard that some women had been arrested, and we feared for you." She turned to the sergeant. "There has been a mistake, these women are honest herbalists." She then addressed Alice, "Your lady mother is safe in the cottage, I hope?"

"She is drowned in the pond," called Alice. She was desperate that her mother's body not be interred in some field without a priest to say the prayers. Her voice hoarse, she shrieked, "See she is given a proper burial, I pray of you!"

"Stop your caterwauling, witch!" ordered the sergeant.

"Yes, of course I will." Abigail wiped tears from her eyes. "Lady Alice, be assured your lady mother will be buried with all dignity in the nuns' cemetery of Syon."

Alice collapsed into herself, exhausted but relieved. She doubted not that the Smiths' money would obtain the services of a priest and a plot in the old convent's graveyard.

"Enough of this!" The sergeant turned to Abigail. "Go about your business, Madam, unless you want to accompany them to Newgate, in which case, climb in." He ordered the driver, "Move on, you lummox!"

Alice felt tears spring to her eyes and remembered her mother saying that only kindness breaks the heart open. Mother would be glad to be interred among the good sisters. But surely Mother could not be not dead. Not Mother, who never hurt anyone in all her born days. No, she would be fine once they got her out of the pond and pumped the water out of her lungs. Tomorrow, or the day after, they would all meet back in the cottage.

The driver cracked his whip, and the horse whickered and moved on.

Alice raised an arm to wave to Abigail, who returned her salute before riding off. Alice felt a dull pain under her ear and something warm trickling down the side of her neck. She touched it and realized it was blood from where the hook had caught her and saved her from a merciful death by drowning.

Alice's mind drifted to William. Could she get a message to him? Could he save her and Goody? "Do you know of a Sir William of Bayston in Newgate?" she asked their driver.

He turned to gape at her. "Sweeting, are you a lunatic? There are hundreds in that gaol." He must have seen her entire frame shaking, for he halted the cart and took off his leather jerkin. "Here," he said. He moved to throw it to her but paused. "You are bleeding," he said, his mouth turning down in distaste. He appeared about to take his jerkin back, but he looked again at Alice and said, "Keep it." He spat over the side.

The jerkin smelled musky, but Alice was glad of the warmth.

The driver switched at the horse and it walked on. He took out a loaf from a satchel and tore off a piece and stuffed it in his mouth. He turned and threw a piece each to Goody and Alice.

Goody ate hers at once. Alice broke off crumbs and nibbled. She was thirsty more than hungry. She gave a low laugh: to be thirsty after being near drowned. Her shoulder throbbed, but she put her arms around Goody, who curled up against her and murmured prayers, pausing only to whimper when the cart wheels struck a rock in the road.

It was dusk when they entered London via Newgate. When they reached the prison entrance, Alice tried to return their driver's jerkin, but she lacked the strength to lift the heavy garment. When the man relieved her of it he seemed to be taking a long time, and Alice felt his hands encircling her waist. *Oh, just like other men*, she thought. He handed the document of charges to a gaoler, told him of Lady Maud's death, then went his way. The gaoler opened the prison doors and ushered the women into a stone-lined passageway, its walls dripping with moisture, and then down a flight of stairs. Alice and Goody, barefooted, had to take care not to slip on the wet steps. They came to a wooden table behind which the gaol keeper was eating a leg of chicken and drinking from a flagon of ale. Alice realized she was famished. The man scowled, looking up from his supper.

"Names and charges?" he asked.

The guard broke the seal on the document and read: "Alice Grantmire and Goody, no surname. Neither married. Both papists of Brentford. The charge is witchcraft and presumed heresy."

The keeper wiped his mouth and wrote the information in a ledger beside him on the table. He grunted, then rose and led the women to a cell. The sound of screaming grew louder as they approached. The keeper opened the lock on the iron door and pushed them inside. Alice retched. The smell of unwashed bodies and excrement was near palpable, and the din was what she imagined souls tortured in Hell would make if only they had voices. The cell was black as a fly's body, but after a few seconds Alice's eyes became accustomed to the dark. The only light was from a single smoking tallow candle over the door by which she could see a dozen prisoners lining each of the walls. Some were manacled. Those that were not sat on the stone floor, rocking back and forth, many of them screaming. The keeper waved his torch and indicated a corner, pushing Alice and Goody toward it. Goody stumbled and slumped to the ground. Both women put their hands over their ears to keep out the fearsome noise. Alice smelled something else that at first she could not identify above the general reek, then realized it was strong ale and that these prisoners were all drunk.

The keeper tugged Alice's hands down. "If you want food other than pottage or drink that does not taste like horse piss, it will be a shilling a day, for each of you."

"We have no money," protested Alice. She had eight halfpennies in her pocket. She was famished. How would she keep her strength up for Goody and for William, when she found him?

"What is that?" The man pointed to a leather purse attached to a string at Alice's waist. She opened it and counted five shillings. *Oh, it was our driver*, Alice realized. *God bless you, my friend.*

"Yes," she said, handing over two shillings. "Bring us something fit to eat."

The throbbing pain in her shoulder was increasing; she must get her cuts tended to before they festered. She said, "Bring me bandages, too."

The keeper took three shillings. "And two more for candles."

"How long will we be kept here?" asked Alice.

The man grunted. "Your trial is set for tomorrow," and he pocketed the money.

Goody sat up and shrieked. "Not tomorrow!" Her face was flushed.

"My nurse is ill," said Alice. "Can you send for a physician?"

The keeper laughed. "Have you ten more shillings for him to come here?"

Alice shook her head.

A few chuckles sounded from the prisoners on either side.

"Listen to her," said one bundle of rags to his neighbour. "The girl is calling for a physician." The bundle laughed aloud until a fit of coughing silenced him.

Alice looked at Goody trembling in the corner. Overcome by despair, she thought, *I would not care if I died now but for hope of seeing William. Mother is back at the cottage, or she is in Heaven. But William is somewhere in this gaol, and I am not going to die before I see him.*

The keeper returned with a bowl of thin pease pottage and a crust of rye bread. He brought clean linen clouts, and Goody managed to dress the wounds on Alice's neck and shoulder. The cell was cold as a January night, yet Alice, holding Goody close, felt her nurse's skin burning and her breath becoming faster.

The women slept, and when Alice woke the next morning, she noticed Goody had cooled to normal temperature. But she made no movement. Alice cried out and continued to scream above the noise even of the other inmates.

The keeper arrived carrying a cudgel. "Stop that infernal racket!" he ordered. Then he noticed Goody's stillness. "She is the fortunate one, isn't she?"

He hauled Alice to her feet. "The judge will see you now."

Alice, disbelieving Goody could have died in the night, stared at the body. "What will you do with her?"

"Bury it in the walls here." He spat on the ground. "Follow me."

"No!" cried Alice. "I must stay with her." She struggled against the keeper, but he shoved her out the iron door and along the corridor.

Another guard marched her up the stairs and into the sunlight. She covered her eyes to keep out the dazzle while the guard guided her across the street to the courthouse. Inside was dim and the air stale, but Alice breathed without gagging. She saw she was the only woman among a dozen prisoners to be tried. A few were in chains, but most appeared too weak to have need of restraint.

Alice felt faint from hunger, and staggered. A sergeant pointed with his halberd to a bench, and she sat. She knew her coif was stained, and in her wet dress, torn at the shoulder, she must look like a slattern, but she did not care. Mother and Goody both dead. She felt she might start to laugh from shock and disbelief, or to cry. If only William would come.

She was the first prisoner to be tried. A clerk with a hairy mole on his cheek called out, "Alice Grantmire, charged with witchcraft." A shudder ran through the room and everyone, including the judge, crossed themselves. He was a portly, bespectacled man of middle age, wearing the black robes of a lawyer.

Alice stood before his great desk and pulled herself erect.

"On what evidence?" asked the judge, shuffling parchments.

"Manufacturing potions from various and sundry herbs, my lord," replied the clerk.

"That, per se, is not witchcraft. Who fell ill or died from imbibing these potions?"

"No one directly, my lord, but the chief accuser stated that the accused's mother gave physic to a woman in order to induce a miscarriage, should one be desired."

"And did a miscarriage result?" The judge scowled down at the clerk, who shuffled his feet.

"Not as far as I know, my lord."

For the first time the judge looked directly at Alice. He removed his spectacles and shook his head. "What is your name, again?"

"Alice Grantmire, my lord."

"Surely not the daughter of Sir Hugh Grantmire?" The judge's voice quavered with disbelief.

"Yes, my lord," replied Alice.

"We were at Balliol, Oxford, together." He passed a hand before his eyes and replaced his spectacles. "I am John Speedwell. I am sorry that your father died." His face coloured and he stared down at his desk. "Few of us are as brave as he." He scowled. "This is a disgrace, that you, a lady, and presumably innocent, should be brought before this bench.

"Clerk," he ordered, "send to my house and ask Lady Speedwell to have one of my daughters' gowns delivered here."

He turned to Alice. "Pray come with me." She followed Lord Speedwell as he strode to his private chambers.

"But my lord," protested the clerk, scratching the mole on his cheek, "the other prisoners!"

"They can wait. Court is adjourned until one o'clock."

Sir John's rooms smelled of old books and leather. Alice was reminded of her father's library and felt herself about to cry but clenched her jaw and willed the tears back. Shelves of law volumes stood against the walls, and a vigorous fire burned in the grate. Sir John indicated for Alice to stand in front of it, and steam rose from her sodden garments.

The judge sat in a chair beside the hearth and asked Alice how she had come to trial for witchcraft. He listened while Alice told of her family's eviction from Hartbourne, Sir Hugh's execution, their descent into poverty, her mother's drowning, and Goody's dying last night in the gaol cell. "She was my nurse since I was an infant, and she was most loyal to my mother and to me." No longer able to control her grief, she wept. Sir John handed her a silk handkerchief, and Alice sobbed into it.

"Will you honour my family with your presence, for so long as you desire?" asked Sir John rubbing at his own eyes. "It would offer me the chance of making some slight amends to your family. I regret I allowed my friendship with your father to lapse because he possessed courage, while I, only cowardice."

"Thank you, Sir John. That is kind but unnecessary," replied Alice, forcing a smile. She twisted the handkerchief in her hands. "I would be glad to wash and have fresh clothes, but my cousin, an innocent, needs me back at Syon cottage." She frowned, "If it is not too much to ask, I would request that Goody be buried in a proper grave." She blushed and crumpled the handkerchief. "Also, I have a friend, a knight, imprisoned here in Newgate."

"What is his name and crime?" Lord Speedwell reached for a quill and parchment.

"William of Bayston, and he is falsely charged with treason." Alice clenched her jaw. "William slashed at a commissioner's face, the one who evicted us from Hartbourne. Master Jenkins had just murdered our unarmed stableman, who was trying to defend us women from his lewd advances."

"Bayston," said the judge. "Why does that name sound familiar?" His cheeks reddened. "Ah, I recall that family also refused the oath. There are times when I wish I had had the ballocks to… Excuse me, my dear, but…" His words trailed off and he stood. "I must finish the day's work, then I shall make inquiries for you."

Before leaving, Sir John ordered refreshments. Alice turned to face the fire and within a half-hour her dress was dry. A ewer of hot water and a tray holding a glass of claret, a hot pork pie, a cheese tart, and dried figs arrived. Alice washed her hands and face with rose-scented soap and dried herself with a piece of soft flannel.

Grief over her mother and Goody and anxiety over William robbed her appetite. *But I must stay strong for William*, Alice thought, and nibbled at the pie and drank the wine. *But what if he has died? For if he were alive, surely by now he would have been tried? Maybe if a person is to be burned alive for treason, they need more time to be sure he is guilty.* She began to pray for him but could not concentrate; feelings of anger toward the apothecary's wife flooded her mind. Because of her, Mother and Goody were dead. Alice hoped justice would soon come knocking on that treacherous woman's door. But the warmth of the room overcame her, and she fell asleep.

Dusk was falling when the judge returned, waking Alice. He set down a large package on a sideboard by the door and lit the candles in their sconces. "I have news for you, my dear. Sir William of Bayston escaped from Newgate three days ago."

Alice gasped and leaped from her chair. "Oh, then where is he now?"

"In one of several houses in London that harbour escapees, I would imagine," replied Sir John, seating himself. "If a man has been chained up a while it takes him a few days before he regains strength enough to ride."

William, free. Alice's spirits rose to the heavens. "Thank you! I must leave at once," said she, smiling.

"Nonsense, my dear. Best wait till the morning. Pray sit you down again."

Alice sat, her face flushed, wringing her hands in excitement. "How did he escape?"

"I understand money changed hands and your friend was smuggled out in a coffin." He stroked his chin. "Someone in the King's household was responsible. And, by the saints, the man chose the best time to escape, with the King taking four thousand guards with him up north. There is hardly anyone left in London to hunt him down."

Lady Joyce, thought Alice. *Thank you!*

"I am glad for your knight." Sir John frowned. "Even after all these years I still cannot stomach when they burn a man." He rose. "It will be near impossible to find him among the city's seventy-five thousand souls. But I have no doubt he will turn up at your dwelling soon. Meanwhile I trust you will honour my home with your presence for this night." He pointed to the package. "I will step outside while you change your garments."

"Thank you, but I would prefer to remain here, rather than impose upon your family," said Alice, yawning. "I can sleep on those two chairs brought together."

"Very well." The judge moved the chairs and gave an almost inaudible sigh of relief.

Alice understood. He would not want his wife and daughters to associate with a woman accused of witchcraft, even if she were innocent. "I shall leave at first light," said she, rubbing her eyes. Fatigue pressed on her like a millstone.

"The quickest way to Syon is by the river. My wherry-man will be waiting to escort you to the boat." Sir John banked the fire and took a purse from inside his lawyer's gown. "Please accept this."

Alice was about to refuse, but his mouth spasmed. "Do not deny me, but take it for your dear father's sake. I hope Sir Hugh, who is now in Heaven, will pray for me, a forsworn traitor to my faith and conscience, when I stand before the seat of judgment."

Alice took the purse. "Thank you."

"I hope you will remember me in your prayers."

"I am not a chantry to take your money, Sir John." Alice smiled, but the judge's face was solemn.

"But you are one of the true faith," he said, and, taking her hand, turned it over kissed her palm. Then wiping his eyes on his sleeve, the judge made his bow and left.

Alice looked inside the purse. A handful of gold sovereigns glinted at her. Even though she was near to falling over from exhaustion, she made herself take off her old clothes. She dressed in clean linen and the fine navy blue silk gown from the package. *It will save time in the morning, and by the time I get home, please God, William should be there.* She snuffed the candles and curled up in her makeshift bed. *This money would keep us for a year, but there are so few of us left. No Father, no Mother, no Goody.* She cried herself to sleep.

ust as the sun rose over the River Thames, Alice set out, carrying her black woolen dress bundled under her arm. From the boat she could see the city, with its myriad houses, one of which contained William. It would be wonderful if they arrived at the cottage at the same time, but it would depend on whether he travelled by land or by boat. *Thank you, Aunt Joyce, for William's escape, the one good thing to emerge from the horror of the past few weeks.*

It took all her self-control to refrain from asking the wherryman did he not have another oar for her to ply. Alice told him where to stop, by the weeping willow, and he helped her to shore. As she disembarked, purple thunderclouds gathered overhead and rumbling sounded in the distance. By the time she reached the cottage, forks of lightning shot down from the skies; rain pelted down and her new silk dress was drenched in seconds.

Alice opened the door of the cottage and heard movement upstairs. She called up to the loft but received no answer. Then a man's legs appeared on the steps, followed by the rest of his body.

"Greetings, Lady Alice," said the man standing before her. Alice's breath caught in her throat. It was Jenkins, the commissioner who had murdered Stewart the day her family was evicted from Hartbourne. Jenkins wore a cap pulled down over his forehead that also covered one side of his face. He smirked and made a mocking bow.

Alice turned and ran to the open door, but Jenkins moved faster and shut it.

"Where are…?" she said out loud, thinking John and Dickie must be close by. And William, he must be on his way. She shivered from the wet clothes clinging to her body and from the terror and loathing she felt toward this man.

"Let me see, now, sweeting," drawled Jenkins. "You are no doubt wondering where your men are." He spat in the grate. "Your beloved, obviously, is not here." He took off his cap and Alice gasped in horror. A cluster of red fungus-like swellings grew around the cut in his cheek. "Pretty, ain't it? You remember, I'm sure, the day he did this to me." Jenkins scowled and clenched his fists. "And so we would have privacy for our little meeting, I made sure the idiot and his minder were headed to the village ere I let myself in."

Jenkins caught up the hem of Alice's dress. "I have been robbed! Your sweetheart should have died a slow and agonizing death, but he escaped, God damn him!" He seized Alice by the shoulders and chuckled. "But you won't."

Alice screamed and kicked out, but in an instant Jenkins had her turned around and bent forward over the table. He held her down with one hand and flung her skirts up from behind. "Now do not make a fuss. I could just as like be poking a white arse same as yours for tuppence in the Bishop of Winchester's Southwark brothels." He gave a guttural laugh. "But here is Lady Alice, begging me to swyve her, hard and deep, like the whores pant for it."

Alice screamed again and Jenkins slapped her head. Alice felt bile rise in her throat. She turned her face to spit at him but missed. Jenkins laughed as he released his grip to unfasten the points of his hose, and Alice used her elbows to get herself nearly upright. But he shoved her face back onto the table and held her down with a hand on the back of her neck. She cried out but without hope of anyone hearing her above the din of thunder and lightning, even had anyone been within earshot.

Alice felt the room shake around her and thought lightning had hit the cottage. But something was different—there was no pressure on her neck. She stood and saw Jenkins lying on his side on the floor, motionless.

"Alice! Alice! That bad man was hurting you. Your face is white as swans' down."

Dickie stood with the iron skillet swinging in his hand. Sobbing, Alice straightened her crumpled gown. Her breath came rapid and her heart galloped inside her chest. She tried to speak but her throat was so clenched she could get no words out.

John stepped through the door. "God's balls, Master Dickon, we will have to wait out this deluge—" He stopped short when he saw his mistress. "Lady Alice!" he cried, then saw the body slumped on the floor. "Are you hurt?"

Alice raised a trembling hand to her head. "He hit me here, and he was trying to..." She was crying so hard she could not finish the sentence. Over and over she smoothed down her skirts.

John nodded. "Please, Lady Alice, sit and I will bring you some ale." Alice could hardly keep the cup from spilling on account of her hands shaking, but she managed to drink a little.

John asked, "Who is he?"

Her voice shook. "His name is Jenkins. He is the man who killed Stewart and assaulted Goody and would have also..."

Dickie's eyes were wide as silver shillings. "I killed him, didn't I?" He embraced Alice. "He was a bad man. I saw him hurting you." Alice held him tight and wept more.

John rolled the body over, and Alice saw the man's open hose and his limp member lolled to one side. She ran to the open door and vomited, again and again. Even once her stomach was empty she continued to retch. Afterwards she stood in the downpour, willing it to take Jenkins's touch away from her body. She kept telling herself that he had struck her face and that was all. But even the thought of how close he had come to raping her made her sway on her feet. Alice willed herself stay upright, to feel the clean rain soak through her dress till it bathed her skin. She reminded herself William would soon arrive. She did not want Jenkins's corpse to be the first thing he saw on entering the cottage. Her face throbbed from the blow, and when she thought of

Mother and Goody dead, and now this assault on her person, for a moment she lost sense herself. As if from a distance, she saw a young woman standing, dripping wet, outside a peasant's cottage. Alice threw back her head and started to laugh. Her eyes shone distant, like two moons reflected in still water.

Dickie stood in the doorway. "Alice, why are you laughing? Don't. You are scaring me. Come inside, now." He took her hand.

Alice forced herself to listen to Dickie. *I cannot give way now.* She put her arm around his shoulder. "Thank you for what you did for me, I will never forget it."

"Where are Aunt Maud and Goody?" asked Dickie, as they walked through the door.

"They are in Heaven," replied Alice, shaking water from her dress.

"I don't want them in Heaven, I want them here!" Dickie cried, and Alice wrapped her arms around him. "You are getting me all wet," he said, and she released him.

John looked up from lighting the fire and blessed himself. "God above, Lady Alice, we heard that Lady Maud was drowned two days ago, but Goody, gone as well?"

"Did that bad man kill them?" asked Dickie, pointing to Jenkins's corpse, which now lay, covered with a blanket, in a corner by the door.

Alice flinched. "No, it was not he." She wanted to change the subject. "Dickie, I am sore famished, is there anything to eat?"

Dickie nodded and pulled a bunch of carrots from a basket on the table. "I can have them cooked in five minutes."

"And what will we do about the body?" asked John, his brow furrowed. "It would require a big hole. The vegetable garden isn't big enough, and besides, it would hardly be the place for it." He grimaced. "Ugh, think about Jenkins flavouring our soup."

Alice had one foot on the bottom rung of the stepladder. "We will use the stones outside the barn to sink him in the river. Now I must change my clothes."

Alice pulled off the sodden silk gown. She found a stiff brush and cleaned off her black woolen dress and mended its torn shoulder with a needle and thread. Her fingers shook as she sewed, and she jabbed herself twice but felt it a relief to be again performing a familiar task.

She re-dressed and descended. "William is alive and should be here soon," said she.

"I am right glad to hear some good news," said John. He nodded and stood back from the new lit fire.

Dickie put the knife down from chopping carrots. He hugged Alice hard. "I love you," he said and headed out the door. "The rain has stopped and I will dig us more vegetables for supper."

"Did they retrieve my mother's…?" Alice, warming her hands at the fire, could not complete the sentence.

John scratched his ear. "They did so and buried Lady Maud yesterday in the nuns' graveyard at Syon. It seems that her ladyship had a fine rosary in her pocket, which convinced the priest that she was a true Christian, besides which she drowned, proving her innocence." John added a log to the fire; it sizzled then caught light. "I wanted to attend the burial but was afeared to leave Master Dickon alone. I heard Mistress and Miss Smith were there. They insisted on providing a fine oak coffin for your lady mother, themselves."

Alice fell to her knees and clasped her hands. "Thank you, God, thank you, Blessed Virgin, for this mercy!" she sobbed. "And thank you, Abigail and Mistress Smith, for I know Mother is now seated on the right side of God in Heaven, where she has always longed to be."

Alice raised herself, tears pouring down her face.

"And, thank you, John, for standing by us in all our sorrows."

John made a bow. "It is my honour to have known your lady mother, God bless her."

"And poor Goody, too," added Alice, wiping her eyes on the back of her hand.

Dickie returned with turnips and onions. "Can we set that outside while we eat?" asked Alice, tilting her head toward Jenkins's corpse.

John and Dickie moved the body. After dinner, Alice set her purse on the table, opened it, and tipped out the gold sovereigns.

"Where did they come from?" asked John and Dickie in unison.

"A gift from an old friend of Father's."

Dickie spent an hour playing with the coins. He built up piles, knocked them down, and then rebuilt them. Twice he asked of John, and also of Alice, "I did a good deed, did I not?" He wore a worried frown.

"A very good deed," they assured him.

Dickie chuckled. "I was just like Sir Bedivere slaying the wicked knight, was not I?"

Later, John and Dickie carried the rocks from the barn door to the river's edge. Alice watched them, hugged herself, and cried. *Those were the rocks that were going to drown me. And that was before Mother and Goody died and that man tried to rape me. Please, William, hurry.* She swept up the coins from the table and placed them in an earthenware jug.

Once night fell, the three dragged Jenkins's body to the river. John placed the rocks in a sack from the barn, and together they eased in the corpse. The sack reached to mid-chest, and John secured it with a length of rope. "This will do," said he. "It will be weeks, months even, before the fishes nibble through and release the body."

"No, don't say that," said Alice, her mouth trembling. "I will have nightmares of him surfacing from the river."

John shook his head. "He will not be bothering you again, Lady Alice."

"And if he does," said Dickie, with his foot on the corpse, "I will kill him again."

The three rolled the body over the edge of the bank. It sank and bubbles rose to the water's surface.

Alice brushed blades of grass from her gown. "Now I shall go to Mother's grave."

John accompanied her to the cemetery, and in the moonlight Alice could make out one newly dug grave, strewn with pink roses. Alice knelt and tried to pray but cried so hard she could not form the words. "I will return tomorrow," said she, swaying as she rose to her feet.

John supported her back to the cottage and helped her make up a bed by the hearth. Alice could not abide the idea of sleeping in the loft without Mother and Goody. She insisted John and Dickie sleep in her old bed so she would not be alone in the cottage. Just before dawn, Alice was woken by the sound of John and Dickie tiptoeing down the stairs.

"Alice, we are going to gather wood," said Dickie. Alice nodded and turned over.

"We will not be far, so call if you need us."

The next thing she knew, William was kneeling beside her.

"My love, what has happened? Why were you asleep by the fire?" He grasped Alice in his arms. "Your cheek is bruised and your hands are shaking."

"I…I…" Alice could not speak, overcome with relief but unable to find words to describe the horrors of the previous day.

"Dear heart, you are not at all well. Let me fetch Lady Maud."

"Just hold me, William." Her body trembled and tears ran down her face as she buried her face in his chest.

William embraced her until she stopped crying. He released her a little so they could talk face to face.

"Mother is dead…and Goody too."

"Oh, Alice, I am most sorry." William crossed himself.

"But that is not all," continued Alice. "That man Jenkins, you remember him from Hartbourne? He came here. I was alone in the cottage yesterday, and he attacked me and tried to…"

"Oh, my love! Did he? Are you…?"

"No, because Dickie came in and…oh, it was horrible. I

was frightened out of my wits, and then it was dreadful as well because…because Dickie…killed him."

"Dickie?"

"Yes, before Jenkins could…" She put her face in her hands. "Together we heaved the body into the river last night."

William sat down hard on a stool. "How much you have had to bear, my darling. I am most sorry I was not here to protect you."

Alice looked into William's face. His cheeks sagged and he had purple bruises under his eyes.

"But you are here now, dearest William, and that is all that counts. And, my love, you must be famished." Alice turned to head toward the cupboard.

"That can wait, sweetheart," said he, grasping Alice's hand. "It was hard in prison, especially as any day I could be sent for and burned alive, and the hour I spent in the coffin was the longest in my life." William took Alice's hands in his. "That was how I escaped, but we can talk of that later. Here we are, my love, together again."

"My darling," said Alice.

William kissed her palms. There was a knock at the door and in flew Abigail.

"Oh!" exclaimed Abigail. "Who are you?"

William rose and bowed.

"Abigail, this is Sir William of Bayston, my betrothed," said Alice. "William, this is my dear friend, Mistress Abigail Smith."

Abigail blushed and ducked a curtsey, then turned to Alice. "I met Dickie and John bundling sticks near the barn. John said that you had returned but that your nurse had died in gaol. And so soon after the death of your dear mother." Abigail's eyes brimmed with tears. "Dickie said he killed a giant last night, but its body's whereabouts is secret. I thanked him and said Mother and I will sleep sounder in our beds knowing he was our protector." Abigail wiped her eyes on her sleeve.

Alice smiled, despite her distress. She and William exchanged knowing looks, and Alice realized she must tell Dickie to keep his brave act secret.

"Thank you Abigail, I understand my mother had a most decent burial on account of you and your mother."

"You are welcome, I am sure," replied Abigail. "Mother has written you a letter," she said, handing Alice a parchment. "She planned to have it delivered to you in gaol, but I told her I felt in my bones that you would soon be released and home again." Abigail smiled at William. "Mother gave it to me, saying the Blessed Virgin would not permit the innocent languish in the prisons of the ungodly."

William returned her smile and bowed. "Your mother puts it well, Mistress Smith."

Alice broke the seal and read aloud, "Honourable Lady Alice, I greet you and send God's blessings and mine. I am heartily sad for the untimely and unwarranted death of your lady mother. Please come to us at Syon House, where my daughter and I will strive our utmost to comfort you during your time of sorrow, Yours Assuredly, Catherine Smith."

Tears started in Alice's eyes. Again her mother's saying came to mind, that it is always kindness that melts the heart. William placed his arm around her shoulders.

Abigail's brow furrowed. "I am sorry, she did not mean to upset you."

"Your mother is most generous. I shall be happy to come." She looked at William.

He nodded. "Yes, my love, it would be best you stay with these ladies until we are wed." He drew her close and whispered, "Besides, you cannot stay here after what has happened."

"My father is gone down to Plymouth," said Abigail. "The King is commissioning two new ships, so…"

"There is no fear of meeting him again," concluded Alice. The young women smiled at each other. "Please thank your mother and say I will come this afternoon. And my thanks to both of you for attending my mother to her grave."

The friends embraced. Abigail looked at William and then back to Alice. "I imagine you two need some time together," she blushed again, "so I will say goodbye." She ducked a curtsey at the door and went away, humming to herself.

William took Alice in his arms. "Oh, Alice, thinking of you was all that kept me alive while I was in prison. If I am to lose you to the great house, at least permit me first to kiss you, as my betrothed wife."

Alice leaned her face up to his. Her lips first met the stubble on his chin. "Ouch!" she cried.

"We could try like this," and William angled his mouth so the softness of his lips met hers, and they drank deep of each other's sweetness. Grief of loss swelled Alice's heart along with the pleasure of their embrace. She held the back of William's head hard and pressed her tongue farther into his mouth. She felt an emptiness inside her and wanted to take him upstairs and sate herself on his body. No, not upstairs, here, now. Only the act of love could, in some way, fill the void that was consuming her. She undid the laces of William's hose, and he, responding to her ardour, cupped her breasts with his hands. Alice pushed them away. It was as if that intimate touch had reined in the bolting horse of her passion. "My darling," she said, panting for breath, "we cannot do this right now."

Alice, her cheeks flushed, looked down, but William lifted her chin up, and she saw her desperate need reflected in his own face. "My most precious love, there will be time, once we are wed." William's breath came in short gasps. "And be assured I desire you, more than I have desired anything or anyone in my life before." He placed a hand on his heart. "But I want you as my wife, first." He retied the laces of his hose then stroked her cheek. "You are the most beautiful woman I have ever seen." He fingered the strands of hair that had loosened from her coif. "And the brilliant red of your hair…oh, it is falling out!" William showed her the strands that had come away under his touch.

"It happens after a great shock, but it will grow back," said Alice, wincing as she thought of all that would not return in her life—Father, Mother, Goody, Hartbourne.

"Alice," said William, taking both her hands in his, "I know we had agreed to wait because of your father's death, and now, moreover, your mother's, but I would urge our speedy marriage." He kissed her on the forehead.

"Yes, I feel that is what my parents would have wanted, and it is what I want also." She smiled and hugged him tight. Then Alice looked around the tiny room and groaned. "Before she took ill, Mother was content here, for she was helping others. Of course, she missed Father…" Alice burst into tears. "I miss them. I know they were prepared to die for the faith. But for Mother to die like that, drowned in a village pond. That was too cruel."

William embraced her. "I will accompany you to the great house now, for your mind is overwrought and you need to rest awhile."

"Oh, I nearly forgot," said Alice. She reached for the earthenware jug and emptied its contents on the table.

"We could buy a cottage anywhere in England with this!" exclaimed William.

Alice explained how she had come by the money. The sovereigns glinted in the sunlight, reminding her of her mother's rosary beads. Alice felt a pang of regret that the rosary had caused argument between them, but at least it had enabled Mother to be buried in hallowed land.

John and Dickie entered, each carrying a bundle of sticks.

"It is right good to see you again, sir," said John, embracing William. Dickie hugged him too.

"I am going to stay at the big house for a few days but will come by every morning to see you," said Alice as she kissed Dickie.

John swept the hearth then arranged a few twigs in the centre and struck a light on his flint.

"And Aunt Maud and Goody will be back soon, won't they?" asked Dickie.

"No, dear," replied Alice.

Dickie frowned. "Maybe they have gone to live with Hessie. I would like to go live with Hessie too. Did you tell William about the giant I slayed?"

"Dickie, that is our secret." Alice put a finger against his lips. "I told William and he is very proud of you, but no one else must know."

Dickie hung his head. "I told Abigail."

"Yes, but no one else, mind."

"If I promise to keep the secret, will you bring me comfits from the big house?"

"I will, of course," replied Alice, smiling.

William and Alice walked to the great house and stood on the top step.

"I will come to see you tomorrow morning," said Alice.

William kissed her cheek. "I look like a scarecrow, my darling, so I will leave you here." He turned three times as he walked away to check that Alice was still there, waving.

Once William was out of sight she rapped on the door. The woman who opened it curtseyed. "Lady Alice, pray follow me."

Alice had a momentary spasm of anxiety; she had slept on the floor in this dress, but she told herself there were far worse things in the world than her appearance.

Mistress Smith and Abigail were dining in a small room at the back of the house. They sat on cushioned benches on either side of an oak table. Mistress Smith sat under a painting of Abraham preparing to sacrifice Isaac, his son, and Abigail sat beneath Jonah swallowed by the whale.

Abigail leaped from her seat. "Welcome," she cried, embracing her friend. "Sit here beside me."

Mistress Smith, too, rose. She did not seem to notice Alice's dishevelment. "Indeed, welcome. We are most sorry for your family's troubles." She had tears in her eyes. "Please join us at our simple repast. We started for we knew not when to expect you."

Alice beheld a brined ham, a loaf of manchet bread, quince jelly, and a custard sprinkled with nutmeg. Abigail brought a ewer and basin so Alice could wash her hands, then loaded her guest's plate with food.

Alice stared at the plate, thinking of William and how famished he looked.

"Oh," said Mistress Smith, "you are thinking of your cousin." She turned to an attendant. "Send a basket of vittles to the cottage, at once."

"Vittles." That is what Goody would have said. Alice smiled ruefully.

She thanked her hostess, and then, discovering she was ravenous, ate half the loaf. She found it so light it hardly needed chewing, and the ham so savoury that she ate three slices.

"No one will disturb your privacy should you wish to be alone," said Mistress Smith, resting her hands on the table. "But of course, Abigail would be glad of your company." Mistress Smith surveyed Alice. "You need a new gown. You are a little taller than she, so we will need to have a few of her dresses lengthened to fit you."

"Thank you, Mistress Smith," said Alice. "Your kindness is too great."

They finished eating and Mistress Smith said, "Abigail, you may show Lady Alice upstairs."

The bedchamber was as large as the solar at Hartbourne. Soft woven rugs covered the marble floor, and vases of roses stood on every table and sideboard. A huge bed with a crimson velvet tester stood by the mullioned window. Alice felt the mattress and sighed. "It is a beautiful room and this feather mattress its crowning glory."

"I shall send the maids up with a tub and hot water for your bath," said Abigail, smiling. "When you have refreshed yourself, please join me in the arbour." She pointed out the window to a wooden seat under a canopy of trellised roses. "That is where I take my books."

"What are you reading?"

"The tale of Lancelot and Guinevere, from *Le Morte d'Arthur*," said Abigail, blushing.

ester drifted in and out of delirium for two days and nights. Sister Agnes and Sister Dorothy took turns sitting with her and, when she was conscious, propped her up to eat and drink. Hester called so piteously for the dress, Sister Agnes asked Gareth to fetch it. The nun later told Gareth that Hester held the dress close and often put the hem in her mouth and chewed on it. Sister Dorothy pronounced this unhealthy, but Sister Agnes said to let Hester be. Sister Agnes told him that Hester called also for Blackie, but the little dog thought his mistress holding the ripped skirt was playing a game, and he barked and tried to tug it away. Sister Dorothy said the barking gave her a headache, so Blackie was sent back to the kitchen.

Gareth worked on the roof during the day, and in the evening he played his harp outside Hester's door. Sister Agnes deemed it unfit he be in the same room with Hester abed, seeing as they were unmarried. Gareth could not bear the sound of Hester crying out for her mother. Sometimes she begged Henry not to hurt her, but mostly she was pleading with Mervyn not to screw her other thumb. Gareth wished she would call out for him, but she never did.

He could not abide doing nothing to help so decided to make Hester a new medicine chest. He found a piece of cherry wood in a cupboard in the infirmary, to which Sister Agnes told him he was welcome. He carved a box two feet long and a foot wide and added compartments with drawers for herbs. Sometimes he whittled in the drying room and sang as he worked, much to the delight of the novitiates. But all the time, he was looking forward to the day he could walk out with Hester in Sister Agnes's physic garden, where she would pick what herbs she needed for her new chest.

Hester awoke to see two nuns standing over her. "Sister Dorothy tells me you passed a calm night," said the older of the two. "The poison is no longer coursing through your body; it is now gathered in your thumb. As you can see, it is greatly swollen."

Hester nodded. "Yes, and I would feel well if not for the terrible pain of it." She looked around the cell and lowered her voice. "I think I may have not been in my right mind recently." She gazed at the older nun. "Who are you, and pray tell, where am I?"

"I am Sister Agnes, the infirmarian of Saint Winifred's shrine, in Holywell, and this is Sister Dorothy." She smiled at Hester. "Gareth, your good friend, brought you here a week ago."

"Oh, I remember now, Mervyn did this and then he…" Hester raised her hands to her face and sobbed. "Holy Mary!" she screamed as her thumb brushed against her cheek, sending jolts of pain through her hand.

"You can tell me about it later, if you wish, my child, but the abscess is ready to be incised, and 'tis best done now," said the nun.

Sister Agnes selected a small steel blade from her leather pouch and turned to Sister Dorothy. "You have the moss with you?"

"Yes, Sister."

Sister Agnes turned back to Hester. "I am going to make a cut to release the poison from your thumb. You must stay very still."

Again, Hester nodded. She uttered a scream as the pale yellow pus gushed out but afterwards exclaimed, "Oh, that feels good!" She felt almost giddy with relief as the swelling subsided, taking the pain with it.

"Sister Dorothy will now dress it with healing moss."

"I have never seen moss that bright a shade of green," said Hester.

"It grows only here in Holywell," said the nun. "Do you know the history of the shrine?"

Hester shook her head. "I know only that my mother is buried here."

"Indeed," said Sister Agnes, "and once you are well, I shall take you to see her tomb. The legend tells that in the sixth century of Our Lord, there lived a noblewoman named Winifred, who aroused the passion of a Prince Caradoc. When Caradoc tried to ravish her, she fled. And, when he caught her, he beheaded her with his sword."

Sister Agnes dismissed the younger nun, and Hester thought of Henry and how men had not changed much in a thousand years; they pursued women and beheaded them.

Sister Agnes continued, "Saint Bueno, Winifred's uncle, placed her head back on her shoulders, and she returned to life. A spring of pure water, which now feeds into our baths, emerged from the place where her head had fallen, and around that spring grows a bright green moss with healing properties." Sister Agnes smiled, and so did Hester.

"What became of Winifred?" Hester asked.

"First a nun, and then an abbess. Holywell became renowned as a site of pilgrimage. King Henry the Fifth prayed here before leaving for France where he won his great battle at Agincourt."

"But this King Henry has destroyed all pilgrimage shrines. Why was Holywell spared?"

"Even he dared not abolish a shrine commissioned by his grandmother, who is a saint of living memory. But our lands have been confiscated, and our buildings are falling into disrepair." Sister Agnes's face clouded over. "In some of our sister convents, Thomas Cromwell's hirelings were not satisfied with desecrating holy places but desecrated the nuns, also…" Her eyes glazed over. "Who will heal this schism? Not Henry's son, Edward, who is in the grip of the most earnest reformers, nor his daughter Mary, who would burn every Protestant outright. Still I pray every day for a ruler who will bring peace to our land." Sister Agnes blinked. "You need not be troubled with these matters, my child. Something came over me. How does your thumb feel now?"

"Much better already, thank you, but I am very thirsty."

Sister Agnes called for Myfanwy, who brought ale. Hester was delighted that she could hold the cup in both hands.

Sister Agnes smiled. "Gareth told me about your family in the south, and I shall write to them." Her smile widened. "Or even better, in a day or two, you will."

Hester stared into her empty cup. "Where is Blackie?"

The nun frowned. "In the kitchen. Let me tell you, Master Gareth, given his own way, would have stayed outside your door, day and night, singing songs of ill-starred lovers. No," she laughed, "not all the lovers were ill-starred. Some eventually were united in happy marriages."

Hester gave a brief smile. She remembered the warmth of Gareth's kiss in the field on St. John's Eve and how he made her laugh about biting her fingernails. She looked at her nails and saw they were a proper length now. But how could she face Gareth again when she could not tell him what had happened with Henry or Mervyn? She felt she had forfeited her honour to both the King and her cousin, but could a maid lose her virginity without knowing a man? And was a coerced marriage valid? Would a nun like Sister Agnes know the answers?

She thought of how Gareth had come for her, sore injured as he was, and brought her to safety here. What further proof of his love could she require?

A raven cawed from the nearby woods, and she shivered. How could she ever consider having a man, even one she loved as much as Gareth, take her in the way of love after what she had suffered?

"Gareth has captured the hearts of all the novitiates with his music," said Sister Agnes. "When he played in the refectory after dinner, Sister Catherine refused to sweep the floor, saying the angels would be angry if she interrupted his song. Eventually I had to send him back up to mending the roof, for the sake of general cleanliness." Sister Agnes paused. "He is greatly devoted to you."

Hester flushed. "I am very much beholden to him, but… "

Sister Agnes waited, but when Hester did not continue, she pronounced, "You will rest in bed today. Tomorrow morning, come to my parlour. There are matters to discuss."

Hester knew that the nun would not be satisfied with anything less than the truth. She sighed with relief as she realized she wanted to tell her everything.

"And, Sister, then will you take me to see Mother's tomb?"

"Very well, child." Sister Agnes left and closed the door.

Hester heard rapid footsteps approaching, then overheard talk in the hall.

Gareth declared, "She is awake, and Sister, surely I may see her."

"She is still weak. Wait until tomorrow."

Gareth groaned.

Sister Agnes counselled, "Patience, now. Much of what afflicts her is her ill-usage at the hands of men. Once she has unburdened her soul to me, she will look to you."

The pair walked away and Hester listened as their words gradually faded. "Now I will take you to Sister Margery at the baths. You can assist her with those unfortunates who cannot descend the steps unaided. They have travelled many miles, and 'twould be hard for them to leave without benefit of our healing waters."

As they walked toward the baths Gareth said, "I understand that this well, dedicated to Saint Winifred, was once sacred to the Lady, that is, to the goddess Brehen-ys-nef. Is she still worshipped, I mean, honoured here?"

"Ah, Brehen-ys-nef, the ancient goddess of the Celts. In this time when no one knows if it be safe to pray their rosary beads, many look to the old ways. I would not say they have reverted to worshipping any goddess, but they sorely need to believe a loving mother watches over them."

Gareth said, "Where I come from, deep in the mountains, food is always left out for the fairy folk at the full moon, but it is as much from fear as love. I wonder if people would love a goddess more than they feared her." It occurred to him that, perhaps here, in this place sacred to the ancient goddess, Hester would meet the deity personified. But the Lady Elizabeth was a mere child, so Peredur must have been mistaken.

"'Tis good for fairies to have full bellies," replied Sister Agnes. "Once a year, the villagers come up before dawn to dress the spring with ribbons and flowers, then flee home, afraid a priest might be watching. As for loving or fearing a goddess, I cannot say, but they have to worship the Mother somewhere, especially now the churches are empty of Our Lady's image." She laughed. "Still, every May Day we must rise early to remove the garlands, lest they clog the spring."

Gareth, hearing a clatter of sticks against the stone floor and the splash of water, knew they had drawn near the pool. The pair turned the corner and the baths' graceful arches and carved, fluted columns came into view.

A dozen old men wearing linen shifts reaching to their knees sat beside the water's edge. They batted at flies buzzing around their heads, then together, uttering a low groan, ducked themselves in the water and quickly re-emerged. This they did twice more, and Sister Agnes explained three immersions were required to reap the benefits of the holy waters.

As Gareth and Sister Agnes passed by, pilgrims reached out to touch the nun's gown. Sister Agnes seemed not to notice. "You talk about a goddess. It is hard for simple folk to imagine there being one God, when for thousands of years they worshipped mountains and rivers, each of which had its own god or goddess. And in the Old Testament, Asherah, Ishtar to the Babylonians is—"

There was a huge splash. "Hell's cockles!" cried an angry voice.

"Sister Veronica!" Sister Agnes called out to a stout nun, her eyes closed, praying her rosary. "Matthew has slipped on the steps."

The nun opened her eyes and, tucking away her rosary, hitched her habit above her ankles. Gareth threw off his shoes, and he and Sister Veronica waded down to the first step. Together, they lifted Matthew, a middle-aged, red-faced man with a protruding belly, out of the pool.

Male laughter echoed off the walls of the shrine.

Matthew spat water. "I beg pardon for profanity, Sisters."

"Never mind, Matthew," said Sister Agnes, smiling. "You are re-baptized in Saint Winifred's waters and your missaid words forgiven you."

Sister Veronica set to towelling off Matthew's head.

Gareth and Sister Agnes walked on. Wishing to resume their conversation, Gareth asked, "The ancient Greeks had Demeter as their mother goddess, did they not?"

"For the harvest, yea. But she was hardly fertile herself. If I recall aright she had but one daughter. It is many years since I read classics." She sighed. "I did enjoy those myths. I liked Athena best, the virgin goddess of wisdom."

"Little of the mother there," replied Gareth, "seeing as she sprang fully grown from her father Zeus's head."

"That is so," conceded Sister Agnes, "but the church made a saint of her, or at least of her Roman counterpart, Minerva." She paused a moment. "Now doesn't 'Saint Minerva' have a pleasant sound to it? I think a warrior queen of heaven would never have permitted the misery of these past—"

A merry female voice could be heard above the muffled coughs and prayers of the invalids at the far end of the pool.

"That is Sister Margery, who needs your help, so I shall leave you here," said Sister Agnes.

"Master Gareth," a cheerful-faced young nun called out,

"Farmer Lloyd here has the palsy and cannot walk. Will you help carry him into the pool?"

Sister Margery's habit was soaked at the hem, and a few strands of frizzy red hair protruded from beneath her coif.

Gareth was struck by the whiteness of the old man's flesh—his legs and arms were pale as bleached linen.

"I don't remember ever being wet all over my body before," said the old man. "Except for when torrents of rain came down last spring, when I was out in the fields a-birthing the new lambs." He scowled. "That was before this happened," he said, pointing to his withered legs.

The pair helped Farmer Lloyd make three immersions, and as they were climbing out, Gareth noticed the coat of arms of Margaret Beaufort, Henry's grandmother, above an archway. He wondered about Henry and Hester. For a moment, all the white flesh around him felt overwhelming. He recalled white was the colour of the Lady of Death and felt a moment's bewilderment. Christians had their good God and bad Devil. But worshippers of the goddess were pledged to embrace her as both creator and destroyer. If Lady Elizabeth was daughter of the goddess incarnate, the future consecrated queen, for which would she stand, life or death?

ester remained in bed the rest of the day and slept on and off. That night she had a vivid dream of a young girl with golden red hair, dressed in tissue of gold and purple, holding a sceptre in one hand and an orb in the other. The sceptre turned into a snake, but the girl just laughed. Hester woke, her heart racing. *Who is this daughter of royalty, and why is she in my dream?* When she fell back asleep, she had another dream, in which a wild boar gored her thigh. She woke up in a cold sweat. She had a vague sense that the wild boar was Henry. *I don't want him in my dreams. Tomorrow I shall tell Sister Agnes everything that happened, and she will tell me how to find peace.*

In the morning Hester, wearing the white robe of a novitiate and with her hand bandaged, found the nun writing at her desk by a window overlooking a flower garden.

Hester curtseyed and sat on a stool looking at a painting above the hearth of Mary with Jesus blowing on a dandelion puffball. The pair were laughing at each other. Hester thought of how she used to be rather puffed up herself, like a bantam cock and needing to be in charge at all times. In this way had she bid defiance to a fate that had made her dependent on others. Now she felt unpuffed; she was grateful to be cared for, knowing that without the nuns' ministrations, she might well have died, or at the very least, lost the use of her hand. She glanced at a book cabinet, which reminded her she would see neither her prized volumes nor her medicine chest ever again. On the top shelf sat a gilded mahogany box, its sides inlaid with mother-of-pearl. The book inside must be precious indeed to be so housed.

Sister Agnes laid down her pen and sanded the parchment.

"Yet another petition to the King, begging him to restore some part of our lands."

Hester nodded. "Sister, I need to tell you something about the King."

"Of course, my child, but first, come and see where your dear mother is buried."

Excitement at seeing her mother's tomb displaced Hester's immediate desire to take the nun into her confidence. *Later,* she thought.

"Such beautiful marigolds and columbine," declared Hester as they passed through the garden, her nerves tingling with anticipation.

"All the flowers here are in honour of Our Lady," said Sister Agnes. "Marigolds speak for themselves. The columbine are Our Lady's earrings."

A stubby plant with frondlike leaves caught Hester's attention. "What is that?"

"*Chrysanthemum parthenium*, feverfew," replied the nun. "It was planted but a fortnight ago, yet it is sprouting up fast."

Golden virgin, thought Hester. She recalled her dream of the previous night: a royal, golden-haired girl holding a sceptre and orb. She dismissed the memory; her heartbeat quickened, for she was about to see her mother's final resting place. Dark clouds threatened rain, but thrushes and chaffinches sang from a nearby thicket of young oaks. Beyond a patch of tall grass, dotted with blue cornflowers and yellow cowslip, lay the cemetery, with a statue of the Virgin at the centre.

"Our Lady stands over Margaret Vaughan's crypt," said Sister Agnes. "I wish I had known your mother, but I have been here only a few years."

Hester's knees shook as she approached. She recalled her promise to the Blessed Virgin, made less than two months ago, to erect a statue of her over her mother's tomb once she was Queen of England. How could she have been so arrogant and witless?

"So this is where Mother lives, I mean, lies," she murmured. She brushed away tears. "I wish Dickie were here, although he would not understand."

She heard a bark and turned to see Blackie racing toward her. She scooped him up under her good arm. He licked her face and the trio made their way toward the tomb.

Many of the statues of saints and angels were missing an arm or a wing, and grass grew in cracks at the bases.

"Is this the work of the wreckers?" asked Hester.

"No, simply the wear and tear of decay."

The statue of the Virgin stood at the head of a rectangular granite slab. Her arms outstretched, she embraced all her children and their sorrows. Behind a wrought iron gate a flight of steps led down to the crypt. Hester peered down into the darkness. There was only one oak coffin in the centre of the chamber.

Sister Agnes started a prayer, and Hester clasped her hands together and mouthed the words, "We beseech thee, O Lord…," but a sudden surge of pain and anger overtook her. She hid her face in Blackie's coat to hide her emotion. Sister Agnes continued, "to have mercy upon the soul of thy handmaid, Margaret Vaughan, and…"

Hester's thoughts strayed from prayer. *Oh God, could you not have spared her, just a little longer, so that I would have some memory of her, instead of none at all?*

She sobbed from a whirling confusion of pain, anger, and guilt, but mostly from sadness of never knowing the one who had given her life.

"I will give you some time here alone." Sister Agnes walked away to pray at another grave.

Hester felt a sudden weakness and leaned against the base of the Virgin's statue for support. A shower of gravel fell away.

Sister Agnes turned to her. "Take care, for the pediment has eroded, and just a little push could send the statue tumbling."

Hester stepped back. *If it fell, would it shatter entirely, or just its head come off?* She thought about Henry's eagerness to decapitate those who displeased him. Anne Boleyn came to her mind, but why think of her here, beside Mother's tomb? A sudden downpour broke her reverie, and the women ran to the parlour door. Hester staggered and Sister Agnes supported her to a chair.

"Myfanwy will bring ale, and I shall return shortly."

Blackie lay down by the grate, licked himself dry, then fell asleep. Myfanwy arrived and the bitter liquid refreshed Hester.

Myfanwy said, "Soon you will be all recovered, and you and your sweetheart will…" She blushed and looked down at her hands.

Hester wanted to cry. She couldn't bear to think of Gareth and of all the things she couldn't say to him. She stared at the mahogany box on the top bookshelf.

Myfanwy followed her gaze. "A beautiful Book of Hours sits up there. No one may touch it, but sometimes Sister shows me the pictures." She lowered her voice. "Sister Agnes would not mind if you looked, for you are a guest, and your mother was our benefactress." Myfanwy's eyes shone. "I cannot reach it, but you are plenty tall enough." She blushed again. "The case is not locked. I did try it once, standing on a stool."

Hester took down the box and removed the velvet wrapper. The book fit in the palm of her hand and fell open at a picture of the Flight of the Holy Family into the desert. Joseph was leading a donkey, which carried Mary and baby Jesus.

Myfanwy giggled. "Is not that donkey the happiest you have ever seen? His mouth is smiling and his tail standing up."

"My Aunt Maud has this very same Office of the Blessed Virgin," said Hester. She turned the pages until she reached a painting of Mary, aged around eight years, standing outside the temple, surrounded by white-bearded men.

"Look at those old fellows! I'm glad I wasn't the Virgin Mary," said Myfanwy. "Not much fun to be had there." She giggled again and crossed herself against the blasphemous thought. Hester could not help but smile at her companion's illicit delight.

"It must have been strange," said Myfanwy, "being brought up by priests instead of her mother, Saint Anne."

Hester mused, "And Mary was never allowed to step on the ground. There was always a white sheet under her feet."

"Then I am glad I wasn't the laundress, either. Imagine all that washing…"

Hester continued turning the pages until she reached the Nativity of Christ, with the three wise men hovering around the Holy Family. "This is my favourite, when they bring gold and frankincense and myrrh."

"Mine too," agreed Myfanwy. "I do not know what frankincense is, and myrrh sounds sad. It's gold we could use around here, though even lead would help." She explained about the King's men stripping the roof. She glanced at Hester. "Will I call Master Gareth? He is up there, mending one of the biggest holes."

Hester stared at the picture and whispered, "No."

"He loves you dearly," pleaded Myfanwy, "and wanted only—"

The pair jumped at the approach of rapid footsteps. Hester quickly rewrapped and replaced the book.

They heard a splash and an irritated "Saints preserve us!"

Sister Agnes entered the room examining the sodden hem of her robe. "At times this place would task the patience of Job himself. One should not have to worry about stepping in puddles indoors." She waved dismissal to Myfanwy, who grinned at Hester and sped away.

Sister Agnes sat wearily on an oak arm chair and gestured Hester to the other. Blackie leaped to Hester's lap, circled twice then settled himself to sleep.

"I am sorry for the death of your father, my child," started Sister Agnes. "Gareth told me it was but recent."

Hester blushed in confusion, not having thought of her father in days. "Sister, I hardly knew him, for he became deranged after Mother's death, and I was sent to England. And by the time I arrived at Dinas Emrys, last month, he was already dying."

"And now you are well again, you are praying for the repose of his soul, are you not?"

"Yes, Sister," lied Hester. She prayed for Alice and Aunt Maud. She prayed for Sir Hugh and Dickie, and she prayed for Peredur and Nia. She felt she had no prayers left over for Father. A wave of sadness overcame her.

Sister Agnes shot her a quizzical glance. "But let us turn to the living. Pray tell about Gareth and about that ruby ring."

Hester blushed again and murmured, "Gareth is my betrothed, but…"

"But," repeated the nun.

"But he would not love me, if he knew what I have done." She frowned and her voice became husky. "Or rather, what has been done to me."

"Ah, and what has been done to you?"

Hester took a deep breath. For an instant she felt overwhelmed by shame but told herself she needed to tell her story to someone who would listen and maybe not blame her. Or at least not blame her as much as she blamed herself.

"I visited the King, the day before I left for Wales, and brought salves for his ulcered legs, but he was near demented with rage against Howard women. My Aunt Maud is of that family, so he thought I was, too. In a frenzy he tried to, to…" Hester faltered. "Ravish me. But when he could not, he thrust his finger inside me, then I fainted. He must have put the ring in my dress pocket, but I only found it later." She stared into the empty grate. "Afterwards, I wanted only to die, which was very bad of me, I know, but then my cousin Mervyn," she shuddered, "brought me to Wales. He wanted my lands but especially the ring. I was forced to marry him." She cried, "I love Gareth, but am too shamed to tell him about any of this!"

Blackie fidgeted but settled back to sleep. Hester stroked his ears. *I know Gareth loves me, but can I love him? The witch tells me I am hers because of all my badness, especially my anger toward Mother. And so I am unworthy of love.*

"I would advise you to tell Gareth all." Sister Agnes fingered her rosary. "Also you must write to Sir Hugh. He will arrange an escort for your return home, once you are a little more recovered."

"But I believe Sir Hugh to be in gaol."

"In that case, you will write to your aunt." Sister Agnes paused. "Yet I hardly think your dear departed parents would wish for you to marry a bard, even if you were free to marry another." Seeing Hester's face crumple, she added, "But you might obtain an annulment since you were forced into marriage. Please God, it was not consummated?"

"No, he did not…" Hester, from the depths of her shame, refused to think of that night. *How could Gareth still love me, if he knew of it?* "Very well, Sister. I shall write today." But Gareth had saved her life, and she felt bound to defend him. "Wherefore should I not marry a bard? Gareth may well attain a great position in a duke's court. Did not Thomas Cromwell, who was but the son of a blacksmith, rise to become Lord Privy Seal?"

Sister Agnes shuddered at the mention of Cromwell's name and clutched her rosary beads so the white showed through her knuckles.

A rapid knocking on the door caused Blackie to jump down and bark.

Myfanwy's face appeared, pale with alarm. "Sister, a man has been brought in with his leg quite cut off."

She and Sister Agnes hurried away down the corridor.

Hester paced before the hearth, and Blackie curled up beside the empty grate. She took down the Book of Hours and opened it to the Holy Family's flight into Egypt. There sat Mary, carrying Jesus on the smiling donkey while Joseph urged the beast on. Hester thought Gareth was a bit like Joseph in rescuing her from Mervyn, her own Herod. But Gareth was young and good-looking, while Joseph was decidedly old and wizened. She felt badly for thinking so of the saint, but when she looked up at the painting of the Virgin Mary smiling down at Jesus, she knew that the Lady, at least, would forgive her.

Hester jolted upright. She remembered Aunt Maud saying that it was unheard of that any sinner seeking refuge with the Mother of God was turned away. Mary would forgive her for going to Henry and for marrying Mervyn.

The rain had cleared and the sun, shining through the window, warmed the parlour. Hester did not hear Sister Agnes enter the room and gave a guilty start when the nun spoke.

"That is a most beautiful book," Sister Agnes said, sitting beside her. "The colours glow as if they were painted but yesterday."

Hester nodded, then asked, "How fares your newest patient?"

"A deep enough wound, but his leg is safe."

"You do marvellous work here," said Hester. "Aunt Maud only let my cousin Alice and myself assist in minor ways, such as preparing willow bark tea for villagers with the rheumatism."

"It is strange how your aunt, as the lady of the manor, was expected to be proficient with her distillery and its remedies, whereas a poor wise woman could easily be accused of witchcraft." Both women made the sign of the cross.

"I pray they are all safe," said Hester. "My Uncle Hugh was drafting a law he hopes to be passed by parliament next year. It is to protect wise women."

"How will that work?" asked Sister Agnes, reaching down to stroke Blackie behind the ears. The dog gave a contented sigh in his sleep.

"Poor folks who cannot afford physicians suffer and die from ignorance of their grandmothers' remedies. This new law says that so long as a wise woman accepts no fee for her services, she will be safe from prosecution."

"Ah, so the physicians stand to lose nothing, and the women will not hang." Sister Agnes gave a wry smile. "I suppose that is an improvement for the women. Here, all healing is due to God's grace, even if we do find autumn crocus gives great relief to our gouty supplicants." Sister Agnes raised her eyebrows, and Hester covered her mouth with her hand to hide her smile.

The nun pointed to the book in Hester's lap. "This is our most valuable treasure. The pigment for the blue of Our Lady's robe derives from crushed lapis lazuli, so the colour never fades; unfortunately, the Latin script is now barely legible. We hid it from Cromwell's men, but we could have spared our pains, for they were more interested in plundering the altar." Sister Agnes closed her eyes a moment. "But we were talking about Gareth and your cousin Mervyn, whom you were forced to marry. How did that come about?"

"Father died." Hester felt grief well up for this man she had never known, except at the beginning of her life and the end of his. She stifled a sob. "And once my uncle Lord Llewelyn knew I was not *virgo intacta* and of no use for his sacrifice, he handed me over to his bastard." Hester spat out the word "bastard"; it felt satisfying on her lips.

"What are you saying?" Sister Agnes's eyes widened. "That Lord Llewelyn planned to have you killed?"

Hester explained that her uncle worshipped the old gods and that he believed they demanded a pure sacrifice of his kin in exchange for a successful attack on King Henry.

Sister Agnes gasped. "This has been a Christian country for near a thousand years. How could this have happened?"

"But it is worse, Sister. It was dreadful." Hester sobbed. "Poor Gwendolyn, my cousin, died instead of me, because she was virgin." The two women blessed themselves.

"This is beyond belief," said the nun, her face drawn in shock. She clasped her hands and began to pray. "Heavenly Father, we implore thee to have mercy upon the soul of thy handmaiden, Gwendolyn—" She was interrupted by rapping on the door.

Myfanwy opened it and said, "Sister, forgive me for intruding, but two men are at the main door. They are come from Master Mervyn to fetch Mistress Vaughan away."

Hester reached down for Blackie and clutched him so hard he yelped.

"Best show them in," said the nun, frowning.

"No, please, Sister," gasped Hester. "They will take me back to…that man!" Blackie escaped from Hester's grip and raced to the door. He squeezed through the gap left by the retreating Myfanwy and headed to the main door, where he barked like the day of doom had arrived.

oments later, two men wearing battered leather jerkins and thick riding boots walked carefully into the room. One was a bearded redhead and the other wore blond greasy hair down to his shoulders. They bowed, tugging their caps from their heads. Blackie yapped at their ankles and ran back to Hester and hid beneath her chair; she felt his breath on her ankles.

"Begging your pardon, Sister," said the bearded man, waving a beefy hand toward Hester. "We are come to retrieve her, what absconded with the bard's apprentice."

Hester stared at the painting of Our Lady with Jesus and the dandelion puffball. Under her breath she prayed, "Lord Jesus, puff really hard and let them vanish."

"Our master tripped over the dog and is abed with a broken leg," said the blond man. He scowled at Hester. "He said we would find you here at your mother's resting place." He coughed, caught the spittle in his hand, and wiped it on his jerkin.

Hester focused on a fluffy dandelion seed caught in midair.

"Is sanctuary meaningless to you, that you intend to remove a supplicant to Saint Winifred's well?" asked Sister Agnes.

The blond man spoke wheedling wise. "She is Master's wife and has a ring that now belongs to him—"

Sister Agnes interrupted, "Mistress Vaughan is not your master's wife. A coerced marriage is no marriage."

The bearded man laughed. "But she will need a man of law to prove it. They were married by a priest with witnesses. Two sisters were there. It's her word against Master's."

Sister Agnes sighed, knowing full well only the husband's word would be believed.

Turning to his partner, the man growled, "Let's take her."

The smell from their sweaty jerkins made Hester gag. "No!" she cried, as they seized her shoulders.

"You are good Christians, are you not?" asked Sister Agnes.

"I know my Pater Noster and creed, but that purports nothing," said the blond-haired man.

The bearded man touched a crucifix under his shirt.

"Good. So you understand that here, Mistress Vaughan is protected against all temporal powers. You both will burn in hellfire for eternity, lest you unhand her."

They released Hester, crossed themselves, and backed out the door.

The blond one hissed, "But she can't stay here forever. We will be waiting, and the minute she leaves—"

Sister Agnes interrupted. "Just mind you wait outside the precincts and away from the cows. We don't want their milk to curdle."

Hester's mind was in turmoil. She felt bound to the ring but knew not why. She hated it yet would never yield it to Mervyn. She also knew she could never set foot in that house again. "Tell Mervyn he may have my property, but not the ring."

"At least we shall not return empty-handed," grunted the bearded man, and they left.

Blackie jumped up into Hester's arms and licked her nose. She rumpled his ears.

Sister Agnes smoothed her robes. "'Tis shame only threat of hellfire makes some people act aright."

Hester gave a wan smile. "Yet it is effective. Thank you, Sister Agnes, for—"

A tremendous crash sounded from down the hall.

Myfanwy entered, gasping, "It is Master Gareth. He fell from the ladder but is up and after them with the sledgehammer."

The three women watched from the window as Mervyn's men rode off. They had but one foot apiece in the stirrups, with an enraged Gareth in pursuit. But Gareth could not match their horses' speed. Shouting imprecations at their departing backs, he shouldered the hammer and returned to the house.

"Gareth is a courageous young man and has the right idea. But I would rather not need to tend to those men's injuries, had he caught them," said Sister Agnes, resuming her seat in an arm chair. She indicated Hester to the other.

"Jesu Christ! I wish he had swiped their wicked heads clean off their shoulders," declared the little maid.

"Myfanwy!"

"Yes, Sister, I know, I will confess and do penance for my unchristian words. May I please be excused?"

Sister Agnes nodded. As Myfanwy left the room she grinned and whispered to Hester, "Well worth it."

Hester could not help but smile.

Breathless, Gareth stood in the doorway and asked, "May I enter, Sister?"

"Certainly," replied Sister Agnes, "but leave your weapon outside the door." She indicated the stool opposite Hester. "Pray be seated."

Hester blushed and stared at her hands.

Gareth was sunburned and sweat trickled down his forehead; he wiped it away with the back of his hand.

He looked eagerly at Hester. "You are not hurt, dear heart?"

She gave him her good hand. "Indeed I am not." *At least not any more than I already was.* She looked into his eyes and saw them dance with happiness. She smiled in response to his pleasure, a pleasure she could not feel herself. How was she to love him, when all she felt about herself was shame?

"I know I am only a bard," said Gareth, "but in loving you, I feel like a king."

"Do not say, 'only a bard,'" remonstrated Hester. "Your music is angelic."

He turned over her hand and kissed her palm. "There will be some remedy for that false ceremony. I know it."

Hester withdrew her hand. Just the idea of being married, and how that would mean allowing herself to be touched in places—no. How could she ever consent to receive, much less desire, a man's caresses? Not even Gareth's. The smell of the men who had just left lingered in her nostrils. Nauseated, she swayed on her chair.

"You are unwell!" exclaimed Gareth. "Sister Agnes and I will take you back to your room."

Blackie scampered behind them. Just inside the door Hester told Gareth, "I said Mervyn could have my property, but not the ring. That is my, I mean, our safe passage home."

"Oh, Hester, fach," groaned Gareth, "without your lands, what shall we live on?" Then he exclaimed, "You do not think I wish to marry you for your lands?"

Hester smiled. "No, not after all that has passed between us."

"Well, I feel I can aspire to your hand more honestly now, in that it will be the sweat of my brow, or at least the songs of my harp, that will provide for us." He kissed her gently on the cheek.

"You rest now, and with Sister Agnes's leave I will pick some flowers to brighten your little cell."

"Not from our Mary garden," advised the nun, "but there are plenty of wildflowers down by the brook. You can leave Blackie in the kitchen on your way out."

Once beyond the precincts of the shrine, Gareth ran through the fields, fairly whooping along. He felt relief that Hester was mending and also for being released from the company of religious women.

He slowed to a walk along the brook, which burbled along over a bed of smooth grey rocks. Flowers and ferns grew along its banks, and demoiselle dragonflies darted above the water's surface. They were mating as they flew, one riding on the other. Gareth smiled to himself. Once Hester was his wife, they too would partake of such pleasure.

He gathered yellow irises and purple marshmallow. The rays of the sun beat down on his back, and so, looking around and seeing no one, he flung off his clothes and lay down in the stream where the cool water washed the sweat from his naked body.

He shook himself dry and lay down in the grass, where he dozed off. But when he woke to get dressed, to his horror he found himself face to face with two nuns. One was young and plump, her brow beaded with perspiration. The other was an ancient wrinkled dame whose wide open mouth revealed a total absence of teeth.

Both women's faces bore expressions of shock, and the old one uttered hoarse shrieks. "Lord bless us and save us! The barbarians are come!"

"Sisters, I beseech you, prithee peace!" cried Gareth. He grabbed his doublet to shield his loins from view. "I mean you no harm. I came to pick flowers for my betrothed, and it became hot, so I went in the water."

The nuns covered their eyes, but Gareth saw the younger one peeping between her fingers.

"I am Gareth ap Fychan and a guest at Saint Winifred's," said he, with as much dignity as he could muster. "I am mending the roof."

"Oh, then you are the bard. They say you sing divinely. I am Sister Anne," said the young nun.

"Thank you, now if you would excuse me…"

The women turned their backs while he dressed.

The older nun wailed, "You should not tell him your name, Sister. I am sure he will track you down and ravish you while you are asleep in your bed." She spluttered, "Wherefore comes a naked young man here? All the men who come to Saint Winifred's are old or infirm, but always clad decently. And this young man has all his members, I mean, his limbs intact."

"Do not be afeard, for he reminds me of my brother Dewi,"

consoled Sister Anne. "He was full of mischief but would not harm a fly."

Once Gareth was dressed the nuns turned round.

"Are you returning to the shrine?" asked Sister Anne.

The three made their way back through the fields to the sanctuary. Skylarks swooped around them, making easy prey of the drowsy insects. Sister Anne told him all about Dewi, her younger brother, and said it was a miracle that they two survived the sweating sickness, when the rest of their family had died. Gareth was impatient to reach Hester's side, but courtesy dictated he slow his gait to match the sisters'. He offered the older nun his arm in an attempt to speed their progress, but she glowered her refusal.

Gareth returned to find Hester asleep. He fetched an earthenware vase from the kitchen for the yellow and purple flowers and left it outside her door. He shared a loaf of millet bread and some cheese with Corwen in his little room under the stair, then worked away at the medicine chest and smoothed out the lid. It was nearly finished, and he felt sure Hester would like it.

ester tossed on her bed, and the pain still awakened her each time she rolled onto her injured hand.

The witch, wearing a white robe with a hood that concealed most of her face, appeared in her dream. Her eyes flashed, but she spoke lovingly. "Join me, dearest daughter, and let me keep you safe forever." They were standing beside her mother's tomb, and Hester tried to run away, but her feet refused to move. "You would be safe in there beside your mother. Why do you hesitate?" She stroked Hester's arm. "You know about poisons: henbane, foxglove, and monk's hood." The witch's voice and face became her mother's, with sad, downcast eyes. Even softer, she crooned, "I will hold you close forever and never desert you." Hester lay down beside the tomb, and the ground opened up beneath her. Then her mother turned back into the witch, who cried out in triumph, "I have you now!"

Hester awoke in the dark, her heart racing and body bathed in sweat. She eventually fell back asleep and woke as Sister Agnes walked through the door, followed by Blackie. The little dog leaped up beside her, and Hester stroked his head.

The nun handed her a cup of peppermint tea. "You look pale, my child."

"I had a bad dream, Sister."

"Gareth left flowers outside your door yesterday evening." As Hester sipped the fragrant brew, Sister Agnes brought in the vase of irises and mallow. "Are they not pretty?" she asked.

"Mm, I suppose so," replied Hester, barely glancing at them.

"Fresh air will do you good. Come, let us walk in the physic garden." She helped Hester into her robe. "Today we celebrate the

Visitation of the Virgin Mary to Saint Elizabeth. But Father Jerome, who will officiate at Mass, will not arrive for another hour or so."

Followed by Blackie, the two women entered a garden divided into four quadrants by a gravel path. Each quadrant contained neatly arranged beds of medicinal herbs. At the centre of the garden grew a lavender bush, spanning several feet across.

Hester surveyed the plants. "Ah, foxglove, *digitalis purpurea*, for making the ailing heart beat stronger." Under her voice she added, "Or for making it stop." Sister Agnes had stooped to pluck strands of grass from a parsley bed and did not hear her charge's last few words.

"Mullein, for the cough," continued Hester. "*Vebascum thapsus*. And there is tansy, which provoketh the bowels, *Tanacetum vulgare*." She looked around and exclaimed with pleasure, "Oh, yes, there is *Aspleniifolius*, which cleanses the spleen and liver."

Sister Agnes placed her hand on Hester's arm. "What happened with Mervyn?"

"I do not want to talk about it."

Sister Agnes spoke quietly. "But you must."

Hester looked around for other plants to identify. Sister Agnes's hand remained gently but firmly on her arm. Hester took a deep breath. "On our...," she could hardly bring herself to say, "wedding night," she faltered, "he...he...ripped my mother's wedding dress, and then he tried to use me, but not as a man is wont to use a woman."

"Oh?" inquired Sister Agnes, with an edge to her voice.

"But as a man would use another man."

"Oh!" Sister Agnes crossed herself. "That is most dreadful!"

Hester felt a quiet satisfaction at having been able to elicit this response from one who never lost her self-control. Then she felt ashamed. The nun had been kind to her, and yet she did not feel gratitude, only resentment.

"Had he gotten his way, he could hang for it," said the nun.

"He would say I lied," returned Hester.

"Yes, and only he would be believed."

They walked a while in silence.

"Sister, he broke his leg because Blackie tripped him on the stairs. Only, I had physicked his wine, which, of course, he does not know."

"You did well to take care of yourself, and let us pray God he never discovers the truth." Sister Agnes paused. "It is important you tell Gareth these things. My child, you must understand, you are not alone in having suffered."

They lingered by the lavender bush in the middle of the garden. Bees hummed, collecting pollen from the tiny purple flowers. The bees kept shifting their weighted legs so as not to lose balance on the delicate stems.

Sister Agnes's brow furrowed, and she took a deep breath. "A month before it was suppressed, I visited the convent of Saint Irene, five leagues to the west of us, which is now a heap of rubble. Saint Irene's owned an exquisite marble statue of the Virgin, and Cromwell's hirelings smashed it. Not only it, but the hands of the half-dozen nuns who held onto it, praying to Our Lady for succour. Then the men hauled the youngest and prettiest down to the crypt, where they first raped and then strangled them."

"I am sorry," whispered Hester, her eyes widening in horror, "but why are you telling me this?"

"The Mother Superior of that convent never spoke a word of what had happened. A year later, to the day, she hanged herself. You see, shame begets silence, and silence never heals."

"That is most dreadful," gasped Hester.

A raven called out from a nearby elm tree, and another, answering its call, flew to join it. Then another, and another, until the air resounded with a cacophony of ravens.

Sister Agnes continued, "So you understand why you must tell Gareth all." Hester tried to interrupt, but Sister Agnes raised her hand. "I do not pretend it will be easy, but he is a good man and will understand."

They walked in silence between the beds of herbs, the scent of lavender wafting around them. "These are difficult times. Of course, we still believe in God and His Son here at Saint Winifred's, but there are places nearby where people do not." Sister Agnes's voice rose. "People ask, why did He not save His church? And they can no longer afford to buy bread, which is an even greater hardship. Some say this land has fallen under Satan, while others have reverted to worshipping the ancient mother goddesses of the Celts."

A thrush warbled from an apple tree at the far end of the garden.

"As did my Uncle Llewelyn," said Hester. Her robe caught on a twig; she reached down and threw the stick for Blackie, who chased after it. "Father Ignatius, who was Llewelyn's ally against Henry, said the villagers in Dinas Emrys honoured Mary more than God or Jesus." Hester explained how Father Ignatius had extorted a confession of heresy from her, so he could permit the sacrifice of a Christian woman on a pagan pyre.

"I do not know which grieves me more, my dear," said Sister Agnes, "that a chief of his people should forsake the Church or that a priest of the Church should misuse another human being so."

The women paused by a black currant bush and ate a few warm, sweet berries.

"Do the people hereabouts worship Mary?" Hester inquired.

"No. With her image gone from churches, the hillside peasants have reverted to worshipping and sacrificing to the three mothers, Ane, Modron, and Arianrhod."

Hester nodded. "Gareth believes in goddesses."

"Yes, we discussed this recently. How in the cities, the Church still holds sway, but many of the country folk, in their hearts, pray for a goddess's return." Sister Agnes continued, "One of the reasons Saint Winifred's was spared was that Henry knows even if he destroys our shrine, people would still come to honour the Lady of the waters." Sister Agnes gave a wan smile. "He cannot risk his subjects reverting to their old faith and their old ways. A fractured

Christian Church is one matter, but one uprooted from its very base is quite another. 'Tis but sixty years since the Turks brought Islam to the gates of Rome."

Hester knew not how to reply. She felt no interest in goddesses or the religion of Mohammed. She just wanted to...she didn't even know any longer what she wanted. She reached to pluck a stalk of rosemary, but it was tough and needed both hands to break it.

"Ouch!" she cried. "My thumb still hurts if I bend it hard. I wish I could help, even if only to hang herbs to dry, or grind roots and seeds." She groaned. "But I could not even lift a pestle, much less the mortar."

Sister Agnes looked straight at her. "And about Gareth?"

Hester looked down. "I feel tainted. I would rather be alone. Sometimes I think if they came to arrest me for a witch, I would almost sigh with relief, thinking, 'They have found me out, at last.'"

"My child, you must not allow yourself to think such thoughts," said the nun. "You cannot deny you love Gareth, and your brother and your uncle's family, even though at times you may feel you do not."

Sister Agnes took Hester by the shoulders and forced her to look at her. "Listen to me," she said, "a witch is someone who is unable to love."

"Oh, I had not thought of that."

The nun fingered her rosary. "And, as you may have gathered, I have changed my mind about your betrothal. Having conversed with Gareth, I believe he is indeed worthy of your hand, and he is devoted to you."

"Oh, Sister, thank you." A smile wreathed Hester's face. "I knew that about him; it was my own self I doubted."

"Never doubt yourself, my child." Sister Agnes returned Hester's smile. "When you write to your aunt, you may say that I am in favour of the marriage."

"I shall write today."

The pair walked on, silent save for the crunching of pebbles under their shoes. As they turned a corner, the statue of the Virgin in the cemetery came into view. Hester looked long at it.

Sister Agnes noticed her stare and smiled. "The Virgin Mary is mother of us all. When I look up at the clear blue sky, I imagine it is her cloak of love, spread over every one of us."

A terrible sense of loss engulfed Hester. She wished with all her heart she had known her mother or at least had some memory of her. As the longing left, a spasm of anger took its place.

"Why should Our Lady care when my own mother didn't care enough to stay to look after me?" retorted Hester, scowling. "Besides, the Virgin has the whole world to mind; she doesn't need any more waifs clinging to her skirts."

Sister Agnes halted and a look of pain aged her face. "My dear, you come very close to committing the worst of sins when you speak in such wise."

"You mean pride?" Hester bit her lower lip and clenched and unclenched her fists.

"Yes. When you were tiny, your mother's death was like a keg of gunpowder ignited inside you." Sister Agnes wiped a bead of sweat from her brow. "And, because your understanding was not yet formed, you might well have thought she left you of her own accord. But now you are grown, you know that was not so, and to deny the love of others, because it is not hers, is willfulness. Pride."

"You do not understand the dreadful emptiness inside!" cried Hester, tears welling in her eyes.

"But I do," replied the nun, her eyes glazing over. "My mother died when I was six, from the sweating sickness. My father was a knight, and I, his only child. Mother died at Easter and Father remarried in the New Year." Sister Agnes sighed. "She was a widow with five children and persuaded Father to send me to a convent and take the veil when I was of age."

Sister Agnes flicked away a damselfly that had landed on her sleeve. "I had no choice, of course, and those nuns were, shall we say, less than kind."

"Oh, I am sorry," replied Hester, flicking her tears away. "But you do not seem any the worse ..."

"You ask, how did I fare so well?" Sister Agnes raised her eyebrows. "I have seen children brought here who not only lost their parents, but were left by the roadside to starve. Myfanwy is one of many such. I count myself fortunate."

"I had not considered it that way before," murmured Hester.

"No," replied Sister Agnes, "I dare say you haven't, but you are young yet."

A cow lowed in the meadow on the other side of the garden wall.

The pair arrived at a strawberry bed, the ripe fruit glistening in the sun.

"We will gather some berries for Father Jerome," said Sister Agnes. "He imposes light penances, so he is always welcome."

The women stooped to gather a few handfuls. Hester ate one. The warmth and fresh sweetness filled her mouth, and she almost gasped at the pleasure.

"They are good, are they not?" Sister Agnes bit into one. "I always think of strawberries when I think of the Feast of the Visitation. I hope the Blessed Virgin took some to Saint Elizabeth and they enjoyed them together. After all, there is nothing pregnant women love more than strawberries."

Hester laughed. "Do strawberries grow in the Holy Land?"

"Only the finest," replied the nun, smiling.

Blackie nosed his way into the berry patch and nuzzled one curiously, then took a bite. He wolfed it down and snapped at another.

"Those are not for you," scolded Hester.

The two women passed back through the kitchen and found a bowl for the berries.

Cook accosted Sister Agnes. "Sister, Master Roger is in his cups more than he is sober. He dropped a basket of fish in the mud yesterday..."

Blackie barked and Cook reached into a saucepan with a

knife and brought out a chunk of thrice-boiled mutton bone. She ordered, "Sit, boy, sit." Blackie did and Cook gave him the bone.

"Yes, Cook, I will speak to him," said the nun.

Sister Agnes turned to Hester. "You may go to my study, child, and compose your letter. I will join you shortly."

Blackie followed Hester down the corridor, chewing on the bone.

She sat down at the desk and took a clean piece of parchment from the drawer. She lifted a quill from its holder, dipped it in black ink, and wrote, "Dearest Aunt Maud."

Hester tucked a stray tendril of hair back under her coif. She pondered writing, "My Uncle Llewelyn planned to sacrifice me to his pagan gods, my cousin tortured me then forced me to marry him, and please send monies so I can procure an annulment and marry the man I love." After fiddling with the quill a few moments, she replaced it in the holder.

Confusion reigned in her mind. *I do love Gareth, I owe him my life. He loves me now, but if he knew what I was really like, he would not. Even before Henry, even before Mervyn, I could not love. No, that is not true. I loved. I mean, I love Dickie and Sir Hugh; I love Alice and Aunt Maud. I just never felt that I deserved their love. And neither do I deserve Gareth's. If I marry him, I will only hurt him, and then he will die, just like Mother.*

ister Agnes entered the parlour just ahead of Gareth, who bounded into the room, holding the medicine chest behind his back.

"Good morrow, Sister. Why, Hester, your cheeks are rosy, for which I am heartily glad. See what I have made for you!"

He produced the cherry wood box, and Hester took it in her hands. Gareth stood behind her, demonstrating his handiwork.

"These are compartments with sliding drawers for your herbs. And here in the centre is a place for your mortar to sit and a groove for the pestle. So this way, everything will stay in its place, even when we travel."

Hester gave a small smile. "It is a cunning little chest. Thank you." She put it on the floor beside her. Fatigue overwhelmed her, down to her very marrow.

Disappointment ravaged Gareth's face. He exclaimed, "I stayed up all last night finishing it, and you have hardly looked at it!"

Sister Agnes sent him a glance of sympathy and left the room, saying, "There is a matter I need to attend in the infirmary. I will be back quite soon." She looked straight at Hester. Her message was clear: *Tell him.*

Hester's eyes filled with tears. She felt dirty, besmirched, and surely it was better to drive him away now than have him find out her true nature and then leave her. She felt overcome with shame. She fiddled with her pen and inkwell.

"Hester, what ails you? Why are you crying? Why will you not look at me? Have I offended you in some way?" Gareth spoke, half-beseeching and half-demanding. He kneeled down beside her and reached over for her hand, but she withdrew it.

Gareth brushed tears from his cheeks. "Why do you use me thus? I know you have suffered, but I promise I will make it up to you. I want only to love you and care for you, as my wife."

Hester stared into the empty grate.

"Just talk to me. I will do anything that will make you happy."

Blackie woke up with a whimper. He ran to Gareth and snuggled inside his doublet. Gareth stood up. "Very well," he declared, "I shall not stay if I am unwelcome." He rose, and holding Blackie with one arm, strode toward the door.

"Gareth!" cried Hester. He returned in an instant.

"I am sorry. I am in much pain with my hand still," she lied.

"Oh, in just a little while more it will mend," he said.

"And my spirits are unsettled. It's because of my mother…"

Gareth reached for her good hand, and she let him hold it.

"When your hand is mended we can gather flowers again together. Did you like the ones I left outside your chamber?"

She nodded.

"Remember when we picked St. John's wort? We were happy that day. We will be happy again, I promise you."

Yes, she was happy that day with him. Very happy. But that was before—

"I have learned a new song, do you want to hear it?" said Gareth, interrupting her train of thought.

Hester nodded again, relieved she was not called upon to speak to him. But she berated herself for being a coward and keeping silent. She knew it would be a dreadful mistake to throw away Gareth's love. Even if he left her once he knew all, she must take the chance and tell him everything. "First I need to tell you about the King and about Mervyn. I did a most foolish thing…"

Gareth smiled at her, waiting for her to continue.

"I was foolish enough to believe I could heal the King's terrible leg sores, so I bribed his niece to arrange a royal audience—"

The door flew open and in strode a short, plump man, dressed in a white robe. Gareth released Hester's hand and bowed. Blackie ran to the priest and sniffed around his feet.

"Oh, my goodness!" exclaimed the priest. "A youth courting one of the novitiates! And a three-legged puppy!"

Gareth picked up Blackie.

Hester made a curtsey. "Not at all, Father. I am Hester Vaughan, and you must be Father Jerome."

"And this young man is?"

Hester blushed and stared at the ground. "He is my...," but she could not finish her sentence. She thought, *He is my rescuer, my friend, my dear companion*, but she could not say her husband-to-be.

"I am Gareth, Mistress Vaughan's betrothed," said he, but as he spoke, Blackie barked and drowned out his words.

"You will be the bard Myfanwy just told me about," said the priest.

Sister Agnes entered the room.

"Good morrow, Sister," said Father Jerome.

Sister Agnes smiled and offered him the bowl of fruit.

"Mm, strawberries. Thank you. My little weakness." He winked at Hester and selected two of the biggest berries.

"I must needs parley with Sister Agnes," he said, and the couple withdrew to the window with Blackie yipping after them.

"The Lady Elizabeth is on her way here," said Father Jerome.

"You mean the King's younger daughter?" asked Sister Agnes, her body rigid with shock.

"The bishop told me over dinner last night."

"But whatever for?" Sister Agnes sat and, without waiting for a reply, exclaimed, "We have no place to house her, much less any dishes fit... I must send word to Cook, to see what can be done. And the roof..."

Father Jerome wiped his lips with a crumpled handkerchief. "The party will not arrive for two weeks because Her Ladyship's governess, Mistress Champernon, needs to travel in a litter. She has the stone, and since the household physician has not cured her, she comes, accompanied by her royal mistress, to partake of the healing waters."

"But surely the King cannot permit his daughter to travel here, just because her governess is unwell?" asked Sister Agnes, her face clouded with consternation.

"His Majesty has a secret motive, but I promised the bishop not to tell," said Father Jerome, reaching for another strawberry.

Sister Agnes raised her eyebrows. "A fortnight should suffice for preparations," she said. "'Tis pity Henry destroyed Shrewsbury Abbey last year; the abbot could have accommodated Her Ladyship nicely."

"But the King's grandmother endowed Saint Winifred's; she did not endow the Abbey." The priest smiled. "However, be not discomfited, for Elizabeth brings tents and bedding for the entire household: cooks, her priest, scrivener, physician, and sundry attendants. It is her desire to be no encumbrance to you." His smile broadened. "But she is prodigious fond of sweets, and perhaps…"

Sister Agnes groaned, cutting him off. "She will give us a purse of gold, so we shall still need to make her a handsome present, and we have nothing fit for the King's daughter." She rubbed her forehead.

"I am sure you will solve that dilemma, Sister, but do you not think it would be good to have some little sweetmeats to offer the poor motherless creature on her arrival?" Father Jerome pouted.

"I would hardly call her a poor creature," retorted Sister Agnes. "And I understand you would be reprimanded most severely by the creature herself, were you to suggest that in her presence." She laughed and took a strawberry from the bowl.

Hester and Gareth pretended to be looking out the window but were following every word of the conversation.

"She is eight years old," declared the priest, "and enjoys marzipan fashioned in the guise of animals, or so I hear."

Sister Agnes bit down on the strawberry. "Father, I am not sending to Chester for almonds for marzipan. I have neither men, nor money, nor horses for such foolishness."

"Ah, well then," murmured the priest, appearing crestfallen.

Sister Agnes, regaining her composure, asked, "Have you been introduced to my guests?"

Gareth and Hester walked over to join her and the priest. Father Jerome bent forward to scratch behind Blackie's ears.

"Indeed I have," he said. "To Mistress Vaughan and her two-legged and three-legged friends."

Gareth smiled at Hester. "But I am not simply your friend, am I?" When Hester said nothing, he whispered in her ear, "I am your betrothed, am I not?"

Gareth frowned and addressed the priest. "We plan to marry, once a legal matter has been resolved."

Hester murmured something inaudible and dropped his hand to examine her nails. Gareth took a step back.

"Hester, I shall not stay and be denied by you. If you cannot acknowledge me as your betrothed before Sister Agnes and this priest, I know not what is to be done."

Father Jerome looked with sympathy at him. "My son, do you fancy a visit to the confectioner in Chester?"

"Why not?" Gareth nearly spat the words. "For it is plain to see that I am not wanted here."

The priest handed him a small purse and made the sign of the cross over Gareth's head. "You are exempt from attending Mass, on account of your high errand."

Gareth bowed to Sister Agnes and Father Jerome, and strode from the room.

The priest sighed. "Well, well, young love."

Sister Agnes looked at Hester. "You did not tell him, did you?"

Hester shook her head. "No," she whispered. "We were interrupted."

"Later then," said Sister Agnes, pursing her lips. "Now we shall go hear Mass."

The three set off down the corridor to the chapel, stepping around the puddles in the flagstones.

Father Jerome turned to Hester. "Your accent is southern, my child, so what brought you to Wales?"

"My father sent for me because he was dying. He passed away last month."

"I am sorry to hear that," said Father Jerome, making the sign of the cross above Hester's head. "What was his name?"

"Dafydd Vaughan," replied Hester.

The priest halted in mid-stride. "Not brother to Llewelyn Vaughan?"

"Yes," said Hester. She felt goosebumps rise on her arms.

"I regret to tell you he, also, is dead," said Father Jerome.

Hester crossed herself. *He planned to kill me*, she thought. *I shall not miss him, but what about his men?*

"I believe two dozen or so were caught and hanged," said the priest, as if reading her mind.

Hester gasped aloud. That was the entire party; all the able-bodied men of Dinas Emrys were dead.

Sister Agnes looked at Hester, compassion in her eyes. "We will talk further after Mass."

"Ladies, I must tell you something, but in secrecy," said Father Jerome. A drop of water from the ceiling fell on his head, and he flicked it away. "The real reason why the Lady Elizabeth comes here is to pray for her father. This Welsh attack on Henry failed, as did another revolt in the spring. But he now lives in terror and has charged his daughter to make a pilgrimage, as it were, to this holy place and offer thanks for his survival." The priest wagged his head. "'Tis said he cannot sleep for nightmares of his grandmother,

Margaret Beaufort, our benefactress. He hopes the prayers of her great-granddaughter can appease her ghost."

"But why send her, a mere child, and not Mary?" asked the nun.

"Mary accompanies the King and her stepmother, the queen, on their royal progress." Father Jerome laughed. "A stepmother who is some seven or eight years younger than herself!"

The trio entered the chapel and genuflected to the altar. Sister Agnes and the priest approached the chancel, while Hester stood at the back with the supplicants. A woman with a swelling the size of a beet in her neck and an old man on crutches made room for her. The scent of incense hung heavy in the air, and the chapel was silent save for the occasional cough.

Paintings of the life of the Virgin adorned the walls, and a stained glass window of Saint Winifred cast blue and green light into the chancel. Carved images of the apostles stood out on the rood screen, and a gleaming silver crucifix and pyx stood on the altar table.

Sister Agnes took her place in the choir, and Father Jerome began: "*Asperges me, Domine, hyssopo, et mundabor; lavabis me, et super nivem dealbabor.*"

Hester wondered why sprinkling someone with hyssop would cleanse him, but she had always liked the second part that said it would render him whiter than snow. She vowed that as soon as Gareth returned, she would tell him everything about Henry and Mervyn. She prayed for him and for her aunt and uncle and for Alice and Dickie. She prayed for her father's soul and that God had seen fit to spare some, at least, of Llewelyn's men, especially Twgardan, Nia's betrothed.

The nuns' singing soared to the rafters, and Hester's thoughts drifted upwards. For a few minutes her mind was still. The service ended and Sister Agnes beckoned Hester to follow Father Jerome and her to the front door.

"Well, Sister, I shall leave you now." The priest wagged his finger at Hester. "Not a word, now, for Henry does not wish people to know of his terror."

They reached the door. "I believe Her Ladyship is worth watching," said the priest.

"How so?" asked Sister Agnes. The nun indicated to Hester to move the pails in the vestibule to better catch the drips from the ceiling.

"Plans are underway to restore Mary and Elizabeth to the succession. Henry fears that Edward will die young, and unless he passes the crown to one of his progeny, he has damned his soul and nigh destroyed our country in vain."

Sister Agnes nodded. "Yes, for no one expects another son."

Father Jerome opened the door. "And the Lady Mary is sick of heart; she will not survive to bear issue. That leaves Elizabeth."

The three stood on the top step, and each drew in a deep breath. Hester inhaled the fragrance of the surrounding meadow and watched a pair of swallows daubing mud on their nest under the eaves of the barn. The depth of the holy-day silence was so deep she thought she could almost hear the birds' wings beating.

"A pretty piece of speculation!" Sister Agnes laughed. "And, if it comes to pass, we shall fare even worse. Henry, from respect for his grandmother's memory, kept a leash on the wreckers here." She grimaced. "Will such a queen, Protestant-fed from infancy, provide us with a new roof? Will she restore the faith her father has well-nigh eliminated?"

"No, Sister," conceded the priest, pursing his lips. "But if she ceased from executing those whose faith differed from her own, would that not be some improvement?"

Father Jerome said his farewell to Sister Agnes. Hester made a curtsey and he signed her with the cross, then the women walked to the parlour.

Hester thought fleetingly of Twgardan's sisters, Bessie and Maire, and whether they had sweethearts among the slain. She wondered about Bronwyn, who would now be just a few weeks from her confinement. Was her husband dead or alive?

Once inside the room, Sister Agnes looked at Hester. "I wonder what gift we can we make to Lady Elizabeth?"

Hester shook her head and sat and gazed at the opening line of her letter: *Dearest Aunt Maud.*

Sister Agnes glanced at it. "You have a fair hand, my child."

"Thank you. I learned that, too, from Aunt Maud."

The nun reached down the Book of Hours from its shelf and unwrapped it. "How long would it take for you to write over the faded Latin script? It would make a fitting present for royalty."

"Perhaps a few days," said Hester. "I would be honoured to work on it." Also she knew she would rather do that than write to Aunt Maud.

Myfanwy knocked and poked her head around the door. "Sister, pray excuse me, but there are two men outside. Father Jerome sent them to help with the roof, but one has a bad morbel on his leg. Would you please to look at it before he goes up the ladder?"

Sister Agnes sighed and left with Myfanwy.

Hester leafed through the book and counted twelve pages. The Latin was still decipherable, so it was simply a matter of inking over the just-visible words. She ground more charcoal for ink and resharpened the quill. A trail of vines intertwined with daisies bordered each page, and when she was bored from writing, she added curlicues to the tips of the vines and extra petals to the flowers. Blackie lay at her feet, gnawing his bone. All the time she worked she thought about how glad she would be to see Gareth again.

areth rode hard with Corwen struggling to keep balanced on his shoulder. The crow shrieked in Gareth's ear until they reached an inn at Chester. "I should have left you at Holywell," he said. The ruffled bird glared back at him.

It was dusk. Gareth was the only guest, so the innkeeper was happy to welcome man and bird but insisted Corwen stay in a cage, which he would supply. After a supper of mutton and parsnip stew, Gareth withdrew to his chamber and lay down, fully dressed, on a straw pallet. Although exhausted, he slept badly because of mice scurrying in the walls.

He rose early the next morning and ventured into Chester market, a press of farmers, fishmongers, ale sellers, and local housewives. Corwen cackled as they passed a butcher's stall stocked with flayed rabbits hanging from a rack above trays of beef liver. Gareth bought a penny worth of liver wrapped in a piece of cloth; he gave Corwen a sliver and put the rest in his pocket.

The crowd was raucous and the smells overwhelming—the rank odour of the tanner's stall with its treated hides mingled with the acrid stench of gutters blocked with rotting vegetables and animal dung.

Gareth startled when a stranger's hand grasped his crotch.

A young woman with a squint in her eye stared up into his face. "A penny is all I ask, Master. I am clean, God's truth." She held a thin woolen shawl over a tattered red dress, and her hair straggled in rats' tails down her back.

Gareth removed her hand, murmuring a decline.

"Give me a penny anyway," she wheedled. "As I am a Christian, I've not had a bite to eat in two days."

He reached into his purse and handed her a coin.

A stout woman called from the baker's stall. "Don't be going with that whipperginnie! I swear she's had half a dozen jacks in there already this morning, and all of them poxed." She sidled up to him, and Gareth could smell the yeast on her. "I'll do you for a half-penny, Master," she cackled. "I could blow on your little soldier an' warm him up."

Gareth smiled and held up his hands to gesture no.

"Do not be afeard I'll bite him off," she cackled. "See, I have no teeth!" She roared with laughter.

Startled, Corwen leaped about on Gareth's shoulder, croaking like a fiend.

The woman sprang back. "God's breath! Get that devil away from me!" She crossed and recrossed herself.

Gareth walked away and gave Corwen another piece of liver. "Who would have thought a crow would make such a fine chaperone?" he murmured to his companion.

He found a confectioner's stall, where he bought a bag each of sugar and almonds. He was headed back to the inn, when out from an alleyway leaped a bedraggled young woman, her face all scratched and her clothes torn. She accosted Gareth, who sighed and reached into his purse, but when he looked closer, he recognized Nia.

"Gareth!" she cried. "It is you!" But she broke out coughing so hard that she could hardly stand, let alone speak. Gareth supported her while the paroxysm passed.

"Nia! What has happened to you?"

"Oh Gareth, I am glad to see you. I have slept in ditches this past week and am fair sick with hunger." She groaned. "Llewelyn and all the men were seized at Saint Alban's, before they had a chance to shoot even one arrow at the King." She sobbed. "Twgardan was killed along with the rest, and now I wish I had died with him, but I was afraid and I hid from the fighting."

"Nia, fach, I am very sorry. Here, let me help you back to my inn, where you can rest."

They were beside a pie man's stall, and Gareth gave two pennies for a meat pie, which he wrapped in his handkerchief and handed to Nia. "Careful, it will burn your mouth," he warned.

Nia took a big bite. "Oww!" she exclaimed, but devoured it all the same. "Can I have another? I shall wait till it cools."

Gareth bought another pie and Nia held it. "And Bronwyn's husband, Dewi, died too, and her soon to have their babe. Llewelyn was taken to the city and hanged in chains," she said, tears running down her face. "Gibbeted is what the English call it. They had to make an extra yard of chain to wrap around his belly." She wiped her eyes on the handkerchief and bit into the pie. "A London drover brought me to Chester in his cart two days ago, and since then I have been trying to get home."

Nia ate the rest of the pie and licked gravy from her fingers. "Oh, but I nearly forgot," said she. "The drover said how Sir Hugh Grantmire, Mistress Hester's uncle, was hanged or beheaded, he didn't know which, back a few weeks ago."

"What? Oh, poor man, and poor Hester, when she finds out. But why?"

"Henry didn't like him, I suppose," replied Nia.

"And what about his family, Hester's aunt and her brother and cousin?"

"I heard nothing of them. But I must get home and tell Twgardan's mother; she will be heartbroken, too," whimpered Nia.

They reached the inn, where Nia was seized with another fit of coughing. She, Gareth, and Corwen went to his room where all three fell asleep on the straw pallet.

By morning Nia's cough seemed to have settled. Over breakfast Gareth declared, "Nia, I must discover what has befallen Hester's family. I cannot return to Holywell without being able to tell her they are safe…or, if they too…" He faltered. "You stay here and regain your strength. I have silver enough to pay the innkeeper and for you to buy some new clothes. When I return in a week's time, we will travel to Holywell together."

"But Gareth, that journey will take ten days at least."

"I shall change horses every few hours." Gareth took a long draw from his mug of ale.

"How will you do that? Have you so much money?" Nia bit into her slice of bread.

"I have enough, but this will help." He pulled the ruby ring out of his doublet. "It should suffice to get me fresh horses on the way. None would dare refuse the King's messenger."

Gareth frowned. "Hester no longer loves me. This ring may as well be some use. I once thought of it as our betrothal ring, but now I would gladly throw it on the midden pile."

"I am sure she loves you," said Nia, between bites, "but her mind is addled, that is all."

"Can you take care of Corwen?" asked Gareth. "He needs feeding twice a day, and if you can let him out of his cage even once, he will be grateful."

Three days of riding gave Gareth time to reflect on what had befallen Llewelyn and his men. He felt some sadness for Llewelyn's pitiful end but mostly anger that his mad venture had cost the life of most every adult male in Dinas Emrys. He must return there as soon as possible, with or without Hester.

He arrived at Hartbourne House in the late afternoon. At the front door he encountered a footman carrying a box of glassware. "Do you know where Lady Maud Grantmire lives now?"

The man shook his head. "No, and you are trespassing. Be off with you."

Gareth led his horse toward the stables. "Halloo there, does anyone know where Lady Maud can be found?" he shouted.

A young lad emerged from a stall. "Sir Hugh is dead," he informed him, "and Lady Maud and Lady Alice, her daughter, are gone to a cottage at old Syon, upriver a few miles."

Gareth gave him a shilling. An hour later he dismounted and knocked at the back door of Syon House. He told the servant who opened the door that he was a friend of the Grantmires. The man looked askance at his travel-stained clothing but seeing no harm in the youth, pointed toward a clump of elms. "There is a cottage behind those trees where they all lived till a week ago. But then Lady Maud and her daughter and her nurse were taken for witchcraft and the mother drowned when they swam her, and the nurse went and died in gaol." He shook his head. "Lady Alice is staying here with Mistress Smith and her daughter."

"What a terrible loss for the poor lady." Gareth's head sank on his breast, and he prayed Modron bless Lady Alice and her family. He looked up. "May I speak with her?" Gareth also felt grief for Hester; nearly all her family was now dead. He was near to falling from exhaustion and had to lean on his horse's flank for support.

"Lady Alice is presently visiting them what's left at the cottage."

Gareth thanked the servant. He reached the cottage and met a young man digging in the vegetable patch. "Hallo there!" he called. "I am looking for Lady Alice."

"She is within," replied the man, resting on his spade and spitting on the ground.

"Who comes hither?" asked another male voice, in the mellifluous tones of the aristocracy. A thin young man with long fair hair, shouldering an axe, appeared from behind the cottage.

"I am Gareth the Bard, and I come from Mistress Vaughan in Holywell."

"Oh!" exclaimed the fair youth, laying down his axe. "I am William of Bayston. I trust Mistress Vaughan fares well?"

Gareth felt a moment's confusion and a brief stab of envy. How did this nobleman come to know Hester? "Mistress Vaughan is well enough, I thank you," he replied with asperity.

"I am Lady Alice's betrothed. This is John, Dickie's minder," William paused, "no, not his minder, his companion. Dickie is Mistress Vaughan's younger brother."

Gareth nodded that he understood who Dickie was. He saluted John, who bowed and returned to his digging.

Gareth, giving an inward sigh of relief, followed Sir William indoors. He saw a young woman wearing a black silk dress sitting beside a rough pinewood table on which sat a jug of pink briar roses. The room was fragrant with rose scent. A boy knelt in one corner weaving a rush basket; his face was scrunched up in concentration. The woman was reading from a book, which she set down as Gareth entered.

"Do not stop, Alice," said the boy. "I like this part where Daniel gets thrown into the lion's den and gets out again."

"We have a visitor, Dickie," said she. Gareth could tell from her red-rimmed eyes that she had been crying recently. He bowed and Alice pointed him to a stool. Overpowered by fatigue, he nearly tripped over it before he sat down. William moved to stand behind Alice, where he hovered protectively.

"Dickie, will you and John go catch us a pair of trout for our supper?" asked William.

"Very well, we can do that," replied Dickie and left.

"Any mention of his sister distresses him," said William to Gareth, who nodded.

William turned to Alice. "My dear, this is Master Gareth. He has news of your cousin Hester."

Alice poured Gareth a cup of ale.

"Hester is well, I hope?" Alice clasped her hands.

Gareth rubbed his eyes in an effort to stay awake. "Indeed, my lady, she is. She is staying at present at a shrine in Holywell." He was on the point of explaining Hester's sham marriage and her illness but did not want to distress her cousin. "Lord Dafydd, her father, died, and you may have heard that his brother, Lord Llewelyn, is also…deceased."

"I am sorry to hear that."

"And please accept my sympathy for your own grievous losses, my lady." Gareth forced himself to sit upright on his seat. "I was told by someone at the great house."

Alice blessed herself and tears trickled down her cheeks. She spoke in a choked voice. "Thank you. It has been very hard." She could not talk for a few seconds. "I have thought about Hester a great deal, and am glad to know that she is with the good nuns of Saint Winifred. I wish I could see her again…" Her voice trailed away, and William gave her shoulders a gentle squeeze. "But you can tell Hester that Dickie and I, at least, are safe and give her our love," said Alice.

Gareth nodded. "I shall be happy to do so."

"Tell her Sir William and I plan to wed, soon," said Alice, her cheeks turning as pink as the roses on the table.

"I wish you both joy," responded Gareth.

"We shall marry in Shrewsbury, where my parents live, and Wales lies just across the border." William looked inquiringly at Alice, and she nodded.

"Hester would be delighted to see you," said Gareth. *Even if she does not want to see me,* he thought. His head slumped forward on his chest.

"You must rest now," said Alice. "You can sleep up in the loft."

He had a foot on the bottom rung when Alice asked, "Did Hester send you here?"

"No, I wanted to be able to tell her you were all well before we parted company." Gareth sighed and stood in front of Alice. "I have loved Hester right well, and I thought she did me, but I know she keeps something important hidden inside."

"You do know that the King misused Hester when she visited him at the end of May?" Alice's cheeks suffused with crimson, and she reached over to rearrange the roses on the table.

"No, I did not know that. Thank you for telling me." *It explains the ring, at least*, thought Gareth.

✦

While Gareth slept, Alice conferred with William.

"It is time for us to leave the cottage," she said, frowning as she looked around the room.

William held her hand in his. "And the sooner we leave England, the better."

Alice's eyebrows shot up. "Why so?"

"Jenkins's cronies will wonder why he went missing the same time as I escaped. They will soon come in search of me."

Alice nodded and tightened her grip on William's hand. "Then Wales it is," she said.

They set off to find Dickie and John and met them returning from the river.

"Four trout!" exclaimed Dickie. "And I caught them all myself."

"Well done," said Alice, kissing him. "Now listen close, for William has something exciting to say."

They headed back to the cottage.

"Lady Alice and I plan to marry at my home near Shrewsbury," said William, "then set off for Wales."

"To Wales, where Hessie is?" Dickie jumped up and down. "But I cannot ride, and I think it must be a very long way to walk."

"Dickie, you are much stronger now and you have not taken a fit in over a week," said Alice. "I think you could ride Mirabel very well."

William took John aside and handed him five gold sovereigns. John shook his head. "I have no need of all this."

"But you will come with us, yes?"

"Yes." John nodded and his brow furrowed. "I feel toward Master Dickon more as if he were my younger brother now. But I must go back to Hartbourne estate to say goodbye to my mother, and she will be glad of a couple of these coins, to be sure."

The next morning Gareth asked Alice for a sheet of parchment. William handed down a piece from the shelf containing the herbal remedies. Gareth explained how there was hardly a single able-bodied adult remaining in Dinas Emrys on account of Llewellyn's failed attack on the King.

"Oh, that is dreadful! Those poor men, and their poor families," said Alice, her hand raised to her mouth.

William placed his arm around her shoulders and kissed her on the head. Alice looked up at him. "They may be glad of our help." She gave a little smile as she realized how like her mother she was.

William's face brightened, as though Alice's smile had lifted a weight from him.

"Indeed they will be glad of your knowledge of healing herbs." Gareth sharpened a quill and Alice set a jar of black ink in front of him. "But even more valuable will be that once you master the Welsh language, you can teach them to read and write."

Alice nodded and smiled again.

Gareth drew an outline of North Wales. "It takes a day and a half from Shrewsbury to Holywell," he said. "I do not know how long Hester plans to remain there, nor I, either."

Alice shot him a quizzical look, but Gareth ignored it.

"The Roman road leads to Caerhun, where there is a good inn, and then on to Caernarfon." He indicated with the pen. "Then follow the central road to Beddgelert, and from there take this bridle path up toward Snowdonia. Watch for a blasted oak stump and take the path to the left. If you miss the turning you will soon be lost." Gareth smiled. "It is the reason only the invited ever find Dinas Emrys."

"It will indeed suit us," said William, clasping Alice's waist and holding her to him.

"You will all be needed." Gareth rubbed at the ink stains on his fingers. "The women cannot tend the animals as well as bring in the crops."

Alice sat down to write to Aunt Joyce, telling her that she was well and that a dear friend from London was visiting. She hoped her aunt would understand from this that William had been safely returned to her. She forbore to give more information, or even her thanks, for should the letter be intercepted, it could place William's life at risk.

nother three days saw Gareth back at the inn, where he found Nia lying in bed, pale and feverish. "You have the pleurisy," said Gareth, frowning with concern. "I should not have left you."

Corwen perched on his shoulder, nibbling his ear.

"Nay, 'tis no blame on you. I was mending well up until yesterday, when I took a turn for the worse." Nia reached for a cloth and spat in it. "No blood," she said, and tried to smile.

"We shall leave tomorrow for Saint Winifred's, where the nuns will heal you," said Gareth, stroking the bird. "Then I will escort you back to Dinas Emrys, for I do not plan to spend long at Holywell."

Nia took a coughing fit so did not hear Gareth's last few words.

The next day Gareth spent the last of Peredur's money on a gentle pony for Nia, and they wended their way back to Holywell.

On the fourth morning following Gareth's departure, Hester wondered what kept him so long. The journey should take no more than a day each way, or perhaps two if his horse lost a shoe on the road. Her heart sank further as each hour passed without sign of him. He must return, if only to deposit his purchases with Sister Agnes. But would he then stay or leave again?

Hester reached the last page of the missal. She penned in the words of the office for compline, opposite the painting of the Flight of the Holy Family to Egypt. She stared at the donkey carrying Mary and the infant Jesus. She suddenly remembered Lady, her own pony. However could she have forgotten her friend?

She sprinkled sand on the page. As she rose, Blackie cocked an ear, leaped up, and followed her outside. Hester walked around the perimeter of the main building. The sun shone and the air was fragrant with the smell of gorse. A raven called from a nearby elm and alighted on a stump so close she could see the white membrane flickering across its eye as it blinked. It wobbled on the stump until Blackie chased it and it flew off, making the strange coughing sound inimical to ravens.

"You are Corwen's relation," Hester called out to it. "Tell him to bring Gareth back to me. Please."

She stopped by a patch of grass and pulled up a few handfuls of herbage. On entering the stables she heard Lady whinny from her stall. Hester ran to her and threw her arms around the pony's neck. She rubbed the back of her hand against Lady's muzzle, and the little mare snorted with pleasure. Lady accepted the fresh grass, and Hester stroked her neck and ran her hands through her mane. She nuzzled her face into the downy hair beneath Lady's ear.

"Soon I shall be able to ride you again," she whispered. "Another week and I will be able to hold both reins." She stood back and proclaimed, "Well, Lady, your coat is shiny as a new minted groat. I must remember to thank Sister Agnes, for her people are busy enough without having additional creatures to tend. Including me." She smiled ruefully.

Hester kissed Lady's muzzle. "I miss Gareth," she said. "Maybe I will go to the drying room and find some herbs to put in that marvellous little chest he made for me. What do you think, Lady?"

Lady gave a snicker, which Hester took for agreement.

She lifted Blackie out of a manger he had settled into and set off back to the house, taking a shortcut through the kitchen garden. Myfanwy was there, cutting parsley. Hester asked her how to get to the drying room.

"It is the third door past the parlour. The top hinge is broken, and the door won't shut properly. You will smell the herbs as you go by." She frowned. "What is keeping Master Gareth? Should he not have been back last night?"

"If Master Gareth chooses to stay away, well…" Hester could not complete the sentence. Tears prickled in her eyes. "He is his own master and must do what likes him best." She picked up Blackie and hid her face in his fur.

"Now, Mistress, I am sorry. Do not take on so," soothed Myfanwy. "Just I thought maybe you were being cruel…" She stopped in confusion. "I know that a maid should not seem too willing, like, especially when her suitor is as handsome as Master Gareth. Not to mention that his voice would put the holy angels' singing to shame." She covered her mouth and giggled. "Not that I have heard the holy angels singing, but you know what I mean."

Hester smiled. "Indeed, I do." She asked, "Would you mind Blackie for a little while?"

Hester fetched the medicine chest from her cell. She opened the broken door to the drying room and found it unoccupied. A long scrubbed oak table stood in the centre, and hooks hanging from the rafters burgeoned with sheaves of drying herbs—rosemary, lavender, and thyme—and their scents filled the air. Hester was reminded of the drying room at Hartbourne. She said a prayer for her family and for Gareth's safe and speedy return. Standing on a stool, she reached up to break off a small branch of thyme. She stripped the leaves from the stalk and placed them in one of the compartments of her chest, then did the same with a branch of rosemary.

Two novitiates entered the room, whispering. One was around eighteen and the other sixteen. "I hope she brings her best robes," said the younger. "I've never seen a lady before, and they say her hoods are made of velvet and sarsenet!"

"Sarsenet," echoed the older girl. "You speak in jest! Lady Elizabeth is but an infant and—" They noticed Hester and dropped curtseys to her. Hester bowed her head in acknowledgement.

"Mistress Vaughan, we did not expect to find you here," said the elder.

"I need herbs for my medicine chest." Hester paused. "But how do you know who I am?"

"Oh!" exclaimed the younger. "You are Master Gareth's betrothed, for whom he made that cunning little chest."

Hester was taken aback by this familiarity with her affairs. "How do you know about the chest?" she asked, more sharply than she intended.

"Sometimes he would bring it here. He sang and polished it, as we ground away." The younger novitiate pointed to a pestle and mortar on a shelf. "It made the time fly by. We powdered a whole gunny sack full of flax seed while you were sick."

"However, we are glad you are recovered," interposed the elder. "I am Sister Monica and this is Sister Catherine."

Sister Monica had a fair complexion and freckles on her nose. Sister Catherine was darker, and deep pockmarks scarred her forehead and cheeks. But her expression was so cheerful that to Hester's eyes the blemishes hardly existed.

Sister Catherine tugged down a branch of rosemary hanging from the rafters. She descended into a low curtsey and addressed Sister Monica. "Lady Elizabeth, allow me the honour of presenting you with the royal rosemary. I only ask in return that you let me admire your ermine-lined sleeves."

"Don't be a silly," retorted Sister Monica, taking the rosemary. "It is July. The Lady Elizabeth will not be wearing ermine." She ran to a tub of water and dipped the branch in it. "She will be wearing cool silks that float in the breeze. Rose pinks and purples and primrose yellows. And now I shall anoint you with water from the royal rosemary in the hope that it will clear your addled brain." She sprinkled it over Sister Catherine's head.

"Oh, the water from the royal rosemary is cold and running down the back of my neck!" exclaimed Sister Catherine, seizing a bunch of fennel and dipping it in the water. Unable to reach the top of her fellow nun's head, she had to be content with flicking it over her chest.

Hester laughed. *I haven't laughed like this since we all went out that day, Gareth and I and Bronwyn.* She remembered Gareth's kiss and became aware of an ache inside of her.

Over the next few days Hester made herself useful in the drying room and distillery. Her hand was well enough mended that she could prepare liniments and brews for the patients. All the time, she wondered what detained Gareth. Blackie kept occupied chasing the flies that buzzed in the hot, still air.

One evening Sister Agnes sent for her. When Hester arrived in her parlour, the nun looked up from a ledger. She sighed. "Lady Elizabeth arrives in approximately a week's time. We have six lambs for the slaughter and three hogs, a sack of fine white flour, and a cheese being delivered tomorrow. The biggest hole in the roof is mended…" She sighed again. "Our first royal visitor in living memory. Well, my child, show me the Book of Hours."

Hester brought it down from the shelf.

"This is splendid," said the nun. "There are but a dozen this fine in the country. Probably most of those are in King Henry's hands, and he, alas, will never open one." She turned the pages. "I wonder how Elizabeth will turn out. I hear she has a formidable intellect, but it must both pain and shame her to have had a mother who was executed for adultery and witchcraft and a father who declared her a bastard."

"I did not know about Anne Boleyn's witchcraft," said Hester.

"Henry had to find the worst crimes he could accuse her of. And any woman charged with that crime is grateful for the mercy of the blade."

"Indeed, that is a grievous burden for a child to bear."

"We know how bitter Lady Mary is, and her mother, Katherine of Aragon, was only divorced, not beheaded," continued Sister Agnes. "I fear if Elizabeth ever reigned she could prove a worse tyrant even than her father." She straightened the crucifix at her neck. "You know her mother was greatly for the reformers?"

Hester shook her head.

"In fact Anne hid at least one of them, at great peril to herself. She may have been a scheming woman, but she had the stomach of a courageous man."

Hester attempted a jest. "Then I am looking forward to seeing her daughter, but from a safe distance."

"Ah, so your pride will not be hurt by encountering a child more learned than yourself?" teased Sister Agnes.

Hester had grace enough to blush.

"Nevertheless, I would like you to present the book to Her Ladyship. After all, you may be related. She, too, descends from Enyfed Fychan, seneschal of Wales, and as you are aware, Vaughan is but another version of that name."

Hester startled. She had no desire to meet Henry's daughter.

Sister Agnes continued, "It is a chance for you to forgive someone who has hurt you, in proxy as it were. That is, if you are ready." She paused and added, "Such chances come but seldom."

Hester's stomach clenched. She knew that the anger and abhorrence she felt toward the King injured him no whit, but they festered inside of her, like a cancre. She wondered if she even wanted to heal from this wound she held inside. For who would she be if she held no resentment against the world?

Her mind in conflict, she paused, then answered, "That is a great honour, indeed, but..." she sought an excuse, "but I cannot, for I have nothing suitable to wear."

"Then we must find something," said the nun. "Besides, you cannot continue to wear the robe of a novitiate, betrothed as you are." Sister Agnes laughed.

"No," agreed Hester, smiling. "But what keeps Gareth away so long?"

"I daresay our bard can fend for himself." Sister Agnes stood as did Hester. "There is a dress that our dear departed Sister Lucy brought as part of her dowry. It is a fine robe and richly embroidered. She planned to make an altar cloth from it but was called to her heavenly reward before the task was even started." The women bowed their heads in prayer. "May light perpetual shine upon her soul."

Hester also sent up a prayer for her mother and father.

"So, we are agreed?" asked the nun, and Hester nodded.

Sister Agnes called for Myfanwy. "There is a package in the cedar chest at the back of the chapel. Bring it here, child."

A few minutes later, the girl returned, half-hauling and half-carrying a linen-wrapped bundle nearly as tall as she. Sister Agnes unfolded it to reveal a forest green velvet dress with gold tissue sleeves and a gold embroidered underskirt. As she shook it out a few dried stalks of lavender fell away.

Myfanwy gasped. "How beautiful!"

Blackie jumped up at the dress. Sister Agnes said, "Pray take Blackie to the kitchen." The little maid reluctantly scooped up the dog and backed out of the room, her eyes glued to the gorgeous robe.

"I will help you into it," said Sister Agnes, holding the dress toward Hester.

Hester removed her white robe and stepped into the underskirt and Sister Agnes tied the kirtle, which was embroidered with pearls in an interlocking rose pattern. Sister Agnes fastened the bodices and attached the sleeves.

The yoke was cut low, and Hester was aware of exposing a goodly amount of bosom. She had not worn such a dress since she visited Henry, and her heart skipped a beat at the unwelcome memory.

A black satin headdress with a pearl biliment completed her costume. "The skirt needs lengthening by an inch, otherwise it is perfect," declared Sister Agnes. "I feel the future bodes well for you and Gareth," she continued. "These are times of great upheaval, and men rise in ways of which their grandfathers never dreamed.

After all, Cardinal Wolsey's father was a butcher, and look how far he rose."

Hester smiled to hear Sister Agnes give her the same reasons for marrying Gareth as she had given the nun but a few days before. "Thank you. Your approval means a great deal to me," she said. She blushed with happiness for having this beautiful gown to wear for him on his return. Surely he would return, soon, and forgive her when she asked his pardon for her rudeness toward him?

"It is late, we must attend compline, and then to bed," said Sister Agnes. She smiled. "If we had a mirror, you would see how well your new dress becomes you, but alas, being a convent, we have none."

Hester thought about her uncle and aunt, and Alice and Dickie; she wished she could share her happiness with them. How strange that she, who had abhorred the idea of being banished to Wales to marry a gentleman farmer, was looking forward with all her heart to marrying a nigh penniless Welsh bard. She prayed Mervyn might somehow die and save all the difficulty of procuring an annulment. But how could a prayer for someone's death, even if that someone was as horrid as Mervyn, be a good start to a marriage?

he next morning Hester sat at the desk before the parchment on which she had written "Dearest Aunt" a week ago. She yawned and turned to Myfanwy, who was letting down the hem of her new robe. Blackie lay, curled up on the window seat.

"How much longer?" asked Hester.

"Patience, Mistress," murmured Myfanwy. "I am stitching as fast as I can so it is ready for when a certain person returns."

Hester blushed and Myfanwy sighed. "You are so very fortunate. You are pretty and have a beautiful new gown, you know all kinds of physic, and Gareth loves you."

"Oh, thank you, Myfanwy," said Hester. "That is a lot of blessings." If only she could feel half as accomplished on the inside as Myfanwy saw her from the outside.

There was the sound of knocking at the main door. A minute later the door to Sister Agnes's study opened, and in staggered Gareth, carrying Nia. Blackie raced to him, and Hester started out of her chair to greet them. Gareth set Nia down on the chair beside Hester, who took Nia's hand and said to Myfanwy, "Fetch Sister Agnes!"

"She has the pleurisy in her lungs," said Gareth to Hester, "but 'tis more grief and exhaustion that ails her. Grief on account of—" He was interrupted by the arrival of Sister Agnes, who took one look at Nia and said, "We must get her into bed, straight away. But the infirmary is still full, and—"

"She can have my little room under the stair," offered Gareth. "I can sleep in the barn."

Only then did Hester note his haggard appearance. His dark

hair was plastered to his skull, and his eyes were bloodshot. He had several days' growth of beard, and his jerkin was torn and mud-splattered.

"You had best sit down, for I have sad news," said Gareth to Hester as Sister Agnes and Myfanwy took Nia to her room.

"Are you not going to embrace me?" asked Hester.

"I expect soon to return to Dinas Emrys," he replied, and sat by her side.

"Gareth, you look sore distressed." Hester leaned forward and took his hands in her own. "Is it on account of our last meeting? Please forgive me, I did not know my mind at all well, then."

Gareth took his hands back and placed his head in them. He sighed. "Twgardan is dead, as are all Llewelyn's men." He hesitated. He could not bring himself yet to tell her about her uncle and aunt.

"Oh, no! Poor Nia!" exclaimed Hester. "I had heard that Llewelyn and his men perished, but I hoped there would be some who escaped."

Gareth groaned. "There is not a man or youth between the ages of twelve and fifty left in the village." He looked up at her. "But it is about your uncle and aunt. I am most sorry. I doubt you will have heard what befell them"

He paused, just in case Hester had learned while he was away.

"No. Oh, please God they are not…"

Gareth took a deep breath. "I am afraid so. Sir Hugh was executed last month, and Lady Maud but two weeks ago drowned when they swam her for a witch, and your nurse died in gaol—"

"No, it cannot be!" screamed Hester, covering her ears. She felt as if the ground surged beneath her and she was being swallowed down into a deep crevasse. She gulped for air. "And what of Alice and Dickie?"

"They are safe and plan to come and live in Dinas Emrys." Gareth explained that William was now an outlaw in England, but Hester was not paying attention.

"Thank God for that," she said. She sat, dazed, and thought how reluctant she had been to write to her uncle, and now he was dead. He had cared for her, and at their very last meeting at Hartbourne, she had disobeyed him. She would never be able to apologize now. Worse still, her aunt had died a horrible death, and poor Goody, too. Hester felt numb and even though she thought surely she must cry, no tears came.

Gareth placed his hands on hers, but she pulled hers away. "I need to be alone," she said in a low voice.

Gareth bowed stiffly and left the room, followed by a silent Blackie.

Hester looked up at the painting of the Virgin and child. "Do not try to tell me there is anything good in this life," she snarled. She sped from the room and ran across the field to the cemetery. She stood facing her mother's tomb. "Oh, Mother!" she cried. "And now your brother is dead and the wife who loved him. It is not fair! I cannot bear this." Still no tears came.

The sun beat down on her back, and sweat collected on her spine. She heard someone approach. "Hester, I am sorry for your grief," said Sister Agnes, "but there is nothing you can do here." She placed a hand on her shoulder, adding, "And Nia would be glad of your company."

"You don't understand!" declared Hester. Her cheeks were flushed and her hair was in straggles around her face. "Uncle Hugh was mother and father to me. I loved Aunt Maud, too, for she was kind, but her heart belonged to the Church foremost. Besides, she was a woman and could die, just like Mother. But Uncle Hugh, as a man, was safe to love, and now he is dead. They are both dead. I cannot, I shall not, bear it."

"Listen to me," demanded Sister Agnes. "Your aunt and uncle are in the hands of the All Merciful. Our duty is to comfort the living. Gareth travelled six days straight to determine that your brother and cousin were safe."

Hester murmured, "Oh, I did not know that. He did not say."

"Did you not think to ask why he was gone so long?"

Hester made no reply.

"What am I to do?" she asked the statue of Mary. Then, "Why am I asking you?" She wiped sweat from her brow and turned to Sister Agnes. "And you, why should I listen to you? You hide in this cloister. You don't know what it means to give all your love to another and risk having them ripped away from you, again and again." Hester paused for breath. "Here at Saint Winifred's, you don't have to take a chance on love. You never have to think, as I do, what if I give everything of myself to Gareth and he dies? I lack courage, I know, but you only ever see other people's troubles from the outside." She shouted, "I hate this place. I wish I had never been born. I want to die!"

"Hester Vaughan, I shall forbear answering you. You sound like a headstrong child who has never learned to grow up. Yes, you have experienced hardship, but how dare you think you are the only one?"

Hester's thoughts tumbled into each other; she thought of the witch and how it felt to be hated, but even being hated was better than being totally alone. Only in pain and anger can you bear to live in this world, because you know if you choose to love again and experience happiness and it is ripped away from you once more, you will sink, and this time you will be unable to stagger away with any shred left of yourself.

Hester screamed, "Leave me alone!" She sobbed, "I am alright on my own. Go! Please go!" She felt so long as she never let herself be touched, never looked outside herself again for anything, she could survive.

Hester was too overwrought to resist when Sister Agnes took her hand and led her back to her cell and put her to bed. Hester fell asleep and when she woke, it was dark. She was feverish and her head ached. She saw Sister Agnes dozing in a low chair by the door and a nearly spent candle that guttered on the windowsill. Hester arose and put on her shoes, but the wooden soles resounded on the stone floor, so she took them off for fear of waking the nun;

she crept away from her cell, barefoot. She pulled back the bolt on the main door and made her way to the cemetery under the light of a half-moon. By the time she reached her mother's tomb, the hem of her shift was soaked with dew.

She faced the statue of the Blessed Virgin. "My uncle believed in you!" she shouted. "My aunt believed in you. Why did not you save them? And poor Goody, who never harmed anyone." She pushed at the statue, trying to force an answer from it. "You have that little smile always on your lips, as if you think everything is well in this world. You are wrong!"

She shoved the marble statue, and it toppled over, breaking at the neck. The Virgin's head landed on the rusted metal grate and blasted it open, then rolled down the steps to the crypt below. Hester leaped back. "Oh my God, what have I done? I am damned for this. But, by Hell, Mother, if I am already damned then I shall have whatever is left of you!"

In the moonlight she could see her mother's coffin. The seams had split along one side. At Hester's feet, masses of insects scurried for safety—woodlice and spiders. Hester pulled back in horror. But then she thought, *No, I have come this far. I cannot go back.* "This coffin embraces you," she shouted. "I cannot even remember your embracing me. I have nothing of yours left to me, but I swear I shall not leave this place without something of you. Something I can hold onto."

Hester crawled through the remains of the grate, descended the steps, and picked up the statue's head. She heaved it at the coffin, and a seam opened further revealing shreds of grave clothes. She braced herself to reach inside, but just then, Blackie came running up to her. Excited to join in the game, he pawed away at the hole in the coffin.

"No, no, Blackie, do not go in there. You will get hurt." He stopped and looked at her, waiting for her praise. His luminous black eyes shone in the moonlight, and she knelt and hugged him. Something broke inside of her, and she wept into his furry coat.

"Oh, sweet Jesus, what have I done?" She carried Blackie up the steps. She turned to gaze in horror at the broken head of the Virgin and the hole in her mother's coffin. She whispered to Blackie, "I have desecrated both Our Lady and my mother's remains."

Hester was too distraught to notice Gareth's approach. When he reached her side, she looked up and saw that he carried a mallet. The expression on his face was grim.

"If your dead mother's bones are so important to you, and they are what you want, then you shall have them. Then you can forget about me, for I shall be gone as soon as Nia is able to ride away from here."

He descended the steps and raised the mallet, poising it over the cracked coffin.

"No, don't do that!" pleaded Hester, running down to join him. "I have made a terrible mistake. She is not coming back. Please do not do more damage than what I have done," she implored. "I have been very foolish." Holding Blackie with one arm, she grabbed onto Gareth's with the other, forcing him to lower the mallet. She wept, "Gareth, I am sorry. Our Lady, I am sorry. Mother, please forgive me. I don't know what I was about." She gasped, "Take me away from here, I pray you."

Gareth put down the mallet and, taking Blackie from Hester, supported her back across the field. They proceeded in silence. The moon revealed their footprints in the wet grass and the swathe Blackie had cut in his race to join Hester.

When they arrived at the door to her cell, they saw that Sister Agnes was still asleep in the chair.

Whispering, Hester asked, "How came you to find me in the cemetery?"

"The crash woke me from the barn. I doubt if anyone inside the house heard it."

"Would you really have smashed into my mother's coffin?" Hester asked in a small voice.

"Probably not, but I was very angry. Angry that you seem only to want to live in the past."

Hester beseeched him, "Please do not leave."

"Let us not wake Sister Agnes. Get some rest now."

Hester's mind spun as she recalled the dreadful things she had said to Sister Agnes. She barely heard Gareth whisper, "We will talk tomorrow."

She pleaded, "Please do not leave Holywell."

He answered in a low voice, "I must take Nia back to the village when she is fit to travel, and I am needed there, with no able-bodied men left."

Hester took his hand. "Oh, of course. Thank you, in any case, for coming to find me."

Gareth bid her goodnight and took Blackie with him. Hester climbed into her cot and listened to his retreating footsteps. She hoped he would return and tell her he still loved her. But his footsteps continued on until there was only silence.

Hester cried, but silently, lest she wake Sister Agnes. She fell asleep and dreamed she was little, in her nightdress and barefoot. The witch appeared. "What a coward you are! You could not face your own mother's bones, all on account of your fear of insects and the dark!"

"No, I am not afraid, truly I'm not. I shall endure them to be with Mother."

The witch changed into a pale young woman, standing by an open coffin. Hester recognized her mother, who spoke. "My daughter, see? I shall lie down here and you shall lie beside me, and I will put my arms around you. Now just be still, and nothing will hurt you." Hester climbed into the coffin and the lid descended on them. She was suffocating. "Let me out! I am alive and I want to live," cried Hester.

"No you don't!" She felt the witch's bony hands at her throat, choking her. "You want to be with your mother. A good girl belongs with her mother. You are a good girl, aren't you?"

"Yes! No!" shrieked Hester, confused. Was she a good girl or not? Then she felt something rise under her. She looked down and saw a great salmon carrying her out of the coffin and up a waterfall. The huge fish sang to her. Was it Gareth's voice or Uncle Hugh's? The fish emitted a golden light, and the song was of love between man and woman, between mother and child.

"No," hissed the witch. "Send the fish away. I cannot bear it!" She shrank until she was tiny enough to fit inside an acorn cup. She changed into a slug and spoke wheedling wise. "If I go, you will have no one. Humans are not to be trusted. They die, you know."

Hester laughed. "But I love Gareth, and though one of us must die and leave the other, we shall be happy between now and then."

The slug shrieked, "I shall leave you now, you horrid, ungrateful wretch. I shall find someone else who needs me."

The golden light became brighter and brighter. Hester woke with the rays of the new-risen sun shining in on her. *I must find Gareth.*

Sister Agnes's chair was empty. Hester threw on her robe. She found Gareth tuning his harp in the garden. His hair was damp; he had just come back from bathing in the stream. Hester ran to him, calling his name. Gareth looked up, his face expressionless.

Hester stood two feet in front of him. She addressed his sandals. "I love you and I am sorry for hurting you." She looked up at him. "You are the most important person in the world to me. I want to be with you always."

Gareth took her face between his hands. "I love you, but are you sure you want to come with me? Will you be happy living in a tiny village?"

"I am just thankful to be alive and loved by you. And I want to help, too."

She thought about Bessie and Maire, who had dressed her in her mother's wedding gown. With all the young men dead, they would, as like as not, never marry. She could teach them about healing herbs so they would at least be able to support themselves.

"Certainly your help will be much needed." Gareth took her in his arms and with one hand smoothed her tumbled hair away from her face.

Hester took a deep breath. "I need to tell you…" It all spilled out: her presumption in thinking she could cure Henry's legs; his molestation of her; the ring; her "pregnancy"; Llewelyn's failed sacrifice; and her coerced marriage to Mervyn.

Gareth's face turned white. "Your cousin Alice said Henry had misused you, but not how. And Mervyn, that foul caitiff…"

Hester rushed on, "But Mervyn didn't want…he wanted… something else. Because of the way he is…with men." She looked down. "So I put poppyseed juice in his wine, then Blackie tripped him on the stairs."

Gareth snarled, "I would kill both Henry and Mervyn."

"Neither is necessary," said Hester, calmly, although in her heart she was glad of Gareth's fury. She looked up at him. "The King will be dead soon enough of his own doing, and if you were to kill Mervyn, you would be hanged. I do not want that for my proper husband."

"Husband," murmured Gareth. "Say that word again."

"My husband," repeated Hester. She reached up and placed her arms around his neck, forcing his head down. His lips rested on hers. She smelled the scent of river and new grass on him, and felt his fine hair shiver through her fingers. She kissed him, timidly at first, but as his tongue gently probed its way inside her mouth, she responded in kind. Her breathing quickened and she felt her knees tremble. If Gareth had not been there, supporting her, she must have fallen to the ground. Hester suddenly drew back. How could she enjoy such bliss with her uncle and aunt only just dead? But she remembered her dream of the salmon leaping and how it had sung to her in Sir Hugh's voice, or it could have been

Gareth's, but in either case it had bid her live and be happy. Her lips searched out Gareth's and they kissed again. She smelled the scent of strawberries as the sun's rays warmed the patch. "I must see Sister Agnes," she stammered.

"That can surely wait, my espoused wife." Gareth returned his lips to hers, and they kissed again. A few minutes later Myfanwy arrived and they were forced to part. Hester found herself short of breath, and Gareth's eyes were dark with desire.

Myfanwy looked down, kneading her apron. "Nia is awake and asks for you both."

"Oh, how is she?" asked Hester struggling to calm her breath. She knew she was flushed, and that awareness made her flush even deeper.

"Sister Dorothy said she spent a good night."

"I will go to her," said Gareth.

"Please tell her I will come as soon as I have seen Sister Agnes." Hester straightened her robe.

Blackie bounded up the path. "And I shall keep this one out of the strawberry patch," said Myfanwy, taking the little dog in her arms.

ister Agnes was seated at her desk in the parlour. Hester flung herself on her knees at the nun's feet. "I am very sorry for the dreadful things I said to you yesterday. And I have done something terrible too."

"Do get up, child. The floor is not yet swept." Sister Agnes spoke sharply, but when Hester looked up at her, she saw the hint of a smile on the nun's lips. "What can have you done that is so terrible? People, when they have been shocked, say witless things, like men do when in their cups."

"Thank you for your forbearance, but there is worse. Pray come with me."

Sister Agnes followed Hester to the cemetery.

"By all the saints, what has happened? The Virgin's statue broken, and the crypt gate smashed. Was there a lightning storm last night? Yet I heard nothing."

"I did it," said Hester, her head hanging low. "I could not bear it. Not having anything of Mother's. And with Uncle Hugh gone..." She faltered. "He was my only remaining connection with her. The hole inside me felt so huge. I wanted her bones. In my hunger I would almost have eaten them, had I been able to reach them."

"But you didn't reach them, did you?"

"No. Blackie stopped me. Then Gareth came and he stopped me too."

"He stopped you with that?" asked Sister Agnes pointing at the mallet lying on the grass.

"No. He pretended he would help me, but he said I must choose between him and Mother's bones." She concluded, "I chose him."

"Ah," sighed Sister Agnes. "That is well, and eventually there will be money for the repairs."

"Are you not very angry with me?" asked Hester, for the first time looking directly at the nun.

Sister Agnes's eyes were sad. "Far worse crimes have been committed hereabouts than the breaking of a statue and a tomb."

"But it is sacrilege and—"

Sister Agnes interrupted. "See those four white crosses by the stone wall?" Hester followed her gaze to the perimeter of the cemetery. "There lie the remains of the sisters I told you of, who were raped and murdered by Cromwell's men. They were brought here from Saint Irene's, and if digging up their bones would bring those nuns back to life, do you not suppose I would have done it long ago?" She added softly, "For all that they are at rest in the company of the angels." She raised her voice and concluded, "So let us hear no more about this affair."

Sister Agnes took Hester's hands in her own. "Lady Elizabeth will be upon us in a few days. I have matters to attend to."

Hester turned the nun's hands over and kissed each palm in turn. "Thank you. I will always remember this." Hester looked at Sister Agnes then up at the clear sky. She remembered the day she and Alice had climbed the hill behind Hartbourne, when she had read the letter commanding her attendance on the King.

"What is it, child?"

"Sister, I had the strangest thought. If Henry had not... molested me, it would be I who was dead, and not my cousin Gwendolyn." They prayed for the repose of Gwendolyn's soul then made their way back to the parlour.

"Send Cook to me, child," instructed Sister Agnes.

Hester bobbed a curtsey, gave Cook the message, and went to Nia's little room. Sister Dorothy was brushing out Nia's hair, while Gareth played his harp. The three looked up and smiled at Hester. She sat down at the edge of the bed and embraced her friend.

"Nia, I am so very sorry. I know you loved Twgardan with all your heart."

"It is a terrible thing to have happened. For all of us." Nia winced then shook her head. "And for you also, dear Mistress, your uncle and aunt."

They wept in each other's arms, then they wiped their eyes and Nia sat up straighter and addressed the ceiling. "Is it true that Elizabeth, the tyrant's daughter, plans to visit here?" She scowled and clenched her fists.

"You are most definitely improving, thanks be to God," said Sister Dorothy.

Hester blushed and murmured about presenting Elizabeth with a gift. Gareth threw her a glance, which Hester pretended she did not see.

Sister Dorothy smiled at the three of them. "You should rest a little now," she said to Nia.

Hester hugged her friend, saying, "I will be back shortly."

Gareth said likewise, then he and Hester took their leave.

They walked to the stables. "What is this about your presenting Lady Elizabeth with a gift?" asked Gareth, his brow furrowed. "She is Henry's daughter, or had you forgotten?"

Hester smiled and reached up to smooth out the lines in his forehead.

"It was Sister Agnes's idea, and I have no quarrel with his daughter." They entered the stables, and Hester sought out Lady, who whinnied when Hester rubbed her neck. "And sometimes, when I forget to be angry, I have no quarrel with the father, either."

"That is all for the good I am sure," said Gareth reaching his saddle from its hook on the wall. "And Nia looks much improved, thanks be to the mothers."

"She is receiving the best of care," said Hester, "and the peace here will, I hope and pray, help mend her heartache."

"I have two surprises for you," said Gareth removing a package from the saddlebag. "The first is that Alice is betrothed to Sir William of Bayston."

"That is marvellous news!" exclaimed Hester, remembering the fair-haired, pleasant young man from Hampton Court.

"They plan to visit you here in Holywell."

"And they will bring Dickie?"

"Yes, Alice says he is much stronger and will be able to ride the distance."

Hester clapped her hands in delight.

"Now shut your eyes and open your mouth," said Gareth. Hester obeyed, and he popped a sugared almond between her teeth.

"Oh, thank you!" she exclaimed. "It is ages since I last had one."

Gareth brushed a wisp of straw from Hester's shoulder and pulled her toward him. She looked up at him from under half-lowered lids. Gareth took her face in his hands and tilted her chin upwards so their lips were within an inch of each other. Hester inhaled his scent of worn leather. He clasped her around the waist and brought his mouth down to hers. His tongue gently caressed the perimeter of her lips. He nibbled on first her upper, then her lower lip. After a few seconds, Hester could stand it no longer. She thrust her tongue inside his mouth to meet his. She felt her knees sink beneath her, and Gareth tightened his grip around her waist. They were forced to break the seal of their kiss to breathe. Hester took a gulp of air then pressed her lips to his again. His kiss felt like warm honey dripping down the back of her throat. The drops fell into the bowl of her low belly and resounded there like the chime of a bell. Hester pulled him closer to her, aware that his yearning for her was the same as hers for him.

ven amid the bustle of preparations for the Lady Elizabeth's visit, Gareth and Hester managed to find time alone together, and often the stables was the place that afforded most privacy. The couple was clasped in a tender embrace beside Lady's stall, when they heard a young but imperious voice call out from the courtyard. "Ho there! Where is everyone?"

"It must be Lady Elizabeth!" cried Hester, springing apart from Gareth. "She has arrived a day early."

The couple emerged from the stables and saw a girl of eight years with golden red hair, dressed in a green riding habit, mounted on a huge stallion.

"You there, help me down." The rider waved a golden-tipped ebony crop at Gareth.

Gareth bowed low. "It would be my honour, Your Ladyship."

He rose and smiled at the girl and assisted her to dismount.

Elizabeth, once on the ground, reached up to pat her horse. "Good boy," she said, then turned to Gareth. "He needs rubbing down, lest he catch cold."

"Of course, Your Ladyship," said Gareth. He grinned and walked past Hester, who stood amazed in the stable's entrance.

Elizabeth tapped her silver-buckled calfskin boots with her crop. "So where is everybody?" she demanded of Hester.

Hester stared at her. She was the *Chrysanthemum parthenium*, the golden-haired virgin of whom she had dreamed. She stammered, "My Lady, they are all within, making preparations. Begging Your Ladyship's pardon, but the royal party was not expected until tomorrow."

Gareth returned with a blanket, unsaddled the stallion, and proceeded to rub him down.

Elizabeth frowned. "Well, you know who I am. Who are you?"

"I am Gareth the Bard, Your Ladyship."

Elizabeth nodded. "Are you going to introduce your lady-love to me? You were kissing in the stables, were you not? So you must be lovers."

Hester blushed and made a deep curtsey. "I am Hester Vaughan, please Your Ladyship."

Elizabeth nodded. She strode back and forth in the yard, swishing her riding crop in the air. "Hah! I outraced all of them." She turned to Gareth. "Will Bucephalus be stabled here?"

"Ah," said Gareth, "Your Ladyship has named your horse after Alexander the Great's."

"Of course," she replied. "See, my stallion has a white star on his forehead just like Alexander's Bucephalus."

"The Delphic oracle proclaimed that he who rode Bucephalus would rule the kingdom," said Gareth.

"You know a good deal about ancient horses," said Elizabeth, smiling.

A groom entered the yard in a swirl of dust. "A thousand pardons, Your Ladyship, I simply could not keep up."

"Hah!" declared Elizabeth. "Your gelding could never hope to keep pace with my stallion."

Hester reflected that Elizabeth was indeed her father's daughter. She was tall for her age, and slender, but it was her pitch-black eyes that compelled the observer's gaze. Anne Boleyn's eyes, Hester assumed, for Henry's were hazel. But both father and daughter had hooded eyelids. Henry's eyes were barely visible between his lids, which made them appear both piglike and reptilian. Hester felt sure it was those barely seeing eyes that permitted him to destroy men and women without compunction. She thought Elizabeth's eyelids could go either way; it was, as yet, too early to tell.

A stableboy came running up. He gawped at the size of

Bucephalus and bowed to Lady Elizabeth. Gareth handed him the horse's reins and whispered to Hester to meet him in the garden after supper. She nodded assent.

"Bard," commanded Elizabeth, "you may leave, but you will sing for us this evening over supper. I wish to hear a tale of Sir Gawain, my favourite knight."

"I shall be honoured, Your Ladyship." Gareth bowed and left.

Hester smiled to herself. Elizabeth was no goddess incarnate but a little girl who liked stories of knights and ladies. Elizabeth dismissed Hester with a flick of her wrist, and Hester curtseyed and returned to Lady in the stables. She took comfort in her pony's calm solidity, stroking her neck and ears. The stableboy entered with Bucephalus and settled him in the neighbouring stall. Elizabeth followed, issuing instructions, then turned to Hester. "Is this your horse?"

"Yes, Your Ladyship. She is called Lady."

"That is a sweet name." Elizabeth reached into her the pocket and brought out a carrot. She broke it in half and gave one part to Bucephalus and the other to Lady. "Show me the grounds, Mistress Vaughan," she commanded. "It will be an hour, at least, before the rest of my party arrives. I want to see the chapel my great-grandmother commissioned, for I have important business there."

"Sister Agnes, who supervises the convent and infirmary, will be best suited to that. Will Your Ladyship do me the honour of accompanying me to her parlour?"

The pair walked along the gravel path, while bees buzzed in and out of the rose bushes.

"What do you know of this place?" asked Elizabeth.

"Little, save that it has been a holy site from before Christian times, on account of the spring."

"You mean back when pagans dwelled here? Like the worshippers of Jupiter and Neptune and Venus?" Elizabeth plucked a rose and proceeded to tear off its petals.

"Mm, though I prefer their Greek names, Zeus and—"

"Poseidon and Aphrodite," finished Elizabeth, with a tilt to her chin. "Yes, I like the Greek names better; they sound more musical." She threw the now-denuded rose to the ground and plucked another.

"But I imagine the people hereabouts would have worshipped their own gods and goddesses," said Hester. Then she remembered. "Although I hear there is a statue of Minerva, just outside the walls of Chester." Hester felt an ache in her thumb and rubbed it with her good hand.

"Minerva? Ah, Athena to the Greeks, the goddess of battles and weaving, who sprang fully armed from her father Zeus's head. Athena is my favourite goddess."

"Why is that, Your Ladyship?" Hester stared at a butterfly that had landed on Elizabeth's hood. It opened and closed its wings once, then flew away.

"Because she never loses." She lowered her voice and frowned. "And her father always does what she asks of him." In her usual tone she asked, "Do you read Greek, Mistress Vaughan?"

"Yes. Does Your Ladyship?"

"No. I know Spanish and Italian and French, because Mistress Kat has taught me. And a smattering of Latin, but I long to know Greek. When Edward, my brother, is big enough to learn, I shall study with him."

They entered the herb garden, and Elizabeth continued, "Father says the Romish saints are no better than those ancient gods and goddesses, and no reasonable Christian would offer them worship."

Hester opened her mouth to speak, but she felt a sudden confusion and could not form a reply. She closed her mouth. Perhaps this child of royal blood was correct. Maybe the saints were superfluous. Hester plucked a stalk of lavender and shredded the fragrant purple flowers in her fingers. "But people are not always reasonable, so they still need saints to whom to pray."

"Not if their King forbids it," replied the girl, her eyes narrowing. She stopped stock-still for half a second and touched her throat with one long, tapering finger. "But perchance they don't need to die for it."

Before Hester could make a reply, Elizabeth cried out, "Oh, look, strawberries!" She skipped across to the patch and stuffed three in her mouth at once.

When they reached the parlour, Hester introduced Sister Agnes to Elizabeth. Sister Agnes rose and made her obeisance. Elizabeth responded with a graceful bend to her head and dipped a curtsey.

"Where is Your Ladyship's party?" inquired Sister Agnes, a bemused expression on her face.

"They are with Kat Champernon, my governess, who is being carried on a litter. I did not wish them to hurry her, but my horse tired of walking and wanted to gallop, so I rode ahead." Elizabeth stood by the hearth and looked around the room, tapping her foot against the fender.

"Will Your Ladyship sit and take refreshment?"

"I thank you, but no. I have an important commission to discharge, so pray show me to your chapel." Elizabeth was already out in the hallway. "I want Mistress Vaughan to come too."

Sister Agnes walked ahead and opened the heavy doors to the chapel, which stood empty.

"Would your Ladyship care to learn about the chapel?" asked Sister Agnes.

"No, permit me be alone here a few minutes." Elizabeth's face flushed. "But pray wait close by, for I fear I may lose my way when I am finished."

Sister Agnes and Hester stood outside the door and could hear the faintest murmuring from within.

After about ten minutes they heard Elizabeth trying to push open the doors. Sister Agnes opened them for her.

Elizabeth's eyes held tears. "I was afraid you had left me in there and I wouldn't be able to get out."

Sister Agnes and Hester bent down to try to comfort the little girl, but she stepped back and thrust up her chin.

"Now I would like to look around the building and perhaps take a look at your sheep grazing outside. Welsh sheep have black faces and look funny. Where we live, sheep are just white all over."

A stout, red-faced woman in a brown velvet riding dress clattered down the corridor toward them. "Your Ladyship!" she gasped. "Wherefore did you race ahead of us? I have been terrified!"

"Pray calm yourself, Lady Troy. How is Kat?"

"Fine, fine, Your Ladyship. Mistress Champernon and the others will arrive soon. The physician said she will sleep for a day from exhaustion of passing the stone."

Elizabeth introduced Sister Agnes to the mistress of her household.

"Will you come to my parlour, Lady Troy?" asked Sister Agnes.

The nun offered Lady Troy a chair into which the woman sank. Sister Agnes introduced Hester, who made a deep curtsey to Lady Troy and received a nod of acknowledgement in return.

"Will Your Ladyship sit, too?" asked Sister Agnes of Elizabeth, offering the other chair.

"No, why should I want to sit when I am barely just arrived?" The girl frowned. "I want to see everything. I want to see the lepers and the sheep. The lepers first."

"No, no, Your Ladyship. Please not the lepers! What would your father, the King, say?" Lady Troy turned to Sister Agnes. "Sister, do you, perchance, own a fan I could borrow?"

"His Majesty will not say anything because he won't know," said Elizabeth, pacing before the hearth. "Father gave permission for me to come here, but I doubt if he thought twice about my health." She added under her breath, "Father only worries about Edward, not about me or Mary." She threw back her shoulders. "So, Sister Agnes, lead me, pray, to the lepers."

"Alas, we have none, Your Ladyship," she replied, suppressing a smile.

Elizabeth pouted and turned to Lady Troy. "Well, I shall visit the sacred pool, then. I have already seen the chapel and offered prayers of thanksgiving for His Majesty's life, and I prayed also for my brother and sister and my moth—" Elizabeth swayed on her feet, and her eyes, unfocused, stared into the empty grate for a few seconds. Then she blinked rapidly and gave a cough. "I meant to say, I prayed also for my stepmother, the queen, so my duty is done until Mistress Champernon arrives."

Lady Troy's eyes were shut, and Sister Agnes was searching in her desk for a fan, so only Hester noticed that Elizabeth had appeared to lose consciousness for a moment, but force of will had prevented her from fainting.

No one ever talks to her of Anne Boleyn, thought Hester. *Poor child, for she worships her father, who ordered her mother's execution. What confusion must be at play in her young mind under all the learning she has accrued.* Hester reflected on how confused she had been before coming here to Saint Winifred's.

"Yes, indeed, Your Ladyship," murmured Lady Troy, fanning herself. "Once I am recovered I can accompany you."

Elizabeth strode to the desk and picked up a quill and wrote her name on a piece of parchment.

"There never was a monk with fairer hand than our Lady Elizabeth's," said Lady Troy observing her charge. The girl's letters were firm and round, and under "Elizabeth" she inscribed a flourish of zigzagged lines.

"King Henry the Fifth came here, did not he, Sister, after his victory at Agincourt?" asked the child.

Sister Agnes confirmed that he had.

"Father is fond of that Henry, even if he was of the old religion. It was not his fault he was Roman Catholic." Elizabeth, bored with writing her name, strolled around the room. "It was like the Jews before Jesus. They couldn't help being Jewish and not Christian, could they?"

Sister Agnes gave a strangled gasp. Just then Blackie pushed open the door and bounded in.

"Oh, look!" cried Elizabeth. "What a darling, and he has only three legs."

Blackie leaped up at Elizabeth, his one front paw reaching just below her knee.

"Get down, dog!" shouted Lady Troy. "Push him away, Your Ladyship. It will dirty your dress."

"I have other dresses, but I have never kissed a three-legged dog before." Elizabeth picked Blackie up and snuffled her nose against his.

"It will be abounding in fleas!" protested Lady Troy.

Hester spoke from between clenched teeth. "Lady Troy, I would hazard sixpence against any flea you might find on Blackie." Immediately she regretted it. She had no sixpences to forfeit in case she was wrong.

"Blackie. How sweet!" enthused Elizabeth. "Did his mother have three legs? Or maybe his father? Was he born with the proper number of legs?" Her brow clouded, and her black eyes narrowed. "Four, but not five. A woman I heard of had six fingers, and she was a queen, but because of that, she…" Elizabeth halted a moment, "and because of that, she died."

"Come now, Your Ladyship," cajoled Lady Troy. "We do not talk of things long past."

A look of wistfulness crossed the child's face. She turned to Hester. "Did his mother push him out of the litter because he had only three legs?"

"I do not know," replied Hester. "But he seems none the less happy now, regardless."

Elizabeth crossed to the window. "I see the carts are arriving. Good, my pavilion will be erected within the hour," she declared.

Sister Agnes spoke to Lady Troy. "I am afraid you find us

rather unprepared. We were not expecting the honour of your visit until tomorrow."

"Yes, Sister, and when Mistress Kat passed the stone yesterday, we were on the point of sending you word that we should return home. But Mistress Kat needs to rest a day or two, and Lady Elizabeth insisted we make our visit." The woman sighed. "I am like to seize up with the strangury if I have to mind Her Ladyship on my own while we are here." She put her hand to her side. "What if the damp Welsh air inflames all our kidneys? I already feel mine swelling."

"Oh, please do not be ill." Elizabeth ran to her and kissed her on both cheeks and hugged her. "I am sure the Welsh air is perfectly fine. My grandfather was Welsh, you know."

"Yes, I know." Lady Troy sighed again.

"Hester, pray call for refreshments for Lady Troy, then show Lady Elizabeth the sacred pool," instructed Sister Agnes.

"Mind she does not touch anyone," warned Lady Troy.

"Can I carry the dog?" asked Elizabeth.

Hester laughed. "Certainly, Your Ladyship." She opened the door and the girl skipped through, cradling Blackie in her arms.

A pair of footmen, waiting outside, followed a few paces behind as the pair made their way down the corridor.

Elizabeth walked briskly. "Poor Mistress Kat, she groaned like a cow in heat all the time she was passing that stone."

Hester laughed but was shocked, also. "How does Your Ladyship know what a cow in heat sounds like?"

"Why, I make it my business to know things. Every morning I rise before dawn. I quietly climb out my window and go look around the fields then return to my bed. When Mistress Kat comes in to wake me, I yawn and say, 'Oh, is it time to get up already?'"

Hester laughed again. A maidservant passed them in the hallway, and Hester asked her to see that Lady Troy was supplied with a light repast.

"I like you, Mistress Vaughan; I believe we shall get along quite well, you and I." She touched Hester's hand with her long tapering fingers, and Hester could feel their coolness and strength.

They reached the pool and saw two old men, bent with rheumatism, sitting on the lower steps. Elizabeth glanced at Hester, as a cue for an introduction.

"Good men," said Hester, "we are honoured with a visit from the King's daughter, the Lady Elizabeth."

The supplicants reached for their crutches and tried to rise.

Elizabeth cried out, "No, kind sirs, do not discompose yourselves." She stretched out her arms to them. "I pray that you receive a cure for your ailments from these healing waters."

Tears welled in the men's eyes. Likely no person of rank had ever spoken kindly to them before. "Long life to Your Ladyship!" They chorused, ducking their heads. "And long live Good King Henry."

Hester thought, *These men would rejoice for days if they heard someone had sped a pike through Henry's gizzard. But this is what royalty is: the touch of God. Or, perhaps in this case, the Goddess.*

Elizabeth made the briefest of curtsies and turned to leave. "I shall go riding now," she declared, "and, Mistress Vaughan, you shall accompany me."

"I pray Your Ladyship excuse me, for I recently suffered a hand injury and may not ride, yet."

"Very well. Inform Lady Troy I have taken my grooms. That will content her." Elizabeth entered the stables. "Men!" she called out. She clapped her hands and the grooms emerged from behind a haystack, hurriedly putting their dice in their pockets. Within minutes, Elizabeth was mounted on Bucephalus and galloping across the fields, her attendants trying to keep up with her.

Hester obeyed Elizabeth's command. Lady Troy scowled, harrumphed, and dismissed her. Then Hester remembered she meant to visit Nia. Her friend was asleep, and Sister Dorothy sat beside the bed, winding bandages.

"How does she?" inquired Hester.

"Her breathing is easy now. She took some pottage earlier, and in another few days she should be up and about, God willing."

"I shall return later," said Hester. "I will go sit in the garden before dinner. I am exhausted having spent all of ten minutes with Lady Elizabeth. It felt like ten hours, her wits are so sharp."

The kitchen was filled with scurrying menials, and the aroma of roasting pork wafted on the air. Gareth filched a sliver of tripe from a pot to give to Corwen.

Cook grumbled, "I have spent this half-hour fashioning a peacock from marzipan." She groaned. "And still it looks like a duck."

"Ah," pronounced Gareth with mock solemnity, "Sister Agnes expressly said that Lady Elizabeth likes not only peacocks, but swans, bears, and lions."

"Lord bless us," replied the dame. She turned to a pair of half-naked boys by the hearth. "You lads there, turn the spit," she screamed. "And do not dare let that suckling pig burn!"

She reached over and cuffed the one closest to her. The lad stumbled backwards from the blow and overturned the salt box.

"You poopnoddy! You have ruined my precious salt!" she howled.

The lad had no doubt received far worse blows, for the next moment he was humming a ditty as he swept it up.

"How about I try my hand at the marzipan?" asked Gareth.

Cook grunted an assent. A few minutes later she exclaimed, "Oh, my, that does look like a swan."

In no time, Gareth had fashioned a menagerie of exotic animals: swans, tigers, and dragons. He smiled at his creations.

Cook asked, "How come you look so happy?"

"I have left Mistress Hester with the Lady Elizabeth," he replied. "Her Ladyship knows Spanish and Italian, which Hester does not. I think it will do my love good to talk to her."

"Ay, bring her down a peg or two. And once you have childer, she'll see what all that foreign learning is good for. Like wings on a pig."

She scowled. "So, Lady Elizabeth has brought her own provisions. Ha! I'll not have them go from Saint Winifred's saying we couldn't serve a repast fit for royalty. My eel pie has no equal, has it, lads?"

"No, Mistress Cook!" chorused the boys.

Gareth arranged the marzipan animals on a platter, then left to meet Hester.

He found her sitting on a bench in the garden. The air was redolent with the scent of warm thyme and lavender. Gareth sat beside her, taking her hand in his.

Hester examined his almond paste–covered fingertips.

"It would seem I have found my true calling in fashioning marzipan animals." Gareth smiled and licked his index finger.

Hester protested, "Do not be so greedy." She took his middle finger and placed her lips around it.

Gareth gasped with the pleasure of her sucking his finger. Hester looked at him mischievously.

"I cannot stand it. Oh, Hester, I love you and I want to have you, for always. Now it is my turn." He examined her fingernail and laughed. "The proper length! This is your destiny, Hester Vaughan, to marry a man who cares for the well-being of your very fingernails."

"Yea, my liege lord and custodian of my fingers," replied Hester and rose to make him a mock curtsey.

Gareth stood and seized her in his arms. He tenderly kissed Hester's eyelids, then turned her face and nibbled her earlobe. He kissed her fully on the lips and felt her responding kiss and her body arch against his.

"Ah ha! Lovers!" cried Lady Elizabeth, striding into the garden.

Hester laughed and curtseyed. "Lovers, indeed, Your Ladyship."

"I am famished after my ride," declared Elizabeth. "It must be nearly dinnertime. There will be cherry pie, I know, because Lady

Troy has brought five, and we have only eaten three, so far. I must send one to Kat, for it is her favourite, too. I will see you both at table," she concluded. "I hope these kisses have not interfered with your singing voice, bard."

Gareth grinned and made a low bow, and Elizabeth skipped off to her pavilion. Hester watched her go and turned to Gareth. "Before she leaves, I would like to give her the ring and ask her to return it to Henry."

Gareth frowned. "Yes, my love, knowing how you came by it, I shall be glad to be rid of it. And there is something else. When I first looked into Lady Elizabeth's eyes, I knew in a flash that she was the daughter of the dragon, the one Peredur foretold, for only dragons have eyes of ebony. And her hair is the colour of Welsh gold. She is the red dragon, sent by the goddess to save this country. Peredur came to me in a vision and told me this. He also said that Elizabeth needs your help."

"I cannot fathom how I might help, but now I see Lady Elizabeth, I recall having dreamed of her." Hester shook her head. "But I must go now to change my robe for the banquet."

"Do you have any other?" asked Gareth.

She blushed. "Sister Agnes found one for me. It is quite becoming."

"I shall be delighted to see you dressed in anything other than a nun's habit."

⁂

"I should have asked you to raise the neckline, for it is cut very low indeed." Hester tried to tug it up over her bosom.

Myfanwy said softly, "Consider the pleasure it will give Master Gareth to see your duckies peeping up, all hello and how are you? But hurry now, you do not want to keep the fine folks waiting."

Hester smoothed down her gold-and-green patterned skirt and hastened to the pavilion. Elizabeth sat at the centre of a trestle table, raised on a dais. Lady Troy and Sister Agnes were on either side of her, and Father Jerome sat beside the nun. Elizabeth's household members and local gentry were seated at a table that ran the length of the tent.

Elizabeth wore a blue damask gown and a black satin hood, trimmed with emeralds, set back on her red-gold hair. Her skin was pale as the full moon, and her jaw set for ceremony. Her black, obsidian eyes darted everywhere, under half-lowered lids.

Gareth was tuning his harp at a side table and gazing at the child. He did not notice Hester as she approached the head table, curtseyed, and took a seat beside Father Jerome.

Two old men in black robes entered and looked around, confused.

"Ah, my physician and surgeon," exclaimed Elizabeth. "Welcome, and sit ye down."

They manoeuvred themselves onto a bench at the lower table beside a portly middle-aged man wearing a velvet cape and a plumed hat. "Master Henshaw, make room for my venerable friends," commanded Elizabeth. The man bared his teeth in a grin and made way for the pair, but his narrowed eyes betrayed his chagrin at being displaced farther down the table.

Gareth finished tuning his harp and looked up and saw Hester. He nearly dropped his instrument at the sight of her in her new dress. A broad smile crossed his face as he looked long and hard at her. Hester felt herself blushing with pleasure. Lady Elizabeth smirked at them both and clapped her hands for the first dish, then motioned to Gareth to play.

Gareth sang of Arthur's knight Sir Gawain, who had fallen into misadventure and could only succeed in his quest if he accepted the aid of a lady under enchantment.

The first two courses were suckling pig and eel pie, and Elizabeth pronounced them both excellent.

Gareth sang how Gawain, in return for the lady's help, was honour-bound to marry her. However, the spell was such that the lady appeared in the guise of a deformed crone during the day but in her true form, a beautiful young woman, at night. The court both pitied and mocked Sir Gawain for being wed to such a loathly lady. One night, his wife asked him, "I can be beautiful during the day and hideous at night, or vice versa. You may choose which is to be." And Gawain, from chivalry and acknowledging that it was the lady who had to bear the pain of enchantment, said, "My Lady, you yourself choose." The spell was broken and the lady became lovely and young both by day and by night.

The assembly applauded, Elizabeth the loudest of all.

"Well told, bard. When we first met, I caught Master Gareth and Mistress Vaughan kissing in the stables. I don't think he was kissing her in her secret place, because he wasn't fastening his codpiece, like the grooms do after they have kissed the housemaids in the loft."

The company laughed nervously, and Hester, blushing deeply, heard Lady Troy whisper in Elizabeth's ear, "Some things are not said at table."

Elizabeth scowled at the rebuke. "Where is the marzipan?" she demanded. "I always have marzipan for dessert."

A platter of Gareth's creations was set before her and her face cleared. "Oh, this swan is so cunningly made. And look at this dragon, Lady Troy, with fire coming from his mouth and scales on his wings. I shall save him till last." Elizabeth turned to Sister Agnes. "Your cook is a prodigal, no, a prodigy, and is to be highly commended." She coloured and dabbed her mouth on her napkin.

Sister Agnes murmured her thanks. Hester caught Gareth's eye and he winked at her.

After the dishes were cleared, Sister Agnes spoke. "Would Your Ladyship do Saint Winifred's the great honour of accepting this small gift?" She beckoned Hester, who stood, curtseyed, and offered the wrapped package to Elizabeth. Elizabeth washed her fingers in a silver bowl and dried them on a linen towel. She unwrapped the blue silk covering.

"A Book of Hours. How delightful! My sister, Lady Mary, has one, for she is a Papist." Elizabeth turned the pages. "Look!" she exclaimed. "The Virgin Mary's dress is the same colour as my own." She addressed Sister Agnes. "Sometimes I think it great pity we no longer adore the Virgin Mary." There was a wistfulness to her voice, but then she sat up straight and said with all the sternness she could muster in her eight-year-old voice, "My father has decreed that God has no mother, and worshipping the Virgin is idolatry."

Lady Troy said meekly, not wanting to offend Sister Agnes and the priest, "Your Ladyship might think of Mary as a very good woman. The best there ever was."

"I have heard it said that Mary is another form of Venus or Aphrodite," said Elizabeth, ignoring Lady Troy. "She even bears the same title of 'Morning Star.'" Elizabeth scoffed. "When she is called the Seat of Wisdom, you might as well call her by her proper name, Athena."

Father Jerome choked on his claret, Lady Troy tittered from embarrassment, but Sister Agnes's face remained composed. Hester thought, *After all, Elizabeth is only a little girl, no matter how cleverly she talks.*

Lady Troy changed the subject. "Why do you not look through the book?"

Elizabeth turned to the picture of the Virgin Mary as a toddler ascending the steps of the temple, where a dozen long-bearded priests awaited her. St. Anne and St. Joachim, her parents, stood at the bottom of the steps, watching their daughter leave them.

"Is this the Virgin Mary as a child?" asked Elizabeth. "I have never seen this painting before. It is not in Lady Mary's prayer book."

"This copy is of a very rare Book of Hours," replied Sister Agnes.

"Why is Saint Anne letting her daughter go live with those old men? Doesn't she love her?" Elizabeth frowned. "Saint Anne. Oh, my mother's name was Anne. But she went away to live somewhere—in a churchyard, I was told, but perhaps it was a temple."

Hester watched as Elizabeth's eyes flickered upwards. The child passed her hand before her face as if wiping the face of an imaginary mirror. "My mother was a queen, though, and not a saint," pronounced Elizabeth. She picked up a marzipan swan and examined its neck.

Someone at the lower table echoed Elizabeth's words, "not a saint," followed by a stifled guffaw.

Elizabeth traced her finger around the swan's neck then bit off its head. She appeared to be close to tears. Gareth called out, "And remember, Your Ladyship, Ane was the great mother goddess of the Welsh!"

"Thank you, Master Bard. So I am the daughter of a goddess!" She laughed, but there was an edge to her laughter.

Father Jerome huffed and Lady Troy fluttered her hands in her lap. Elizabeth fingered the marzipan dragon, then stood and addressed the diners. "Dear and honoured countrymen, I am the granddaughter of a Welshman, Henry Tudor. As my father, King Henry the Eighth's, royal coat of arms bears the lion and the dragon of Wales, so shall mine."

She pressed her slender fingers to her temples. "My head aches, now."

"Her ladyship is having a megrim," observed Lady Troy, who stood to usher her charge from the pavilion. The aged physician and surgeon rose with difficulty to follow the pair.

"Mistress Vaughan, I want you also to attend me," said Elizabeth.

A large feather bed stood in the centre of Elizabeth's tent, and beside it, a carved oak table. Fine green-and-red woolen rugs covered the ground and hung on the walls. Lady Troy took Elizabeth behind a screen to undress and a minute later handed a glass bowl of urine to one of the old men.

Elizabeth, clad in her shift, laid down on the bed, and Lady Troy drew a blanket over her.

The physician's hands shook as he poured some of the liquid

into an alembic, which he held up to the light. "Ah, this is your water, Lady Elizabeth. Last time you played quite the jest, giving me your horse's urine to diagnose. Not all my charts could help me there." He unfurled a map of the stars on the table. "It is an auspicious time to be bled from the antecubital fossa," said he.

The surgeon ambled over and rolled up the sleeve of Elizabeth's shift to above the elbow. He brought out a scalpel and made a half-inch incision into the vein. The girl remained as impassive as the oak table.

Hester thought, *Look how pale she is! Surely she does not need bleeding.* But it was not her place to decry the venerable gentlemen's remedy. She remembered, with chagrin, scoffing at Henry's physicians less than two months ago. Hester left the pavilion and went to the drying room, where she took down a bunch of dried feverfew. She brewed it in a kettle in the kitchen and strained it into a cup. After adding a little honey to the decoction, she returned to Elizabeth's tent to find the surgeon repacking his instruments.

Elizabeth clutched her head in her hands. The bleeding had not helped.

"Your Ladyship may find this gives some relief from the megrim." Hester offered her the cup.

"Give it to me, Mistress," demanded Lady Troy. "I am sworn to taste any physic before it passes Lady Elizabeth's lips. I must answer to the King himself." She took it. "It smells quite pleasant."

"It is feverfew and honey, my lady," said Hester.

"I have tried to administer feverfew in the past," said the physician, "but Her Ladyship has always refused. The honey is a good idea. I will remember that." He smiled at Hester, who ducked a curtsey.

Lady Troy passed the cup to Elizabeth, who drank it and sank back against the pillows.

"Recite a poem, Mistress Vaughan," she whispered. "Tell me the story of Polyphemus, the ugly Cyclops, and the lovely nymph he adored. You know how he shaves off his beard with a scythe and rakes his hair to make himself handsome, but it only makes him look worse."

Hester began, "*Acis erat Fauno nymphaque Symaethide cretus magna quidem patrisque sui matrisque voluptas.*"

Elizabeth fell asleep, and Lady Troy gave Hester a quizzical look. Hester translated, "'Acis was the son of Faunus and the nymph Symethis, who was very much loved by his mother and father.' The poem tells how Acis was even more loved by the nymph Galatea. But the Cyclops loved Galatea too. The story has a sad ending."

Hester looked at Elizabeth, asleep. She appeared very young and vulnerable. *She has been caressed to sleep by a dead language.* Hester recognized that she, too, had sated herself on book learning, absorbing knowledge and languages like it could keep starvation at bay. Like sponges, they both sopped up anything that might fill the void left by a mother's death.

Hester curtseyed to Lady Troy and returned to the banqueting tent, where Gareth was singing of King Arthur's final battle to a small group of guests.

"How fares Her Ladyship?" asked Sister Agnes.

"Resting now," whispered Hester.

Gareth finished the song and lay down his harp. Sister Agnes declared the banquet over, and he and Hester left the tent.

"Let us go the garden," said Hester.

They sat on a bench and Gareth handed the ruby ring to her.

"Henricus Rex and Elizabeth," read Hester. "I wonder if one day, 'Elizabeth Regina' will be engraved here."

"I expect so." Gareth told Hester how Peredur had foretold that she would succour Elizabeth, the daughter of the dragon, to prevent her following the example of Henry's vicious reign. Gareth added how happy Peredur would have been to witness their encounter with the firesome young Lady Elizabeth.

"I shall help, if I can," replied Hester, turning the ring over in her hand. "She carries an air of both dragon and goddess about her. I can envisage her as Queen of England and Wales."

Gareth looked into Hester's eyes. "She may become Queen of the realm, but is you I want for queen of my bed and board. Particularly of my bed."

A page approached and bowed. "Pray pardon, but Lady Elizabeth desires the attendance of Mistress Vaughan, forthwith."

Hester kissed Gareth on the cheek. "I will see you in a little while."

Elizabeth sat in an armchair, a green silk shawl over her shoulders. A tiny brown stain on the sleeve of her shift indicated where she had been bled. She held a silver bowl of sweetmeats on her lap. Lady Troy, seated beside her, worked at her embroidery.

"Mistress Vaughan, what do you desire above all else?" Elizabeth crunched down on a sugared almond.

Hester blinked, being rather taken aback by the question, but answered, "Why, Your Ladyship, to marry my beloved." She paused, then added, "And to see my brother, Dickie, and cousin Alice again."

"I shall arrange the first part, your marriage, on one condition," said Elizabeth, using her forefinger to dislodge a piece of nut from between her teeth.

"How shall Your Ladyship do that?" asked Hester, her eyebrows raised in surprise.

Elizabeth beckoned to a man standing by the entrance. Hester recognized the plumed cap from the banquet. "This is Master Henshaw, my scrivener."

He made a slight bow and Hester returned a brief curtsey.

"I overheard Sister Agnes mentioning to Lady Troy that you are encumbered by an unfortunate marriage to your cousin, is that not so?"

Hester's eyes widened and she nodded. Lady Troy frowned but did not look up from her needlework.

"I understand that this marriage is invalid on several accounts." Elizabeth held up her fingers to count them, starting with her thumb. "First of all, you were pre-contracted to Master Gareth."

"Yes, I was," replied Hester, recalling the night Gareth asked her to marry him. It seemed a very long time ago.

Elizabeth raised her index and middle fingers. "You did not receive a dispensation for cousins to marry, and you were forced into marriage." Lifting her ring finger, she added, "He did not kiss you in your secret place, and so the marriage was not...," she paused, "consumed. I think that is the right word." Elizabeth stared at her little finger and frowned, disappointed she could produce no fifth objection. Lady Troy sighed, and Hester, amazed by the child's precocity, could only stare at her.

Elizabeth scowled. "Come now, Mistress Vaughan, do not play the simpleton. Unless a man kisses his bride in her secret place, the marriage is not consumed and is hence invalid." She turned to her scrivener. "Is that not so, Master Henshaw?"

The man hemmed. "Well, yes, in so many words, Your Ladyship."

"Quite," continued Elizabeth. "The King, my father, put away Princess Anne of Cleves last summer on two accounts. First, she had been pre-contracted to the son of the Duke of Lorraine, and second because the marriage was not consumed."

Lady Troy gasped. "Your Ladyship must not speak so of His Majesty!"

"Hah! All he does now is kiss Cate Howard in her secret place. Yet there is no sign of another prince, because she's barren."

Lady Troy exclaimed, "Not another word! The queen gave you a fine ruby bracelet at New Year's."

"Pieces of red glass. She thought I could not tell the difference." Elizabeth pursed her lips.

"Perhaps they were garnets, but definitely not coloured glass," argued Lady Troy.

"She gave me a bauble," declared Elizabeth, "and my father has squandered a treasury on her." She turned to Hester. "In any case, Mistress Vaughan, I propose that Master Henshaw requests from the Bishop of Saint Asaph the necessary documents for an..." She paused.

"Annulment, Your Ladyship," completed Master Henshaw.

"Then I shall have the papers delivered to my friend Wriothesley, one of the King's chief counsellors. You will have your annulment by the end of the month, whereupon you and Master Gareth may marry."

Hester continued to stare, speechless, at Elizabeth.

"In return, you will join my household as my apothecary. My physician and surgeon grow long in the tooth and will soon need replacement." She drummed her fingers on the arm of her chair.

"Surely—" objected Lady Troy, but Elizabeth's voice rose higher.

"And Master Gareth shall be my household musician."

"But Your Ladyship," pleaded Lady Troy.

"His Majesty has granted me one musician, and my sister, Lady Mary, will not object. Master Gareth has strange views concerning religion, but Mary despises only the new religion and this new queen. Mary kept to her room for days after the marriage." Elizabeth laughed. "But His Majesty, my father is the King, the best King England has ever had, and can do what he likes. Though I do wish he liked to see me a bit more…"

She blinked hard, fighting back tears, then her voice gravelled over and she looked straight into Hester's eyes. "So we understand each other. We each get something we want." Her eyes became hooded, rendering her gaze inscrutable. Hester felt a shiver of repulsion, aware that inside this child's mind lurked the potential embryo of a tyrant.

"Your Ladyship," she began, "I am deeply sensible of the honour done to me, but I fear I must decline. Gareth and I want to return to the village of Dinas Emrys and help its women and children."

"What?" exclaimed Elizabeth. She stood and clenched her fists. "'Twas but recently that foul rebels from there attempted the King's life." She glared at Hester. "His Majesty bade me offer thanks for his victory over them here at my great-grandmother's shrine." She scowled. "He had their leader hanged in chains from the city walls."

Hester murmured, "Llewelyn was my uncle."

"Do you have any quarrel with your anointed King, Mistress Vaughan?" Elizabeth's jaw set like an iron clamp.

Hester thought of Henry—grossly repulsive, cuckolded, and lying abed tortured by his leg ulcers. "No, Your Ladyship, I do not, but the village widows and orphans will need help to survive the coming winter."

Lady Elizabeth's face softened. "And would you ensure their loyalty to their King?"

"Indeed," replied Hester, reaching into her pocket. "And, on another matter, I hope Your Ladyship can see fit to return this to His Majesty, at some time."

Lady Troy and Master Henshaw gasped. Elizabeth took the ring in her slender fingers and read the inscription aloud, "Henricus Rex and Elizabeth." She asked, "How came you by this?"

"I performed some service in the tending of His Majesty's leg ulcers." *What more can I say?* thought Hester.

Blackie bounded into the tent and leaped up into Elizabeth's lap. She handed the ring to Lady Troy and stroked Blackie. She motioned her scrivener to a chest opposite her bed. Master Henshaw handed her a purse. "Mistress Vaughan, I rather like this little creature. How much will you take for him?"

The money would be most useful in the village, thought Hester, and she was sore tempted to accept, but she knew she must not. This girl may one day rule England and must learn something more about love.

"Your Ladyship," interjected Lady Troy. "Wherefore needs you such a mongrel?"

Elizabeth ignored her and handed Hester the purse. "Ten sovereigns will rebuild every house in your village."

Hester's mouth opened in shock; the girl had read her mind. Elizabeth grinned.

"Ten sovereigns!" echoed Lady Troy. "I must forbid it."

"It is my Christmas gift from Princess Anna, and I shall do with it as I like." She stared at Hester, awaiting her acquiescence.

"Your Ladyship is most generous," said Hester, returning the purse, "but Blackie is not for sale."

The atmosphere in the room thickened, as air before thunder. Lady Elizabeth's black eyes burned like anthracite. "Get you from my sight!" she shrieked. "You refuse to join my household, and now you refuse to sell me this dog!" Blackie jumped down to the floor. Elizabeth's voice broke; she was close to sobbing. Her face crumpled. Its habitual veneer of sophistication cracked, revealing her as the motherless child she was. Hester's heart went out to her.

"Your Ladyship mistakes me. I wish to offer Blackie as a gift. He has been a good friend to me, and I pray he will be likewise unto you."

To Hester's surprise, Blackie leaped back onto the girl's knees and licked her under her chin. He curled up in her lap, as if somehow knowing she needed him, now, more than did Hester.

Lady Troy sniffed. "I suppose that would be acceptable, but however will you go a-hunting with a three-legged dog?" She and Master Henshaw chuckled.

Elizabeth murmured, "I am fond of the poor creature. He reminds me somehow of somebody missing…" She raised her hand to her throat, and Hester realized Blackie reminded the child of her mother. "I don't know…" stammered Elizabeth. She quickly recovered herself. She stroked Blackie's ears and kissed his nose. "I shall call him Trivium."

Lady Troy tittered. "Ah, Trivium," said she. "How clever, naming him after what every grammar school boy learns—his triad of grammar, logic, and rhetoric."

Master Henshaw sniggered. "He was born a quadrivium, like a university scholar with arithmetic, geometry, music, and astronomy, but alas, cruel fate rendered him a trivium, instead."

Hester's eyes darkened and she spoke with feeling. "No, Your Ladyship, his name is Blackie. And Blackie he shall remain."

Elizabeth's face turned white with rage. "Be gone from my presence this instant, Mistress Vaughan." She clutched Blackie's coat and he yelped.

"Lady Elizabeth can name it anything she chooses," spluttered Lady Troy.

Hester curtseyed and said, "Names matter, Your Ladyship. Did you know the word 'matter' comes from the Latin 'mater,' for mother?"

"Why mother?" Elizabeth sighed and nuzzled the dog's ears. "Mothers matter. Very well. Blackie, he will stay." She stared at Hester. "I was named for my grandmother, Elizabeth of York, who once owned that ring. For whom were you named?"

Hester smiled. "I know not, but Blackie was named Blackie because he is black."

Elizabeth repeated, "Because he is black. Oh!" Then she laughed.

A slender young woman with a pale complexion entered the tent and curtseyed to Elizabeth.

"Ah, Mistress Kat, I am heartily glad to see you arisen, but you still look tired. Meet my new friend."

Hester curtseyed to the young woman, then realized that Elizabeth meant Blackie.

Kat stroked the dog and smiled at Hester.

"I feel recovered, now," said Elizabeth. "Mistress Vaughan, let's you and I walk in the garden. Lady Troy, pray help me dress and ensure that Kat does not overtire herself." She turned to her scrivener. "Master Henshaw, you have a task. To the bishop. So go."

lackie chased a bumblebee into a flower bed of yellow poppies.

Hester pointed across the field to the cemetery. "My mother is buried over there; she died when I was very young."

"My mother died when I was three, and she is buried in the Tower of London," said Elizabeth. She frowned in concentration. "She lies in a chapel named Saint Peter ad Vin…"

"Saint Peter ad Vincula," said Hester.

"That is correct. Her head was cut off with a sword for she refused to kneel on the block. She was Queen of England." Elizabeth tore the flower head from a yellow poppy and shredded its petals.

"Your mother was a courageous woman," said Hester, smiling.

"What do you know of her? Whenever I ask Lady Troy or Kat, they pretend to have forgotten all about her, then Kat tells me a story from the *Odyssey*, about Circe or the sirens, and I forget to ask again." Elizabeth stared at the remains of the flower in her hand. "Neither knew my mother, but there is no need to pretend she never existed. My sister, Lady Mary, prays daily for Mother's soul. Sometimes, she calls her 'The Whore.'" She flung the poppy stalk down and ground it with her heel.

"Queen Anne sheltered priests who would have burned for heresy, which put her own life in danger. And she was learned. Your mother persuaded His Majesty to accept an English translation of the Bible." Hester was talking too fast, but she wanted to impart all she knew of Anne to the late queen's young daughter. "So it is thanks to Your Ladyship's mother that the common folk can now understand the Lord's word without having to struggle with Latin, which so few of them know."

The pair reached a rose trellis arbour and sat beneath it. Butterflies fluttered among the flowers, and the perfume of roses wafted in the air.

"Mary says my mother was also a witch for casting an enchantment on His Majesty, our father, to make him besotted with love for her. It was only due to his great mercy that she was not deemed a witch and a heretic and burned. Sometimes I have dreadful nightmares where I am chained on top of a pyre and my mother is about to light it, but just before she does, I fall through the logs and wake up."

"No, Your Ladyship," said Hester, her eyes filling with tears. "Your mother was not a witch, and she loved you very much." *Just like in my own nightmares, a witch has taken the place of her mother.*

Hester took Elizabeth's cool hand in her own hot, perspiring one.

Elizabeth cast Hester a look of disdain for having taken this liberty but let her hand rest where it was.

"How do you know that my mother loved me very much?" asked Elizabeth, her eyes dark with scorn.

"My aunt's sister has been keeper of the queen's wardrobe these past dozen years. She remembers your mother sewing your nightshirts and how much labour she spent on them, making sure the stitches were even. Queen Anne was not a good seamstress and never even bothered trying to sew the King's shirts."

Elizabeth laughed. "Oh, I never knew that. Is there more?"

Hester brushed her tears away. "And she was beautiful."

Elizabeth nodded. "I want to show you something. Kat and Lady Troy must know I have it, but they pretend they don't." She reached into the bodice of her dress and withdrew a tiny locket, the size of her thumbnail. She opened it.

"Ah, it is your mother, Queen Anne Boleyn," said Hester. "You have her eyes."

"Oh, you said her full name," murmured Elizabeth. "No one ever says her full name in my hearing. It is whispered about, but that is different."

"Yes, it is different," agreed Hester.

"Why are you crying?" Elizabeth released Hester's hand. "I am not and we are talking of my dead mother."

"I think because my mother is buried close by, and I had never seen her tomb until a few weeks ago."

"I would like to see it."

"Oh, but you cannot." Hester shook her head.

Elizabeth frowned and pursed her lips. "You forget yourself, Mistress Vaughan. What mean you, I cannot?"

"I did something I very much regret, just recently. I smashed the statue of Our Lady that stands over my mother's tomb. I was sick, but I still knew what I did. I tried to break into her coffin so I could touch her bones."

"Oh." Elizabeth pondered this, her eyes narrowing. "And did you touch them?"

"No. Master Gareth came and made me realize what I was about. And Blackie came, too, thinking it was a game." Hester gave a rueful smile.

A bee landed on Elizabeth's sleeve, and Hester brushed it away.

"Yet you loved her," said Elizabeth, looking puzzled, "even as, in your anger, you made to dishonour her remains."

"I loved her very much, as I know she loved me. Just as your mother loved you."

"I was very angry with Mother, too," said Elizabeth, plucking a rose from the trellis. Her brow furrowed. "One day I was a princess, the next day I was only a lady. But that would not have mattered to me at all, just so long as she hadn't gone away, I mean, died." Her eyes filled with tears. "Sometimes I think I would be happier as a scullery maid with a mother that loved me than as a princess with a huge hole inside. Is not that a terrible thing to say?" Elizabeth pulled off the pink rose petals. "What is worse is that I killed her as surely as any blade did." Hester opened her mouth to protest, but Elizabeth continued. "Everyone knows had I been a boy, the King would not have needed her to die, to make way for Queen Jane and Prince Edward." She squeezed the remains of the rose in her fist and stood.

"Pray sit, Your Ladyship," said Hester seizing the child's hand.

Again Elizabeth cast a look of scorn at Hester, but she sat and permitted Hester hold her hand.

"I thought for a long time it was my fault my mother died," said Hester. "Even though I had been forbidden, I opened the door and saw her bleeding to death after the birth of my baby brother." She looked into Elizabeth's dark, unfathomable eyes. "For years I was sure that if only I had not opened that door, Mother would have lived. Only recently have I come to see I was wrong in thinking that."

"What of it, Mistress Vaughan? It was a little naughty of you to open the door when you had been told not to, but it was an innocent mistake." Elizabeth released Hester's hand and stood to pluck another rose from the trellis.

Hester stood also. "Dear Lady Elizabeth, if I made an innocent mistake, then how much more innocent were you for being born a girl and not a boy? You had absolutely no choice in your sex. Yet when the dreadful thing happens, we blame ourselves."

Elizabeth's eyes widened a moment. "But someone must be to blame. If not me, then it must be Father, or God, and I dare not think either."

Hester knew whom she blamed but did not see how her saying so would help Elizabeth, who seemed to worship her father along with God.

"Sometimes terrible things simply happen," said Hester.

Elizabeth's eyes filled with tears. "Oh," she cried and dropped the rose to the ground. Hester opened her arms and the child leaned into her embrace and wept.

Within a few seconds, Elizabeth had regained self-control

and dabbed her eyes with a lace handkerchief. Blackie emerged from the flower bed and yipped at her feet for attention. Elizabeth picked up a long stick from the ground and pointed it up in the air.

"Sit, Blackie," she commanded, and Blackie sat.

"Just please, Majesty," continued Hester, "remember wisdom and compassion together."

"What did you call me?" asked Elizabeth, in a low voice.

"I said, 'Majesty.'" Hester paused a moment. "Your Ladyship, holding that stick, reminded me of the goddess Athena, wielding her spear."

Elizabeth laughed and threw the stick for Blackie to chase. "That is a fine conjecture, but more important for the present is the matter of your impending nuptials. I shall have to make you a wedding present." She pulled her purse from a pocket. "This will help your villagers and restore your mother's tomb." Elizabeth blushed. "This is the same purse as I proffered earlier, only with a few more sovereigns added that Lady Troy knows nothing about."

"Your Ladyship is most kind." Hester took the purse, stood, and curtseyed. "I have something I need to say. It is as like as not that you will rule this kingdom in good time."

Elizabeth looked at her, but her eyes were inscrutable.

"The King, your father, has secured peace for the realm." Hester felt her breath catch, as she recalled how much misery he had caused his subjects, including herself. She continued, "Your Ladyship will inherit a united country. I pray you let your people have the privilege of worshipping in their own way without fear of death."

Elizabeth gave an almost imperceptible nod. Hester took a deep breath. Blackie returned, dragging the stick, and Elizabeth scooped him up in her arms. The trio returned to the dining pavilion from whence issued the strains of the harp. Gareth was playing as the servants cleared away the remains of the feast.

"I shall leave you lovers to your own devices," declared Elizabeth. "I shall visit Sister Agnes, for I wish to examine her library." Hester dipped a curtsey and Elizabeth headed toward the parlour, Blackie following at her heels.

Hester showed Gareth the purse. "It is Her Ladyship's wedding present to us and her gift to the village."

He took her hands in his. "We will live in Peredur's apartment, yes?"

"I loved the light in there," she replied, smiling, "but will you not find it hard, with him gone?"

"He would be happy, knowing of our happiness, and we will name our first son after him."

"You never answered me when I asked before." Hester kissed him lightly on the lips. "What is your surname?"

"Why, Vaughan," said he, laughing. "But I go by the Welsh version, ap Fychan."

"Why did you not tell me?" protested Hester. "How closely are we related? Can we marry?"

"Have no fear. My father was second cousin to Llewelyn, which makes us only third or fourth cousins. Besides, King Henry is a Vaughan too, by descent, and that didn't stop you from setting out to beguile him into marriage."

Hester gasped from shock of Gareth's speaking in jest of that dreadful event. Then she laughed, realizing that if he could laugh about it, then he held it not to her account. He had forgiven her. She gave a sigh of relief as she forgave herself.

⁓⁕⁓

The next morning bore witness to the royal party's departure. Lady Elizabeth and her retinue were assembled in front of the main steps, their horses saddled and waiting.

Elizabeth handed Sister Agnes a purse. The nun's face wreathed in smiles when she opened it. "Why this will finish repairing the roof with monies to spare! Thank you, Your Ladyship."

Elizabeth beckoned Hester over and kissed her. "I wish you

well and expect you to write and inform me of your progress in Dinas Emrys." She donned her riding gauntlets, and Gareth helped her mount Bucephalus.

Beside her, Lady Troy sat upon her mare, quite overshadowed by Elizabeth's massive steed. Blackie poked his head out of the pannier strapped to Bucephalus's side.

The party set off. "God be with you all," called out Sister Agnes, and her household echoed the blessing.

Later that afternoon, Gareth, Hester, and Sister Agnes stood in the drying room selecting herbs for the couple to bring back to the village of Dinas Emrys. Sister Agnes gave a sad smile. "Nia will soon be well enough to travel, and then you will depart." She reached down a bunch of sage. "I miss Blackie and I will miss you both."

"As we shall miss you," said Hester. "The thanks I owe you cannot—"

The door flew open and in bustled Father Jerome. "I am come too late to say goodbye to Lady Elizabeth," said he. "Last rites for my oldest parishioner, God bless him." He smiled at Gareth and Hester. "But I am in time to marry you two, in the interim, as it were. Sister Agnes told me of an impediment, but 'twill soon be removed, God willing."

Hester set down the parsley in her hand and looked at Gareth, who raised his eyebrows and grinned at her. "Thank you, Father," he said and bowed to the priest.

"This is not the regular order of things," sighed Father Jerome, "but alas we live in irregular times, and better you be married in the sight of God before you leave here and proceed to...," he coughed, "as young people will."

"But I am wearing this workaday gown," said Hester, looking down at her skirt. "I do have that beautiful dress..." She paused, blushing as she remembered how much bosom the low neckline exposed. Then she thought of her mother's wedding gown but could not recall where its remains were. Yet it signified not, for it was a thing of the past. Her mother would be delighted she was marrying such a fine young man as Gareth, and that was all that mattered now.

Sister Agnes nodded and smiled at Hester. "Very well, child. Myfanwy will help dress you." She called to a nun in the corridor, "Fetch Myfanwy, pray, and ask Sister Dorothy, and as many as the sisters as are at liberty, to assemble in the chapel in one half-hour."

Myfanwy arrived short of breath from running. Her face beamed as she embraced Hester, who choked back tears of happiness.

A half-hour later, Hester, dressed in her sumptuous green and gold gown, knelt with Gareth before the stone altar in the chapel. Light poured down upon them through the stained glass painting of Saint Winifred.

Father Jerome instructed the groom, "Repeat after me, 'I, Gareth, take thee, Hester, to be my wedded wife, to have and to hold, from this day forward, for better, for worse, for richer or poorer, in sickness and in health, till death us do part. And thereto, I plight thee my troth.'"

Gareth's eyes shone and his face radiated happiness as he recited the words.

Hester repeated the same vow with the addition: "And I promise to be bonny and buxom in bed and at board."

Father Jerome pronounced, "Therefore in the presence of Almighty God and these witnesses, I declare you man and wife."

Gareth reached into his jerkin pocket and produced a gold ring that glinted in the sunlight.

"From whence came this?" asked Hester, in a low voice.

"Elizabeth," replied Gareth, who slid the ring on her finger then bestowed a brief kiss on her lips. After a concluding prayer, the party proceeded to Sister Agnes's parlour.

The priest withdrew a small bottle from under his cassock. "For the nuptial libation!"

Sister Agnes coughed. "Father, I do not think—"

Father Jerome interrupted. "Today, Saint Winifred grants us a holiday from abstention."

"Very well," replied the nun, laughing. "A wedding and the promise of a new roof are cause for celebration."

A dozen nuns traipsed through the door. Father Jerome poured wine, and a toast was offered to the newlyweds. The novitiates spluttered and giggled as they drank. Gareth seized Hester by the waist and swung her around, while the others clapped.

After the party dispersed, Hester took a glass of wine to Nia and told her the news. When Nia offered her congratulations, both young women burst into tears. Nia became drowsy from the wine. "I want to go home," she said. "Twgarden's mother will be heartbroken, as he was her only son, and my poor cousin Bronwyn near to delivery." Nia tried to smile and took Hester's hand. "But it is your wedding day, and soon your wedding night, so should you not be with your bridegroom?"

"I am glad to be here with you now. Besides, I would like our first night as newlyweds to be under the stars, not to mention there is no bed for two here at Saint Winifred's."

Nia managed a half-smile, and once she was asleep, Hester disengaged her hand, kissed her friend's cheek, and left.

Two days later, soon after cock crow, Nia and Gareth were mounted and Lady saddled, awaiting Hester. Corwen clucked and hopped on Gareth's shoulder.

Hester found Sister Agnes in her parlour. "I have come to say thank you, and goodbye."

"You are hardly the same girl who came under this roof a few short weeks ago."

Hester blushed and dipped a curtsey. They embraced.

"Thanks to you," said Hester, "I have healed from an even deeper wound than my hand. I have peace in my heart, and even joy now."

Both women brushed tears from their eyes.

"I sent a letter of introduction to Bishop Astley of Saint Asaph," said the nun. "You may lodge there tonight."

Hester blushed and looked down. "I had hoped tonight Gareth and I could sleep under the stars and—"

Sister Agnes interrupted. "I am sure you could find a pleasant copse and you both warm enough that you would not risk contracting pleurisy." The nun raised her eyebrows.

"Oh, but Nia cannot sleep outside!" exclaimed Hester.

"Quite so," replied Sister Agnes, smiling.

"Thank you," said Hester, taking Sister Agnes's hands. "I would like to wait here for my brother, Dickie, and my cousin Alice to arrive, but Nia is most anxious to be with her family again. Will you please...?"

"I shall direct them to Saint Asaph and thence to Caernarfon. From there they will need to ask directions to Dinas Emrys," said Sister Agnes. She laughed. "I believe Saint Dewi himself would get lost trying to find it."

Hester brought the nun's hands to her lips and kissed them. Sister Agnes signed her with the cross, then the pair joined Nia and Gareth in the yard. Hester embraced a tearful Myfanwy, and Gareth and Nia said their farewells to Sister Agnes, while Corwen shrieked and set off a cacophony amongst the neighbourhood crows.

our days after Gareth's departure, Alice stood in a field shielding her eyes from the afternoon sun.

"Well done, Dickie!" she shouted.

Dickie, mounted on Mirabel, had just completed his first gallop over the fields. William helped him dismount. "I can do it!" cried Dickie, waving his arms in the air. "Now we can set off to see Hessie."

The three walked back to the cottage. "We need supplies for the journey, plus another couple of horses," said William, his brow furrowed in concentration. "We shall leave tomorrow. I would write to inform my parents of our visit, except we shall probably be there ahead of any messenger."

"I look forward to meeting them, William dear," said Alice, smothering a yawn. She was not sleeping well, despite the feather bed at Syon House. Her freckles stood out dark brown against the daisy white pallor of her face, and purple shadows sat under her eyes.

"I must return to the big house and say goodbye," said Alice, "but first I need to say goodbye to Mother."

"Will I come with you?"

"No, my love, I need a little time alone, and besides, you have to go to market." She saw his face droop in disappointment so reached up and kissed him on the cheek. William mustered a smile, then went with Dickie to unsaddle Mirabel.

After praying at her mother's grave for both her parents' and Goody's souls, Alice rose and walked to Syon House. She felt a dull, lingering ache inside. She had worried about William for so long, and he was now safely returned; she had fretted over monies, and they now had more than sufficient for their wants. *I should feel joyful. Mother and Father and Goody would want me to be happy.* She felt she betrayed them by being miserable. But she often woke from nightmares in which her mother emerged from the river leading Jenkins by the hand and saying, "Look, Alice, who I have found; I think he is yours."

At the house, Alice curtseyed to Mistress Smith and embraced Abigail.

"Please visit if you are ever in this area again," said the mother.

"Close your eyes and hold out your hands," said Abigail. "I would like you to have this," and she unfastened the pearl pendant from her throat and handed it to Alice.

"Thank you!" said Alice. "I know what it is even with my eyes closed." She opened them and held her friend close again. "That was the last pearl from Mother's necklace, so it means more to me than all King Minas's gold."

Alice spent that night at the cottage and early next day the little party set out on their journey. Because of the need to shelter from occasional summer thunderstorms, it took them a week to reach Shrewsbury. They spent the night in a hostelry there, and before dawn the next day were on the road to Bayston. As the day warmed, the roses in the hedgerow opened, scenting the air with their fragrance. Some flowers had already lost their petals, and a green nubbin of a rosehip grew in their stead.

When they reached Bayston castle, they saw most of the roof was missing and two of the walls were mere piles of rubble with grass growing in between.

"How very sad," Alice said, drawing close to William. He removed his hat and blessed himself.

"Our home was slighted five years ago," he said. Alice looked at him, puzzled. The lines of weariness on William's face deepened. "You can see that two walls remain intact." He sighed and continued, "'Slighting' is when, instead of destroying the entire building, parts are left standing to remind all who pass by of the penalty of incurring the King's wrath."

"Oh, rather like a gibbeting," said Alice, frowning, "where the corpse is left as a warning to other would-be criminals."

"Exactly, my dear. I am sorry to show you such a mournful sight, but I needed to stop and pay my respects."

Dickie shouted up to a pair of crows perched on a broken chimney pot, and they cawed back at him. "I am hungry," said he, turning to Alice.

"And I am fair parched," added John.

"It is just a little farther to my parents' new home," said William.

They continued along a pathway lined with oaks in full leaf. Sparrows hopped in front of the horses' feet, darting away a split second before a hoof landed on them.

An old man in a tattered cloak approached them, waving a staff. "Sir William, is that you?" he called.

"Simon, my dear friend, how fare you?" William signalled to the party to dismount.

"I am middling, Master, but Lord and Lady Bayston are gone…," the aged retainer looked around him, "gone to France," he whispered.

"When was that?" William's face paled and Alice touched his arm. He covered her hand with his own.

"Saint John's Eve it was," said Simon. "The King's man came to arrest them, but he sickened with a fever, and while he were a-bed, your parents set out for London town and thence to France." The old man wheezed and leaned on his stick.

William shook his head. "But the King has never threatened their lives before. Why now?"

"His progress." Simon scowled. "He wanted to leave no one of the true faith alive that might foment trouble while he is away."

William's brow creased in anxiety. "Wherefore did my father not write to me?"

"Your dear father was afeard if the letter were seized, his whereabouts would be discovered. But he left one for you."

William nodded. "Thank you, Simon."

William ran a hand over his forehead, then placed his arm around Alice's shoulders. "Alice, let me present to you Simon, who has served my family for over fifty years, is that not right?"

"Aye, and in far better times than these," replied the old man.

"And, Simon, this is Lady Alice Grantmire."

Alice smiled and offered her hand. Simon bowed and took her hand in both his.

"Bless you, my lady. A sight to gladden the eyes is what you are."

William introduced Dickie and John, and the four travellers followed the old man along an overgrown path.

"And your poor grandparents, their wits be sore addled. They will not know you from this here stick in my hand." Simon stared at his blackthorn staff and sighed. "The King's man, cranky because he lost his prey, evicted them from your parents' house, and now they live with me and my old goodwife." They reached the doorstep of a shambling cottage. Simon pointed to a bench on a tiny porch. "Marry, there is no room for all inside, so you two lads sit yourselves here and keep an eye on your horses, who can graze around as they like."

Simon called inside, "Goodwife, look who is upon us!"

An elderly woman, wearing a spotless white apron, opened the door. The smell of fresh-baked honey cakes wafted out toward the travellers. The woman tucked a strand of grey hair into her coif and gasped. "Master William, if my eyes do not deceive me! But look at you, poor dear, so pale and thin looking. Come in, come in!"

She embraced him and made a curtsey to Alice. Simon produced a flagon of ale and pewter mugs and set them down on an oak table carved with ivy vines.

"Matilda was my mother's nurse," William told Alice.

"Sit, sit," said Matilda, shoeing a marmalade cat from a chair and removing a basket of linen from another.

"Lady Alice is my betrothed," William said to Matilda.

"Bless us and save us," exclaimed the old woman. "I remember when you were a wee little lad, no higher than this table, and now you are going to be married." She turned to Alice. "Such a lovely child he was, and never so much as a froward glance from him."

William's cheeks turned pink. "Ah, dear Matilda," he said.

Simon poured ale for William and Alice, then carried mugs and a loaf of rye bread outside to John and Dickie. Matilda set a loaf of wheaten bread, a roundel of cheese, and a platter of honey cakes on the table. Alice nibbled on a crust.

"How are you going to breed if you don't eat?" demanded Matilda.

Alice blushed and stuffed a piece of cheese in her mouth. William cast her a commiserating glance, and she attempted a smile with her mouth full.

"Better," said Matilda, nodding approval.

The sound of gentle snoring came from the next room.

"Those are your dear grandparents," said Matilda to William. "They sleep most of the time now."

"I shall not wake them, then, until just before we leave," said William. He grinned as he bit into a honey cake. "No one bakes these as well as you, Matilda."

The old woman smiled. "Our Lady has blessed us in bringing you both here today." Her eyes filled with tears, and she clasped William's and Alice's hands in her own. "Why cannot you stay?"

Simon returned with a knife and set to work opening a niche beneath the window frame.

William explained his escape from prison after being wrongfully accused of attempted murder. "Rather than be always fleeing the law, Alice and I shall remove ourselves to the mountains of North Wales, where Alice's cousin lives."

Matilda dabbed her eyes with the edge of her apron. Simon withdrew a parchment from the windowsill and handed it to William. "Here is the letter your dear father left for you."

William broke the seal and read aloud. "William, my dear son, Greetings. These are perilous times, as well you know. Your mother and I will take refuge with our friend, the priest of Saint Genevieve, close by the Hotel Dieu in Paris. One day, when the

True Faith returns to England, so shall we, please God. The Lord keep you, Your loving Father." William wiped a tear from his eye and tucked the letter in his sleeve.

"Yes, Paris is what they told us," said Simon, "only we could not remember the other Frenchie names."

"I know they had been sending what little monies they could spare to that church," said William.

"Yea," said Matilda, thumping her mug on the table, "ever since the King determined to set aside good Queen Katherine and start his own religion, one that would countenance his lewdness and other wicked ways."

A feeble groan, followed by "Where are you, Simon?" came from next door.

"Oh, dear Lord, I have awakened your grandfather." Matilda pursed her lips and turned to William. "Come see them."

The four entered a tiny chamber, the entire space of which was occupied by a large bed. Two ancient, withered creatures lay with heads poking out from under the blankets. Their hair was white and fluffy like lamb's fleece, and their eyes bleared with sleep. The room smelled of cedar mingled with the musk of old people and a faint, acrid whiff of the piss pot.

"Here is your grandson and his espoused wife," said Simon in a loud voice. "They are both deaf as newts," he explained to William.

William shouted, "Grandfather, Grandmother, do you not remember me, William?" But not a flicker of recognition registered in their faces. He embraced each of them. His grandmother stared at the ceiling.

"Who are you?" asked William's grandfather.

Shocked, he stepped back. "I am your grandson, William." He turned to Alice. "He taught me how to lure trout down by the river when I was six," he said, rubbing his knuckles into his eyes. Alice took his hand, and he gave her a rueful smile.

"They took to their beds just after you parents left," Simon told William as the four left the room.

William said, "It is hard to see them so. But 'tis evident they are very well cared for." He took Simon's hand. "Thank you for your hospitality, but we must be setting off, for Alice and I plan to wed this day, please God, in Saint Alkmund's church."

"Oh no, Master William! It will break your heart!" cried Matilda, wringing her hands.

"What? Getting married?" asked William, frowning.

"No, the church."

"Has so much changed in the past two months?"

"Just a fortnight ago, they came and tore down the rood screen," said Matilda, her voice catching. "Then they hauled away the statues of the saints."

"But what else would you expect from a king who calls himself pope of England?" said Simon, frowning.

"Old Mouldwarp, that's what we call him." Matilda grimaced. "And the precious gold reliquary that held Saint Anthony's finger, all covered in rubies and emeralds, is gone too, now. Gone to line King Greedy Guts's coffers."

"Sad times, indeed," said William, shaking his head. "Is Father Ambrose still priest at Saint Alkmund's?"

"He is," said Simon.

"What about the banns?" Matilda asked, her head to one side.

"Father Ambrose has known me since I was a child. I am hoping he can dispense with them." He placed his arm around Alice's shoulder.

"Where will you spend the night, once you are married and all?" asked Matilda.

"John will ride on ahead and bespeak us a good inn in Chester."

"Mind the mattress is well aired and the sheets and blankets too, but I dare say you pair will be hot as coals and able to heat the whole inn with your nuptials."

Alice's cheeks turned rose red.

"Matilda, say no more," said Simon, wagging his finger at his wife.

In the silence that ensued, William took out his purse and counted out six sovereigns. "These are for you," he said.

"Gold!" exclaimed Matilda, accepting the coins. "Thank you, Master William. I haven't seen gold since they took away poor Saint Anthony's reliquary, the one with all the—"

"We don't need half this much," interrupted Simon.

"Please take it. No amount of gold can repay your kindness to my grandparents..." William's voice cracked. "But we must leave now if we are to be married and reach Chester before dark."

Matilda leaned up and kissed him on the cheek and made a bobbing curtsey to Alice.

"I wish you both great joy. And set about making childer this very night, do you hear? Do not be letting the grass grow under your feet."

Alice smiled and hugged their hostess. "Thank you, Matilda. God bless you both."

The travellers remounted; John and Dickie had drunk too much ale and needed to dismount every few minutes to pass water, but in half an hour they reached the old Saxon church of Saint Alkmund. Brambles and purple vetch covered the graveyard's neglected headstones, and chaffinches flew among the stones, calling to each other.

William asked John and Dickie to wait by the lychgate with the horses. The betrothed couple proceeded up a yew-lined path to the church door. The mottled brass handle shook when William turned it. Inside, the church was dark and the air heavy with smells of incense, musty fabrics, and beeswax candles. The only sound was of whispered prayer.

Once her eyes became accustomed, Alice could see an old, bald-headed man kneeling in the chancel. His surplice was riddled with holes.

"Who comes to Saint Alkmund's this fine day?" asked the priest. As he stood to greet them, he stumbled on the hem of his gown but steadied himself on the altar rail.

"Father Ambrose, it is I, William, Lord Bayston's son," said William, leading Alice up the aisle. He embraced the aged cleric, whose rheumy eyes filled with tears.

"William, my child, it is indeed good to see you again. Your family is a brave one, defying the King." The old man shook his head. "I thought you had gone into exile with your parents."

"No, Father, and here I am come with my betrothed, Lady Alice Grantmire, asking you to marry us."

"Grantmire," said the priest. "I know that name, my dear. Was not your father executed, but recently, for refusing the King's Oath?" Alice nodded. "You belong to another courageous family, and I would be honoured to officiate your marriage."

He turned to William. "On what date do you desire to be wed?"

"Today," replied William, smiling down at Alice.

"By Our Lady, at this very hour?" The old cleric looked dumbfounded.

William nodded.

"But the banns?" asked the priest.

"Dear Father Ambrose, can you see fit to dispense with them? We need to be in Chester by this evening." William explained their anxiety to reach the highlands of North Wales, and safety, soon.

"Yes, under such circumstances, I can. But witnesses are essential, and do you have a ring?"

"We have no ring yet," said William, looking at Alice.

"Well, well, the ring can wait, but…"

"Father, pray come with us," said William and the trio walked to the door.

William tugged it open to reveal Dickie holding a posy of wild roses wrapped in a handkerchief. Dickie was sucking his thumb. "Mighty sharp thorns, but I've taken off the worst," he said. Grinning, he bowed and handed the flowers to Alice.

"Your name, my son?" asked the priest.

"Dickon Vaughan, Father, but mostly I am called Dickie."

"Very good, Dickie." Then Father Ambrose turned to John. "And, my son, you are called?"

"John Haywood, Father."

"Excellent, we are all gathered here in the porch, so I shall proceed with the ceremony," said the priest.

"And this is for your head, my lady," said John, producing a garland of purple vetch and daisies from behind his back. "Your husband-to-be may crown you," he said, and handed it to William. Alice smiled, removed her coif, and unpinned her braids. Her red hair, albeit thinner than before, fell loose and tumbled over her shoulders. Her tresses shone gold and amber in the sunlight.

"My beauty," said William, placing the wreath on her head.

"See, Mirabel has one too, for she is your bridesmaid," said Dickie. Alice looked to where Mirabel stood under the lychgate, chomping on daisies from the very long garland looped around her neck.

Alice laughed aloud as did Father Ambrose and William.

Father Ambrose coughed. "My dear," he said to Alice, "are you of marriageable age?"

"I shall be sixteen come All Saints Day."

"Good." He turned to William. "And as for you, dear lad, I remember your birthdate all too well." Alice looked with puzzlement at the priest, and William's mouth turned down at the corners. "January third, 1521, Anno Domini, the day the Pope excommunicated Martin Luther for his heretical writings."

Father Ambrose clasped his hands together. "William of Bayston, are you aware of any impediment to your marrying Alice Grantmire?"

"No, I am not."

"Alice, is there any impediment, of which you are aware, to your marrying with William of Bayston?"

Alice, likewise, replied in the negative.

"I wish my parents could have been here," whispered William, "and your dear mother and father also."

The priest bowed his head. "*Requiem aeternam dona eis, Domine, et lux perpetua luceat eis.*"

Dickie nudged John. "What did he say?"

John shrugged his shoulders.

"Eternal rest grant unto them, Lord, and may light perpetual shine on them," whispered Alice.

The couple exchanged vows and Father Ambrose declared them man and wife. After they had kissed, he concluded, "What God has joined together, let no man rend asunder."

William and Alice thanked the priest, and William placed a gold sovereign in the poor box.

The friends remounted and struck off on the road to Chester. Once they reached Wrexham, John rode on ahead to bespeak a room for the bride and groom at an inn for the night.

The travellers were glad of a near-full moon to light their way, as the sun had long set by the time they reached Chester. The innkeeper, a stocky, black-bearded man wearing a white apron around his middle, greeted them.

"You must be the newlyweds," he said, bowing from the waist. "Pray follow me to the separate dining room. Your companions will be served with the regular guests."

William nodded and Alice blushed. Alice felt too nervous to eat, but the aroma from the beef pie set before her worked on her appetite. She and William devoured it and a fruit tart, accompanied by a bottle of malmsey.

William looked at her over his glass; Alice was not able to meet his eye. But smiling she set down her knife and rose from the table. She took his hand and together they climbed the narrow staircase to their chamber, and William opened the door. Alice beheld a large bed with a kingfisher blue coverlet strewn with daisies. "How beautiful, and how thoughtful!" she exclaimed.

"I have this for you," said William. He reached inside his doublet and withdrew a single pearl. "A wedding present, though it was you who gave it to me."

"William, is it...?" exclaimed Alice, taking it and holding it in her palm.

"Yes, my darling, it is one of the two you gave me. The other kept me from starving in gaol."

Alice reached up and kissed him on the lips. "Now I have two of Mother's pearls, but best of all, I have you."

William turned and closed the shutters. Alice felt her heart racing, but she stood stock still, more than half afraid of what would come next.

William stroked her hair and kissed her forehead. He nibbled her ear, which made Alice giggle. She tilted her head up, and he kissed her mouth and she stopped giggling. A little breathless, she ran the tip of her tongue around his lips, and William groaned and pulled her closer, inserting his tongue into her mouth. Alice responded in kind to its velvet, firm movement. But when William cupped her breast with his hand, her body stiffened and she drew away. Alice observed his darkened eyes and flushed skin, and shuddered.

"Did I hurt you, my dearest?" asked William, his voice hoarse with desire.

"No, not at all, but I became afraid." Alice scrunched her eyes closed. "Because of that man. Because he grabbed my breast, before he tried to..."

"My darling Alice," said William. "Look at me." Alice opened her eyes. "Do I look like him?"

"No, my love, except your eyes, they have gone black, the way his did. I have never seen them look that way before."

"My precious one," said William. "Yes, it is lust. I cannot help but desire you." He kissed her eyelids. "But I desire you with my heart first and only second with my body. You are my own true wife, and I would not hurt you any more than I would hurt myself."

"I understand, my sweet," replied Alice. "And I desire you and want to open myself to receive you. Only I am afraid." She frowned.

William smoothed her brow with his forefinger. "Don't frown, my darling. Let us see how we get along. If it fares well tonight, wonderful, and if not, there is always tomorrow night."

Alice nodded in agreement. William took her face in his hands and nibbled at her throat, then slid his thumb down the front of her neck, from the angle of her jaw to her collarbone. He repeated the motion. Alice gave a moan and pressed herself against him. William fumbled with the fasteners and buttons on Alice's dress. A minute later she stood in her shift. William inhaled deeply as she stepped out of it.

"You are perfect…every inch of you glows." He gathered her into his arms. "My beautiful wife." He kissed her face all over while she held him tight. After a minute he released her, and she climbed between the sheets. William shed his clothes in seconds and was in bed beside her. Alice ran her hands through his hair. Then William lowered his head and kissed each of her breasts in turn. Alice gasped at the pleasure. He nudged her thighs apart and lowered himself onto her. Her body rose to meet his.

"You must tell me to stop if I hurt you," said William. "But don't just say 'stop'; push on my chest."

"Very well," replied Alice. She guided him inside. "Stop," she said, putting a hand on his chest.

"Does it hurt very badly?" asked William, his voice cracking with urgency.

"No, and now you can go in a little more." Alice felt a mixture of pleasure and discomfort. "Are you all inside now?" she asked.

"Very nearly, my love." William, breathless, and unable to hold back longer, gave a thrust. Alice cried out at the momentary pain, then as she felt him deep inside her womanhood, she knew he was hers, and she was his, absolutely and for all time.

Alice slept soundly for the first time since leaving Hartbourne. She woke just before dawn. She felt a moment of panic before realizing the man beside her in bed was William, her dear husband. She stroked his arm and gave a prayer of thanksgiving to the Virgin for restoring him to her.

ester, Gareth, and Nia travelled through the woods under a canopy of full-leaved trees. An occasional hare ran across their path, and several deer bounded away into the thicket at their approach.

At noon they dismounted beneath an old oak tree. Gareth lit a fire and they shared a cold roast pheasant, a loaf of fine white bread, and a flagon of ale.

Nia did not eat. "I am anxious, that is all. I am afraid that I will be the bearer of the terrible news." She coughed and held her rib cage. "The pain is not too bad." But sweat pooled on her brow and her breathing was rapid. She could not mount unaided, so Gareth lifted her into the saddle.

They stopped several times for Nia to rest, and it was dusk when they reached St. Asaph and the bishop's palace.

A servant greeted them at the door and, on beholding the seal of Saint Winifred on Hester's letter, bowed low.

"I will inform my lord bishop of your arrival." He beckoned a groom who took the horses and Corwen.

"Behave like a Christian," Gareth warned the crow, "and you will dine well, for bishops keep a fine table."

The servant conducted the travellers to a well-appointed receiving chamber. Velvet-cushioned benches and finely carved sideboards lined the walls on which hung paintings illustrating the lives of the saints. Beside the marble fireplace stood four comfortable armchairs upholstered in tooled leather.

Hester and Gareth stood on a white-and-green Turkey carpet, supporting Nia between them. Hester could feel the heat radiating from her friend's body and led her to a wide bench to lie down.

With a fan she found on a side table, Hester was fanning Nia when the bishop strode in. He was a soft-jowled, tall young man wearing a fine black velvet doublet and riding breeches.

"Ah, the newlyweds!" he exclaimed, and turned to Gareth. "Welcome to Saint Asaph."

Gareth bowed and Hester approached, curtseyed, and kissed the ring on the bishop's plump right hand. She handed him Sister Agnes's letter.

Bishop Astley opened it and scanned its contents. "I have already received news of you from Lady Elizabeth's scribe." He stared at Hester. His eyes protruded a little from their sockets. "You enjoy an exalted acquaintance." Hester coloured and dropped her gaze. "My clerk works on your annulment even as we speak."

Nia coughed and the bishop looked over at her, and, seeing her distressed breathing, stepped backwards and signed a cross in the air. His pink cheeks blanched.

"'Tis only pleurisy," Gareth explained. "Our friend Nia has been ill for some time now. It is not the sweat."

Bishop Astley inhaled. He, like everyone in the country, understood that the sweat killed in hours.

"Well, then, your friend is welcome too, but best get her to her room."

Hester and Gareth helped Nia upstairs and into a spacious bedchamber. A maidservant removed a warming pan from between the sheets, then she and Hester helped Nia undress and ascend the soft feather bed. Hester asked for a bowl of bone broth, which appeared within minutes. Nia drank but a couple of spoonfuls of the steaming liquid then fell asleep. Her breathing was shallow and rapid, and when Hester felt her forehead, it was hot as the broth she could not drink.

Gareth waited outside. "Let me show you our bedroom," he said with a smile on his lips, though his eyes were tired. He led her to the adjoining chamber. A tapestry of the three wise men's attendance on the infant Jesus, picked out in gold thread, dominated one wall.

Glassed windows spanned floor to ceiling. It was the brightest room Hester had ever been inside. The great bed's four posts supported a tester carved with scenes from the Old Testament.

Hester gave a wry laugh. "Who could experience the raptures of love lying beneath a painting of the siege of Jericho?"

The couple rejoined the bishop in his receiving chamber, where he and Gareth proceeded to set up a chessboard.

"I fear our friend is most unwell, and we shall need to trespass on your hospitality for a few days, my lord," said Hester.

"Do not discompose yourself," said the bishop. "My servants do little more than play at dice all day long, so some useful employment comes not amiss." He moved a knight on the board. "How are your archery skills?" he asked Gareth.

"Of those, I have little, but I play the harp well." Gareth moved a pawn.

"Excellent. I should like to hear a few melodies over dinner." The bishop moved his other knight.

Hester wandered over to an oak desk on which sat a guilded, leather-bound copy of Chaucer's *Canterbury Tales*. She carried the book to a cushioned chair and opened to the first page where the author relates how springtime is the season to embark on pilgrimage.

This king has not left many places for pilgrimage, she reflected. *The great shrine of Saint Thomas a Beckett, to which Chaucer's pilgrims were bound, is with us no more, nor that of Our Lady of Walsingham. In fact, only Saint Winifred's remained.*

Please God let Nia's fever break and that she mend, she prayed. A tear fell on the page and she brushed it away before it could smudge the fair print. Hester set down the book and gazed into the empty fireplace.

"Checkmate!" cried Bishop Astley.

A servant entered to light the candelabra. The bishop led his guests to a dining chamber, where a table was set with a repast of sliced roast goose and quince marmalade. Neither Gareth nor

Hester could eat, but their host displayed a hearty appetite. Gareth played the song of Gawain and the Green Knight that the Lady Elizabeth had enjoyed so much, then Hester and he bade the bishop good night and ascended to their room. In the gloaming light of their candle they could still discern the high walls of Jericho carved in the bed's canopy.

Hester shrugged herself out of her grey workaday dress and, clad only in her shift, climbed into bed. Gareth followed suit, but when he tried to kiss her, she brushed his lips away and turned her back to him.

"So we will wait, then?" asked Gareth, with a sigh of disappointment. "This should be our night, our first night where I can embrace you as my wife."

"Yes," said Hester. "If only Nia were well, how different it would be, but…" The mattress was so soft she fell asleep midsentence.

When Hester awoke next morning, Gareth had already risen and gone from the room. His place in the bed was cold, and she felt her heart sink. Perhaps she should not have rebuffed him last night. Then she remembered Nia. Hester leaped out of bed, snatched up a blanket to drape around herself, and raced to Nia's room.

Nia was sitting up in bed eating a piece of bread and cheese and drinking ale from a silver cup. Her face was pale, but her breathing was normal. Hester's eyes shone with relief as she ran to her friend.

"The fever broke last night," said Nia with a smile. "Feel my hands, they are cool as yours!"

Hester did, then embraced her. "This is marvellous!" Tears poured down her cheeks.

Nia nodded and gave a cough. "I think tomorrow I shall be able to ride again." She took another drink of ale. "Do you think they know of the carnage yet in Dinas Emrys?" she asked as tears filled her own eyes.

"Perhaps," replied Hester, frowning. She wiped her face with the back of her hand. "Caernarfon folk would have heard by now and sent word to the village." She clasped Nia's hands. "But we will be there soon enough." She kissed Nia on the cheek. "You finish your breakfast and rest more."

Hester returned to her chamber and stared at the imprint of Gareth's body in the feather mattress.

When did he leave? she wondered. *And why? Our Lady, pray bring him back soon.*

A maidservant entered carrying a ewer of water. She drew back the curtains to reveal rain streaming down the windowpanes. "You must wonder where your husband is," said she.

Hester nodded and washed her face in the basin so the maid might not see her misery.

"Bishop was called before dawn to the governor's house," continued the girl as she passed Hester a linen napkin. "His wife birthed her fourth and it was feared it would not survive, so his lordship was obliged go baptize it."

"What concern was that of my husband?" asked Hester in a querulous voice.

"His lordship thought music might console the unhappy parents. The governor is no mean harpist himself. This is his first son; the other three are girls."

Hester now remembered being gently shaken and Gareth whispering something to her. "Oh," she said. "I think he did try to tell me."

The girl assisted her in dressing, then Hester sat and looked out the window as her hair was being braided. "There's a sorry looking group just arrived," Hester said, then gasped. "It is Dickie and Alice and the others!"

Hester ran from the room and down the broad staircase to the door. She sped past the attendant, who was looking askance at the bedraggled party pulling rein before the palace steps.

Hester, ignoring the pelting rain, reached up to embrace her brother atop his horse, even though she could grasp only his knee. "Dickie, my dearest. It is wonderful you are here. Let me help you down."

"Hessie! It is so very good to see you, but, no thank you, I can do it myself."

Once he was down he hugged Hester and lifted her off the ground.

"How strong you are grown!" she said. "I have missed you very much."

William assisted Alice to dismount, and the two cousins embraced.

"Alice, I thought this day would never come!" said Hester, kissing her.

"But here we are," replied Alice, beaming. "It is lovely to see you again." The women released their grasp on each other.

"It is good to meet you again, Sir William," said Hester, making a brief curtsey.

"Likewise, Mistress Vaughan," replied William, lowering his head.

She turned to John. "Welcome, John, I am right glad you are here."

John bowed. "Thank you, Mistress Vaughan. Where will I take the horses?"

Hester pointed to a group of outbuildings. "The stables are just behind there."

She mounted the front steps and addressed the servant standing in the door. "Pray admit Lady Alice Grantmire, Sir William of Bayston, and my brother, Master Dickon Vaughan."

The attendant's eyes widened. He bowed and stood aside as the sodden travellers entered.

"Dickie and Alice, come to my room," said Hester. "Can you find dry clothing for Sir William?" she asked the attendant.

"I will go with William, thank you, sister," said Dickie. He grinned at her and embraced her again.

Oh, he is no longer my fragile little brother, thought Hester.

Once in her chamber, Hester and Alice held each other close.

"I am most sorry for all your losses—your father, your mother, Goody," said Hester.

"It was horrid," replied Alice, "but William is everything I had ever hoped for in a husband."

Hester unfastened Alice's dress.

"I have no other robe," said Alice.

"You can wear this." Hester produced the green and gold gown. "I was married in it."

"Does that mean you have…?" said Alice, arching an eyebrow.

"No," sighed Hester, "but I hope tonight…"

Alice held Hester's face in her hands. "Why cousin, you are blushing."

"We have kissed, deeply," said Hester, "and I felt the longing inside that only—"

The maidservant arrived with a square of flannel, ending the conversation. Hester dried her cousin's hair.

"We were married two days ago in Shrewsbury," said Alice, her smile irradiating the whole of her face, "then we travelled to Chester, and then last night reached Saint Winifred's. Sister Agnes said you had left that very morning, but that we would find you here. She found space for us to sleep, and now here we are."

"And most wondrous it is to see you again," said Hester, as the maid helped Alice dress.

Hester dismissed the girl, and Alice explained how William was now an outlaw and they hoped Dinas Emrys would prove a safe haven for them.

"The safest haven in the world," replied Hester, pinning up Alice's hair. "Barely anyone knows of its existence."

Alice admired herself in the mirror, but a moment later turned to her cousin.

"Oh, Hester, it has been so hard!" she cried, unable to hold back her tears. "As well as Mother and Father and poor Goody, I was nearly hanged for a witch and could have burned for heresy, and a wicked man tried to…"

Tears pricked in Hester's eyes as she held Alice to her. "I am sorry for all that happened to you," she said. Her own ordeals were minor compared with her cousin's. True, her father, too, had died, but she had barely known him, and he had died of natural causes, not executed as a traitor, and Mother was long dead. Also, like Alice, she had nearly died, but she saw happiness ahead, married now to the man she loved. As was Alice, thank God. *Poor Uncle Hugh and Aunt Maud, who only ever wanted to help others. And Goody, too. The Lord bless them all in Heaven. And Father and Mother.* Hester ducked her head a moment. The women separated from their embrace and smiled at each other.

"Let us go downstairs," said Hester. "It will be lovely for us all to sit at table together. Have you breakfasted?"

"No, we were in such a hurry to reach you here," Alice replied, wiping her eyes on a handkerchief.

In the great receiving room, William, wearing a clerical black gown, and Dickie, likewise garbed, sat beside a bright, crackling fire, playing a game of chess.

An attendant at the sideboard carved a roundel of soft cheese and sliced an apple tart. The four gathered at a table, and as they sat to eat, in walked the bishop and Gareth.

Hester made introductions, and it transpired that William's and Bishop Astley's fathers had attended the same college at Oxford, although separated by some years.

Gareth embraced Hester. "Did you miss me?" he whispered, tilting her chin up and bestowing a brief kiss on her lips.

"Yes, but I forgive you," she said, smiling into his eyes. "Did the babe survive?" she asked.

"Indeed it did. Our bishop performed his duties, I played a few merry tunes, and then we saluted the joyous occasion with a glass of fine hippocras. And I have a bottle for us to celebrate our own joyous occasion come the evening." He raised his eyebrows and Hester blushed and ducked a mock curtsey.

Bishop Astley excused himself to rest. Dickie, wanting to make sure their horses were well tended, joined John in the stables. The cousins and their spouses spent the remainder of the day beside the hearth, sharing tales of their adventures.

Nia, looking vastly improved, joined them for supper. John, seated beside her, tried to engage her in conversation, but Nia only murmured inaudible replies.

The bishop invited the group to stay longer, but Nia was adamant they leave in the morning.

As the company rose, Gareth took Hester by the hand. "My wife and I have need of each other's company." They meandered around the garden. The rain had stopped and the air was heavy with the fragrance of roses and lilies. The couple watched as the sky turned violet and a crescent moon appeared. "Do you see Venus up there?" asked Gareth.

"I do, and I surmise you are making an invitation?"

Gareth took Hester in his arms and kissed her on the mouth. A frisson of pleasure spread from her lips down her spine. After a few minutes Hester felt her knees tremble. "Let us go inside," she gasped, "while I can still walk."

"In a little whiles. I shall be happy to carry you, if needs must." He grinned at her and his eyes glinted. Gareth guided Hester to a great elm tree and leaned her against the trunk. He kissed her again, this time deeper and longer. Hester, aware of Gareth's desire, moved her hips to meet him.

"It was my wish to spend our wedding night under the stars," said she, pausing for breath. "But the grass is sodden, and besides, it would be a sad waste of a fine feather bed."

"You sound like an old sensible housewife!" Gareth laughed and took her hand. "We may never be offered such luxury again." They made their way back to the house and entered their chamber. Gareth opened the bottle of hippocras, and they shared a crystal goblet. Gareth took a deep breath. "Well, my bride, what do you say?"

"I say yes, and yes again."

He untied Hester's bodices and helped her out of her dress until she was clad only in her shift. Shyly she lifted her undergarment over her head and let it fall to the floor. She heard his admiring gasp at the sight of her naked body. He gently held her breasts and kissed them.

The shock of pleasure coursed through her veins and centred in her low belly. Hester climbed between the fine linen sheets while Gareth stripped himself. She lay down and Gareth descended to her. He kissed the notch of her throat, and her body arched toward him as his tongue caressed her lips. As he moved into her she felt herself soaring like a comet into the heavens. For a single moment everything went dark, followed by a cataclysm of blue light. She was bathed in light. She was that light.

A little while later Gareth asked, "Happy, wife?"

"Happiest I have ever been, husband."

In the little cottage by Snowdonia, Master Mervyn sat by the fire in his living room, his leg propped on a bolster.

Iestyn, his old servant, approached. "Master, the bed had to be moved, for the rain was coming through the ceiling, and I found this."

Mervyn took the little phial, opened it, and inhaled the sweet smell of poppy juice. A slow, dark smile spread across his pain-ravaged face.

"So my wife tried to poison me." He clenched the phial in his fist. "Do you know the punishment for poisoning a husband?"

"Nay, Master, I do not," replied Iestyn.

"Boiling alive in a cauldron of oil. Or if the judge be lenient, burning at the stake. Either way I shall watch her die, and it will be the most beautiful sight I have ever seen."

He drained his glass of claret and poured himself another.

Acknowledgements

My first and greatest thank you is to Marianne Ward for her editing. Without her wisdom, humour, and encouragement, *The Tudor Prophecy* would never have materialized as a book. Writing a novel is like running a marathon, and Marianne was there on every street corner with refreshments and shouting out, "You can do it… you are nearly there!" She made me feel believed in, and that has made all the difference between the manuscript mouldering in a cupboard versus now, being in readers' hands.

I would like to thank my two younger, adult children, Taigh and Kit MacManus, for accepting without demur my disappearances into the library many weekends during their childhood.

I am grateful to Elizabeth Peirce who edited the first draft and likewise to my sister, Gillian Webster, who gave it her thoughtful consideration.

I tender heartfelt thanks to those who read through the near-finished manuscript: Dagmar Moulton, my eldest daughter; Stephen Barbour, a fellow violist; Elizabeth Eve, retired editor; and Anne MacAlpine, a dear friend.

Much gratitude is due to the following authors who gave of their own precious time to endorse my novel: Carol Bruneau, Elizabeth Edwards, and Apple Gidley, thank you all so very much. I am also grateful to the authors of the following reference books: *Henry VIII: The King and His Court* (Ballantine Books, 2001) by Alison Weir and *Elizabeth: The Struggle for the Throne* (Harper Perennial, 2001) by David Starkey.

I wish to thank Paula Sarson, erudite proofreader extraordinaire; Rebecca Wilson, creator of the beautiful cover illustration; and David Edelstein, designer, who has transformed a manuscript into a work of art.

Finally, I wish to thank Anne O'Connell of OC Publishing. Anne is a publisher with vast and intimate knowledge of the profession and has encouraged me to manifest as an author. Whenever I meet with Anne for tea, I have to be careful to swallow before she says anything, as it is likely to make me laugh so hard I will expel tea through my nose. Such qualities in a publisher—dangerous laughter and excellent guidance—have been of immense importance to me as I offer my first novel to the world.

About the Author

Julie Strong is a recently retired family physician in Halifax, Nova Scotia; she has an ongoing shamanic practice where she addresses the spiritual causes of illness. Julie grew up in England, Wales, and Australia and emigrated to Canada in 1980. Her medical degree is from Trinity College, Dublin University, Ireland, and she holds a BA in Classics from Dalhousie University, Halifax. Her shamanism training is from the Foundation for Shamanic Studies.

Dr. Strong has presented internationally on insanity in ancient Greek literature and on shamanism. She delivered a course on The Goddess in Antiquity in spring 2024 for the Seniors College Association of Nova Scotia, which emphasized humanity's need to reconnect with Nature and the Divine Feminine

Julie's essays appear in several anthologies, including *Letting Go* (Bacon Press Books, 2016) and *Much Madness, Divinest Sense* (Pottersfield Press, 2017). Her story "Alice's Bonfire" won the Budge Wilson Short Fiction Prize from the Writers' Federation of Nova Scotia in 2010, and her play *Athena in Love* was awarded "best new play" in the Halifax Fringe Festival in 2012. *The Tudor Prophecy* is her first novel. Julie is working on a memoir, *Keeping It Together Down Under.*

Julie has three grown children and three grandchildren and plays viola in an amateur string quartet and orchestra.